T0338640

THE HUMAN FACE
OF COMPUTING

Advances in Computer Science and Engineering: Texts

Editor-in-Chief: Erol Gelenbe *(Imperial College London)*
Advisory Editors: Manfred Broy *(Technische Universität München)*
Gérard Huet *(INRIA)*

Advances in Computer Science and Engineering: Texts   Vol. 9

THE HUMAN FACE OF COMPUTING

editor

Cristian S Calude
University of Auckland, New Zealand

Imperial College Press

ICP

Published by

Imperial College Press
57 Shelton Street
Covent Garden
London WC2H 9HE

Distributed by

World Scientific Publishing Co. Pte. Ltd.

5 Toh Tuck Link, Singapore 596224

USA office: 27 Warren Street, Suite 401-402, Hackensack, NJ 07601

UK office: 57 Shelton Street, Covent Garden, London WC2H 9HE

Library of Congress Cataloging-in-Publication Data
The human face of computing / [edited by] Cristian S Calude (University of Auckland,
New Zealand).
    pages cm. -- (Advances in computer science and engineering. Texts ; vol. 9)
  ISBN 978-1-78326-643-2 (alk. paper)
  1. Computers and civilization. 2. Computer scientists--Interviews. I. Calude, Cristian, 1952–
QA76.9.C66H833 2015
303.48'34--dc23
                              2015017458

British Library Cataloguing-in-Publication Data
A catalogue record for this book is available from the British Library.

In-house Editors: Catharina Weijman/Sree Meenakshi Sajani

Typeset by Stallion Press
Email: enquiries@stallionpress.com

Printed in Singapore

Contents

v

Part 3. Social Aspects of Computing 351

Anil Nerode: Foreword

Over the last 64 years of immersion in computability I have watched the confluence and interdependent development of mathematical logic, materials science and control engineering, culminating in the scientific discipline of computer science. Computer science has by now permeated all human and machine activities which can be executed by algorithms. It is so successful that it has already fragmented into many separate interdisciplinary departments such as bioinformatics, data mining, and even computer art.

These interviews show the breadth and depth of computer science and will fascinate anyone interested in how a science evolves. The scientists interviewed for this volume range from early pioneers to recent innovators. Early figures came already trained in fields such as mathematics and engineering, and philosophy and linguistics before there were any computer science departments or any recognition that such a subject made intellectual sense. Now computer science departments provide the expertise in concentrated form.

As a mathematical logician and computer scientist, I regard the first theoretical basis for computer science as having been developed by logicians before there was any hint of computer science. By this I mean the mathematical definition of the general notion of an algorithm investigated in the 1930s by Church, Kleene, and Turing. Their interest was to determine the scope of Gödel's incompleteness theorems. My introduction to their work was when I was a graduate student in mathematics in 1950 at the University of Chicago. The only professor there who understood Gödel well was the philosopher Rudolf Carnap, who had written the first complete exposition of the incompleteness theorems. Under him I read all the 1930s papers of these authors. Each had a formal system in which they gave a definition of an algorithm. Among these papers, the one closest to founding modern computer science was Turing's. He visualised a human being executing an algorithm by hand, in the same way that for 4000 years specific algorithms were executed by hand: first, recording the execution by wedges impressed on Mesopotamian clay tablets, then execution with ink on Egyptian papyrus, perhaps Archimedes' calculations in the sand and finally, pencil on European paper. Intermediate steps of the execution were often recorded in ephemeral form by human hands manipulating an abacus or stones on a counting table or equivalent. I am emphasising that Turing did not describe there the execution of algorithms by physical devices. He described only execution of algorithms by human beings.

The joint efforts of these mathematicians demonstrated that from any algorithm in any one of their formal systems, one can compute an algorithm in any other of their formal systems such that the execution of the first can be simulated by the execution of the second. This insight was incorporated into universal algorithms which, given a suitable code for an algorithm, can read that code and simulate execution of that algorithm. I find no prior hints before these authors either that there could be a mathematical definition of an algorithm, or that there might be a universal algorithm which could simulate any algorithm using a code for that algorithm. (I even read Babbage–Lovelace dealing with a special class of algorithms intended for computing mathematical tables, a now obsolete preoccupation.)

Now each of the formal systems would be viewed as a computer language, each code for an algorithm as a program, each universal algorithm as an interpreter.

In 1950 no one I knew was aware that in the secret world of cryptanalysis Turing had already designed and built electronic computers, or that von Neumann, who knew the work of these mathematicians, had designed a practical computer architecture based on the materials science then available. Computers evolved in the 1950s with substantial industrial financial support for materials science and solid-state physics in the US. By the early 1960s Cobol, Algol, Fortran, the IBM 360 had arrived. Those of us developing computer science concluded that the best way to advance the discipline was to form self-standing academic degree programmes in major research universities. At Carnegie Mellon it was recognised early on that computer science would permeate almost all disciplines, and at that university it has. Here are some of my personal recollections. At Cornell we founded our computer science department in 1964. The university did not risk startup funds, rather we obtained a founding grant from the Sloan Foundation. I and Robert J. Walker proposed a major in computer science to our arts and science faculty. This proposal was greeted with some derision by the scientists present, who expressed the view that computer science was Fortran programming. I explained that computability theory was under rapid development. Walker explained that investigation of new algorithms for numerical analysis of partial differential equations was essential for the advancement of science. This carried the day. Cornell was extraordinarily lucky to hire Juris Hartmanis as our founding chair. A little later at my *Alma Mater*, Chicago, I persuaded my friend Felix Browder, chair of mathematics, that computer science could not be developed in a mathematics department, because neither computer engineers nor software specialists would come. He initiated the appointment of my former student Robert I. Soare, then of the University of Illinois at Chicago, to a professorship in mathematics at Chicago. Soare put a lot of effort into convincing the then president, Hannah Grey, that a computer science department was essential for the future of science at Chicago. Soare became the founding chair. Another recollection, my friend Burton Dreben of Harvard told me at that time that the suggestion of introducing a computer science department at Harvard was met with the response that if the subject developed, they could hire in the 21st century. Fortunately, they changed their minds. A last recollection. US federal agencies gave strong support to academic computer science starting in the 1960s. But even in the 1970s and early 1980s, European industries did not see that they would gain by sharing EU research funds with university computer science. departments. My former student George Metakides, while on leave in the EU from the University of Patras, proposed and succeeded in getting funded the Esprit program creating circles of excellence in computer science throughout Europe.

Incremental advances in electrical and control engineering, and solid-state physics have resulted in the vast inexpensive computing power ubiquitous in our present everyday life. Each advance was the impetus for the discovery of new algorithms for new applications, and improvement of old algorithms, leading to a science of algorithms and their implementation, which I identify in the abstract as computer science. In 1950, I believe that neither von Neumann nor Turing, nor any engineer in industry or academia, imagined that their ideas would so change the world.

Acronyms

AADL	Architecture Analysis and Design Language
ACM	Association for Computing Machinery
AMS	American Mathematical Society
ARPANET	Advanced Research Projects Agency Network
ASL	Association for Symbolic Logic
ASLA	Amerikan Suomen lainan apurahat, or Grants from Finland's American Loan; today called ASLA-Fulbright program
BDD	Boolean decision diagram
BIP	behaviour, interaction, priority (framework)
BPP	bounded-error probabilistic polynomial time (complexity class)
BQP	bounded error quantum polynomial time (quantum computing)
C&O	combinatorics and optimization
CADP	construction and analysis of distributed processes
CALG	Computational Geometry Algorithms Library
CAV	Computer Aided Verification (conference)
CiE	Computing in Europe (conference)
CMO	collateralized mortgage obligation
CMU	Carnegie Mellon University
CNOT-gate	controlled NOT gate
CNRS	Centre National de la Recherche Scientifique
CAV	Computer Aided Verification (conference)
CMO	collateralised mortgage obligation
CPN	cognitive packet network
CRC	Canada research chair

CS	computer science
CST	Constructive set theory
CUP	Cambridge University Press
CZF	constructive Zermelo–Fraenkel
DBLP	Digital Bibliography & Library Project
DNS	domain name system
EASA	European Aviation Safety Agency
EATCS	European Association for Theoretical Computer Science
ETH	Eidgenössische Technische Hochschule (Zürich)
FAA	Federal Aviation Administration
FFT	fast Fourier transform
FOCS	Foundation of Computer Science
GCSB	Government Communications Security Bureau (New Zealand)
GPAC	general purpose analog computer
GRA	graduate research assistant
GSIA	graduate school of industrial Information,
HTML5	hypertext markup language 5
IANA	Internet Assigned Numbers Authority
IBC	information-based complexity
ICALP	International Colloquium on Automata, Languages, and Programming (conference)
ICANN	Internet Corporation for Assigned Names and Numbers
ICM	International Congress of Mathematicians
IETF	Internet Engineering Task Force
IF	IF computing toolbox
IFIP	International Federation for Information Processing
INRIA	Institut national de recherche en informatique et en automatique
IPL	instruction-level parallelism
IPv6	Internet Protocol version 6
IRSES	International Research Staff Exchange Scheme
ISI	Institute for Scientific Information
ISO	International Organization for Standardization

ISP   Internet service provider

IZF   Intuitionistic Zermelo-Fraenkel

LEDA   Library of Efficient Data Types and Algorithms

LIPIcs   Leibniz International Proceedings in Informatics (conference proceedings)

LLPO   Lesser Limited Principle of Omniscience

MC   Monte Carlo

MFCS   Mathematical Foundations of Computer Science (conference)

MRC   method of relativized conceptualisation

NoE   Network of Excellence

NSA   National Security Agency (United States)

NSF   National Science Foundation

NSF   The National Science Foundation

NYAS   New York Academy of Sciences

NZIMA   New Zealand Institute of Mathematics and its Application

NZMRI   New Zealand Mathematics Research Institute

NZMS   New Zealand Mathematical Society

OEM   original equipment manufacturer

OR   operations research

ONERA   Office National d'Etudes et de Recherches Aérospatiales (French aerospace research organisation)

PCI   peripheral component interconnect

PRNG   pseudo-random number generator

PTAS   polynomial-time approximation scheme

QIPC   quantum information processing and communication

QM   quantum mechanics

QMC   quasi-Monte Carlo

R&D   research and development

RSNZ   Royal Society of New Zealand

SAT   Boolean satisfiability problem

SCADE   Synchronous Design and Validation of Embedded Software Control (synchronous programming environment)

SIAM   Society for Industrial and Applied Mathematics

SOF-SEM	Current Trends in Theory and Practice of Computer Science (conference)
SPIRE	Symposium on String Processing and Information Retrieval (conference)
SQL	structure query language
SRI	Strategic Resources International (Company)
STOC	Symposium on Theory of Computing
TCP	Transmission Control Protocol
TCS	Theoretical Computer Science
TCTL	timed computation tree logic
UICI	University of Illinois at Urbana-Champaign
UML	Unified Modeling Language
UN	United Nations
URL	uniform resource locator
UWO	University of Western Ontario
VLSI	very-large-scale integration

PART 1

Computing Science

Chapter 1

Dines Bjørner: Formal Methods

Professor Dines Bjørner, http://www2.imm.dtu.dk/~{}dibj/, *is a well-known computing scientist working on formal methods for the specification, development and verification of software and hardware systems. Professor Bjørner worked on* **VDM:** *the Vienna Development Method at IBM and was involved in producing* **RAISE:** *the Rigorous Approach to Industrial Software Engineering formal method and tools support.*

He co-founded **VDM-Europe,** *which subsequently became* **FME:** *Formal Methods Europe, an organisation that supports conferences, education and related activities and* **ForTIA:** *the Formal Techniques Industry Association. Professor Bjørner's chef d'oeuvre is a three-volume book* Software Engineering *published in 2005–2006 by Springer. He is a knight of the Order of the Dannebrog and a winner of the*

John von Neumann Medal (1994) and the Ths. Masaryk Gold Medal (1996), has received a Dr.h.c. from Masaryk University (2004), is a member of the Academia Europaea (1989) and the Russian Academy of Natural Sciences (AB) (2001), and is a Fellow of the IEEE (2004) and ACM (2005).

CC: Could we start by telling us the subject of your PhD thesis?

DB: Aha! Yes, I thought one associated with EATCS would ask that question. The title of the PhD thesis (1969) was: *The Theory of Finite State Transductions*. I have much regretted the *"The"*. At most an *"A"* might have been more appropriate. In effect I had no tutor; no one at my department, for the last two-thirds of my study, had any background in computer science, let alone in automata theory and formal languages.

But a Danish PhD is not the highest academic degree one can obtain in Denmark. A PhD is society's blue stamp of approval. Institutions hiring PhDs should be assured that PhDs from the **Technical University of Denmark** can be placed into advanced engineering and applied research work.

There is also, for example, a **doctor technices** degree. To obtain such a degree one has to have shown more than ability. One has to have also demonstrated that one's research has influenced engineering in industry. Normally technical universities should not appoint (full) professors unless they have a Dr. techn. degree. Well, I had not at age 38, when I became a full professor, having spent 11 of my professional years, since my master's degree, at IBM, accumulated much in the direction of original, "path-breaking" work worthy of a Dr. techn. degree. And, it was then customary that a royally appointed professor would not consider submitting a Dr. techn. thesis. Can you imagine what would happen if it was rejected! Would that professor have to step down?

CC: When did you join the EATCS?

DB: I believe it was in the late 1970s. The EATCS is the right organisation for European computer scientists. I would wish it also covered computing science. (Instead we have a bewildering set of programming, software engineering, etc., associations — each founded by someone who wanted to be "President".) To me a distinction is necessary: **computer science** is the study and knowledge of the things that can exist "inside" computers as well as the science of the special techniques and theories of how computer science is pursued. **Computing science** is the study and knowledge of how to construct those things that can exist "inside" computers as well as the study and knowledge of how to apply the techniques of computing science than other to software (and hardware).

CC: Please reminisce about your relation with the Bulletin.

DB: Grzegorz (Rozenberg) asked me, in the late 1970s, or was it in the very early 1980s, to orchestrate a funding drive to cover the EATCS membership for colleagues in Eastern Europe and the (then) USSR. I had travelled somewhat in several of these countries by then. The EATCS lent me their then current membership list and I wrote to "all" members asking them to contribute. Their willingness was most gratifying. And the EATCS was able to provide up to 200 memberships — I think — and for several years.

Grzegorz — what a man, without outgoing, active, almost "shameless", people like him where would we all be? — also invited a private informatics R&D centre of which I was one of the two initiators, DDC: Dansk Datamatik Center, to become an EATCS sponsor. So DDC was an EATCS sponsor for almost eight years. Later, when I "co-founded" and directed UNU-IIST: the United Nations International Institute for Software Technology, UNU-IIST became an EATCS sponsor — at least in the years I was the director at that, I shamelessly pronounce, very successful research and post-graduate/postdoctoral training centre in Macau.

CC: Do you consider yourself mainly a computer scientist, a computing scientist or a superposition of both?

DB: I consider myself a computing scientist.

CC: What is your view on "software engineering"?

DB: Software engineering is applied computing science. Most software engineering textbooks, in my opinion, fail to cover advances in computing science, such as formal techniques.

CC: What do you mean by "domain", "domain engineering" and "domain modelling"?

DB: *Domain* is understood to be a universe of discourse, such as physics, literature, musicology, banking, etc. Something for which there is a reasonably delineated set of terms that cover the simple entities, functions, events and behaviours of the domain: (i) entities that represent phenomena of the domain that one can point to, i.e., be seen, smelled, touched, heard, tasted, or be measured by physical (incl. chemical) instruments, or that one can conceptualise from these simple entities or concepts thereof — with some subset of observed domain entities defining a domain state concept, (ii) functions that apply to entities and yield entities, i.e., functions that observe properties of entities, parts of entities or create new entities, etc.; (iii) events that "occur", in some domain state, and, usually, change that state (that is: events are characterised by certain predicates and transition relations over states) and (iv) behaviours — set of sequences of applied functions, i.e., actions, and events. Examples of domains are: [(a) the container line industry, (b) the financial service industry, (c) railway systems, (d) "the market" (consumers, retailers, wholesalers, producers and the supply chain), (e) health-care] etc.

Domain engineering is understood to be the analysis and description of a(ny) domain. Many stages and steps are needed to do domain engineering properly: identification of domain stakeholders, domain acquisition, domain analysis, domain terminologisation, domain modelling, domain verification, domain validation and domain theory formation. Some of these stages (and/or their embedded steps) are of a pragmatic nature, but several (most in terms of time spent on pursuing these stages) are based on computing science — and domain theory formation requires deep insight into computer science.

Domain modelling is understood to be the specific tasks of creating a domain model in the form of a precisely narrated and — hopefully also — a precisely formalised description of the domain. The descriptions are of the domain, **as it is**, with no reference to requirements let alone software.

CC: How relevant is theory for software engineering?

DB: "There is nothing so practical, that is, of use in engineering, as a good theory", as Ludwig E. Boltzmann is quoted to have said. The techniques of software engineering, whether for domains, requirements or software, mostly have a theoretical foundation. Where physics deals with what can be measured and hence favours mathematics that can express measurable properties, software engineering deals primarily with domains about which we wish to express logic properties. Where classical mathematics focuses on continuity, computer and computing science, the theory foundations of software engineering, deal with discreteness and hence modern algebra plays a role alongside mathematical logic.

A cornerstone of today's software engineering, and hence a central focal point of computing science research is "formal specification" and "verification". A number of formal specification languages and related proof systems have evolved over the years. The first, apart from classical predicate calculus, was VDM. Some others are, in more or less chronological order, `Z`, `RSL (RAISE)`, `B`, `Event B`, `Casl`, `CafeOBJ`, `ASM` and `Alloy`.[1] Using any one of these, the software engineer can express dynamically evolving systems that grow and shrink in a number of entities etc., something that classical calculus is not good at. Early notations of automata and formal language theory are steeped, it seems to me, in classical discrete mathematics — where use of the more modern formal specification languages, in addition to rather sophisticated theorem proving systems, is more appropriate for expressing much of today's computer science work. The result is twofold: (i) published papers that attempt to formalise some, otherwise fascinating software-relevant notations or techniques, are fraught with errors, and (ii) the creators of these notations and techniques remain ignorant of progress in computing science and software engineering. A derivative, but far more "dangerous" effect, is that many of our candidates remain sceptical of formal techniques

---

[1]See the Springer EATCS Series book: "Logics of Specification Languages" (ISBN 978-3-540-74106-0).

since their teachers never took these seriously. This is a strange phenomenon: It is normal to expect that all mathematicians of a mathematics department understand basic tenets of all branches of mathematics that are taught to students. But not so in the average computer science department. It is a disgrace.

CC: Can you comment on one of your most preferred results?

DB: Well, first of all, since I work in programming methodology: the study of the sets of principles whereby the phases, stages and steps of software development can select analysis and synthesis techniques and tools. The results are not simple 18 page papers where some beautiful set of theorems are postulated and proved. The results are bits and pieces, "bricks and mortar", of methods. Together with (the late) Hans Bekič, Cliff Jones and Peter Lucas, I was one of the originators of VDM — whose VDM-SL was the first ISO standardised formal specification language. And I instigated and co-led the work that led to RAISEs RSL. So I consider my contributions here to be among my "preferred results". But, in the last 20 years my work has been focused, not on further research into formal specification languages and their proof systems, but in conceiving the concept of Domain Engineering and by populating that concept with a number of principles and techniques; and in conceiving how one can "derive", major formalisable parts of requirement prescriptions in a systematic theory-based manner — those results, I think, will stand and ought to lead to a rather dramatic reappraisal of so-called requirements engineering. I am of the unabashed opinion that core parts of today's research into requirements engineering are seriously flawed.

Before software can be developed one must understand its requirements. But before requirement prescriptions can be developed one must understand the domain. Electronics, automotive, aeronautics and aerospace, etc., engineers all have a sound education in physics and a specifically deep one in those areas of physics that are related directly to their engineering field: plasma physics, mechanics, and aerodynamics and celestial mechanics. So they understand their domain. Not so for today's software engineers. Oh, well, yes, for those who develop compilers, database management systems and operating systems. But not those, and they are the vast majority, who develop software for container lines, banks, railways, the market, hospitals, etc.

Most computer science and informatics departments, by far the majority, do not offer anywhere near a professional degree in software engineering.

My founding and directing UNU-IIST, the United Nations University's International Institute for Software Technology, based in Macau, China SAR, I also count as one of my "preferred results".

CC: You have worked for companies and universities. Can you please compare life at IBM with that at the Technical University of Denmark or JAIST?

DB: IBM, in my years, 1962–1976, was a very good company — also for us development engineers (1962–1970) and researchers (1970–1976). But a software development methodology, such as VDM, first conceived at the IBM Vienna Lab. (1973–1975), should not be developed in a competition and profit-oriented company, whether IBM or other. IBM's decision not to make room for the R&D of VDM inside IBM was a "blessing in disguise". VDM would never have thrived if only inside IBM. Such software development techniques should primarily be R&D'ed in open, peer-reviewed research centres — and those you found, in the past, in universities. So IBM offered great management, good salaries and exciting projects. Universities offer poor management, low salaries and freedom to pursue what is important. Well, the last seems to be a bit of a problem these days. Today, informatics departments now have, however, a serious problem. Due to political pressures, spurred on by industry spokesmen, our informatics departments are caving into teaching "ready-to-wear" subjects, *viz.* database design using Oracle SQL-developer version 1.5.2 or Microsoft Project Standard 2007 or UML or Ada,[2] etc. There is nothing essentially wrong with these products — but they are just instantiated technology versions of more fundamental techniques and hence theories. Considerable progress in our sciences is getting lost by not being taught due to far too many "ready-to-wear" courses.

---

[2]These were typical project prerequisites of the 1980s and 1990s.

Hence we see that these fields (of progress) are less researched —
and eventually disappear. I am rather pessimistic about the future
of real education, in German 'bildung', in our sciences.

CC: Please describe the Informatics Section of the Academia
Europaea, its history and goals.

DB: You can read about Academia Europaea (AE) at `http://`
`www.ae-info.org/` and about its Informatics Section (IS) at
`http://www.ae-info.org/ae/Acad_Main/Sections/Informatics`.
(By the way, you, Cris have been the editor of its web pages
for a few years.) AE/IS comprises a reasonably fair selection of European computer scientists with a few overseas ones
as well (cf. `http://www.ae-info.org/ae/Acad_Main/Sections/`
`Informatics/InformaticsMembers`). AE/IS has organised, so far,
two events, one in Budapest in 2006, cf. `http://www.jaist.ac.jp/`
`~bjorner/ae-is-budapest/` (by me), and one in Liverpool, 2008
(by you). Suggested by Wolfgang Reisig, we plan to organise an
event, together with members of other AE sections (linguistics, literary studies, musicology, social sciences, mathematics, physics, engineering, earth and cosmic sciences and the four life sciences sections)
on *Models and Modelling*. It should be possible for the AE/IS members to issue, on request (as has been done) or at their own volition, as
will be done, 3–5 page State-of-the-Informatics Sciences manifestos or
position papers that could advise national government, international
organisations, the EU Commission, for example, its newly founded
EIT, etc., on crucial issues before these institutions. The field of computer, computing and informatics science is far from enjoying the status, neither among fellow scientists, at university management levels
and in relevant national ministries, that I think it ought to enjoy.
AE/IS should try to address this problem. But first AE/IS need to
delineate in a reasonable fashion the field of informatics. I was the
chairman of AE/IS from early 2004 to April 2009. In my time as
chairman we enlarged our membership from 23 members to 83.[3]

---

[3] As of April 2014 there are around 200 members of AE/IS.

CC: I was very honoured to be elected a member of AE during your term as chairman. Does AE/IS relevance in Europe and the world grow in sync with its membership?

DB: I would hope so. But what do we mean by "relevance"? AE is neither a government-nor an EU-sponsored academy. One might wish to ask a "pre-"question like: are academies still relevant in free societies? When not tightly connected to governments will they be heard on societal matters with respect to our field? Also: an academy needs funds to act, and it seems that Academia Europaea has little funds: membership fees, always subject to internal haggling, and small donations is all. And academy sections need active member. Oh, yes, many would like to become members, but I see few who really "contribute", by, for example, organising section events and finding funds for these events. Our chairmen have and are putting a lot of work into AE/IS. I trust them.

CC: Your latest book *Domain Engineering. Technology Management, Research and Engineering* was published in Japan in 2009. Could you give us details?

DB: This JAIST Research Monograph (ISBN 978-4-903092-17-1) binds, under one cover, 10 reports that I wrote during my one year sabbatical in 2006 at JAIST. You can all request that monograph from Professor Kokichi Futatsugi, 1-1, Asahidai, Nomi, Ishikawa 923-1292 Japan. My answers to your questions on domains etc., give a hint of what is contained in this monograph. The chapters and appendices of this approximately 500 page monograph span from technology management *via* science of domain engineering to experimental evidence. You may view the monograph at `http://www.imm.dtu.dk/~db/jaistmono.pdf`. It has 76 nice photos from Japan. Look it up, if just for the photos. If your camera has a good telephoto lens then you can indeed find beautiful spots in a Japan full of otherwise ugly buildings, absent city planning, etc.

CC: And your three-volume *Software Engineering* book has been translated in Chinese in 2010.

DB: Initially five, eventually just one, bright Chinese PhD students at JAIST proposed and carried through this translation. It started during my stay at JAIST. Dr. Liu Bo Chao took the initiative: gathered the group, doing most of the translation, contact the publisher (Qinghua Univ. Press), etc. Liu is a wonderful young man.

CC: One of your recent papers is about the "Foundation for Computation for Humanity". What an interesting idea!

DB: Well, you see: this term "Humanity" (with a capital 'H') is a fashionable one. Sociologists and others, maybe, think they understand that term. So I was approached by a dear acquaintance of mine, Pieter J. Mostermann, and invited to write a paper. So I looked the term up and found references to works by Christopher Peterson and Martin E.P. Seligman, and by Abraham H. Maslow. I took their detailed characterisations of the term and, on the basis of the methodological steps of domain analysis I postulated how some of these steps could contribute to what these authors found relevant with respect to "humanity".

CC: What gives you most pleasure in life?

DB: So far, 49 years with my wife — and our children and grandchildren.

Chapter 2

Erol Gelenbe: Computer System and
Network Performance Analysis

 Erol Gelenbe, Professor in the Dennis Gabor Chair of the Electrical at Imperial College London http://www.ee.ic.ac.uk/gelenbe, *is an alumnus of the Middle East Technical University in Ankara, Turkey. He received a PhD from the Polytechnic Institute of New York University (Brooklyn Poly) and the Docteur ès Sciences degree from the University of Pierre et Marie Curie (Paris VI). Professor Gelenbe, one of the founders of the field of computer system and network performance analysis, is well known for his work on Random Neural Networks (RNNs) and G-networks. He created the team that built the Queuing Network Analysis Package (QNAP) and pioneered an object oriented flexible manufacturing simulation system known as Flexible Manufacturing System Simulator (FLXESIM), and both became successful commercial products. Two of his four books were published in English, French, Korean and Japanese. Elected to the Hungarian, Polish and Turkish Academies of Science, the French National Academy of Engineering (Académie des Technologies) and*

the Academia Europaea, he is a Fellow of IEEE (1986), Fellow ACM (2001), and has received "honoris causa" doctorates from the Universities of Liège, Boğaziçi (Istanbul) and Rome II. He has graduated more than 65 PhDs including many women computer scientists and engineers, and was awarded the Parlar Foundation Science Award (1994), the Grand-Prix France Telecom (1996) of the French Science Academy, the ACM SIGMETRICS Life-Time Achievement Award (2008), the UK IET Oliver Lodge Medal (2010) and the "In Memoriam Dennis Gabor Award" of the Hungarian Academy of Sciences (2013). He has been decorated with the honours of Grande Ufficiale in the Order of the Start of Italy, of Commander (Commedatore) in the Order of Merit of Italy, of Officer in the Order of Merit of France, and of Chevalier des Palmes Académiques by France.

CC: Tell us about your experience of studying and working in so many countries.

EG: No two countries and no two environments, and indeed no two institutions, are identical. There is no "best" way to do things and each institution has evolved or adapted according to the personalities of its leaders and the specific context within which it is operating. Moving from one institution to another is particularly interesting and challenging, especially from one country to another, and can be a source of fun and learning (for me, at least). However, being a foreigner almost everywhere, I can group countries and institutions into two very broad categories: those that are open to "allogens" and are willing to be inclusive, and those which have (sometimes in subtle ways) significant barriers to "foreign" penetration. It is quite different if you are a visiting professor: you are there temporarily and do not constitute a threat to others. If you are a permanent addition, matters are different, more challenging and more interesting. Similar things can be said about being a foreigner needing to acquire a residence permit and work permit.

I have held chairs in Belgium, France, the USA and UK. In several countries there can be non-explicit, but widely practiced illegal barriers to foreigners. One hears about illegal immigrants, but seldom does one hear about barriers to legally established foreigners, in matters of promotions, awards, employment, etc. Such practices can continue even when an individual acquires the nationality of the country where he/she is working, and can even happen to EU citizens with regard to another EU country, as we have seen even very recently in countries such as France. My strangest experience was in Italy with my candidacy, at the request of Italian colleagues, to become Institute Director at CNR; I am fluent in Italian. My application was eliminated from consideration because they officially stated that they could not read my signature: *"firma non leggibile"*! Yet I have always used my credit card in Italy without problems about accepting my signature. On that particular instance, a large number of CNR Institute directors were being appointed, and they deftly managed to avoid appointing a single foreign candidate. The CNR was reserving the positions for their local friends, and they succeeded. Even more strangely, a couple of years ago, the lady at a *"Metro guichet"* in Paris refused to sell discount day tickets to two of my Greek and Greek Cypriot PhD students, on the grounds that she just refused to sell discount tickets to foreigners!

CC: As a Computer Scientist, Engineer and Applied Mathematician you have done a lot of theory, part of which was used in commercial products. For example, your early work was incorporated into the QNAP2 software package.

EG: I have indeed attended to theory, but my work, except for my early work on stochastic automata,[1] is motivated by "practical" problems or direct physical inspiration. For instance, I got involved in performance modelling and then in queueing theory because of two main practical drivers. Shortly after defending my PhD, I spent two summers at the Phillips Research Laboratories in Eindhoven, where I was asked to work on memory management algorithms for stack-oriented re-entrant programmes. I knew nothing about the subject but was annoyed by the *"ad hoc"* nature of the design choices that were being made. So I felt that some theory was needed, for instance,

---

[1] E. Gelenbe. On languages defined by linear probabilistic automata, *Information and Control*, 16: 487–501, 1970.

in the choice of the page and memory segment sizes, so as to optimise the overhead. Similarly, at my first job at the University of Michigan (Ann Arbor) as an assistant professor, they asked me to teach computer architecture: everyone already there had "taken over" the courses on automata theory, formal languages, etc,. so I (the newcomer) was "stuck" teaching the subject that others did not wish to teach. Well, there again, I became involved in developing a more quantitative and seemingly rational (at least to me) approach to computer architecture and operating systems, which has given rise to the field of computer and network performance analysis and evaluation. For instance, I was able to prove results on paging algorithm performance which attracted the attention of some Hungarian and Russian mathematicians and physicists, as well as on memory space optimisation which drew theoretical design conclusions from Laszlo Belady's earlier measurements at IBM on "life-time functions". My development of novel "product form" networks which are also linked to statistical mechanics and theoretical chemistry, was motivated by listening to presentations from neuroscientists while visiting the National Aeronautics and Space Administration (NASA) Research Centre in California, but that is yet another story to be told below.

So yes — much of my work has had a theoretical bent, but it has almost always been driven by a strong link with engineering requirements or by observations from nature. Another example inspired by engineering is the research I did on "optimum checkpointing" in databases which appeared in the *Journal of the ACM*, but was motivated by a practical issue that was recounted to me by Claude Delobel in relation to the automatic storage in a database of "hits" during some fencing championships that were taking place in Grenoble, when the computer being used for this was having some intermittent failures! This work gave rise to a few PhD theses around me, and to much more work around the world. Other results were motivated by a property observed in a simpler context, and on the intuition that it actually holds in a much more general framework.

The QNAP2 (then Modline) software tool for performance evaluation was developed by my group at IRIA (now INRIA), and the specific technique that I personally contributed was on "diffusion approximations" that I first published in the *Journal of the ACM*.[2] This software tool has generated some 200 million euros of income over 20 years for the companies that commercialised it (initially SIMULOG, an INRIA spin-off company). The developers and inventors themselves hardly got anything; we were naive about such things. Throughout my career I have been involved with industry, *via* patents, *via* tools such as QNAP2, *via* consultancies or short-term assignments inside industry, and also *via* contracts to my university that are directly funded by industry. Of course, many of my PhD students have gone on to work for industry, most recently in the financial sector.

CC: You are a pioneer in the adaptive control of computer systems.

EG: I am bit like the elephant in the dark room: someone comes into the room, touches the leg of the elephant and thinks it is a tree, another person feels the tail and thinks it's a rope, and yet another catches the elephant's nose and thinks it's a hose! Some people think that I am a pioneer of computer system performance evaluation (at least that is what they say on my ACM Sigmetrics Award, and on my IEEE and ACM Fellowship Awards). The French Academy in 1996 gave me the France-Telecom Prize for developing mathematical models of communication networks. The Hungarian Academy of Sciences, in its recent election, mentions both my work on system and network performance and on neural networks and learning. As you indicate, in the last six or seven years I have been involved in developing ideas on adaptive computer systems and networks such as the "cognitive packet network" and this has helped generate research projects in "autonomic communications" in Europe. I was asked to write a paper about this work in the July 2009 issue of the *Communications of the ACM*. The Internet is largely a legacy system based on principles that find their origin in the computers and data communication systems of the 1970s, and it is working pretty well. Thus

---

[2]E. Gelenbe. On approximate computer system models, *Journal of the ACM*, 22(2): 261–269, 1975.

it is hard to introduce new concepts and methods. Much of the current networking research only addresses tweaks to well-understood aspects.

CC: Tell us about RNNs. You developed their theory — mathematics and learning algorithms — as well as some applications to engineering and biology.

EG: Let me first tell you what the RNN[3] is, and then I will get round to telling you how it came about. Consider a system composed of N counters, and let them be numbered $i, j = 1 \ldots N$. Each counter can have a value which is a natural number. At any instant t, only one of the following *events* can occur: the $i\,th$ counter increases by one (external arrival of an excitatory spike to neuron i), or if a counter has a positive value it may decrease by one (neuron i fires and the spike is sent out of the network), or a counter i may decrease by 1 and simultaneously some other counter increases by 1 (neuron i fires an excitatory spike which arrives instantaneously to neuron j), or i decreases by 1 and so does j if both start in a positive value (neuron i fires an inhibitory spike to j), or finally, at time t nothing happens. What this is modelling is a network of N neurons which are receiving and exchanging excitatory or inhibitory spikes. The system operates in continuous time so that t is a real number, making it a continuous time network of counters. It is quite extraordinary that this very simple model has some very powerful properties including the ability to learn,[4] and the ability to approximate continuous and bounded functions and also some very neat mathematical properties such as "product form".

It all started when I was visiting the RIACS Research Centre at NASA Ames, in Moffett Field, California, in the summers of 1987 and 1988. This was a lot of fun because at lunchtime, going out from the back of the laboratory one ended up directly on an airfield where the U2 spy aircraft was taking off. The body of this airplane

---

[3]E. Gelenbe. Random neural networks with positive and negative signals and product form solution, *Neural Computation*, 1(4): 502–510, 1989.

[4]E. Gelenbe. Learning in the recurrent random network, *Neural Computation*, 5: 154–164, 1993.

is very small and thin, with just enough room for one pilot and his instruments and commands, but the wings are very long. In fact, the wings have small wheels at the edges which support them at take-off; if they did not have the wheels they would be scraping the runway because the wings are long and too heavy to stay in a horizontal position. From Moffett Field, the job of the U2s was, officially, to fly along the US Pacific coast to try to spot and track Russian submarines. The Director of RIACS at that time was my friend Peter Denning who had just recently left Purdue University where he had been department head. My official job at RIACS was to work on the performance of parallel processing systems, since I had just published my small monograph on *Multiprocessor Performance.* NASA Ames had some of the largest supercomputers at that time since they were supposed to eventually replace wind tunnels (another specialty at NASA Ames) for the testing of aircraft and rockets. It is amusing to note that both supercomputers and windtunnels are "energy-vorous".

Another funny thing about my stay at NASA Ames, and these were the days before September 11, was that since it was supposed to be a very secure facility, and I was a "non-resident alien" (...what a funny name for a non-US citizen without a green card!), I was not allowed to enter the airbase officially and had to work in an external building just at the border of the base. But the funnier thing is that the building's back door was unlocked, so I could walk onto the tarmac and observe the U2s, also I could just walk over through the back door to the RIACS. Anyway, this is just to set the tone about my working environment. Peter Denning had recruited an interesting man called Penti Kanerva from Pat Suppes' entourage at Stanford. Penti was originally a forestry engineer from Finland who had completed a PhD in Philosophy with Suppes. He had invented a model of computation called "sparse distributed memory" (SDM) which is not too dissimilar from the Kohonen maps that you may know about. SDMs offer a nice adaptation or learning algorithm both for numerical and non-numerical data based on slowly modifying a data representation based on new data that is presented. As a result, Penti was also interested in natural neuronal networks, as were some other people who worked at RIACS, so they had organised a series of seminars by prominent neuroscientists. My work on the random neural network started in those circumstances. In the meanwhile I published a paper on the learning properties of SDM, which has remained rather obscure.

As many people of my generation, I was familiar with the McCulloch–Pitts model of neurons, and the Minsky–Papert controversy concerning non-linear perceptrons. I knew of John Hopfield's model and his results concerning "optimisation through relaxation", and of the work of the PDP Research Group at San Diego, and the contributions of Dave Rummelhart and Terry Sejnowsky, and about the backpropagation algorithm. At that time, Françoise Fogelman in Paris was a strong proponent of these techniques. My former student Andreas Stafylopatis from Athens was also quite interested in these things and we had tried our hand at some "collective stochastic models" for large numbers of neurons. But I felt, after listening to several presentations by neuroscientists, that none of these models actually captured the spiking activity of natural neuronal ensembles, and furthermore (except for John Hopfield's work) the PDP Group's work did not address the important issue of feedback in natural neuronal systems, or "recurrence" as people say in that area. Filled up with all these interesting neuroscience lectures I set to work upon my return to Paris in September of 1987. Also, I had the good luck of being hired by ONERA (French Aerospace Research Organisation) as a consultant in AI which was not my area, and I felt obliged to produce something significant. In six months I had developed the spiked RNN model, and obtained its analytical solution, but the people at ONERA could not understand what I was trying to do. The following summer I was back at RIACS, and met Dave Rummelhart who had moved to the Psychology Department at Stanford. I dropped abruptly one day into his office without knowing him personally, and told him what I had done. He was very friendly and interested, and invited me to give a seminar the following week. After the seminar he told me to submit my work to the journal that Terry Sejnowski, Dave and others had started a few years back, *Neural Computation*, and the first paper was rapidly accepted and published in 1989.

Several papers followed in the same venue over the years, and since the journal indicates the name of the handling editors after the papers were published I owe a debt of gratitude to Dave Cowan and Haim Sompolinsky, neither of whom I know personally. My learning algorithm came later in 1993: it was the first algorithm which established that learning for an N neuron recurrent network is of time complexity $O(N^3)$, while it was well known that the backpropagation algorithm for a feed-forward network is of time complexity $O(N^2)$. In the course of this work, there were applications to imaging, adventures and complications related to non-linear mathematics; there have been several other applications and extensions, and a return to biology while I was at Duke, but that would lead to an even longer story.

CC: Please describe the famous G-networks.

EG: Queueing theory has been around for at least as long as telephone systems have existed. The literature contains many tens of thousands of papers which appear either in publications related to the application domain (e.g., manufacturing systems, computer systems, the Internet, road traffic, etc.), or in more mathematical journals related to probability theory or operations research. It is a theory based on mathematical probability that considers a dynamical system composed of "service centres" and customers. The latter move around the service centres according to a designated probabilistic or deterministic behaviour, and at each service centre a customer waits in line and is then served according to a service discipline, e.g., First-in-First-Out, Round-Robin, Last-In-First-Out as in a push-down stack, or according to some priority scheme and so on. The service time of each customer in a service centre is typically given in the form of a probability density function or probability distribution, and this will typically differ in each service centre. In addition, customers may belong to "classes" so that the service time distributions and the routing of customers among different centres, may both depend on the class to which the customer belongs. Often independence assumptions are made about the service times and the routing of different customers even though they may belong to the same class. This is a very useful theory in that it is widely used in industry to design telecommunication systems, manufacturing systems, transportation, parts handling and assembly, etc. When such systems have a steady-state or long-term solution in which the joint probability distribution of the number of customers in each of the queues can be expressed as the product of the marginal distributions in each of the queues, despite the fact that the distinct service centre queues are in fact coupled, then we say that the queueing network has "product form"; examples include the Jackson Networks (that Len Kleinrock used in his very early work to model packet switching networks), and the Baskett–Chandy–Muntz–Palacios (BCMP) networks. Product form is a remarkable property which in general reduces the computational complexity of using queueing networks, from an enumeration of all possible states, to a polynomial time and space complexity.

G-networks extend a network of queues, to include certain new types of customers that can modify the behaviour of others. Thus "negative" customers[5] destroy other customers; for instance, they can represent external decisions that are made to reduce traffic because of congestion, or to remove packets in a network that may contain viruses. Triggers are yet another type of customer which can simply move customers from one queue to another. Multiple class G-nets are also discussed. Resets are customers that replenish queues when they are empty, to represent (for instance) a situation where we wish to keep some part of the system busy, or when queue length represents the degree of reliability so that "replenishment" corresponds to repairing a component. Thus, you can think of G-networks and queueing networks that also incorporate some useful control functions: for instance, the ordinary customers can be packets in a network, while these special customers can represent control signals that may travel through the network and affect the ordinary packets at certain specific nodes. The link between G-nets and neural networks is discussed.[6] All of these G-network models,

---

[5]E. Gelenbe. Product form queueing networks with negative and positive customers, *Journal of Applied Probability*, 28: 656–663, 1991.

[6]E. Gelenbe. G-networks: An unifying model for queueing networks and neural networks, *Annals of Operations Research*, 48(1–4): 433–461, 1994.

and other aspects discussed by my colleagues Jean-Michel Fourneau and Peter Harrison, lead to product forms. However, the solutions obtained differ from the earlier Jackson and BCMP networks in that they rely on *non-linear* "traffic equations" (rather than linear equations such as in BCMP models), which describe the flow of customers of different types and classes throughout the network. Because of this non-linearity, one also has to address questions of how and when the solutions that are obtained actually exist and are unique. My first paper on G-networks was turned down at an ACM-SIGMETRICS conference because the reviewers did not quite believe that new models in this area could be found and also solved analytically. Thus, I turned to journals dealing with applied probability... and some of my most cited papers are in this "strange" area which has attracted much attention over the last 20 years.

CC: Tell us about the design of the first random access fibre-optics local area network.

EG: This was a very interesting experience. In the mid 1970s, thanks to Louis Pouzin, who was finally recognised in 2013 as one of the pioneers of the Internet when he received the Queen Elizabeth II Prize, and an extremely sharp and amusing individual, I was put in contact with the group developing the Arpanet. In particular I met Bob Kahn in Washington. At that time, a new packet communication scheme using satellites had been devised: the ALOHA Network, which was implemented by Norman Abramson at the University of Hawaii. Of course, ALOHA is the "father" of the Ethernet. Abramson and Kahn had published papers that described the scheme and computed its maximum throughput; Leonard Kleinrock and his students were also studying the problem. I felt that the initial models were addressing steady-state analysis, in a context where the steady-state might not exist because the system was intrinsically unstable. Together with my collaborators Guy Fayolle and Jacques Labetoulle, we obtained a strong result, which after some delay appeared in the *Journal of the ACM* proving that the slotted random access communication channel (i.e., known as "slotted ALOHA") was intrinsically unstable due to potential simultaneous transmissions between uncoordinated transmitters, and that it could be stabilised and even optimised under a "$1/n$" policy, which was to retransmit previously collided packets at a rate that is inversely proportional to the number of backed-up transmitters. Strong results sometimes upset your colleagues. But Bob Metcalfe, who implemented Ethernet, was very positive about this work, as he wrote a few years ago to Jeff Buzen, his then advisor at Harvard.

This work started while I was at the University of Liège and at INRIA, and then I moved to Orsay (where I was one of the co-founders of the LRI, *Laboratoire de Recherche en Informatique*). At Orsay, I told Wladimir Mercouroff, a senior member of the university, that this work could have practical applications to locale area communications. He suggested funding *via* the *Délégation Générale à la Recherche Scientifique et Technique* (DGRST) jointly with a company called *La Calhène*, to build a fibre optics local area communication system for environments with strong electromagnetic perturbations. I would have been happier to use coaxial technology but the funding agency favoured fibre optics. So we ended up building a prototype called Xanthos, which used DEC-LSI11 processors as access nodes, and fibre optics for transport with the random access protocol using our optimal control algorithm along with a clever scheme we had devised to estimate deviation from optimality based on the frequency of the fibre channel's "silent" periods. Once the system was up and running, I presented it to the French Telecommunications authority for possible commercialisation. They told me that this work was of academic interest, but because we were using random access, we could only guarantee delivery times on average and in probability, rather than with fixed maximum delays; being rather naive at the time, I believed them. So the project was set aside. A couple of years later Ethernet appeared, and I am sure that some French Telecom people were biting their nails. As I said, Bob Metcalfe knows this story. As a consolation prize, the French Telecom hired me as a consultant for a few years and I was able to do several other things for them, but they (and I) missed out on a major opportunity. What happened to Louis Pouzin and his team at INRIA, for similar reasons and regarding the Internet as a whole, is a far more tragic-comic story.

CC: You patented an admission control technique for ATM networks.

EG: This was an application of my earlier theoretical paper on diffusion approximations for queueing systems which was rejected for a prestigious French conference. My results then appeared in the *Journal of the ACM* and *Acta Informatica*, motivated by the need to simplify the calculations of queue lengths, server utilisation and so on, when you have "non-exponential" assumptions. Diffusion approximations and Brownian motion are well known, and there is a wonderful book on the subject by Albert Einstein. This approach had been suggested to approximate road traffic congestion by G.F. Newell (Berkeley), and then by Hisashi Kobayashi (IBM) for computer system performance. My original contribution introduced a mixed discrete-continuous model to address "low traffic" conditions which were ignored in earlier work. This gave rise to mixed differential and partial differential equations which I solved in "closed form". In the mid 1990s, IBM was designing its N-Way switch for ATM (Asynchronous Transfer Mode) networks. The design was carried out at Raleigh (North Carolina) near Duke University where I was department head; the hardware was being designed at IBM's *La Gaude* Laboratory. The fashionable approach at that time to admission control was to use "large deviations", whose originator Varadhan from the Courant Institute in was 2010, like me, was elected to the Hungarian Academy of Sciences, but large deviations only provide "order of magnitude" estimates of packet or cell loss, which is the primary metric of interest in ATM. I was awarded a contract by IBM-Raleigh to look at the problem and we developed an algorithm that used the predictions of my model to decide whether to admit a new flow into the network, based on predictions for packet or cell loss. One of my students, Xiaowen Mang (now at AT&T Labs), performed the simulations. Because it all seemed to work well we patented the technique together with IBM engineers Raif Onvural and Jerry Marin. The US Patent was awarded in 1998 or 1999. Links to these ideas can be found in my recent work on packet travel time in networks.

CC: What is the "cognitive packet network" routing protocol?

EG: Call it CPN[7] to make things simpler. It is an algorithm that runs on specific network routers within an IP (Internet Protocol) or similar network (including sensor and *ad hoc* networks), which adaptively chooses paths with desirable properties such as better delay or loss characteristics, lower energy consumption, lower economic cost, greater security or a combination of such criteria. The combination of criteria is incorporated into a "goal" or objective function, whose instantaneous value is established based on measurements collected with the help of "smart packets". CPN is based upon online measurements, and responds to observations which are being made and which will in general change over time so that CPN's choices also change. CPN offers the end-user the possibility to make such choices, although the end-user may delegate the decisions to an agent which manages its access to the network or which manages several end-users. CPN uses two mechanisms; the first is the use of "smart packets" which act as scouts and collect and bring back measurements. The second is the use of recurrent RNNs which are installed in routers that take part in CPN's decisions (not all routers need do this) and which act as oracles; the excitatory and inhibitory connections of these RNNs are updated using the reinforcement learning rule based on the goal function, as a result of the measurements constantly collected by the smart packets. The RNNs are used to route the smart packets (i.e., to inform the ongoing "search"), while all the resulting measurement information concerning the goal is returned to the end-user or to its decision agent. The decision agent may then decide to follow completely or only partially, the advice it receives, so as to select the best paths in the network. For instance, the decision agent may wish to reduce the frequency with which it makes changes in paths so as to avoid needless oscillations; in that case it may only decide to change a path if the estimated benefit is very high. CPN has been implemented in several wired and wireless network test-beds.

---

[7]E. Gelenbe, M. Gellman, R. Lent, P. Su. Autonomous smart routing for network QoS, *Proc. First International Conference on Autonomic Computing*, IEEE Computer Society, 232–239, Washington D.C., 2004.

It has also been considered as a means to direct people in crowded environments, or in emergency situations.

CC: You have collaborated with the telecommunication and computer industry in various capacities. How useful/relevant are theoretical results for this industry?

EG: I think that the value of theory in our field, when it is based on realistic assumptions and sound evaluation, lies in its ability to provide tremendous short-cuts that avoid a lot of tedious work based on experimentation and testing. My first inroads into the telecommunications industry were related to the performance evaluation of the E10 electronic switch in the late 1970s. The E10 was in fact a large-scale computer, together with electronic equipment, that was going to be used to establish and automatically manage large numbers of telephone calls. It was to replace the previous "dumb" electronic switching systems. The French Telecom research centre CNET had been involved in trying to evaluate whether the E10 was performing up to specification, and they were relying on simulations which were taking orders of magnitude longer than the time it took the E10 system itself to execute the corresponding task. The team studying this was at the end of their tether, and the team leader finally had a (real) nervous breakdown. Together with my PhD student Jean Vicard we stepped in and within six months we had a mathematical model based on queueing networks which was quite accurate and which could be solved in seconds of computer time, rather than in hours or days of simulation time. Thanks to this work, I continued being funded by CNET for 20 years and they hired several of my former PhD students. This also explains why many of my former PhD students teach in France at schools such as *Institut National des Télécommunications and École Nationale des Télécommunications.*

CC: In France in 1982 you designed and implemented a national vocational training in computer technology called the *"Programme des Volontaires pour la Formation à l'Informatique."*

EG: This was a very interesting experience. At the suggestion of Jacques Gualino, who was one of INRIA's managing staff, I started working with the people who had launched the "Centre Mondial pour l'Informatique" in Paris, namely Jean-Jacques Servan-Schreiber, Nicholas Negroponte and Seymour Papert. The latter two wanted to help the third world *via* personal computers, while Jean-Jacques was actually (I think) on a mission to transform the French bureaucracy through a greater use of information technology and to attain some form of political power or political role in the process. The year was 1982, soon after the elections that had brought François Mitterr and the Socialist Party to power, so there was an opportunity to make some changes — but the question was what this centre could do. While these people aimed at lofty and global goals, I decided to tackle a relatively small project. I felt that much of the vocational education in France was obsolete and essentially taking misguided teenagers and turning them into disgruntled unemployed people, simply because vocational education was essentially dispensed by obsolete technical educators in obsolete machine shops which "trained" young people to operate obsolete equipment for jobs that did not exist. On the other hand, both industry and the service sector were looking for people who had some simple computer education that could be used in technical and service jobs. However, instructors who were knowledgeable computer scientists and engineers were just too expensive to provide instruction cheaply. Furthermore, computer equipment was scarce and expensive. In conversations with Jean-Jacques Servan-Schreiber, Pierre Lafitte (then President of the École des Mines in Paris) and myself, we came up with the idea of using newly graduated engineers who could do a "vocational education" service for youngsters instead of their military service where they were often getting very bored. Though conceptually simple, the whole programme had to be "engineered", which I did, so that several hundred young graduate engineers could do this new form of civilian service instead of going into the military for one year. Several ministries had to be convinced. Several million francs for equipment, wiring and room security (against computer theft) were needed to get started, and the network of training centres for unemployed young people also had to be incorporated into the task. The long and short of it is that we were successful: up to 700 young graduating engineers and computer scientists got involved in this programme each year. Personal computers from a variety of sources were purchased and installed in small groups of 10 PCs per training centre. Tens of thousands of young unemployed people were trained and many entered the job market successfully. For the first two years I ran the programme and collected detailed statistics about what was happening. Then the programme was taken over by existing social and government bodies. It came to an end towards 1989 after Jacques Chirac became Prime Minister and some things introduced by the Socialist government were abrogated.

CC: You also served as Science and Technology Advisor to the French Minister of Universities, and member of the Executive Board and of the Science and Technology Board of the Data and Information Fusion Defence Technology Centre in the UK, and chaired the Technical Advisory Board (TAB) of the US Army Simulation and Training Command.

EG: The VFI programme that I discussed before attracted the attention of the then French Minister for Universities, Professor Roger-Gérard Schwartzenberg. Normally, I should never have been in his group of advisors: I was a recent immigrant who had not studied at a *Grande École*. All of his other advisors, except the three political appointees from his party who had been to *Sciences Politiques* (Sciences Po in Paris) had either studied at *École Nationale d'Administration* (ENA) or at *École Polytechnique*. There was a Professor of Medicine who advised the Minister on the medical side of things, and then this strange individual: me. Some of the other people in his group of advisors and higher civil servants in the ministry obviously thought I was totally out of place. But I was a young professor from the best science campus in France, Orsay and I taught part-time at *École Polytechnique*, so I could not be all stupid. I spoke and wrote French well, and the Minister's parents had been immigrants, so he was open-minded. I was offered the job because the VFI programme had shown that I was a "go-getter", able to handle large projects and deal with the arcane administration. Sure enough I did bring together another large project. The year was 1984, and most students in French universities and *Grande Écoles* did not have an introductory course in computer science. The barriers were the usual ones: where to find the lecturers, where to find the computers, where to find the space with appropriate electrical and network connectivity as well as security, and what to teach. The whole funding issue needed to be dealt with because we needed to buy 800 PCs and install them in groups of eight or ten, and the installation itself would cost quite a bit of money. We had to open many junior faculty positions for teaching. We set up working groups to design the material that would be taught by group of disciplines: maths-physics, biology, economics, humanities and so on. I will not dwell on the details, but it worked out well; and also made many of my colleagues unhappy because they thought they could use the equipment funds much better for CS research, without realising that we could not attract such a large investment in research alone and that the equipment and new faculty were in themselves an investment in research as well. In my role as advisor, I had several other jobs too: monitor and expand the different scientific disciplines that I was dealing with, monitor the engineering schools, deal with the transformation of the *École Normale Supérieuere* (a very interesting story to tell separately some day), the transformations of PhD programmes and so on. An initiative which proved very useful was *"Arrêté"* which has allowed some of the *Grande Ecoles* to deliver the PhD degree: it has significantly increased the research activities at many of the elite schools in France. At the end of two years of doing this job from 8 am to 8 pm, I was totally exhausted. I was delighted (!) when in the spring of 1986 the Socialist Government lost the elections and I could leave this harassing activity to return to my lab. In those two years I did manage to write one or two decent papers and to graduate some PhD students, but it was tough.

You mentioned the TAB of the US Army Simulation and Training Command. I spent 1993 to 1998 at Duke University as Head of Department, and then moved to Orlando, Florida. There I was the Director of the School of Electrical Engineering and Computer Science (SEECS) from 1998 to 2003, which I founded by merging several programmes at the University of Central Florida. I was in contact with the neighbouring modelling and simulation facilities for the US Army where much of the training is heavily computerised. I was asked first to sit on the TAB for a year, and then to chair it for four years until I moved to Imperial College. This offered possibilities for interaction with a sophisticated organisation in areas such as virtual and enhanced reality, games, simulation, networking and distributed computing. At UCF I was also Associate Dean of Engineering and headed an organisation with three departments, a total of 2200 students, nearly 100 professors and lecturers, three Master's and three PhD programmes, and four distinct undergraduate degree programmes in computer science, computer engineering, electrical engineering and information technology. In the five years I was there, we also secured $ 15 million for a new building, and it was nice to participate in its design. I have visited it several times since my departure, and have enjoyed seeing my "creation" which is probably the nicest building on the UCF campus.

In 2003, when I joined Imperial College, the UK Government had decided to transfer much of its defence-related research (except for the top secret stuff) to universities. I was one of the writers of a proposal to start a research centre around Imperial College joining with other universities and industry. We succeeded in securing a budget of £10 million per year for six successive years, with half of it from three companies: BT, General Dynamics UK Ltd and QientiQ, which ran until 2009. Since I was involved in the inception, I become one of two Science and Technology Directors, and a member of the Executive and Science Board of the *Data and Information Fusion Defence Technology Centre*. It meant weekly travel around the UK, and was a good way for me to learn about the UK. Now that it has ended, I do appreciate the opportunity to spend more time on my own research.

CC: What is your vision about the future of academic publication?

EG: The deluge of conferences, and of call for papers, is something I have a hard time dealing with. On the other hand, they do keep us informed about which areas are emerging, so it all comes at the price of clicking the delete button many times in the morning! There is this race for citations, and also the excess in publications, both facilitated by word processing software and multiple conferences. I wonder about myself when I see that I may have published some 20 papers in a year. In a way we seem to have all started to imitate the biology community, and I also wonder about papers with so many authors. I still try to keep a traditional zone of work for myself, just working by myself on certain more theoretical problems, and many of my best cited papers are single author. But we are of course part of a dying breed, and we are encouraged to have large collaborative and well-funded projects and to have many PhD students and post docs. I also read with amusement some papers, coming in particular from India, which seem to have copied in their own way material that has long been in the open literature.

The deluge has an inevitable consequence in that we may not know what a person in a related field has actually contributed in terms of scientific output, but we just know whether that person has many citations or not. I find it strange to be introduced by my "h-index" when I give a talk. It is so much easier and more neutral for someone to say something numerical about someone else, rather than to make a qualitative statement or to actually try to understand another person's contributions. It is a bit like bureaucrats who can list statistics without understanding what they actually mean.

In the future I do hope that we can return to more focus on quality rather than just numbers or statistics. However, I certainly do appreciate the role of tools such as Google Scholar, which allow us to know about people, including graduate students, across the world whom we may never meet but who share some of our own scientific and technical interests. By looking at the papers that cite me, I learn about the work and interests of others in a wide range of countries. This is indeed of great human value since it tells us what we all share despite great distances in travel, time and cultures.

I subscribe to the principle of open access with refereeing, but I also think that someone has to pay for it. The cost probably needs to be part of the cost of research since academic research cannot exist without adequately refereed dissemination.

CC: What gives you most pleasure in the academic work?

EG: I think that we are so lucky to have such a fun job. That's probably why we are not good at getting a decent salary in relation to the number of hours that we put into it. Exercising my curiosity and learning new things, being able to talk to experts about subjects that are new to me, being a bit of clown when I lecture, and enjoying the interest of young people, these are some of the things I really enjoy in my work.

I find it so interesting to be constantly in touch with a new generation of younger people with different interests and skills from the previous generations. The way I teach today is very different from my teaching 30 years ago, since I have to adapt to the students' interests and skills. Similarly, the research topics I may suggest today for beginning PhD students also reflect these changes. Having met and worked with young people from so many different countries, ranging from the Sudan and Egypt, to Brazil, Italy, China, France, Russia, Greece, India, Turkey, Venezuela, the USA, Hungary, Macedonia, Korea, Poland, Taiwan and so on, has been such a fantastic privilege of my profession as a teacher and academic.

CC: Did you ever miss a target? How did you cope?

EG: I miss targets all the time, and one reason is that I am rather dispersed as to the subjects that interest me. Right now they are computer networks, gene regulatory networks,[8] viruses in nature and in computers, economics, synthetic chemistry and a few other things (!). I have given up pursuing conference deadlines. I try to publish papers on my work in the best relevant journals, and I benefit from serious refereeing and criticism: referees are my best teachers these days!

---

[8]E. Gelenbe. Steady-state solution of probabilistic gene regulatory networks, *Physical Review E*, 76(1): 031903, 2007.

Chapter 3

David Harel: From Theoretical Computer Science to Behavioural Programming, Biology and Smell

Professor David Harel, http://www.wisdom.weizmann.ac. il/~harel, *is incumbent of the William Sussman Professorial Chair at the Weizmann Institute of Science and until recently was the head of the John von Neumann Minerva Center for the Development of Reactive Systems.*

Professor Harel has received honorary degrees from the University of Rennes, the Open University of Israel, the University of Milano-Bicocca and Eindhoven University of Technology. He is a Fellow of the ACM, the IEEE and the AAAS, and is a member of the Academia Europaea and the Israel Academy of Sciences and Humanities, and a Foreign Associate of the US National Academy of Engineering. His long list of awards includes the ACM Karlstrom Outstanding Educator Award (1992), the Stevens Award in

Software Development Methods (1996), the Israel Prize (2004), the ACM SIGSOFT Outstanding Research Award (2006), the ACM Software System Award (2007), the ACM SIGSOFT Impact Paper Award (2008) and the Emet Prize (2010).

CC: How was computer science during your studies at Bar-Ilan University (BSc), Tel Aviv University (MSc) and MIT (PhD) in the 1970s?

DH: At Bar-Ilan University in the early 1970s, I took mathematics as a major and computer science as a minor (there was no major in CS then). Studies in CS were mostly technical: languages, programming, operating systems, etc., but there was also a wonderful course on computability and automata given by Yaakov Choueka. Incidentally, Moshe Vardi and Nachum Dershowitz were my contemporaries there, as was Assaf Marron, who now works in my group at Weizmann as a research fellow. I remember reaching a point in the first year there (before taking Choueka's course), where I said to myself, "OK, great. I can now write a program that computes the average of a series of numbers; what else is there to learn in computer science?" So a CS degree at that time was very different from what one would get these days, especially for someone with an inclination towards more mathematical topics. Our entire final year, by the way, was jeopardised by the 1973 Yom Kippur War, for which I was mobilised as a reserve officer for nine months; we had to take all the senior year courses during the summer of 1974.

At that point, since my impression of CS was that it was more or less just programming and some system stuff, I started an MSc programme in algebraic topology at Tel Aviv University. After a year of courses, I was about to give up, when a chance conversation with an elderly numerical analyst, Phillip Rabinowitz, changed my life: he suggested that I have a chat with Amir Pnueli, who was then a young Professor at Tel Aviv University, which I promptly did. I ended up switching to CS on the spot, doing my MSc thesis under Amir's supervision on program proving and the logic of programs. And I remember that the first thing Amir asked me to do was to study Zohar Manna's wonderful book, *Mathematical Theory of Computation.* That is when I started to get a deeper appreciation for the theoretical facets of computer science.

MIT was fine, though I kind of rushed in and out, getting the PhD 20 months after arriving. (This was more out of necessity than out of any special talent: I simply had a young family with two small children and had to start earning fast...) My time there under the supervision of Vaughan Pratt and Albert Meyer was extremely eye-opening. Vaughan and Albert are two very different personalities, both brilliant in their own different ways. This work launched my career. And taking courses from the likes of Ron Rivest and Ed Fredkin did not do any harm either...

CC: I remember reading and using a nice paper by Choueka and Amihood Amir on loop-programs and polynomially computable functions, published in 1981. Did Choueka's course include this topic?

DH: That's indeed a really nice paper, and I have taught its contents myself. However, without using quantum-driven time machines there is no way Choueka could have included it in our course, which took place in 1972.

CC: The first period of your academic activity was devoted to theoretical computer science: computability theory, logics of programs, database theory and automata theory. Can you choose one result from each area and comment it?

DH: In computability, I would mention two. The first is the *STOC* 1979 (journal version: *JCSS* 1980) completeness result for computable queries, with Ashok Chandra. At the time, we presented this as work on the theory of database queries, but it is actually a lot more general. We like to think of it as a natural extension of the classical Turing–Church–Gödel notion of computability, from words and numbers to general (not necessarily ordered) structures. Good examples are graphs, relational databases or hierarchical web-like structures. The important thing was to provide the "right" definition of the set of all computable functions over structures. We did this (after choosing the framework of relational structures as the one to work on) by requiring that in addition to having to be computable in the classical sense one requires the functions to preserve isomorphisms, so as not to use information that is not available in the structure itself. We were then able to prove that there was a simple complete language (which can be viewed as the first-order relational algebra or calculus augmented with simple loops), which captures exactly the set of computable queries. Over the years, this result has been generalised to cover essentially all manner of well-defined structures.

While we are on the topic of computability on general unordered structures, I should mention the problem Chandra and I posed in our second (1980) paper (journal version: *JCSS* 1982), which was whether the set of polynomially computable functions over such structures is recursively enumerable (or as Yuri Gurevich later put it, whether it has a logic). This problem is still open now, after almost 35 years, and is considered one of the most important problems in finite model theory and structural complexity.

The second result in computability I'd like to mention is the high undecidability of detecting Hamiltonicity in recursive graphs, from *STOC* 1991. This is a Σ_1^1/Π_1^1 result, and I particularly like it because of its rather "cute" picturesque proof...

In logics of programs, the various axiomatisations of dynamic logic from my 1978 PhD thesis might be noteworthy, as well as the high undecidability of many different logics, such as context-free PDL (1981). In automata theory I'd mention the 1988 work (journal version: *JACM* 1994) on extending automata with — in addition to non-determinism and classical parallelism — the new notion of bounded coordinated concurrency, which originates in the language of Statecharts. This comes with a set of results on the exponential power of succinctness that this gives, over and above that offered by non-determinism and parallelism.

CC: Are there any results you obtained in theoretical computer science that have proved useful in applications?

DH: Not directly, although I like to think of the work with Chandra on computability over structures, and a year later on the complexity theory thereof, as something that may have influenced practical work on query languages for databases. Also, I think that the aforementioned work on the succinctness of Statecharts viewed as automata might have influenced the seriousness with which languages like Statecharts are taken by engineers out there in the real world.

CC: What was your motivation to switch from theoretical to more applied computer science?

DH: Well, I didn't actually switch; there was no conscious decision. In 1983, I was invited to consult for the Israel Aircraft Industries on an avionics project, which is when I started to think more seriously about the problems of specifying the behaviour of what Pnueli and I later identified as *reactive systems*. It was then that I was able to come up with the Statecharts language and the methods around it. (This process is described in a rather personal 2007 *HOPL* paper, with a short version appearing in *Communications of the ACM* in 2009.) Over the years, this line of work became more central to my overall activity. The turning point can be said to have occurred with the publication of my last pure theory paper, the 1991 one on Hamiltonicity in recursive graphs. Since then, the only theory I have done is directly related to the practical issues that come up in the other areas of my work.

So, returning to the phrasing of your question, I think that in most cases this kind of move isn't done by premeditated motivation; you simply get caught up in it. Of course, seeing that people actually use your work in real world applications can have a more conscious influence on one's decisions about future research. In addition, it's often an individual issue of talent and ability: I've never thought of myself as being able to do the deepest and most profound work in theoretical computer science. Thus, in time, the more practical facets of our field seemed to be more fitting.

CC: What is the language of Statecharts and, more generally, behavioural programming?

DH: Well, this is very hard to answer in a brief interview like this. Both the language of Statecharts (1984) and the more recent language of *live sequence charts*, LSCs, (1999), the latter defined together with Werner Damm and later extended with Rami Marelly, are visual formalisms. They are languages for specifying reactive behaviour, which are both formal and rigorous like any other language or any other mathematical concept, but are also inherently visual and diagrammatic. The visuality does not come from using icons, but from using topological and geometric artiefacts in the syntax.

We have recently started to use the term *behavioural programming*, as a more general way to capture a programming paradigm that allows people to program complex reactive systems in a way that is driven by, or oriented towards, behaviour, rather than structure. Perhaps I should point the reader to a 2008 *IEEE Computer* paper on "liberating programming" and a more recent *Comm. ACM* paper (July 2012) on behavioural programming, in order to get the gist of the idea. In this approach, modularity is not necessarily achieved by the structure, but can be done by behaviours. You don't have to think of your system's behaviour as being "chopped up" into objects or tasks or components; you can chop it up any way you want according to the way you like to think about the behaviour. These ideas were inspired by the rich structuring of Statecharts into multi-level states, but really took off with the LSCs. LSCs offer the ability to program using highly modular scenarios, which can be broken up any way you want, but which are also very modal, in the sense that the behaviours can be specified as necessary, possible, forbidden, etc. Something that is not allowed is considered a first-class-citizen behaviour, just like something that has to be done and which you imperatively instruct the program to do. The modularity and the modality are both taken into account in full in the execution engines that run behavioural programs.

In addition to LSCs, we also have non-visual versions of the behavioural programming approach. Of particular interest is a Java version, which allows one to program behaviourally with standard Java tools and compilers, enriched with a small new Java library. And there are versions in other languages too, such as C++ and Erlang. More details can be found in the *Comm. ACM* paper.

In this way, our work is a step towards liberating the programmer not only from the need to specify behaviour according to the structure of the program or the system, but also of the need to specify two artiefacts — what you want your computer to do and your expectations of the program, i.e., its requirements — since both can actually be part of the same fully executable artefact.

CC: Over the years, your work on languages and methods for software and systems was accompanied by your participation in the design of the tools Statemate (1984–1987), Rhapsody (1997) and the Play-Engine (2003).

DH: Yes, I have always made a point of accompanying this kind of research with the building of actual tools. Statemate and Rhapsody were built in a company I co-founded in 1984, I-Logix, which was later acquired by Telelogic and which, as of 2006, is part of IBM. So both of these tools are now IBM products and I'm no longer involved in any of that. The Play-Engine, and our more recent tool, PlayGo, were built here in my group at the Weizmann Institute. They are not commercial and are available to download, but hopefully one day they too will become (or will inspire) commercial tools. Statemate and Rhapsody essentially are the central tools for using Statecharts in the non-object-oriented and object-oriented versions, respectively. The Play-Engine and PlayGo are geared towards LSCs and behavioural programming.

CC: Please tell us about your "sniffer" and, more generally, about your work on the synthesis and communication of smell.

DH: Actually the work is not about a sniffer *per se*. The scientifically significant facet of my work on olfaction has to do with trying to solve what I think is the major problem in this area: the ability to carry out the olfactory analogue of taking a digital photograph and then printing the picture on a piece of paper. Here you would first of all need an input device, a sort of electronic nose, the sniffer, which can take some kind of digital signature of any odour, even an unknown one. Then comes the interesting part: complicated mathematics and algorithmics have to be carried out, following which a set of instructions is given to an output "printing" device, which we call the whiffer, to emit a particular mixture of a predetermined set of odorous materials that are inside the whiffer (the "ink" colours). This emitted mixture must have the property of being as close an approximation of the original odour as is possible under the whiffer's circumstances.

Now, since odour is not captured by waves, unlike audio or video, you cannot simply do a Fourier or reverse-Fourier transform. We sniff molecules, and so your system must whiff molecules, otherwise the human nose and brain will not sense them. So the problems are a lot more difficult. They involve psycho-physical issues, comparing human perception with the chemical setup and structure of odorants, and many other things.

Around a decade ago, with two colleagues, I published a viable scheme for how this can be carried out. Still, the scheme requires a tremendous amount of research and understanding about olfaction, much of which is not yet available. On the other hand, we've had some exciting results published on "understanding" odour, including a paper a few years ago showing that it is possible to artificially predict what is known as the most significant and robust component of our perception of odour — pleasantness. So by sniffing with an electronic nose, and with a high rate of success, you can tell how pleasant an average human would rate a given odour. Still, it is a long road ahead before we can achieve the grand challenge of being able to communicate and synthesise unknown odours; that is, to sniff them and reproduce them in a different location accurately and reliably.

CC: Few top researchers spend time in academic administration, but you did as head of the department, then dean of your faculty, and then head of a research centre. How did you manage? What did you achieve?

DH: Well, first of all, in our particular institute these tasks are not as difficult as in, say, a large university. The main reason is that we do not have undergraduates. So one could say that roughly being Dean of the Faculty of Mathematics and Computer Science at the Weizmann Institute is similar to being a department head in a conventional university, because the faculty is relatively small and we have only graduate students, but no undergraduates.

How did I manage? I think I was an OK dean, but nothing spectacular. Instead of coming to work in the morning thinking "what can I do for the faculty today?", I'd come in and think "when will I be able to get through this administrative paperwork and all these meetings and be able to sit down to do the things I really like?"

I don't think I have some of the characteristics required of a really good manager. This is also one of the reasons I've always refused to head an entire institution. I've been approached to "run" for president of our own institute, and of several universities, and have always refused, not even giving serious thought to such offers. I don't think I could do a very good job there. Also, I'm still heavily involved in research and in the midst of a demanding research program. Thus, even with managerial talent, which I personally happen not to have, I wouldn't feel like spending 90% of my time in management.

CC: The citation for your most recent honorary doctorate has the following statement: "he has put forward the grand challenge of liberating system development from the straightjackets of programming." How will programming evolve in the next decades?

DH: Well, again, I would have loved to talk at length about this, but can't. So, again, the reader is referred to the 2008 "dream" paper in *IEEE Computer*, titled "Can Programming be Liberated, Period?", as well as to another paper that was published in *SoSyM*, jointly with Assaf Marron, titled, "The Quest for Runware: On Compositional, Executable and Intuitive Models". Both give a relatively detailed — if personal — point of view about how programming will evolve in the next decades. But, very briefly, I think that programming should, and will, evolve to become something much closer to the way we "program" other people, as when we bring up our children, supervise our students or give instructions to our employees or to our broker, real-estate agent or whatever. This is the most general notion of programming: to cause other entities to do what we have in mind for them.

I think this kind of intuitive, informal means should be applicable to programming computers too. Sometimes you'd give an explicit instruction, like "do the dishes now!", and sometimes you'd just show by example how something is to be done. Sometimes you'd give a constraint, like "do whatever you want but be home by 11:00 pm", and very often you'd give a forbidden instruction, such as, "never do so-and-so; I forbid this". The idea is to turn programming into an activity that would be natural and intuitive, using, e.g., natural language and very easy-to-do interactions. Clearly, the programming tools would have to be embodied with a tremendous amount of understanding, learning, theorem proving, verification, analysis, synthesis and heuristics, all of which would be active under the table, so to speak, turning this informal, intuitive interaction into an actual executable program. I believe that for many kinds of systems this will be the way things will be done in the future, and we have done quite a bit of work in this direction already.

CC: What is your opinion about the central dogma of digital computing: "computers cannot compute without programmers"?

DH: I don't have a strong opinion about this, as it seems more like a philosophical question. There will always be a need for programmers. The question is whether in the future they will do what most of them do today, which is to write code (or in the best case, to come up with an algorithm and then code it, or to write pieces of code that have to interact with other pieces of code). I think the activity of future programmers will be on a much higher level of abstraction, and will be far more "objective-oriented" (if I may use a pun), with a much larger amount of their time devoted to the deeper issues of how you want your system to behave, leaving a lot of the details about how that is to be achieved to powerful computing tools behind the scenes.

CC: I had the pleasure of reading your book *Computers Ltd.: What They Really Can't Do*. Your book *Algorithmics: The Spirit of Computing*, as well as the series of lectures on radio and programmes on television, have all been aimed at a broader audience. What was the response you got?

DH: Thanks for the compliment...I have actually received an incredibly good response to this expository work, which includes those two books and some other things too. However, one has to be careful because there is a saying that the worst thing that can happen to a scientist is that he or she is considered a good expositor or populariser...I hope that's not something that people think of seriously when they see this work.

Maybe I should add that what I am most proud of is not a particular book or a particular series of lectures, but the fact that I had the lucky opportunity, relatively early in the computer science game, to decide what, in my humble opinion, were the most fundamental issues in computer science. The self-test here was to try to choose — already in 1984, 30 years ago — those topics that I thought would still be relevant in 20 years time. To a large extent, I feel that the decisions I took then turned out to be valid. For example, the *Algorithmics* book was published in 1987 and in 2012 there was a new printing of its third edition, in which very little had to be changed. Of course, there are many new results and new ideas, but apart from programming languages, which have changed quite a bit since the 1980s, and new chapters on system development, most of the issues that were included in the original version are still included in today's edition of that book, almost unchanged. So the test of time regarding what is fundamental and important in computer science seems to have met with success, and that is really my greatest joy in this expository work. People who write about computers and the Internet, or about languages and methods, know that 10 years later, and often just five, they have to rewrite everything because things will have changed. On the other hand, if you concentrate on algorithms and their complexity, on intractability, undecidability, correctness and efficiency, and to some extent even on AI, you have to add and extend, but the basic issues remain the same.

CC: What advice would you give a talented student wishing to start graduate studies in computer science?

DH: Hmmm... One thing that comes to mind is not to be afraid of rejection. My 1984 Statecharts paper took three years to get published, after being repeatedly rejected from several of the most widely read CS journals, including *Comm. ACM* and *IEEE Computer* (and it now has almost 8000 citations...). Do serious research, have confidence in what you do, and be persistent in exposing it.

Another point is more relevant to undergraduates or to graduate students who have not yet settled on the exact field of research in which they want to work. My advice would be to go for mathematics and computer science, or physics and computer science, and in this day and time maybe the best is to go for biology and computer science. A person with a good background in maths and physics, or maths and biology weaved with computer science, is prepared for doing cutting-edge 21st century science. In fact, perhaps it is best to end this interview with the following statement, which appears in a couple of my recent papers on modelling biology, and which captures my belief about the role computer science will play in the coming years: "computer science is poised to play a role in the science of the 21st century, which will be dominated by the life sciences, similar to the role played by mathematics in the science of the 20th century, much of which was dominated by the physical sciences".

CC: Speaking of rejections: we have all read about famous papers being rejected. The very long list includes Turing's "On Computable Numbers", Shannon's "Mathematical Theory of Communication", Hoare's "Axiomatic Basis for Computer Programming" and Bernes-Lee's first paper on WWW. How can one avoid serious mistakes in the peer-reviewed process?

DH: Well, humans write the papers and humans review them. Such things will always happen and I wouldn't even call them mistakes. At the time, no one could have known how these things would work out, and for a reviewer or editor in a serious publication venue it is safer and more professional to prefer not to publish something about which you are doubtful, and to risk erring on that side of the issue than to publish crap and err on the other side of it...

Chapter 4

Juris Hartmanis: Computational Complexity

Professor Juris Hartmanis, a Turing Award Winner, is the Walter R. Read Professor of Computer Science and Engineering, Emeritus, Department of Computer Science, Cornell University, Ithaca, USA. He is a pioneer, founder and a major contributor to the area of computational complexity.[1]

Professor Hartmanis' eminent career also includes a strong service component: he served on numerous important committees (Turing Award Committee, Gödel Prize Committee, Waterman Award Committee); he was director of NSF's Directorate for Computer and Information Science and Engineering. Professor Hartmanis has been honoured with many awards and prizes. He was elected a member

---

[1]http://en.wikipedia.org/wiki/Juris_Hartmanis.

of the National Academy of Engineering and Latvian Academy of Sciences, and a fellow of the American Academy of Arts and Sciences, the Association for Computing Machinery, New York State Academy of Sciences, the American Association for the Advancement of Science and the National Academy of Sciences. He has an Honorary Doctor of Humane Letters from the University of Missouri at Kansas City and a Dr.h.c. from the University of Dortmund, Germany.

CC: Your early studies took you from Latvia to Marburg in Germany and then to the University of Missouri–Kansas City and Caltech in the USA. You studied physics and mathematics. Could you reminisce about those years?

JH: My education took place in three different countries on two continents and in three different languages. It all started in Riga, Latvia where I was born into a prominent Latvian family and had a happy childhood. My father was a high-ranking officer in the Latvian army and later Chief of Staff of the Latvian army. In Riga I attended the French Lycee and spent happy summers on our country estate. This all ended in the summer of 1940 when the Soviet Union occupied the Baltic countries, Estonia, Latvia and Lithuania. The Russians arrested my father and our country estate was nationalised. The Russian occupation was indeed horrible: not only were high-ranking military officers and government officials arrested, tens of thousands of people were deported to Siberian Gulags. In school we learned about the great achievements of the Soviet Union.

In the summer of 1941 Germany attacked Russia and in a matter of weeks the Soviets were driven out of Latvia and the German occupation started. Our country estate was returned and was instrumental in easing food shortages during the four-year German occupation. The French Lycee became a public school and French was replaced by German as the obligatory foreign language.

For the summer of 1944 the family again moved to our country estate, in Western Latvia. By this time, the war was going very badly for Germany and by late fall much of Latvia was in Soviet hands and all land routes out of Western Latvia were cut off. Our family was lucky to be given a chance to leave Latvia by ship for Germany. In late

October 1944 we landed in Danzig (Gdansk, Poland today) and found refuge in Marburg, a small German university town. I attended a German high school for a short time: air-raid alarm interrupted the school year that ended in May 1945 when the Americans occupied Marburg. In 1947 I finished the Latvian high school in the Hanau displaced person camp and enrolled in the University of Marburg to study physics. Intellectually these were very stimulating times, but Germany at this time was a very sad place struggling to recover from the horrible devastation of the war. We took the first chance to leave Germany for the USA and landed in Kansas City, Mo, in late 1949. The University of Kansas City (now the University of Missouri–Kansas City) judged, to my surprise, that I had the equivalent of a bachelor's degree and gave me a fellowship for graduate work. Since they had no graduate programme in physics I studied mathematics and earned a master's degree in one year, in only three years of academic study.

In 1951 I applied to Caltech for a PhD to study mathematics or physics. They admitted me to the mathematics programme judging that I looked like an applied mathematician (with never having taken a course in applied mathematics!). Caltech was and is a superb school and I truly enjoyed my graduate work and Southern California. I earned my PhD in mathematics in four years in 1955 with a dissertation in lattice theory under Professor R.P. Dilworth.

CC: How did you get into computer science? Tell us about some of your early work.

JH: My road to computer science was not very direct. Shortly before my graduation from Caltech, Bob Walker from Cornell visited Caltech and, on the recommendation of Bob Dilworth, offered me and my friend and fellow graduate, John B. Johnston, instructorships in mathematics at Cornell (in the 1950s academic careers started at the instructor level). We both accepted and I spent two delightful years in Ithaca. I loved Cornell University, the campus and the Finger Lakes region. I continued my work on lattice theory. During my second year at Cornell, Dick Shuey from the GE Research Lab in Schenectady, NY, visited Cornell and invited me to visit the GE Lab. After a short interview at the lab I was offered a summer job in the newly formed Information Studies section headed by Dick Shuey. (At that time I could not accept a permanent position at GE since I had already accepted a position as Assistant Professor at Ohio State University to work with Marshal Hall on the lattices of subgroups of groups.)

The summer at the GE Lab was an exciting and productive experience. The Information Studies section was exploring what research should be done to lay a scientific foundation for the emerging information and computing technology. In short, they strived to define and contribute to computer science. Intellectually, it was a very intensive and gratifying time for me. By the end of the summer I knew that I was going to dedicate myself to the emerging computer science and that, after nine months at Ohio State University, I would return to the GE Lab as a Research Scientist. Indeed, I did return the following year to the GE Lab and spent seven happy years in Schenectady working on computer science.

My early work at GE dealt mostly with finite automata and their decomposition into smaller automata, and exploitation of the decomposition theory to the state assignment problem for finite automata. At GE I learned about Shannon's theory of information and I was very impressed by it and one of my early papers "The Application of Some Basic Inequalities for Entropy" is a fumbling try to use entropy in a formulation of a quantitative theory of computing. It turned out it was Turing's work that was the key to the quantitative theory of computing. Only after Dick Stearns and I studied Turing's work did we have the right tools to define such a theory.

CC: In your Turing-award winning paper with Richard Stearns you introduced the time complexity classes and proved the time hierarchy theorem. Tell us about the cooperation with Richard Stearns.

JH: The Information Studies section at the GE Lab had a tradition of inviting highly gifted graduate students and young faculty for summer jobs. Dick Stearns, a mathematics graduate student at Princeton, came to the lab for a summer job shortly after I had joined the lab. Dick was working on a dissertation in game theory at Princeton, but at the lab he joined me working on the state assignment problem for sequential machines. By the end of the summer we completed our paper "On the State Assignment Problem for Sequential Machines, II". Dick was a highly gifted person and we worked very well together. He returned to Princeton for a year, finished his game theory thesis, and, as we had planned, joined that GE Information Studies section. We resumed our collaboration and at the same time we intensively studied material related to computer science.

It is interesting to note that neither of us was familiar with Turing's work on computability (certainly I was not) and we studied material on Turing machines with excitement. We quickly realised that Turing machines may be the right model to explore the complexity of computations. Turing had shown that adding tapes to Turing machines did not change what they could compute. Our problem was to explore how the computational complexity of problems changed with changes to the Turing machine model. We very quickly showed that various changes to the Turing machine had minor effects on the computational complexity and we could quantify the changes. For example, the computation of a multi-tape Turing machine, or one with two-dimensional tapes or even with multi-dimensional memory space could all be performed on a one-tape machine in the square of the computation time of the other models. These results assured us that the Turing machine was the right model to study computational complexity. With excitement we defined time-bounded computational complexity classes and investigated their properties. Using time-bounded diagonalisation we showed that a slight increase in the asymptotic time bound yielded a bigger complexity class. This showed that there are computations with very sharp computational complexity bounds.

Manuel Blum showed in his MIT dissertation that this is not the case for all problems by constructing exotic problems without sharp complexity bounds. We presented our first results on computational complexity in 1964, "Computational Complexity of Recursive Sequences", at the IEEE Annual Symposium on Switching Circuit Theory and Logical design. Other results quickly followed. With P.M. Lewis we investigated tape or memory bounded computational complexity classes, derived hierarchy theorems for tape-bonded computations and other interesting results. We also introduced a new version of the Turing machine by separating the work tape from the read-only input tape. This allowed the investigation of the rich class of computations which required little memory. For example, we showed that context-free languages can be recognised on square of $\log(n)$ tape and that any non-regular language require at least $\log\log(n)$ tape (for inputs of length n). By this time, we fully realised that computational complexity was an exciting, rapidly growing and an important part of computer science. After seven happy and productive years in 1965 I left the GE Research Lab for Cornell to chair the newly authorised Computer Science Department.

CC: You created the computer science department at Cornell University and served as its first chair.

JH: During the summer of 1965, Professor Bob Walker (the same person who brought me to Cornell) called me and invited me to visit Cornell to discuss the newly authorised computer science department. I visited Cornell and at the end of my visit I was essentially offered a full professorship and the chairmanship of the computer science department. The prospects, support and environment for computer science at Cornell looked so good that a short time later I accepted the offer. I have never regretted this decision.

My goal was to create a first-class Computer Science department at Cornell with a great, informal and congenial environment for a cohesive group of scientists who would help define computer science and contribute to its development. We were very fortunate that our early hires, which included John Hopcroft, Bob Constable and David Gries, shared this vision, brought visibility to the department and helped to shape and develop the department and computer science. I am delighted that they are still active at Cornell. I had a great time helping define computer science education, establish light teaching loads, to find the best possible faculty and create an informal, friendly and cohesive environment.

Besides leading the department I had a great time doing research with some outstanding students. Jointly we explored the structure of complexity classes, studied the nature of complete problems and our conjectures initiated lively research activity in this area, we struggled with the P and NP problem and explored relativised versions of this and other problems. The role of sparse sets in complexity theory was explored and led to some interesting conjectures that stimulated some very good results. For me it was a real joy to work with my students, most of whom worked in complexity theory and made a beautiful contribution to computer science.

CC: You have 20 PhD students and 198 descendants (cf. `http://ge-nealogy.math.ndsu.nodak.edu/id.php?id=10404`), many of whom are prominent researchers themselves. Can you comment on your role as a supervisor and mentor?

JH: My move from the GE Research Lab in 1965 to head the new Computer Science department at Cornell was a very well-timed move. At the lab I had immersed myself in CS research and had learned a lot and created some computer science results. In particular, computational complexity theory was very well received and started to attract other computer scientists. Cornell provided me with an ideal base to expand my involvement with shaping computer science education, teaching theoretical computer science and, particularly, computational complexity. On the national and international stage I promoted the computational complexity theory and actively participated in building the international theoretical computer science and computation complexity community. In all these activities, I was supported and worked with a stream of highly gifted and well-motivated students. I have already discussed some of the topics I explored with my students without explicitly mentioning their names; since all of them wrote fine dissertations it would not be fair to just single out a few without reviewing all their contributions. At the same time, I have to acknowledge that working with my students and seeing them succeed was one of the greatest experiences. They were all great individuals. I met regularly every week with my students for creative arguing and shouting matches about broad topics in computer science as well as about the most recent results from our group or outsiders. I met individually with my students for searching discussions of research. I have suggested very specific problems to some of my students and gladly listened to others who picked their own topics. I believe that creativity is highly individual and must be so understood and that the mentor-student relationship has to be built on mutual respect and even friendship. We also met on the volleyball court and delightful trips to conferences. It is a pity that volleyball has now been replace by hockey.

CC: Please comment on your beautiful result regarding trivial theorems in formal systems with arbitrarily long proofs.

JH: I admire deep results in mathematics and computer science, but I am not particularly impressed by just the difficulty of a proof and certainly not just by its length. On the other hand, I had heard a lot of bragging about the difficulty and length of proofs, and I started reflecting on how the length of proofs was related to the theorem it proved. After a while, I realised that in any reasonable formal system one can construct very simple sets of theorems (say a regular set) whose length of proofs grows faster than any prescribed recursive function in the length of the theorem. I had, somewhat mischievous fun deriving this result and it has made me even more suspicious of the long proof worshippers.

CC: Tell us about Gödel's lost letter and P=NP.

JH: Some time before June 1989 Dr. Gerhard Heise showed up in my office to discuss some matter in a handwritten letter in German from Gödel to von Neumann, unrelated to complexity problems. It did not take me long to realise that in this letter Gödel in essence asked von Neumann about the computational complexity of an NP complete problem about theorem proving.

Dr. Heise left me a copy of Gödel's letter which I found very fascinating and I was impressed by Gödel's curiosity about computational complexity of theorem proving. I translated the letter into English and published a note in the EATCS Bulletin, "Gödel, von Neumann and the P=NP Problem". I spent some time searching for a possible reply from von Neumann but could not find it nor has it been found since then. von Neumann was not well at that time and we now have to assume that he never replied to Gödel's letter. I do not know if Gödel raised the same computational complexity problem with anybody else. A complete translation of this letter has been published since then with comments (my note on the letter contained only quotes of the parts relevant to the computational complexity question).

CC: What is "The Real Conjecture of Hartmanis"?

JH: I do not think that there is "The Real Conjecture of Hartmanis". There are several of our conjectures that stimulated a lot of work and others that should have. One of my early conjectures that there are no sparse complete sets for NP, unless P=NP, was verified by Maheney's beautiful dissertation and the sparse sets raised many other interesting questions in computational complexity theory. The Berman–Hartmanis conjecture that all NP complete sets are polynomial time isomorphic stimulated a lot of work and some great oracle constructions to twist it either way. My feeling is that this conjecture may not be true, as stated, but it holds for all NP complete sets with a simple padding property which is possessed by all known NP complete sets. The conjecture also holds for NP complete sets defined under less powerfull reductions.

The conjecture that I like very much states that: a real-time computable real number is either rational or transcendental, stated differently no irrational algebraic number is real-time computable. If true, this would give an amazingly powerful method to prove if the numbers are transcendental. This conjecture emerged from Sterns and my failure to prove that the square root of 2 is real-time computable.

CC: This conjecture was called "The Real Conjecture of Hartmanis" by Lipton in https://rjlipton.wordpress.com/2009/02/24/a-conjecture-of-hartmanis/. My guess is that Lipton called it this because he believes it's the most important conjecture you proposed. Does this seem reasonable?

JH: As stated above, I do like this conjecture very much, and it may be mathematically the most profound of our conjectures. At the same time, I am sure that it will be very difficult to prove, should it be true. There seem to be no mathematical results or techniques to attack this problem and, in general, proving numbers to be transcendental has in many cases been very difficult. Also, it is a conjecture about concepts from two different disciplines and thus not fully appreciated in either one of them. So far I know of only a few attempts to try to resolve this conjecture and so its impact on research in mathematics and computer science has been limited. Contrary to some of our other conjectures that have initiated a lot of good research. It is interesting to note that Steven Cook in his Turing Award lecture discusses our 1965 paper and particularly singles out this conjecture as an "intriguing question that is still open today."

CC: You have led NSF's Directorate for Computer and Information Science and Engineering. . .

JH: I accepted the position of Assistant Director of NSF for CISE partially in gratitude for continue NSF research support at Cornell and for the opportunity to help guide the development of computer science in a new capacity. NSF is a great institution that has been and is vital to computer science research. For sake of brevity, I will just say that I truly enjoyed my two years at NSF and I am impressed how well CISE operated. It expanded my horizons about computer science and government research support and I would urge computer scientists to seriously consider serving some time at NSF or other government research organisations. Finally, Washington is a delightful city and I enjoyed it very much.

CC: What are your most preferred results?

JH: I do not have a preferred result. I had a lot of fun doing research and working with very original and interesting people. When I look back and think about specific results I almost always enjoy recalling how they were obtained and how they fit into the development of computer science. Somewhat like a father feels about his sons, I feel about my results, I like them all, some a bit more some a bit less, but all of them were a pleasure to create.

CC: You have been quoted as saying: "it's been a magnificent ride, like sitting in a cockpit and observing a brand new science being created. I am delighted and surprised at what impact computer science is having." . . . "when I decided to be a computer scientist, I couldn't imagine the dramatic impact it has had."

JH: Indeed! We can all take great pleasure and pride in what computer science and computer technology have achieved. It is awesome!

And I take particular pleasure in the elegance and beauty of computer science.

CC: How do you see complexity theory evolving?

JH: I am delighted to see how computational complexity is evolving and growing. Already in the late 1960s and early 1970s one could see that computational complexity theory was going to be an essential part of theoretical computer science. Today its relevance to computer science and even other sciences is fully recognised. I am particularly impressed by the widening scope and importance of computational complexity. For example, its relevance to cryptography and the impressive results about interactive proofs and non-approximability results. I am very grateful that I could participate in the founding, shaping and development of computational complexity and computer science.

Chapter 5

Kurt Mehlhorn: From Theory to Library of Efficient Data Types and Algorithms (LEDA) and Algorithm Engineering

Kurt Mehlhorn http://www.mpi-inf.mpg.de/~mehlhorn *is the Head the Algorithms and Complexity department of the Max-Planck-Institut für Informatik, Saarbrücken, a Professor at the Universität des Saarlandes, a co-director of the Indo Max Planck Center for Computer Science, the chairman of the Scientific Board, IST Austria and a member of the Joint Advisory Board, Carnegie Mellon, Qatar.*

He was educated in computer science and mathematics at TU München and obtained his PhD at Cornell University, Ithaca, USA with the dissertation "Polynomial and Abstract Subrecursive Classes" (at the age of 25). He has published more than 250 papers in various areas of informatics as well as the influential books Algorithms and Data Structures — The Basic Tool Box, The LEDA Book, Data Structures and Algorithms (*three volumes*) *and* Programming Languages.

Professor Mehlhorn was awarded 17 distinctions (1986–2013) including elected Fellow of ACM (1999), elected member of Academia Europaea (1995), Berlin-Brandenburgische Akademie der Wissenschaften (2001), Deutsche Akademie der Naturforscher Leopoldina (2004), Acatech, Konvent Technikwissenschaften (2004), Bayerische Akademie der Wissenschaften (2012), and United States Academy of Engineering (2014), and many prizes including the Leibniz-Award (1986), Karl–Heinz–Beckurts Award (1994), Konrad–Zuse Medal (1995), EATCS Award (2010), ACM Paris Kanellakis Theory and Practice Award (2011), Khwarizmi International Award (2013), Erasmus Medal of Academia Europaea, and honorary doctorates from the Otto-von-Guericke Universität (2002), the University of Waterloo, Canada (2006) and Aarhus University, Denmark (2008).

He has 24 students and 93 scientific descendants.

CC: Please reminisce about your studies in Munïch (1968–1971) in both computer science and mathematics.

KM: It was clear to me since the age of 14 or so that I wanted to study mathematics; not, that I knew what a mathematician would do for a living. I did not know any mathematicians besides my high school teachers. However, the subject fascinated me early on. I started to study maths at the Technical University in Munich in 1968. This was the year, when Informatik (computer science) was introduced as a new field of study at the Technical University in Munich and six other German universities. A friend of mine convinced me to also attend the introductory computer science lectures. I had little idea what computer science was about. I had read about computers in popular science magazines, I knew them from pictures, but I had never experienced a program at work. The course was taught by F.L. Bauer, a German computer science pioneer.

So, I started with mathematics, physics and computer science. I dropped physics after the end of the second year. I remember the lectures in mathematics and computer science to be very different. Whereas, the maths lectures were polished, the computer science lectures were rough, and the content was of quite uneven difficulty.

It was obvious that the instructor taught most of the material for the first time. The course also introduced us to programming. The programming language, F.L. Bauer used in class, was Algol 68. I tried to read the Algol 68 Report, which is a 168 page definition of the language. This report is one the most difficult documents I have ever tried to read. I never made it through.

In the lab, we used Algol 60 and later Euler as our programming languages. We ran our programs on the *Programmierbare Elektronische Rechenanlage München* (PERM) and later on a Telefunken TR4. I was fascinated by programming from the very beginning. It is an act of creation. Programming creates an artefact, the program, that "lives". It consumes inputs and returns outputs. In order to program, one has to understand a problem so well that one is able to teach a machine to solve it. And amazingly, the machine does it faster and more reliably than the creator himself.

CC: Then you obtained your PhD in computational complexity from Cornell University with Professor Robert Constable as advisor. Why did you move to the US? How was computer science at Cornell in early 1970s?

KM: Back then, German students had to take a major exam at the end of the second year. I did well; so my professors organised a one-year scholarship to the US for me and two of my fellow students. I was sent to Cornell and entered Cornell in 1971 as a special student. Cornell only had a graduate programme in CS at that time. I took the courses in the PhD programme, did well, and so the department offered me a scholarship for PhD studies. This was the summer of 1972. We had long planned that my then girlfriend, now wife, would come to the US in the summer of 1972 for a trip to the West Coast. We went on the tour and we discussed our future. We had been intensive letter writers for the past year and did not want to continue that way. My girlfriend agreed to move to the US. We then briefly returned to Germany in the fall and got married.

Back then, Cornell was a small department, but with an excellent faculty, e.g., Juris Hartmanis, John Hopcroft, Robert Tarjan, Bob Constable, Jerry Salton and David Gries. I was particularly fascinated by Bob Constable's lectures and so wanted him to become my advisor. I remember being afraid that he would say "no", it took me days to build up the courage and actually ask him to become my advisor. Luckily, he said "yes".

Bob's interests spanned complexity, constructive mathematics, logic, and semantics, and so I was introduced to all four subjects. I also received a profound introduction to algorithms by Hopcroft and Tarjan. The fact that I was recently able to publish on a framework for verification of certifying computations (*Journal of Automatic Reasoning*) goes back to Bob's influence.

CC: As a student I read with great interest your first paper "On the Size of Sets of Computable Functions, in *Proceedings of the 14th IEEE Symposium on Automata and Switching Theory*, 190–196, 1973". Later, I have used several times a constructive form of the Baire category theorem to measure the size of various sets of objects in discrete spaces which you introduced in that paper.

KM: I am flattered. At that time, many researchers in complexity theory studied recursion theory, the mathematical study of degrees of non-computability. We explored which of the notions would carry over to the study of degrees of computability. I had come across a paper that used the Baire category theory in recursion theory, and I transferred those ideas to the domain of computable functions.

CC: You have made important contributions in many areas of theoretical computer science: in computational complexity, data structures, computational geometry, computer algebra, parallel computing, VLSI design, combinatorial optimisation and graph algorithms. What was the motivation for such a variety?

KM: This was never a conscious decision. It just happened. I talk to colleagues, I listen to talks, I read, and when something catches my attention, I start thinking about it.

Of course, some of my work follows a long-term plan. I have recently published some papers on isolating real roots of univariate polynomials. The fact that I worked on this problem, can be traced back more than 30 years. I developed an interest in computational geometry soon after the field was introduced by Shamos and Preparata. The third volume of my 1984 book on data structures and algorithms deals with computational geometry. It never occurred to me at that time, that the implementation of (geometric) algorithms might be difficult. The book starts with the sentence that the machine model used in computational geometry is the Real-RAM, a RAM that can compute with real numbers. It did not occur to me that this machine model is far away from real machines and that the gap to real machines might be non-trivial to bridge. I asked students of mine to implement some of the algorithms as part of their master's degree. A very good student (he later got a PhD and is now a leading figure in a software company) implemented Voronoi diagrams of line segments. It was a beautiful piece of work, but it only worked for some examples. I tried myself, but could not do it any better.

What had gone wrong? We had implemented the Real-RAM by substituting floating point arithmetic for real arithmetic. The round-off errors killed us. Geometric programs branch on geometric predicates, e.g., does a point lie left of, on, or right of a line. The outcomes correspond to the sign of an arithmetic expression in the coordinates of the points and the line parameters. If the sign is computed incorrectly, a wrong branch is taken, and the computation may go astray. Let me give a simple example. Consider a polygon in the plane, a point outside the polygon, and assume that the edges of the polygon are oriented counter clockwise. Then the point sees a contiguous set of edges of the polygon, but it does not see all of them, where a point sees an edge if it lies to its right. Therefore, one can find all visible edges by finding one and then walking in a clockwise and counterclockwise direction until one reaches an invisible edge. Due to round-off errors it may happen, that the point sees all edges of the polgygon. Then the strategy just outlined will never stop. It is not too hard to find concrete points, where exactly this happens. The paper "Classroom Examples of Robustness Problems in Computational Geometry" contains many other illustrative examples.

This experience spurred my interest in laying theoretical foundations for the efficient and correct implementation of geometric algorithms. In the 1990s we and others did so for linear geometry: rational arithmetic, floating point filters, LEDA geometry and CGAL. Let me explain the idea of floating point filters. The evaluation of the arithmetic expression underlying a geometric predicate usually returns the correct sign; only in nearly degenerate cases, an incorrect sign may be reported. In these cases, the value of the expression is close to zero. The approach is now as follows. We first analyse the arithmetic expression and prove a theorem of the form: if the absolute value of the expression is larger than some *epsilon* then the floating point evaluation gives the correct sign; the value of *epsilon* comes out of the analysis. If the value is smaller than *epsilon*, the sign may or may not be correct. In this case, we re-evaluate using exact arithmetic. In this way, we always compute the correct sign, but pay the higher cost of exact arithmetic only when needed. Experience shows that the necessity for exact arithmetic is rare. In this way, we arrived at correct and efficient implementations of the algorithms for linear geometry.

At the beginning of this century, we moved to geometry with curved objects. The problem of providing the appropriate Real-RAM becomes much harder. Notice that the intersection point of two lines with integral coefficients have rational coordinates. However, the intersection of a quadric and a line may have non-rational coordinates. Thus, the reliable implementation of geometry with curved objects requires algebraic arithmetic. A key subroutine is the computation of the real roots of a univariate polynomial. More precisely, one wants to compute disjoint intervals with rational endpoints, one for each real root, such that each interval contains exactly one real root. This is a fundamental problem in computational algebra. Algorithms for polynomials with integer coefficients were available, but we needed an algorithm for polynomials with arbitrary real coefficients, where a real number is given as a dyadic number with a potentially infinite number of bits after the binary point. The algorithm would be allowed to ask for additional bits when needed. There were algorithms by Schönhage and Pan which could handle the situation, but nobody had ever implemented them. I started working on the problem and got Arno Eigenwillig, Michael Kerber and Michael Sagraloff interested. I had never worked in computer algebra before. We soon had our first success and now had a simple algorithm that matches the asymptotic performance of Pan's algorithm. We were lucky in the sense that the solution of the problem did not require any deep knowledge of computer algebra.

CC: Can you discuss one of your theoretical results you like most?

KM: It is actually one of my early results, obtained in 1981 and 1982 together with Scott Huddlestone. We studied balanced trees. After an insertion or deletion, balanced trees need to be rebalanced by rebalancing operations. It was known that in the worst case a logarithmic number of rebalancing operations is necessary, and it was also known through experiments, that the average case is much better. Nobody knew how to analyse the average case. We found that a stronger theorem is much easier to prove. We studied two-four trees and showed that the total number of rebalancing operations required for any sequence of insertions and deletions is linear in the length of the sequence, i.e., the amortised number of rebalancing operations per insertion/deletion is constant. For the analysis, we associated a bank account with the data structure. Such accounts are now called potential functions. Our analysis was one of the first examples of an amortised analysis. The theorem is now taught in many data structure courses and the proof method has numerous applications. Previously, Norbert Blum and I had proved a similar result for weight-balanced trees.

CC: You are one of the developers of LEDA, the LEDA. Please explain the goal of the project and how LEDA is currently used.

KM: In the mid 1980s, Thomas Lengauer and I started a project on VLSI-design. As part of the project, we wanted to build a system that translated high-level descriptions of VLSI circuits into compact layouts. The implementation effort encompassed postdocs, PhD and master's students. Progress was very slow. When analysing why, we identified that one of the reasons was that several data structures and algorithms had been implemented several times. In the late 1980s, there was no easy way of reusing implementations and there was no repository of good implementations.

Based on this experience, Stefan Näher and I started the LEDA project in 1988. We first reported about the project at MFCS 89 and ICALP 90. The reaction by our colleagues was lukewarm. The goal was to provide fundamental data structures and algorithms as easy-to-use, efficient and correct modules. We spent the first six months of the project on selecting the programming language and defining the interface of the priority queue data structure. We implemented priority queues and Dijkstra's algorithm. We wanted a specification of the priority queue data structure that would work in Dijkstra's algorithm without prior knowledge that it would be used in this algorithm. We tried C++, Modula, Eifel, C and a few other languages, and decided that only C++ with its template mechanism would allow us to reach our goals. C++ was still in its early infancy at that time. In Dijkstra's algorithm one associates distances with vertices, from time to time the distance of a vertex decreases, and each iteration needs to select the node with minimal distance. We found the interface descriptions in the algorithm textbooks (including my own) not very useful, since the insert as well as the decrease-key operation would have a vertex as an argument, a violation of the goal, that the data structure needs to know nothing about its later use. We decided that the argument of an insert operation would be a priority and the insert would return a handle to the object storing the priority. In LEDA, we use the word "item" instead of "handle". In the graph data structure, we would associate the item returned by the insert with the appropriate node. The decrease-key operation has two arguments: a handle and a new priority. In this way, we had completely separated the data structure and the graph algorithm. The item concept is used throughout LEDA.

The project developed nicely and we soon had a sizeable user community. However, by 1994, we were also facing some serious problems. First, none of our geometry algorithms worked for all inputs. All of them would break on some or even most inputs. This was due to the naive use of floating point arithmetic as a substitute for real arithmetic. It spurred my work on exact geometric computation mentioned above. A first paper appeared in the ACM Geometry conference in 1995.

Second, even the implementations of some combinatorial algorithms were incorrect. For example, the first version of the planarity test, declared some planar graphs non-planar. The program had been written by one of my master's students. One day, Stefan Näher came to my office holding a letter in his hand. The letter contained the planar drawing of a graph that our system had declared non-planar. Stefan said: "Kurt, it was one of your students, who implemented this program". It was clear, that Stefan expected me to fix the mistake. I did. More importantly, Stefan and I started to discuss how we could make our implementations more reliable. We came to the conclusion, that, if possible, all programs in LEDA should be certifying, i.e., for every instance compute a witness (proof) that the output is correct for this particular instance. For example, the planarity test now also outputs a planar drawing whenever it declares a graph planar, and it outputs a Kuratowski subgraph when it declares a graph non-planar. Over a period of five years, we succeeded in making most of our programs certifying. The LEDA book of 1999 and a survey article of 2011 give more details.

Certifying algorithms became a theme for me. Whenever I develop a new algorithm, I ask myself whether it can be made certifying. Certifying algorithms come with a checker program, that inspects the witness and verifies its validity. In other words, the checker validates the work on the main program. "And, who validates the work of the checker?" I have been often asked. I used to answer that the checkers are very simple programs and hence their correctness is self-evident. I now reply that the checkers are so simple that they are amenable to formal verification. Over the last two years, we have formally proved the correctness of several witness theorems and of the corresponding checkers. A witness theorem states that a witness of a certain type proves the correctness of an output, e.g., a Kuratowski subgraph proves non-planarity of a graph.

Stefan Näher, Christian Uhrig and I founded Algorithmic Solutions in the mid-1990s. It markets LEDA, develops it further, and offers algorithmic consulting. We have a solid academic and industrial customer base.

I see LEDA also as a role model for other library projects such as CGAL and LEDA-XXL.

CC: What is "algorithm engineering" and what are your contributions in this area?

KM: There are many definitions of algorithm engineering. I will give you my personal one. Treat programs as first-class-citizens in algorithms research and not as an afterthought. A number of research directions follow immediately from this. Care about constant factors in the running times of programs and also algorithms. Study the implementation process. Can it be improved by algorithmic means? How to go from a correct algorithm to a correct program? Study machine abstractions. Are they a useful abstraction of reality and do they allow for meaningful predictions? If a prediction made by a model conflicts with experimental evidence, try to find the reason and then either refine the prediction or revise the model. Care not only about the worst case, but also about the typical case and the best case. What are typical inputs? Can one characterise them?

Algorithm engineering is not only a subdiscipline of algorithms research. More importantly, it is a mindset. I frequently say that I am a mathematician in the morning and an engineer in the afternoon. I like to do maths, in particular, maths that can be made operational. I also like to turn maths into systems. It gives me great satisfaction to see my systems used. The experimentation with systems generates well-motivated new research problems and sometimes suggests theorem.

CC: You have played an important role in the establishment of several research centres for computer science in Germany. What was the driving force?

KM: I helped establishing the Dagstuhl centre and also the Max Planck Institute for Computer Science. Dagstuhl, because it was decided to locate it near Saarbrücken (Günther Hotz and Heinz Schwärtzel were the driving forces behind this decision) and I was chairman of the computer science department at that time. The Max Planck Institute, because Harald Ganzinger and I were selected to be the founding directors of the institute.

I have served in many other functions, e.g., as a member of the senate of the German Research Foundation, vice president of the Max Planck Society and member of the senate of the Max Planck Society. I believe that every individual owes part of his/her time to the societies he/she is a member of; my yardstick is about 10 to 20%. I love to work in organisations that function well and I am willing to invest time in keeping them that way.

CC: You are serving on the editorial boards of many international journals. New models of scientific publications have recently appeared. How do you see the future of scientific publication?

KM: This is a very difficult question. I strongly believe that all results of publicly funded research should be openly accessible. I do not conclude from this that all journals and conference proceedings must be open access. For example, the theory community has realised open access through the arXiv and institutional and personal repositories to a large extent, although most journals and conference proceedings in the field are not open access. Nevertheless, I believe that scientific publishing will move to the author-pays open access model over the next 10 years. Of course, author-pays has to be implemented as "the institution or funding agency of the authors pays".

Publishing is also about long-term archiving. Academic institutions and also publishing houses are such institutions. I am sceptical when well-intentioned individuals create a new journal without the backing of an institution that can guarantee sustainability.

Publishers (both for-profit and not-for-profit) provide useful services. For example, electronic access to journals was widely introduced at around 2000. At that time, this required substantial investment which only major publishers could make easily. Publishers will also play an important role in the future. The switch to electronic distribution of content has led to great increases of productivity. However, some of the for-profit publishers have forgotten to share the resulting savings with academia, and, as a consequence, the profit rates of some publishing houses have reached unfair heights. In their own interest, publishing houses must return to a fair cooperation with academia.

CC: How do you manage to juggle between so many jobs in different countries?

KM: I try to follow some simple principles.

I avoid multi-tasking. I set aside time for particular tasks and then concentrate on them. For example, when I was writing my 1984 books and the LEDA book, I would work on the book every work day from 8:00 am to 12:00 pm. I would not accept phone calls or interruptions by students during this time. Now, 8:00 am to 12:00 pm slot is reserved for reading, thinking and writing. The no-interruption rule still holds.

I clean my desk completely every evening when I leave my office, so that I can start with an empty desk the next morning.

When I accept a new responsibility, I decide, what I am going to give up for it. For example, when I became vice president of the Max Planck Society in 2002 (for a six-year term), I resigned as editor of *Algorithmica, Information and Computation, SIAM Journal of Computing, Journal of Discrete and Computational Geometry, International Journal of Computational Geometry & Applications,* and *Computing.*

And most importantly, I am supported by many people in what I do, in particular, my co-workers, my students, and then administrative staff in the institute and the department. Cooperation and delegation are very important.

CC: How do you treat your own mistakes?

KM: Of course, I try to avoid them in the first place. Also, I easily forgive others for making mistakes. I treat myself no differently.

Let me be serious. I restrict your question to mistakes that I make as a scientist. I also make mistakes as a manager and these mistakes are a different story.

Scientific mistakes are, in principle, easy to deal with. Dealing with them might be a lot of work, but it is usually clear what one has to do. If one finds a mistake in a proof, one tries to fix it. If one cannot fix it and the result is already published, one admits the mistake. If one makes a mistake in a lecture, one corrects it in the next lecture or in a handout.

I have actually profited a lot from "scientific mistakes". All my work on certifying algorithms and reliable computational geometry was spurred by mistakes. An incorrect implementation is a mistake. Most of the time it is a mistake made by the programmer, but sometimes it leads to something deeper. Namely, if the mistake points to a deficiency in the state of the art. Then one has to try to advance the state of the art. If one succeeds, the mistake turns into a fortunate event. This has happened to me several times.

Chapter 6

Arto Salomaa: Theoretical Computer Science

Professor Arto Salomaa is one of the most important theoretical computer scientists. His many articles and books not only influenced, but also shaped, areas of theoretical computer science. Professor Salomaa has been awarded many prizes, awards and distinctions, clearly more than one can enumerate in this short introduction: among them, nine honorary doctorates, membership in various learned academies, Professor of the Year in Finland in 1994 and winner of the yearly prize of the Nokia Foundation in 1998 and of the 2004 EATCS Award. He is one of the 12 Academicians of the Academy of Finland, Festival Colloquia and 10 books have been dedicated to him.

CC: Let me start this dialogue by citing a paragraph in your recent email: *One issue there was a list of people who did not get the Fields*

Medal. Did it ever occur to you that Gödel did not get it, although he was fully eligible in 1936? It didn't, maybe because I see Gödel beyond the recognition mortals get. Why do you think Gödel did not get it? Could it be because mathematical logic is not mainstream mathematics? Or because Gödel's results are negative?

AS: Certainly mathematical logic was not in the mainstream, especially if you think of those who decide about the medal. It is often much easier to recognise somebody who solves a problem that you yourself tried hard to solve without success than to give credit to a person whose work now seems obscure but is much later quoted as the greatest mathematician of the century. The rules for the Fields Medal (age limit) exclude persons whose contributions become visible only after some time. Also John von Neumann missed the Medal the same time as Gödel.

CC: Yuri Matiyasevich also did not get the Fields Medal for his work on Hilbert's tenth problem (also a negative result) completed when he was 24 or 25.

AS: I don't think negativity is an issue here. Besides, it is often difficult to tell whether or not a result is negative. What about the result of Andrew Wiles? The theorem is true but there are no solutions for the Diophantine equation.

When you give out a prize, an evaluation of some kind is needed. The latter is always difficult. History is full of examples where posterity does not agree with the result of the evaluation. Mozart, Beethoven and Schubert are not honorary citizens (Ehrenbürger) of Vienna, whereas many much lesser composers are. Kubrik and Hitchcock never did get the Oscar for the best director. And so forth.

Let me continue a little bit about evaluations. I have been on many committees evaluating departments, etc. It is only very natural that people getting bad evaluations protest: usually the booklet of counterarguments is much thicker than the original committee report.

Computer scientists have to approach wealthy patrons, whoever they are, in their applications for projects. I have always emphasised to my students and colleagues the importance of a carefully written application for a successful evaluation. Horace approached the original patron *Maecenas* (whose name stands for "patron" in many languages) with the famous words *Maecenas atavis edite regibus* (*Maecenas*, born of monarch ancestors). Apparently, you have to use a different approach nowadays to sell your work. It seems that right now you should use the words *bio* and/or *nano*.

To conclude, I am very happy that I do not have to write applications any more and choose research topics by their eventual applicability.

CC: What attracted you to mathematics in the first instance?

AS: My family constituted a very good starting point, my father was the Professor of Philosophy at the University of Turku. As a small boy I used to think of questions such as the dependence of the parity of the sum on the parities of the summands. (Of course I did not use these terms.) Children were very much left alone during the war because all adults were somehow involved in war activities. Opposing gangs were formed, and I used to be good at breaking codes. There were also other kinds of mathematical problems around. I came up with the rule to find out the number of games when everybody meets everybody else in a league of football teams. My friends did not believe that there could be such a general rule and came to me with a counterexample. They had chosen 14 Finnish teams and made a list of all the games. The list contained only 90 games. But a careful examination showed that the game between two Turku teams, TPS and TuTo, was missing. Maybe this suggests that the referees of scientific papers should be careful before making very negative claims.

It was not at all clear that I would start studying mathematics at university. I went to a classical lyceum and was also very interested in Latin. However, I wanted to become a researcher, and Latin seemed to me as a thoroughly investigated and bounded area, whereas mathematics is growing all the time. This turned out to be very true: my impending research areas did not exist or were very small when I started my university studies in 1952. Actually my father wanted me to become a lawyer since I was "arguing all the time". I wanted to have a broad start and, in addition to mathematics, I studied philosophy and history.

CC: Please tell us more about your graduate studies in Turku, Berkeley and Helsinki. Who influenced you during those years?

AS: It is very hard to imagine the attitudes in the academic circles in Finland in the 1950s. I was strongly advised against going to Berkeley because "American universities are mostly football and other sports". My friend, a physicist, was also recommended to get a doctorate in Finland, although he had one from Oxford. Publications were almost without exception in Finnish annals and journals. This is also true of my first publications.

There were two professors, Kustaa Inkeri and Lauri Pimiä, in mathematics when I started my studies in Turku. Inkeri was a well-known number-theorist. He was also an excellent lecturer who demanded perfectionism in mathematical writing. Pimiä had bad eyes but an unbelievable geometric intuition. I think he would have made excellent an contribution to computational geometry.

In Berkeley I noticed at once how shallow my background was. But I did a lot of reading and there were many good courses given by great people. Alfred Tarski gave a course on the foundations of geometry, the material appeared later as a book. He was dressed up elegantly and chain-smoked Winston cigarettes. Almost everybody smoked those days, including myself. Tarski and Leon Henkin conducted a seminar in logic with visitors such as Roger Lyndon and Robert McNaughton. Henkin was brilliantly clear in every sentence he spoke, also in conversations. Tarski hosted parties in his home up on Berkeley Hill. I also met Alonzo Church there, he later in the 1970s visited Turku. G. Polya wanted a discussion with me a few times; he had intricate questions about the Finnish language.

The course that influenced me most was John Myhill's seminar during the spring of 1957, where the topics were chosen from the newly published red-cover Princeton book *Automata Studies*. Myhill also gave lectures himself. He was very impressive but also out of this world, and occasionally taken to a sanatorium. My own work was about self-reproducing automata. In the construction I gave detailed instructions for all specific configurations. The necessary components were randomly scattered around on the plane, a welding operation was introduced, and so forth. There were even plans for a publication but it never came into being.

Berkeley was a wonderful place also because famous people gave public lectures there: many Nobel Prize winners, Martin Luther King... People were studying very hard, reading rooms were full until 11:10 pm. My stay was funded by the so-called ASLA grant. The grants originated from the fact that Finland was the only country who continued paying its First World War debts to the US. Then at some stage it was decided that the payments would be converted into grants.

I always liked classical music. San Francisco is a wonderful place for concerts, and also opera for a short season. Very cheap tickets were available for students for standing places. Karajan, Bernstein, Szell, Rubinstein, Gould, Menuhin, Björling, Schwartzkopf, Tebaldi were all there. I also went to concerts by Louis Armstrong and Elvis Presley with some of the logicians.

But it was not my intention to stay in America. My father, mother, sister and brother were in Finland, as well as my wife-to-be, and I was not sure how long she was going to wait for me. Because of the reasons discussed already above, I preferred to get my PhD in Finland. In many discussions and in library searches I had come up with a nice topic on many-valued logic, more specifically the composition theory of many-valued truth-functions. I already had some preliminary results when I returned. Automata theory would have been much too esoteric to qualify as a thesis topic in mathematics in Finland. Of course, no such thing as computer science existed.

This answer has become quite long. As regards Helsinki, I never had any actual studies there but took an intermediate degree, because of formal reasons.

CC: You have graduated 24 PhD students; this gives you a huge experience in supervision. What should a new PhD student know before starting his graduate studies?

AS: It is hard to imagine anybody having a better group of PhD students. I have learned enormously when working with them. I have had a few students during my visits abroad. I have also had some foreign students in Finland, especially during the time of the *Turku Centre for Computer Science, TUCS.* But the majority of the students have been Finnish. Many of them are really well-known scientists, some of them have already retired. Most of my students have become university professors but there are also other careers: Nokia, army cryptography, software development ...

What should a PhD student know at the beginning? It depends very much on the topic. Perhaps one can say that some areas of theoretical computer science require rather little previous knowledge, and you can still get good results if you work hard. One of my students did not know anything about formal languages when she started but after three years her paper was accepted to ICALP.

CC: How do you choose a problem to work on? Do you work on a single problem at a time or, in parallel, on more problems?

AS: It depends on the problem. Sometimes you want to settle something really furiously, and cannot get rid of the problem. In general it is better to have several problems to work on. If you get stuck on one of them, you can work on the next one. Maybe after a while something new opens up about the first problem.

CC: Please tell us about the famous MSW (H. Maurer, A. Salomaa, D. Wood) team?

AS: My cooperation with Hermann Maurer and the late Derick Wood started in 1975 and continued to be very active until early 1980s but an MSW paper was published in 1991. Between us we were called MSW1, MSW2 and MSW3, and we were also wearing T-shirts with those names. Why the cooperation kind of faded out around 1984 was explained by saying that we got more involved with other MSW: Hermann with *Mupid*, Arto with the *sauna* and Derick with his *wife*.

But during the high period we really worked hard and were enthusiastic. Close to 40 MSW papers were published in main journals, including several in *Journal of the ACM*. We also presented the stuff at many conferences, although rather seldom all three of us were present. As a matter of fact, we always worked as follows. Two of us got together in the other's place and wrote the paper. Later the third one checked it. I don't recall a single instance where we would have produced a paper when all three were present. But each of the combinations MS, MW, SW met at least once a year. In those days it was difficult to get travel money. Most of the time the guest stayed in the host's home. This of course meant that working days could be some 14 hours. When we were in Finland, the work continued also in the sauna. Indeed, we used to speak of "three-sauna problems" instead of "three-pipe problems" of Sherlock Holmes.

When two of us were together, we realised how much more we could produce together than alone. Somehow the members complemented each other. A new idea usually comes from an individual but the partner is essential in the further development. He can often immediately tell whether the idea is nonsense. If you work alone, you can spend days in a blind alley. Another factor that made the MSW work so fruitful and pleasant was that nobody ever counted the amount of work he did. Everybody tried his best and did not worry if the amount of work was evenly distributed.

Apart from MSW and G. Rozenberg, I have been lucky to have many scientific collaborators who have been great to work with. Of the senior people Karel Culik, Ferenc Gécseg, Werner Kuich, Gheorghe Păun, Sheng Yu, yourself and the late Alexandru Mateescu come to mind.

Coming back to MSW, I would like to emphasise the wonderful social atmosphere around the group. I quote here a part of a song during ICALP-77 in Turku.

Oh Finnish Sauna (Melody: Oh! Susanna). Adapted by MSW1 and MSW3 for MSW2, Turku, July 1977:

> We have come from all over the world / with towels on our
> knee.
> We have gone to Arto and Turku / in sauna there to be.
> Oh Finnish sauna / o do we wait for ye
> we have come from all over the world / with towels on our
> knee.

> A Wood he cannot swim that well / is rotten and not dry.
> His problems they could soon be solved / 'cause sauna heat
> is high.

Oh Finnish sauna / he cannot wait for ye
he's come from lower Canada / with towel on his knee.

Then Hermann says he'll go to Graz / we really don't know
why.
His problems they will soon be solved / 'cause sauna heat
is high.
Oh Finnish sauna / he cannot wait for ye
he's come from Karlsruhe / with a towel on his knee.

When opening the conference / friend Arto wore a tie.
His problems they will soon be solved / cause sauna heat
is high.
Oh Finnish sauna / he cannot wait for ye
he wants to be there all the time / but this can never be.

CC: Please tell about your collaboration with G. Rozenberg.

AS: I met Grzegorz for the first time in May 1971. He had been in Holland for about one and half years, and was running a countrywide seminar in Utrecht, where foreign speakers were also invited. I got an invitation (by ordinary mail, not by phone) from G. Rozenberg. I was not familiar with the name previously. He waited for me at the airport and arranged our meeting through loudspeakers. He looked much younger than I had anticipated. He drove a small Volkswagen. We got immediately into a very hectic discussion about parallel rewriting and L systems. After about one hour I started to wonder why we had not yet arrived at my hotel in Utrecht. It turned out that we were still on some side streets of Amsterdam.

L systems and biologically motivated stuff in general turned out to be an area where our scientific cooperation has been most vivid. The most important outcome is the book *Mathematical Theory of L Systems*, and L systems also play an important role in the *Handbook of Formal Languages*, as well as *Cornerstones of Undecidability*. I would like to explain about the *Handbook*. What I say illustrates very well Grzegorz's friendliness, efficiency and professionalism.

In March 1994, Grzegorz suggested to me: "Let us make a handbook on formal languages." We started planning it immediately. It was lots of work but also lots of fun and good jokes. Everything worked out very smoothly. In less than three years, a copy of the *Handbook* (three volumes, more than 2000 pages, 3.6 kilos altogether, more than 50 authors) was in the library of Turku University. Are there similar examples of such speedy editing of such an extensive handbook-type scientific work?

Already very early in our relationship grew much closer than just scientific collaboration. Grzegorz often says that he has no biological brothers but two brothers of choice, Andrzej Ehrenfeucht and me. Also nowadays we keep close contact, and I often ask his advice in difficult situations and for hard decisions.

My brother has an immense supply of jokes and anecdotes, always suitable to the occasion. Often a somewhat sad situation entirely changes by his comments. One year I missed the meeting of the editors of the EATCS Texts and Monographs Series. My right shoulder had been operated on, and outer rotations of the arm were strictly forbidden. Grzegorz called me from the meeting telling me that it had been decided that Arto Salomaa would be asked to write a book about the geometry of outer rotations.

Grzegorz also lives in the world of *magic*. He surely is on a true professional level in close-up magic, mainly cards. His name as a magician is *Bolgani*. Actually this was his name in my family already before he started to use it as a magician. Let me tell about my own impressions during one of his typical shows. *Bolgani* often presents a sequence of illusions within the framework of a story.

Bolgani explains that in Chinese the names of the suits *hung tao* (heart) and *hei tao* (spade) are similar, and therefore some confusion may rise. But now we try to be careful. He then shows the audience some hearts and puts them on the table, as well as some spades and puts them also on the table, far from the hearts. "So this pile is *hung tao*?" The audience agrees. "And this is *hei tao*?" Again consensus. *Bolgani* then entertains the audience and talks about various matters. About owls. About the sauna. That laughter, and for him nowadays the grandson Mundo, is the best medicine. That one should never assume anything. That the only place where success comes before work is in the dictionary. Then *Bolgani* goes back to the cards. "So this is *hung tao* and this *hei tao*?" General agreement. But when he shows the cards, it is the other way round. "Too bad, let us see what happens if we put everybody in the same pile." He puts first the pile of hearts on the table and the spades on top. Again some entertainment. "Now let us see if they interchanged again." *Bolgani* picks up the cards and shows them. "This is absolutely crazy. They are all *zhao hua* (club, grass flower)!"

CC: May I ask you about your current projects?

AS: I cannot speak of any projects. As you know, I am retired and have no possibility in Finland to apply for funding for projects. But I surely continue my own research. Recently I have been interested in some basic questions about automata and formal languages: decompositions of languages, counting the number of (scattered) subword occurrences in a word, state complexity of finite automata. Recently I studied formal questions concerning reaction systems, a model introduced by Ehrenfeucht and Rozenberg. I also have various editorial jobs: some collective volumes, EATCS Monograph and Text Series, various journals. But you work much less when you get old.

CC: You have authored or co-authored 46 influential books, translated in many languages. *Formal Languages* (1973) made the list of the 100 most cited texts in mathematics in 1991. In retrospect, which one gave you most pleasure and satisfaction?

AS: I would rather speak of 11 than of 46 books. Writing a book is quite different from editing it. However, the *Handbook of Formal Languages*, already referred to earlier in this interview, caused a lot of work, also because I wrote several chapters myself.

You always like a book you are currently working on, so it is difficult to state any preferences. In retrospect, perhaps my first book *Theory of Automata* gave me the most satisfaction. This in spite of the fact that the publisher, Pergamon Press, did an awful job in printing and screwed up the marketing.

CC: With only 12 Academicians, the Academy of Finland seems the smallest Academy in the world, certainly smaller than the 40-member *Académie Française*. Tell us more about it. You have been a member of the Finnish Academy of Science and Letters for many years. From outside it seems a bit strange to have two academies...

AS: This is really confusing. Finland has two "normal" academies (of sciences and letters). The Swedish-speaking one was already established in the 1830s, the Finnish-speaking one in 1908. The latter was established because it was difficult for Finnish-speaking researchers to become members of the former. As you know, Swedish is still an official language in Finland. The members of these two academies are not called academicians.

The government institute corresponding to, say, NSF is called the Academy of Finland. It distributes funding for research projects and also has positions for junior and senior researchers. I was a for a long time an academy professor, associated with the Academy of Finland. It can also convey the honorary title of an academician as recognition of research achievements. By law the number of such academicians is restricted to 12.

CC: What areas of theoretical computer science will probably be taught in 2114?

AS: I don't want to predict. Let me quote some well-known predictions made some 60 years ago. Optimistic: computers of the future will weigh only five tons. Pessimistic: there is a true market for at most five computers in the world.

However, I would like to add that mathematics will be there and so will the problems and areas that are really interesting mathematically.

CC: You are serving on the editorial board of many journals. What is the future of academic journals, paid subscriptions, open-source, mixture?

AS: This is a very broad question, and I cannot say much. Clearly the tendency is towards electronic publications. Really many journals are not any more available in our university library as paper copies. However, I have the feeling most people still want to see their work printed in a journal. It then seems more finalised. The first electronic journal in our field, *Journal of Universal Computer Science*, is ideal in this respect. Contributions are also available as thick yearly volumes.

Whoever publishes, be it electronically or otherwise, needs some compensation. Somebody has to organise the refereeing etc. It is impossible to avoid payments.

CC: Finland is an economical and scientific miracle. Can you briefly explain this phenomenon?

AS: If I give only one reason it is that Finland was able to defend itself, in the Winter War, against the attack of a vastly superior military power and thus avoid foreign occupation. There are very few instances of small countries in history who could do that. This gave real motivation and impetus for war reparations and building up the country. Talented people wanted to stay here instead of moving abroad, legally or illegally. Just compare Finland with the Baltic countries who, in a definite sense, lost 50 years.

This is my answer. Somebody else might give a different answer. But I was five years old when the Winter War started, and still remember the day very well.

CC: Finland is also an international role model in education. May I ask you again to explain this?

AS: This is surely changing. Finland used to have the advantage of a uniform body of students but, with growing immigration, this is no more the case. This is also visible in international rankings such as the Pisa ranking. Finland still gives good education for teachers. The profession of a teacher is ranked higher in Finland than in many other countries.

CC: Your webpage[1] lists two "official" pastime interests: grandchildren and the sauna. Please tell us about your grandchildren.

AS: The webpage is outdated, and all my grandchildren are now adults. They have given me much happiness. By now, one of them is a practicing medical doctor, one specialises in bio-informatics technology, and the third studies medicine. Last year I made a book with pictures and text, *The Golden Years of a Grandfather*.

---

[1] http://www2.math.utu.fi/projects/staff/asalomaa/.

But I still often think of the days when they were small. I have a big picture of myself with Grzegorz, with the subscript *Happiness is being a grandfather*. My grandchildren used to live 300 kilometres from Turku but the distance was never long for me. I have always liked children, and many children call me *Äijä*, grandfather. I like to talk with children. They don't pretend to be anything and are honest. "*Äijä* eats like a pig", was a statement about my table manners. No recognition could be better than the one my grandson, then six years, gave on a trip where we had to cross several borders: "it is so easy for us to travel because *Äijä* knows all languages!"

CC: Your passion for the sauna is well known. For example, Salosauna was presented by Abel and Salamander in *Badplätze*, Oase, 2008, 291–297. At least two articles about sauna have appeared in this book: "What computer scientists should know about sauna" (1981) and "Myhill, Turku and Sauna Poetry: Recollections arising from the EATCS Award" (2004). You have introduced me to the Finnish sauna in 1991 (during my visit to Turku, still vivid in my memory), and, being so impressed, I had a dream that one day we would have one (this dream came true in 2001). What is Salosauna and why it is not only unique, but also the best?

AS: Indeed, a couple of German sauna books have recently published my views about the sauna. Finland, a country of 5.5 million people, has 2 million saunas. Only recently the number of cars exceeded the number of saunas. I could have answered your previous question, about Finland's success, by referring to the sauna!

Every true sauna lover thinks his sauna is the best. Salosauna was built of thick logs from the 19th century. I made some reparations, trying not to destroy the original atmosphere. The decisive criterion in comparing saunas is the quality of sauna heat, *löyly*. The most common mistake, especially in foreign saunas, is that the stove is much too small. No luxury in the surroundings can compensate the stove being a tiny miserable metal box. I always wonder why sauna builders become stingy when the heart of the sauna is concerned. I want to add that, during the three ICALP's in Finland, Turku 1977 and 2004, Tampere 1988, an excellent sauna session has been included in the conference programme.

Let me end by quoting a few lines by Hermann Maurer.

> Salosauna, once again
> heightens joy and heightens pain.
> Underlines what maybe counts
> what this life in truth amounts.
> Through this sauna's windowpane
> past some sunshine, wind and rain,
> our hearts and eyes and ears
> cut through all the passing years:
> see the friendships that stay strong,
> newborn faces, happy song.
> Memories taste sad and sweet
> as they rise in sauna's heat.

Chapter 7

Joseph Sifakis: Concurrent Systems Specification and Verification

Professor Joseph Sifakis, http://www-verimag.imag.fr/
~sifakis and http://people.epfl.ch/joseph.sifakis is a
leading researcher well known for his pioneering work in theoret-
ical and practical aspects of concurrent systems specification and
verification, notably the area of model-checking. His current research
activities include component-based design, modelling and analysis of
real-time systems with focus on correct-by-construction techniques.

Educated at the Electrical Engineering Department at the National
Technical University of Athens and the University of Grenoble, Pro-
fessor Sifakis received a doctorate (1974) and a state doctorate (1979)
from the University of Grenoble, and a Dr.h.c. from the École Poly-
technique Fédérale de Lausanne, Switzerland (2009).

Professor Sifakis is a Professor at the École Polytechnique
Fédérale de Lausanne. He is the founder of Verimag, a lead-
ing research laboratory in the area of critical embedded systems

established in Grenoble, in 1993. He is a member of the French Academy of Sciences, a member of the French National Academy of Engineering and a member of Academia Europaea. He is a Grand Officer of the French National Order of Merit, a Commander of the French Legion of Honour and a Commander of the Greek Order of the Phoenix. He received the Leonardo da Vinci Medal in 2012. As of March 2014, Joseph Sifakis is the President of the Greek National Council for Research and Technology.

Professor Sifakis received the CNRS Silver Medal in 2001 and the Turing Award in 2007.

CC: Please tell us about your education and the people who most influenced your academic career.

JS: I studied Electrical Engineering at the National Technical University in Greece. As a student I was inclined to be more concerned with theory than with practice. I came to Grenoble in 1970 for graduate studies in physics. An encounter has been decisive for my career: I had the chance to meet Professor Jean Kuntzmann, who was the Director of the Institute of Informatics and Applied Mathematics (IMAG). My interest in computer science grew and I decided to quit my studies in physics and start undergraduate studies at IMAG. Jean Kuntzmann was an inspired mathematician. I did my engineering thesis under his supervision on modelling the timed behaviour of circuits. I learned a lot from him, and I remember that he always recommended not looking at the bibliography before coming up with one's own solution to a problem. This is a rule that I have strictly observed throughout my career. After my engineering thesis, I became interested in the theory of concurrency.

In 1974, I met Carl Adam Petri and then visited him and his colleagues in Bonn several times. I was really impressed by his erudition but I could not really understand why "true concurrency" was such a big idea. In contrast to the prevailing approach, I considered in my papers that Petri nets are merely transition systems.

In 1977, I definitely left Petri nets for program semantics and verification. Dijkstra's papers and books had a deep influence on my work as well as discussions with Michel Sintzoff who was working at that time on program verification. They drew me the idea of fixpoint characterisation for temporal modalities, and this opened the way to the results on model-checking. My student Jean-Pierre Queille developed the first model-checker in 1982. I met Ed Clarke and Allen Emerson at CMU in November 1982 and we realised that we had been working independently on the same problem. From Patrick Cousot I learned about abstract interpretation — our offices were in the same corridor and we were both members of the "Programming Languages" team.

In the autumn of 1983, I met Amir Pnueli for the first time at a workshop on "The Analysis of Concurrent Systems", organised in Cambridge. This was the beginning of a continuous interaction and collaboration for more than 25 years. Amir had a deep influence on my career. For more than 10 years, we have set up several European projects in collaboration with Willem-Paul de Roever, on system modelling and verification. We jointly organised with Ed Clarke the workshop on the "Verification of Finite State Systems" in Grenoble in 1989. This workshop is considered to be the first edition of the CAV conference. Amir Pnueli opened my horizons and contributed to the visibility and recognition of our work at Verimag through his international network of connections and collaborations. He brought me into contact with leading researchers and teams working on timed and hybrid systems. Thomas Henzinger came to Verimag as a post-doctoral student. Oded Maler, Amir Pnueli's PhD student, joined my team as a permanent researcher. We had a strong team that contributed significantly to the development of the state of the art in hybrid and timed systems. Amir Pnueli has frequently visited Verimag for over 10 years and we greatly benefited from his wisdom and support.

The interaction and collaboration with researchers in my own team also had a deep impact on my career. I will mention Ahmed Bouajjani, Saddek Bensalem, Susan Graf, Oded Maler, Sergio Yovine and Stavros Tripakis as well as Paul Caspi and Nicolas Halbwachs who designed and developed the Lustre synchronous programming language.

In the late 1990s my research interests progressively shifted from verification and formal methods to system design. This was not a result of the direct influence of a single person but rather through an increasing awareness that verification was hitting a wall and only incremental improvements in the state-of-the-art could be expected. I stepped down from the Steering Committee of CAV and started a research programme on embedded systems design. Interactions with colleagues such as Hermann Kopetz, Lothar Thiele, Thomas Henzinger, Alberto Sangiovanni-Vincentelli and Edward Lee contributed to elaborating a system perspective for computer science. I worked actively set up the Emsoft conference and organic the Embedded Systems community in Europe through the Artist coordination measure followed by the Artist2 and ArtistDesign European Networks of Excellence. Although this incurred some considerable effort in administrative work, I learned a lot through the scientific management of world-class research teams.

CC: Please present the Verimag laboratory you have founded and directed.

JS: In January 1993, I founded the Verimag laboratory, a joint venture between IMAG (Computer Science and Applied Mathematics Institute) and Verilog SA. This has been an exciting and fruitful experience. Verimag has transferred the Lustre language to the SCADE synchronous programming environment. SCADE has been used by Airbus for over 15 years to develop safety critical systems and has become a *de facto* standard for aeronautics. SCADE has been qualified as a development tool by the FAA, EASA and Transport Canada under DO-178B up to Level A. It is currently been commercialised by Esterel Technologies. We also transferred functional testing and verification techniques to the ObjectGeode tool for modelling real-time distributed applications. This tool has been commercialised by Telelogic which was purchased by IBM in 2008.

Since 1997, Verimag has been a public research laboratory, associated with CNRS and the University of Grenoble. It plays a prominent role in embedded systems by producing cutting-edge research and leading research initiatives and projects in Europe.

As the director of Verimag I have sought a balance between basic and applied research. I have used resources from industrial contracts and collaborative projects to develop new research activities and strengthen the potential in basic research. For me, participation in industrial projects has been a source of inspiration. It allowed the definition of new research directions that are scientifically challenging and technically relevant. I believe that this virtuous cycle of interaction between academic research and applications is the key to Verimag's success.

CC: What are Artist2 and ArtistDesign?

JS: ArtistDesign was a European network of excellence federating the European research community in embedded systems design. It brought together 31 of the best research teams as core partners, 15 Industrial and SME affiliated Industrial partners, 25 affiliated Academic partners, and 5 affiliated International Collaboration partners who participate actively in the technical meetings and events.

The central objective for ArtistDesign was to build on existing structures and links forged in the FP6 Artist2 Network of Excellence, to become a virtual Centre of Excellence in Embedded Systems Design. This was mainly achieved through tight integration between the central players of the European research community. These teams have already established a long-term vision for embedded systems in Europe, which advances the emergence of embedded systems as a mature discipline.

The research effort aimed to integrate topics, teams, and competencies, through an ambitious and coherent research programme of research activities which are grouped into 4 thematic clusters: "modelling and validation", "software synthesis, code generation and timing analysis", "operating systems and networks", "platforms and MPSoC", "Transversal Integration" covering both industrial applications and design issues aims for integration between clusters.

The NoE had a very dynamic International Collaboration programme, interacting at top levels with the best research centres and industrial partners in the USA: (NSF, NASA, SRI, Boeing, Honeywell, Windriver, Carnegie Mellon, Vanderbilt, Berkeley, UPenn, UNC Chapel Hill, UIUC, etc.) and in Asia (Tsinghua University, Chinese Academy of Sciences, Seoul National University, East China Normal University, etc.).

ArtistDesign also had a very strong tradition of summer schools, graduate courses, and major workshops.

CC: Why is model-checking so important for today's IT industry? What are your main contributions in this area?

JS: The first results on "Property Verification by Evaluation of Formulas" are in my thesis (*Thèse d'Etat*) presented in June 1979. These results have been published in the paper "A Unified Approach for Studying the Properties of Transition Systems" — Theoretical Computer Science, Vol. 18, 1992. They include a fixpoint characterisation of a simple logic with two modalities: possible and inevitable.

The results of my thesis led to the development of the first model-checker CESAR, in 1982. The tool allows translation of finite state CSP programs into Petri nets, extended with finite-valued variables. The verification method is symbolic, representing sets of model states as boolean expressions. My team developed, in the 1980s, several model-checkers for the verification of distributed systems, by using enumerative techniques such as CADP and the IF toolbox. We also developed in collaboration with Telelogic the TGV testing tool that generates test suites for communication protocols from their specification in a simple temporal logic.

My research for more than a decade focused on increasing the efficiency of model-checking techniques. I investigated compatibility between equivalences induced by temporal logics and behavioural equivalences based on bisimulation relations that can be used to reduce models. I also produced results relating model-checking and abstract interpretation that have been successfully applied in tools such as Invest at Verimag and SAL at SRI.

In the early 1990s we studied, in collaboration with T. Henzinger, X. Nicollin and S. Yovine, the first symbolic model-checking algorithm for the verification of TCTL. This algorithm has been implemented in the Kronos tool at Verimag. I also worked on the verification of hybrid systems, in collaboration with researchers from Verimag, and Rajeev Alur and Thomas Henzinger. These general results are complemented by work on the verification of specific classes of hybrid systems, in particular, in collaboration with Amir Pnueli. Finally, in collaboration with Oded Maler and Amir Pnueli,

I produced results on the synthesis of controllers for timed systems. These have been applied for schedulability analysis of real-time systems.

Today model-checking is a mature technology used by companies such as Intel, IBM and Microsoft. These have developed proprietary technology for verifying complex systems. Model-checking can also be used for debugging or generating suites for testing real implementations. I see two main obstacles to the application of model-checking to complex systems. One is of course the size of the state space which may increase exponentially with the number of components of a system. The other, equally important obstacle, is generating faithful models from system description formalisms, in particular for mixed software/hardware systems.

CC: What is component-based construction and BIP?

JS: We need theory, models and tools for cost-effectively building complex systems by assembling heterogeneous components. This is essential for any engineering discipline. It confers numerous advantages such as productivity and correctness.

System designers deal with heterogeneous components, with different characteristics, from a large variety of viewpoints, each highlighting the different dimensions of a system. They often use several semantically unrelated formalisms, e.g., for programming, HW description and simulation. This breaks the continuity of the design flow and jeopardises its coherency. System development is often decoupled from validation and evaluation.

System descriptions used along a design flow should be based on a single semantic model to maintain its overall coherency by guaranteeing that a description at step $n + 1$ meets essential properties of a description at step n. The semantic model should be expressive enough to express different types of heterogeneity:

* Heterogeneity of computation: The semantic model should describe both synchronous and asynchronous computation to allow in particular, modelling mixed hardware/software systems.

* Heterogeneity of interaction: The semantic model should enable the natural and direct description of various mechanisms used to

coordinate the execution of components including semaphores, *rendezvous*, broadcast, method call, etc.

* Heterogeneity of abstraction: The semantic model should support the description of a system at different abstraction levels from application software to its implementation.

Existing theoretical frameworks for composition are based on a single operator, e.g., product of automata, function call. Poor expressiveness of these frameworks may lead to complicated designs: achieving a given coordination between components often requires additional components to manage their interaction. For instance, if the composition is by strong synchronisation (*rendezvous*), modelling the broadcast requires components for choosing the maximal amongst several possible strong synchronisations. We need frameworks providing families of composition operators for the natural and direct description of coordination mechanisms such as protocols, schedulers and buses. These should provide a unified composition paradigm for describing and analysing the coordination between components in terms of tangible, well-founded and organised concepts. In addition, they should be equipped with tractable methods for ensuring correctness-by-construction to avoid the limitations of monolithic verification. These methods use two types of rules:

* Compositionality rules for inferring global properties of composite components from the properties of constituent components, e.g., the composition of deadlock-free components is — under some conditions — a deadlock-free component. A special and very useful case of compositionality is when a behavioural equivalence relation between components is in congruence. In that case, substituting a component in a system model by a behaviourally equivalent component leads to an equivalent model. Today, we lack compositionality theory for progress properties as well as platform-dependent properties.

* Composability rules ensuring that essential properties of components are preserved when they are used to build composite components. Consider for instance, two components. One is the composition of a set of components sharing a common resource

accessed in mutual exclusion. The other is obtained as the composition of the same set of components scheduled for optimal use of the shared resource. Is it possible to obtain a single component integrating this set of components such that both mutual exclusion and the scheduling constraints hold? System engineers face this type of non-trivial problem every day. They use libraries of solutions to specific problems and they need methods for combining them without jeopardising their essential properties. Feature interaction in telecommunication systems, interference among web services, interference in aspect programming are all manifestations of the lack of composability.

This vision has motivated my research over the past decade, during which I studied BIP, a component framework for rigorous system design. BIP allows the construction of composite hierarchically structured components from atomic components characterised by their behaviour and interface. Components are composed by the layered application of interactions and priorities. Interactions express synchronisation constraints between actions of the composed components while priorities are used to filter amongst possible interactions and to steer system evolution to meet performance requirements, e.g., to express scheduling policies. Interactions are described in BIP as the combination of two types of protocols: (a) rendezvous to express strong symmetric synchronisation and (b) broadcast to express triggered asymmetric synchronisation. BIP offers a clean and abstract concept of architecture separated from behaviour. Architecture in BIP is a first-class concept that can be analysed and transformed. BIP relies on rigorous operational semantics that have been implemented in three execution engines for centralised, distributed and real-time execution. The combination of interactions and priorities to describe coordination between components confers BIP expressiveness not matched by any other existing formalism. The usual notion of expressiveness does not take into account features such as primitives for structuring and composition. It considers as equivalent (Turing complete) a wide variety of formalisms from high-level programming languages to counter machines. I have proposed a notion of expressiveness that characterises the ability of modelling formalisms to describe coordination mechanisms between components.

CC: What is your vision for the development of computer science?

JS: Computer science is a young and rapidly evolving discipline due to the exponential progress of technology and applications. It is a scientific discipline in its own right with its own concepts and paradigms. It deals with problems related to the representation, transformation and transmission of information. As such, it studies all aspects of computing from models of computation to the design of software and computing devices.

Information is an entity distinct from matter and energy. It is a resource that can be stored, transformed, transmitted and consumed. It is immaterial but needs media for its representation. Information is any structure to which one can assign a meaning. The number "4" can be represented by the symbols "100", "four" and "IV". All these representations have the same meaning defined by a semantic function. This concept is different from "syntactic" information measured as the quantity of symbols, pixels or bits needed for a representation. According to Shannon's theory, the informational content of a message of length n on an alphabet of b symbols is $n \log(b)$, that is, the number of yes/no questions one would have asked to completely resolve ambiguity. This measure ignores meaning. It is like saying that one kilo of gold and one kilo of lead are equivalent.

Computer science is not merely a branch of mathematics. As any scientific discipline, it seeks validation of its theories on mathematical grounds. But mainly and most importantly, it develops specific theory intended to explain and predict properties of computations which can be tested experimentally.

More than 95% of the chips produced today are for embedded applications. These are electronic components integrating software and hardware jointly, and specifically designed to provide given functionalities, which are often critical. They are hidden in devices, appliances and equipment of any kind: mobile phones, cameras, home appliances, cars, aircraft, trains, medical devices etc. In 2008, a person used about 230 embedded chips every day: 80 chips in home appliances, 40 chips at work, 70 chips in cars, 40 chips in portable devices. In the near future, another anticipated important landmark will be the advent of the Internet of things as the result of a convergence between embedded technologies and the Internet. The idea is to use Internet technologies to integrate services provided by hundreds of billions of embedded systems. This will require an upgrade of the Internet infrastructure to make it more secure, safe and reactive. Current features for exchanging multimedia documents will be extended to encompass real-time monitoring and control. Systems are becoming ubiquitous. The state of almost everything can be measured, sensed and monitored. People and objects can communicate and interact with each other in entirely new ways. Intelligent systems allow enhanced predictability of events and optimal use of resources.

It is hard to imagine what computer science will be in two decades. More than any other discipline, it is driven by applications and exponential progress in technology. The broadening of its perimeter is accompanied by a shift in focus from programs to systems.

CC: Please illustrate with a simple example the difference between programs, on one hand, and systems, on the other.

JS: Programs usually compute a single function. They transform input data into output data. They must terminate and are deterministic. A system interacts continuously with a physical environment. It combines the execution of several functions. Its behaviour can be understood as a relation between input data streams and output data streams. It is, in general, non-terminating and non-deterministic. Consider for instance, a controller for a lift. Depending on external stimuli (pushing a button by a user) it will execute a function that moves the cabin to a destination. Its behaviour is non-terminating and may be non-deterministic.

Existing models of computation deal with functions. They ignore physical time and resources. Computation is a finite sequence of steps corresponding to the execution of primitive operations. Complexity theory is based on abstract notions of resources such as time and memory. Programs have behaviour that is independent from the physical resources needed for their execution. In contrast, the essential properties of systems strongly depend on physical resources.

New trends in computing systems bring computer science closer to physics. Marrying physicality and computation requires a better understanding of their differences and points of contact. Is it possible to define models of computation involving quantities such as physical time, physical memory and energy? There exist significant differences in approaches and paradigms adopted by the two disciplines. We badly need holistic rigorous design approaches taking into account the interaction of mixed software/hardware systems with their physical environment.

CC: What and how should we teach CS?

JS: Computer science complements and enriches our knowledge with theory and models enabling a deeper understanding of discrete dynamic systems. It proposes a constructive and operational view of the world which complements the classic declarative approach adopted by physics.

Computer science curricula seldom recognise the importance of systems and fails to provide a holistic view of the discipline. I have the following recommendations.

- Teach students how to think in terms of systems (design process, tools, interaction with users and physical environment). Computer science curricula should be extended and enriched by including principles, paradigms, techniques from control theory and electrical engineering.
- Teach principles rather than facts (foundations, architectures, protocols, compilers, simulation...). Very often courses are descriptive and present details that can be acquired later as needed in professional life. Students should be prepared to deal with the constant change induced by technology and applications. They should also be kept aware of the limitations of the existing theory of computing. Very often theory makes assumptions oversimplifying reality.
- Put emphasis on information and computation as universal concepts applicable not only to computers and provide the background for triggering critical thinking, understanding and mastering the digital world.

CC: Theories are not famous for leading to technologies. What do you think about research in computer science and its impact on industrial practice?

JS: Unfortunately, the current scope and focus of research in computer science fail to address central problems for the IT industry, in particular problems raised by system design and engineering. Following well-beaten paths rather than taking the risk of exploring new ideas is a prevalent attitude by researchers from all scientific communities. More than in other disciplines, research in computer science has been over-optimistic regarding the possibility for solving hard problems and overcoming obstacles. This can probably be explained by the strong demand and incentives for innovation by funding agencies as well as the strong push from applications and market needs. Very often, scientific roadmaps and position papers present "challenges" that are mere visions and take desires for reality. All of the following were once hyped as main breakthroughs: artificial intelligence, fifth generation computers, program synthesis, true concurrency and web science. The proper goal of theory in any field is to make models that accurately describe real systems. Models can be used to explain phenomena and predict system behaviour. They should help system builders do their jobs better. A very common attitude is to work on mathematically clean theoretical frameworks whether or not they are relevant. Very often, simple mathematical frameworks attract the most brilliant researchers who produce sterile "low-level theory", that has no point of contact with real computing. This leads to a separation between theoretical and practical work that is harmful for the discipline. The opposite extreme is also observed. Frameworks exist intended to describe real systems such as UML and AADL constructed in an *ad hoc* manner. These include a large number of semantically unrelated constructs and primitives. It is practically impossible to obtain rigorous formalisations and build any useful theory for such frameworks. We need theoretical frameworks expressive enough to directly encompass a minimal set of high-level concepts and primitives for system description which are amenable to formalisation and analysis.

CC: Is it possible to find a mathematically elegant and still practicable theoretical framework for computing systems?

JS: Computer science deals with building artefacts. The key issue is *constructivity*, that is, the ability to effectively build correct systems. As system synthesis from requirements is intractable for complex systems, we should study principles for building correct systems from components. The aim is to avoid *a posteriori* monolithic verification as much as possible. There already exists a large body of constructivity results in computer science such as algorithms, architectures and protocols. Their application allows correctness for (almost) free. How can the global properties of a composite system be effectively inferred from the properties of its constituents? This remains an old open problem that urgently needs answers. Failure in bringing satisfactory solutions will be a limiting factor to system integration. It would also mean that computer science is definitely relegated to second-class status with respect to other disciplines.

CC: What is "system design"? Is it a science?

JS: First, I would like to say a few words about design in general. It is the process that leads to an artefact meeting given requirements. The requirements include functional requirements describing the functionality provided by the artefact and extra-functional requirements dealing with the way in which resources are used for implementation and throughout the artefact's lifecycle. My initial interest was in the design of reactive mixed hardware/software systems. It extended to general systems, in particular the design of cyber-physical systems which are complex systems integrating physical and electronic components. Designers deal with two often antagonistic demands: (1) productivity, meaning cost-effectiveness and (2) correctness, meaning compliance to requirements. I consider that in pursuit of these demands, any design process moves through three stages. The first, specification requirements, describes the artefact's expected behaviour and any applicable techno-economic constraints. The second, proceduralisation, generates an executable description, e.g., application software, for realising the anticipated behaviour by executing sequences of elementary functions. The third, materialisation, produces systems by following the procedure using the available physical resources.

Design is an essential component of any engineering activity. By its nature, it is a "problem-solving process". As a rule, requirements are declarative. They are usually expressed in natural languages. For some application areas, they can be formalised by using logics. When requirements are expressed by logical specifications, they can be treated as axioms; proofs that the artefact meets them can start from there. Proceduralisation can be considered as a synthesis problem: procedures are executable models meeting the specifications. Unfortunately, model synthesis from logical requirements often runs into serious technical limitations such as non-computability or intrinsically high complexity.

Design formalisation raises a multitude of deep theoretical problems related to the conceptualisation of needs in a given area and their effective transformation into correct artefacts. So far, it has attracted little attention from theoreticians. One reason is the predilection of the academic world for simple and elegant theories. Another reason is that design is by nature multidisciplinary. Its formalisation requires the consistent integration of heterogeneous models supporting different levels of abstraction including logics, algorithms, programs, physical system models, risk models, statements about user practices and statements about aesthetics.

Despite the challenges, providing systematic and well-founded design techniques is of paramount importance for two reasons. The first is that we need to construct artefacts of guaranteed quality and performance based on scientific evidence. This is the case for airplanes, cars, critical resource management systems as well as for critical computing and communication infrastructure. The second reason is the need to master as much as possible, through automation, the complexity and development costs of increasingly sophisticated artefacts. This need can be illustrated by numerous manufacturing setbacks experienced by the aircraft industry, e.g., the A380 delivery delay or safety concerns with Boeing's Dreamliner. Ideas for "scientising" design emerged in the beginning of the 1960s. I consider that science is a disciplined and systematic method for building, organising and using knowledge about the world. Scientific investigation intimately combines two interdependent processes. The first process is about understanding/predicting the world; it is descriptive and intended to develop theory connecting some observed reality through abstractions to the world of concepts and mathematics. The second process involves design; it is prescriptive and consists in applying a theory in order to assess its explicability and predictability, as well as to invent things that do not yet exist. Interaction and cross-fertilisation between these two processes is key to the progress of scientific knowledge. Today, more than ever, the two processes are involved in an accelerating virtuous cycle for the advancement of scientific knowledge. Design science is concerned with deriving from scientific knowledge appropriate information in a form suitable for the designer's use, e.g., design flows supported by methods and tools. I believe that despite inherent technical difficulties and limitations, the study and formalisation of design can bring interesting insights about the very nature of artefact creation.

CC: *Rigorous System Design* is the title of a short monograph you published last year in "Foundations and Trends in Electronic Design Automation". What does "rigorous" mean in the title? Rigour is essential in mathematics: however, even there, standards of rigour have changed throughout history, and not necessarily from less rigour to more rigour.

Do we need rigour in computer science? Can we afford rigour in computer science?

JS: The monograph advocates rigorous system design as a coherent and accountable process aimed at building systems of guaranteed quality, cost-effectively. The quest for correctness, that is full compliance to a set of well-formalised requirements, is too ambitious. Instead, I require rigorousness, meaning that at each step of a design flow we know which requirements are met and which requirements may not hold. This is a more realistic goal, if we can formalise design as an iterative process based on divide-and-conquer strategies, and consisting of a set of steps leading from requirements to implementation. At each step, a particular humanly tractable problem must be solved by addressing specific classes of requirements.

A rigorous design flow is such that if some requirement is met at some design step, its validity is preserved by all subsequent steps. It clearly identifies segments that can be supported by tools to automate tedious and error-prone tasks. It also clearly distinguishes points where human intervention and ingenuity are needed to resolve design choices through requirements analysis and confrontation with experimental results.

Rigour has a number of meanings depending on the context. For me rigour of the design process means, in particular, accountability; that is the designer deeply understands the impact of his choices and is able to explain them to third parties, e.g., clients, certification authorities. Rigour is essential in any scientific and engineering activity. The main problem with the current design flows of computing systems is that they are empirical and thus, lack rigour. The need for rigorous design is often directly or indirectly questioned by developers of large-scale systems (e.g., web-based systems) who privilege experimental/analytic approaches. They claim that rigour is too costly or even unfeasible and instead we should develop experimental techniques for improving systems after they are developed: "On-line companies... do not anguish over how to design their websites. Instead they conduct controlled experiments by showing different versions to different groups of users until they have iterated to an optimal solution". My opinion is that experimental approaches can be useful only for optimisation purposes, e.g., for improving performance or enhancing resource utilisation. Nonetheless, trustworthiness is a qualitative property and, by its nature, it cannot be achieved by the fine-tuning of parameters. Small changes can have a dramatic impact on safety and security properties.

CC: You recently moved to École Polytechnique Fédérale de Lausanne. What changes did the move determine? Did the focus of your work change?

JS: I took a professor position at EPFL in October 2011, where I created the "Rigorous System Design" laboratory. The focus of my work did not change. I still have very strong links with my team at Verimag. Of course, EPFL provides a very stimulating research environment including very good students, interaction with first-class researchers and a lot of opportunities for scientific collaboration, in particular in the framework of national Swiss projects.

CC: An even bolder move was to accept in March 2014 the position of the President of the Greek National Council for Research and Technology...

JS: As a native Greek, I am very much concerned with the economic crisis that my country undergoes. I have accepted this responsibility as have many other scientists of the Greek *diaspora* members of the Council, in order to help with reforming the Greek research system and making its connection with the real economy more effective. There is an increasing awareness in the country that the remedy to the current crisis is economic development, and solutions should be sought beyond tourism, agriculture, maritime revenues and exploitation of natural resources. Setting up a modern and competitive economy requires a substantial effort for research, technology and innovation.

CC: The talk about changes brings to mind a poem by Edmond Haraucourt which I remember from my youth. It starts with[1]:

> *Partir, c'est mourir un peu,*
> *C'est mourir à ce qu'on aime:*
> *On laisse un peu de soi-même*
> *En toute heure à tout lieu.*

JS: Over my career, I have considered change and the quest for new problems and ideas as a means for self-fulfilment. I know researchers that made a very successful career by staying in the same area and dealing with variants of the same problem. Forty years ago, I believed that we could develop a theory based on formal methods that is a combination of logic, calculi, formal languages, semantics, type systems and abstract data types, for building correct computing systems exactly as civil engineers build bridges, electrical engineers build circuits etc. I have worked on the theory of concurrency, temporal

---

[1] An English translation (`http://ratiocinativa.wordpress.com/2013/03/19/partir-cest-mourir-un-peu-edmond-haraucourt/`): "to go away is to die a little, it is to die to that which one loves: everywhere and always, one leaves behind a part of oneself."

logics and verification. Twenty years ago, my faith in this vision was shaken. I worked on abstraction, timed systems, hybrid systems and synthesis. I progressively got interested in systems and system design, in particular. Ten years ago, I was convinced that we would never have the all-encompassing "nice theory" I was dreaming of and that the classical system design paradigm is not transposable to computing. I considered that verification is a stopgap until other alternatives for achieving correctness work. It is a "speciality" of computing no other scientific discipline gives it such a prominent place. I believe that a discipline is not worthy of scientific merit if predictability can be achieved only through verification. Of course, any change of research area implies risks. It is not easy to be accepted and recognised by scientific communities which are usually closed to newcomers. But what matters for me is the "trip" as one of my preferred Greek poets says in his poem "Ithaka":

> As you set out for Ithaka
> hope the voyage is a long one,
> full of adventure, full of discovery
> . . .
> Hope the voyage is a long one.
> May there be many a summer morning when,
> with what pleasure, what joy,
> you come into harbours seen for the first time;
> . . .
> Keep Ithaka always in your mind.
> Arriving there is what you are destined for.
> But do not hurry the journey at all.
> Better if it lasts for years,
> so you are old by the time you reach the island,
> wealthy with all you have gained on the way,
> not expecting Ithaka to make you rich.
> Ithaka gave you the marvellous journey.
> Without her you would not have set out.
> She has nothing left to give you now.
> And if you find her poor, Ithaka won't have fooled you.
> Wise as you will have become, so full of experience,
> you will have understood by then what these Ithakas mean.

Chapter 8

Joseph F. Traub: Information-Based Complexity

Joseph F. Traub is the Edwin Howard Armstrong Professor of Computer Science at Columbia University and External Professor, Santa Fe Institute http: // www. cs. columbia. edu/~traub. He is the author or editor of 10 monographs and some 140 papers on computer science, mathematics, physics, finance and economics. In 1959 he began his work on the optimal iteration theory culminating in the 1964 monograph which is still in print. Subsequently he pioneered work with Henryk Wozniakowski on optimal algorithms and computational complexity applied to continuous scientific problems (IBC). He collaborated in creating significant new algorithms including the Jenkins–Traub algorithm for polynomial zeros, as well as the Kung–Traub, Shaw–Traub, and Brent–Traub algorithms. One of his current research areas is quantum computing. From 1971 to 1979 he headed the Computer Science department at Carnegie Mellon University (CMU) and led it from a critical period to eminence (see the Joseph Traub digital archive at CMU at http: // diva. library. cmu. edu/ traub). From 1979 to 1989, he was the founding chair of the Computer Science department at Columbia University. From 1986 to 1992

he served as founding chair of the Computer Science and Telecommunications Board (CSTB), National Academies and served as chair again 2005–2009. Traub is the founding editor-in-chief of the Journal of Complexity (*since 1985*).

His numerous honours include election to the National Academy of Engineering in 1985, the 1991 Emanuel R. Piore Medal from IEEE and the 1992 Distinguished Service Award from the Computer Research Association (CRA). He is a Fellow of the Association for Computing Machinery (ACM), the American Association for the Advancement of Science (AAAS), the American Mathematical Society (AMS), the Society for Industrial and Applied Mathematics (SIAM), and the New York Academy of Sciences (NYAS). He has been the Sherman Fairchild Distinguished Scholar at the California Institute of Technology, and received a Senior Scientist Award from the Alexander von Humboldt Foundation. He was selected by the Accademia Nazionale dei Lincei in Rome to present the 1993 Lezione Lincee, a cycle of six lectures. Traub received the 1999 Mayor's Award for Excellence in Science and Technology. The award was presented by Mayor Rudy Giuliani at a ceremony in New York City. In 2001 he received an honorary doctorate of science from the University of Central Florida.

EG[1]: To what do you ascribe your very successful career?

JT: The short answer is mostly just plain dumb luck. Of course I also took advantage of some opportunities. I will give you some examples. I entered Columbia in 1954, intending to take a PhD in theoretical physics. In 1955, on the advice of a fellow student, I visited IBM's Watson Laboratories at Columbia. At the time this was one of the few places in the country where a student could get his hands on computer. I was hooked. Due to that piece of luck, I've spent the last 55 years involved with computation. My PhD thesis on computational quantum mechanics was done on the IBM 650, a 2000-word drum memory machine. I believe that the need to be very economical on this computer may have led to my early interest in optimal algorithms and computational complexity.

---

[1]This discussion starts with Erol Gelenbe's questions.

The next stroke of luck was being hired in the research division of Bell Laboratories in 1959. This was a golden age at the labs. You were free to work on whatever interested you; if your work had impact on the company, all the better. I had the freedom to spend some four years doing research which culminated in the creation of the optimal iteration theory and the publication of a monograph in 1964. If I had been an assistant professor at a university, it would have been very dangerous to create a new area while publishing very little, but I could do it at Bell Labs.

The next stroke of luck occurred during a sabbatical at Stanford in 1966. I met a student, Michael Jenkins, who was looking for a PhD advisor. We developed the Jenkins–Traub algorithm as well as high-quality portable software for polynomial zeros.

In 1970 I was at the University of Washington. I advertised for a GRA, and interviewed about a dozen students. I selected H.T. Kung, and the following year, brought him with me to CMU. He eventually joined the CMU faculty and today is a chaired professor at Harvard.

In the spring of 1971, I was selected to be Head of the Computer Science department at CMU. I was 38 years old and had this opportunity because I had gotten into the field so early. If I'd been in a mature field, I would never have had such an opportunity. Alan Perlis the department head, was leaving to become founding chair of the department at Yale. Al did not publish much but was a towering figure at CMU. Allen Newell, Alan Perlis, and Herbert Simon had founded the department in 1965. Perlis and I overlapped by just a few days but he gave me invaluable advice. One of the things I recall is that he advised me to rapidly tenure Bill Wulf, who was then an assistant professor. Soon Bill was a full professor, and he later succeeded me as chair of the CSTB of the National Research Council, and then became President of the National Academy of Engineering.

The department was quite small, including Gordon Bell, Nico Habermann, Allen Newell, Raj Reddy, Herbert Simon and William Wulf. Just prior to 1971, many faculty had left the department to take positions elsewhere. Those professors who remained formed a core of world-class scientists recognised as leaders of the discipline.

I worked with the faculty to recruit new members and diversify research funding. I was deeply concerned whether we would remain a leading department. Perhaps it is just as well that I didn't know of a commitment made by the senior faculty to stay at CMU for at least one year to see if the department could be turned around. I often had the feeling that the department and I had been created for each other. By the time I left Carnegie in 1979, we had some 50 teaching and research faculty.

Another opportunity occurred in 1972. Lawrence Livermore Laboratory planned to acquire a STAR computer and hired me as a consultant. I became fascinated with parallel computing, which I saw as a very interesting new direction for computing. Perhaps I was too early. I remember giving a talk at a major research university on why parallel computing was going to be very important. The first question after the lecture was from a very well-known professor: "Joe, you do not really think we are ever going to use these computers to solve our problems?"

In 1972, a stroke of luck occurred that was to change my scientific work. I received a registered package containing a paper and letter from someone named Henryk Wozniakowski in Warsaw. A Polish professor had pointed him to my 1964 monograph. The paper proved conjectures I'd framed in the 1964 book but in much greater generality. Henryk visited me at CMU in 1973 and that was to be the beginning of a collaboration that has extended for almost 40 years. We were to start and build the field of IBC.

By 1979 the department was thriving in every aspect. I had been head of CMU for seven years and I could think of moving on to new challenges. Then came the next stroke of good timing. With some exceptions, the Ivy League universities had lagged behind in the building of computer science departments. Now Columbia decided to start a department, and invited me to return and to build it. I accepted, and went to Columbia in 1979.

By the mid-1980s many papers were being written on IBC and there was no obvious place to publish them. I was not particularly interested in starting a journal, but there was a need. I noted with surprise that there was, as far as I could tell, no journal with the word complexity in the title. In 1985, I started the *Journal of Complexity*. It's now in its 26th year and is much broader than only publishing papers in IBC.

In 1986, a different opportunity came knocking. I was asked to start a Computer Science Board at the National Academy of Sciences. More precisely, it was a board of the National Research Council, which is the working arm of the National Academies. I was told two previous boards had failed — I was determined there would not be a third failure. I called the new board the CSTB and appointed leaders from academia and industry to serve as members. About a year after the establishment of CSTB, I was fortunate to hire a superb staff director, Marjory Blumenthal. Around 1988, Frank Press, the president of the National Academy of Sciences, told me that the Board on Telecommunications (BOTCAP) was failing, and that the decision had been made to terminate it. He asked us to add telecommunications to our responsibilities. Marjory and I wanted to preserve the abbreviation CSTB, so we renamed the board the Computer Science and Telecommunications Board, which has remained its name to the present day.

Another opportunity came in 1990, when I was asked to teach in the summer school of the SFI. I was greatly stimulated by the variety of topics studied at SFI and have been associated with the institute ever since. Currently I'm serving as an external professor.

In the early 1990s, we were lucky to be given a collateralised mortgage obligation (CMO) by Goldman Sachs. This involved computing integrals in 360 dimensions. A PhD student, Spassimir Paskov, computed the integrals by Monte Carlo (MC) and quasi-Monte Carlo (QMC). To our surprise, and later to the surprise of Wall Street, QMC always beat MC by one to three orders of magnitude.

Of course the greatest stroke of luck of all was meeting and marrying Pamela McCorduck. I'm also blessed with two loving children, Claudia and Hillary, and four wonderful grandchildren.

EG: You've done a great deal of research. Could you tell us about some of your early work?

JT: Shortly after I joined Bell Labs in 1959, a colleague asked me how to compute the numerical solution of a certain problem, which involved the solution of a complicated nonlinear equation. I could think of a number of ways to solve the problem. What was the optimal algorithm, which is a method that would minimise the required computational resources? To my surprise, there was no theory of optimal algorithms. (The phrase "computational complexity"which is the study of the minimal resources required to solve computational problems was not introduced until 1965.) I set out to construct a theory of optimal algorithms for the solution of the non-linear equation $f(x) = 0$. I had the key insight that the maximal order of an iteration depended on the available information about f and not on the structure of the iteration. (Maximal order is closely related to computational complexity). This was such a powerful idea that I was sure someone else would announce it. I scanned the world literature, fearing such a publication. To my immense relief, no one published this idea. Wouldn't it be useful for researchers to be automatically notified of papers in which they would be interested? This led to work on such a publication notification system.[2]

I first presented the work on what was to become the optimal iteration theory at the 1961 National ACM conference.[3] In those days the national ACM conference was a big deal, and many of the researchers in computing attended. I kept building the theory and soon had a manuscript of some 120 pages. Being a very young and naive researcher, I sent this manuscript to Mario Juncosa, the editor-in-chief of the *Journal of the ACM*, who wrote back that it would be a long time before he could read the manuscript. Just then, Prentice-Hall asked me if I wanted to write a book. I set to work and wrote

---

[2]W. S. Brown, J. R. Pierce, J. F. Traub. The future of scientific journals, *Science*, 158: 1153–1159, 1966. W. S. Brown, J. F. Traub. 'MERCURY — A system for the computer aided distribution of technical papers', *Journal ACM*, 16: 13–25, 1969.

[3]J. F. Traub. Functional iteration and the calculation of roots, *Proceedings, National ACM Conference*, 5A-1–5A-4, 1961.

the monograph, "Iterative Methods for the Solution of Equations".[4] The editor of the Prentice-Hall Series in Automatic Computation was George Forsythe, who was to become founding chair of the Computer Science Department at Stanford. I'm pleased that this book is still in print, going on 50 years since its publication. The book would have been better titled "Optimal Iteration Theory". It marked the beginning of a lifetime's work on optimal algorithms and computational complexity for continuous problems. The introduction begins with: "The general area into which this book falls may be labelled algorithmics. By algorithmics we mean the study of algorithms..."Don Knuth credits me with coining "algorithmics".[5]

So far I'd worked on general non-linear equations. For such problems, convergence could not be guaranteed. Was there a class of non-linear equations for which one could guarantee convergence? The answer is yes, for polynomial equations.[6] In 1966 I was a visiting professor at Stanford, where I met a PhD student, Michael Jenkins. We continued the work on global convergence which led to what is usually called the Jenkins–Traub algorithm.[7] The algorithm consists of three stages, of which the third is the most important. It can be shown that this stage is equivalent to applying a Newton iteration to a sequence of rational functions, which converges to a first-degree polynomial whose zero is one of the desired answers. Although Newton iteration requires the evaluation of a derivative at each step, the Jenkins–Traub algorithm does not require the evaluation of any derivatives. It can be shown that under mild conditions, the algorithm always converges, and that the rate of convergence is faster than the quadratic rate of Newton.[8] Jenkins wrote a high-quality

---

[4]J. F. Traub. 'Iterative Methods for the Solution of Equations', Prentice-Hall (1964). Reissued, American Mathematical Society, 1998.

[5]D. E. Knuth. 'Algorithms in mathematics and computer science', in Lecture Notes in Computer Science, G. Goos and J. Hartmanis, (eds.,), 122: 82–99, 1979.

[6]J. F. Traub. 'A class of globally convergent iteration functions for the solution of polynomial equations', *Mathematics of Computation*, 20: 113–138, 1966.

[7]M. A. Jenkins and J. F. Traub. 'A three-stage variable-shift iteration for polynomial zeros and its relation to generalized Rayleigh iteration', *Numerische Mathematik*, 14: 252–263, 1970.

[8]See the Wikipedia article "Jenkins–Traub algorithm".

portable program implementing the algorithm. This algorithm is still one of the most widely used methods for this problem and is included in many textbooks.

In 1972 I became fascinated with parallel computing and organised a symposium at CMU in 1973, which may have been the first on this subject.[9] I spoke on this topic at the 1974 IFIP Congress.[10]

In the 1970s I became interested in algebraic complexity. Mary Shaw was a student in my class when I spoke about Horner's method for evaluating polynomials, which was known to be optimal. I conjectured that if one wanted to evaluate all the derivatives of a polynomial, the optimal method would take a quadratic number of multiplications. Mary showed me that she could beat that, and we worked together to get the number of multiplications to linear.[11] Mary is now the Alan J. Perlis Professor at CMU.

Next, my student H.T. Kung and I showed that computing the first n terms of any algebraic function was no harder than multiplying two nth degree polynomials.[12] This problem has a long history; Isaac Newton missed a key point.

Richard Brent and I were able to show that computing the qth composite of a power series was no harder than computing a single composition where q is any number.[13] One day, I got a call from Don Knuth who had heard about our work. I told him I could mail him a preprint in a few days. Don replied that he didn't want to wait, since he was working on that part of his book just then. He had redone parts of our analysis and just wanted to check that it agreed with what we had done.

---

[9]'Complexity of Sequential and Parallel Numerical Algorithms', J. F. Traub, editor, Academic Press, 1973.

[10]J. F. Traub, 'Parallel algorithms and parallel computational complexity', *Proceedings IFIP Congress*: 685–687, 1974.

[11]M. Shaw, J. F. Traub. 'On the number of multiplications for the evaluation of a polynomial and some of its derivatives', *Journal of the ACM*, 21: 161–167, 1974.

[12]H. T. Kung, J. F. Traub. 'All algebraic functions can be computed fast', *Journal of the ACM*, 25: 245–260, 1978.

[13]R. Brent, J. F. Traub. 'On the complexity of composition and generalised composition of power series', *SIAM Journal of Computation*, 9: 54–66, 1980.

This ended my work on algebraic complexity because I was about to move in an entirely new direction.

EG: Can you tell me what happened next?

JT: I mentioned earlier that Henryk Wozniakowski visited me at CMU in 1973. That was to be the beginning of a collaboration that has spanned almost 40 years. Initially, we continued the work on the optimal iteration theory. Then in 1976 there came an event that changed the course of our research. A PhD student named Arthur Werschulz, now a professor at Fordham University and part of our research group at Columbia University, gave a seminar, where he used some of the techniques from non-linear equations to attack the complexity of integration. Our reaction was that integration is inherently different from solving non-linear equations; one doesn't solve integration iteratively. Because these problems are so different, there must be a general structure that underlies this and many other problems. Our search for the general structure led to our monograph.[14] We called this new field analytic complexity. This was to differentiate it from algebraic complexity, which was a very active research area in the late 1960s and 1970s.

Algebraic complexity deals with algebraic problems such as the complexity of matrix multiplication, where information about the input is complete, while analytic complexity deals with problems from analysis, such as the complexity of high-dimensional integration, where information about the continuous input is partial. Let me elaborate this last point. In calculus, students are taught to compute univariate integrals exactly. But most integrals cannot be expressed in terms of elementary functions; they have to be approximated numerically. This is especially true of real-world high-dimensional integrals, such as the integrals common in mathematical finance. We sample the integrand; that is why the information about the mathematical input is partial. Other problems studied in analytic complexity include optimal algorithms and computational complexity of

---

[14] J. F. Traub, H. Wozniakowski. 'A General Theory of Optimal Algorithms', Academic Press, 1980.

systems of ordinary differential equations, high-dimensional approximation, partial differential equations, continuous optimisation and non-linear equations.

Greg Wasilkowski joined Henryk and I to write the monograph.[15] We renamed the field *epsilon*-complexity. One day, Pamela asked me why *epsilon*-complexity? I replied that *epsilon* denotes a small quantity and that it measures the error in the answer. She did not seem impressed. Since Pamela is the author of numerous books, I took her lack of enthusiasm seriously and started thinking about a new name. One day I was chatting with my friend, Richard Karp, who, as you know, was a pioneer in the study of NP-completeness. He suggested IBC, which we adopted as the name of the field. It was the name of our monograph.[16] For brevity we often refer to the field as IBC. Typically, IBC theory is developed over abstract linear spaces such as Hilbert or Banach spaces. The applications are often for problems with a very large number of variables.

Because the information is partial, IBC is able to use powerful adversary arguments at the information level. The general idea behind an adversary argument is the following: the adversary creates a situation where the inputs are indistinguishable but the outputs are quite different. It is therefore impossible to compute a good approximation because if we claim an approximation to one output as the answer, the adversary will say the second output is the correct one. Adversary arguments are often used to find a good lower bound on the information complexity and hence tight lower bound on the computational complexity.[17] This may be contrasted with the rest of theoretical computer science where researchers work on discrete problems with complete information and have to settle for conjectures on the complexity hierarchy. We find these adversary

---

[15] J. F. Traub, G. Wasilkowski, H. Wozniakowski. 'Information, Uncertainty, Complexity', Addison-Wesley, 1983.

[16] J. F. Traub, G. Wasilkowski, H. Wozniakowski. 'Information-Based Complexity', Academic Press, 1988.

[17] See, for example, A. Papageorgiou, J. F. Traub. 'Qubit complexity of continuous problems', *J. Fixed Point Theory and Applications*, 6(2): 295–304, 2009, Section 2.

arguments very natural but we've learned that this way of thinking is so different that many of our colleagues in theoretical computer science find them difficult. An expository account of IBC was published in 1998.[18]

IBC has grown vastly over the past 20 years.[19]

In the early 1990s, I had a PhD student named Spassimir Paskov. Spassimir was very strong in theory, but I wanted to broaden him. We had gotten a CMO from Goldman Sachs. (A CMO is a bond that represents claims to specific cash flows from large pools of home mortgages.) This involved computing integrals in 360 dimensions. I asked Spassimir to compute the integrals using QMC and MC. It was believed by experts that QMC, which uses deterministic sampling, was not good for dimensions greater than 12. To the amazement of our research group, Paskov reported that QMC beat MC by one to three orders of magnitude. The results were presented to a number of Wall Street firms, who were initially skeptical.[20] Other researchers then got similar results. QMC is not a *panacea* for all high-dimensional integration. It is still an open question to explain why QMC is superior to MC for financial instruments.[21]

Moore's law, which has explained the exponential increase in computer power over some five decades, is coming to an end. Starting in 2001 our research group has been applying IBC ideas to solve continuous problems such as the Schrödinger equation and path integrals on quantum computers. Among other objectives we want to answer the question posed by Nielsen and Chuang.[22] "Of particular interest

---

[18] J. F. Traub, A. G. Werschulz. 'Complexity and Information', Cambridge University Press, 1998.

[19] See J. F. Traub. 'A brief history of information based complexity', in "Essays on the Complexity of Continuous Problems", European Mathematical Society: 61–71, 2009, for a brief history see E. Novak, I. Sloan, J. F. Traub, H. Wozniakowski. "Essays on the Complexity of Continuous Problems"European Mathematical Society (2009) for a survey.

[20] S. Paskov, J. F. Traub. 'Faster Valuation of Financial Derivatives', *Journal of Portfolio Management*, 22(1): 113–120, 1995.

[21] See the Wikipedia article "Quasi-Monte Carlo methods in finance", for a survey.

[22] M. A. Nielsen, E. L. Chuang. 'Quantum Computation and Quantum Information', Cambridge University Press, 2000.

is a decisive answer whether quantum computers are more powerful than classical computers". To answer this question, one must know the classical and quantum complexities, which can sometimes be obtained using IBC techniques. A survey on solving continuous problems on a quantum computer may be found in a *Springer Encyclopedia*.[23]

EG: Can you tell me about some of the organisations you've built?

JT: As I mentioned earlier, by getting involved in computing so early I had opportunities I would not have had in a mature discipline. The first was being selected as Head of the Computer Science department at CMU when I was 38 years old. As I told you earlier, the department was very small but the faculty formed a core of world-class scientists. It was crucial to add outstanding faculty and diversify research funding. We decided to revamp the PhD programme. One of the innovations was the creation of the Black Friday Meeting, which was held at the end of each semester. The entire faculty reviewed every PhD student. Every student received a letter regarding his or her progress. I thought this was a very effective management tool. Allen Newell, Herb Simon and I talked about the "greening"of CMU and Pittsburgh, using computers. That has come to pass, big time.

In 1979, Columbia invited me to start a new computer science department. At the time there were two efforts in computer science: an electrical engineering and computer science department and a group in the statistics department. The two groups were at loggerheads, and unable to recruit good junior faculty. The plan was that both these efforts were to be terminated.

I was able to negotiate some very good things for the new department. We would get our own building and I would select the architect. I pointed out that the teaching load in computer science departments at leading private research universities was one course a semester, and

---

[23] A. Papageorgiou, J. F. Traub. 'Quantum algorithms and complexity for continuous problems', in Springer Encyclopedia of Complexity and Systems Science, 8: 7118–7135, 2009. For a more recent work see A. Papageorgiou, J. F. Traub. 'Measures of quantum computing speedup', *Physical Review A*, 88, 022316, 2013.

got the same at Columbia. I accepted the position and started on 1 July, 1979.

It was to be the toughest challenge I ever had. At CMU, the department had enough DEC computers to heat the building. At Columbia, the entire engineering school had a single DEC machine; an 11/45 model, as I recall. There were three tenured faculty inherited from the terminated efforts, as well as a number of junior faculty. None of the junior faculty belonged in a department with national ambitions; they were all gone within two years. I set out to hire outstanding new PhDs. Since many universities and corporate research laboratories were hiring at this time, the competition was very tough, but we succeeded in hiring some outstanding young faculty. With almost no faculty, we were trying to teach several thousand students who were taking our courses. I didn't advertise to our newly hired hotshots that they'd be teaching some 200 students per course.

But we had some great successes. We received a substantial grant from IBM. I took the new faculty to meet Bob Kahn, the DARPA IPTO director. He was so impressed with the new faculty that he decided to give us major funding. Furthermore, for the first time Columbia had a connection to the ARPAnet. We started bachelors, master's, and PhD programmes, and taught computer science to all of Columbia University.

As I mentioned earlier, I started the *Journal of Complexity* in 1985. In the early years, all papers funnelled through me. I realised I was a bottleneck, so I created an Editorial Board, who could independently accept or reject papers or require revisions. The journal is going strong in its 26th year.

In 1986 I was asked to create a Computer Science Board for the National Research Council (NRC). It's now called the CSTB. Our first report, for which the late Michael Dertouzos did much of the writing, was called "The National Challenge in Computer Science and Technology". We had a fairly difficult time getting it through the very thorough NRC review process. Much of this report was devoted to policy, whereas my impression was that NRC was more comfortable with technology. CSTB continued to work on policy as well as technology, and in time, that became highly appreciated at the NRC. I rotated off CSTB in 1992 and then served as chair again in 2005–2009. To see what reports CSTB has completed and what projects are currently underway, visit `www.cstb.org`.

I had a hand in building four organisations: the CS department at CMU, the CS department at Columbia, the *Journal of Complexity*, and the Computer Science and Telecommunications Board. The common ingredient for success was excellent people.

EG: You mentioned your role in building organisations. Did you also play a role in the creation of other entities?

JT: Because I got into computing so early, I had such opportunities. For example, I was one of the founders of the Computer Research Association (CRA) in 1972. We decided to create what became the Federated Computing Research Conference (FCRC) at a meeting which I believe was held in Washington, D.C. I was a founding member of the scientific advisory committee (ISAT) of DARPA in 1986.

EG: Do you have any regrets about something you did not pursue?

JT: There is something important I should have done. Starting in 1985, I noticed various ways in which our information infrastructure was vulnerable to electronic or physical attack. I imagined myself to be a terrorist, or an enemy country, and targeted aspects of what we would today call the national information infrastructure. I felt it was just because we were the most advanced country in our use of information technologies, we were and are the most vulnerable. I also felt we were vulnerable to physical attack. Let me give you an example. I was given the opportunity to visit the floor of the New York Stock Exchange one morning just before it opened. The only visible security was one guard, equipped with a revolver. There may, of course, have been security that was not visible to me, but I doubt it. I thought what a tempting target the symbolic heart of our capitalist society this would make, and the damage a couple of hand grenades would inflict. The actual processing of trades was executed across the river in Brooklyn but I doubted that it was sufficiently secure against physical or electronic attack.

I did not go public with my concerns because I was worried about giving individuals or countries ideas. That was foolish; our enemies are very smart. I now feel I should've spent a considerable amount of my energy and time alerting the country.

I finally went public when I gave the keynote address at a symposium at the National Academy of Sciences celebrating the tenth anniversary of CSTB.[24] I pointed out the vulnerability of what I called the "virtual estate", which consists of bank accounts, equities, CDs, pension accounts, etc. I called it the virtual estate because it's recorded in electrons. If you were a terrorist, and wanted to do a great deal of damage to American institutions and individuals, a natural target would be the virtual estate. Our virtual estate is just one example of a potential target. Others include the power grid and our communications systems.

Who should be in charge of protecting our infrastructure? I argued for strong Federal government leadership, centred in the executive branch.

EG: Can you say something about the future of computing, especially as it relates to your interests?

JT: That is such a deliciously open-ended question—I'll confine myself to just four issues.

The first has to do with scaling laws. Perhaps the most famous scaling law is Moore's law, an empirical law which has driven computing for almost half a century. Moore's law is running up against a number of fundamental physical limits. For a while we will benefit from multi-cores, many cores and massive parallelism. But there are considerable impediments to parallel computing. Parallel machines are difficult to program and some problems are difficult to decompose. That is why there's much interest in radically different kinds of computing, such as quantum, photonics, molecular and biological computing. Of course Moore's law is not the only important scaling law. Another example is the doubling rate of bandwidth, which is much shorter than that of chip density. How should we plan our computing and networking in light of this effect?

---

[24] J. F. Traub. 'From infoware to infowar', in 'Defining a Decade: Envisioning CSTB's Second Ten Years', National Academy Press: 1–7, 1997.

A second area is IBC. Quite a few years ago, I ended an MIT lecture by stating some open questions. Afterwards, Marvin Minsky told me he saves his good questions for his students. I replied that there were lots more where those came from. That's always been the case in IBC. We end many papers and talks with a list of open problems. For example, Erich Novak and Henryk Wozniakowski have written a three-volume monograph, *"Tractability of Multivariate Problems"* published by the European Mathematical Society (2008, 2010, 2012). They contain 149 open problems, a number of which have already been solved.

Why are there so many open problems? I believe it's because we're asking new questions about many continuous scientific problems, a vast domain. Furthermore, when the technology changes, or might change, that alters what algorithms are permitted. A good example is quantum computing, where, for example, we're investigating the power of quantum computing for solving the problems of quantum mechanics.

A third area is cybersecurity, far more than just the protection of the virtual estate. Two very different issues have recently been studied by the CSTB. One is deterrence strategies for the US government towards preventing cyberattacks. Many reports on this topic are available at `www.cstb.org`. Another is in regard to US acquisition and use of cyberattack capabilities; a recent CSTB report is available. Cybersecurity can only become still more important.

I'll end with concern about computer science majors. There is an odd dissonance between the feelings of prospective students and their parents, on the one hand, and university computer science faculty, on the other. Students seem reluctant to study computer science for two reasons: concern jobs will be outsourced; and a feeling that the big advances are behind us. But my colleagues and I feel that computer science is more exciting than ever. Bill Gates has expressed concern about not being able to hire American computer science majors. We worry that women are not attracted to computer science, which cuts us off from half the brains of the country. This is at the very time that China is making huge investments in computer science education.

The key to the country's future is innovation, and it's vital that computing attracts some of our country's best and brightest.

CC: In your 1998 paper "Non-Computability and Intractability: Does It Matter to Physics?"you write "I'm not convinced that non-computability need be of concern". What is your current position regarding this statement.

JT: I will briefly summarise the issue for the benefit of the reader.[25] Consider, for example, partial differential equations with computable initial conditions but non-computable solutions. The equations can be very simple. Examples are the wave equation with initial conditions which are not twice differentiable and the backwards heat equation. The renowned physicist and mathematician Roger Penrose is concerned by the result that the wave equation with computable initial conditions can have non-computable solutions; he called this a "rather startling result".[26] Is this really a startling result? Let's have a deeper look.

The differential equations mentioned above are special cases of ill-posed equations. Werschulz[27] proved that if a problem is ill-posed it is impossible to compute an ε-approximation to the solution at finite cost even for an arbitrarily large error ε. But this is a worst-case result. There is a surprising result that every ill-posed problem is well-posed on the average for every Gaussian measure; a survey of the work leading to this result was published in 1994.[28] Thus the non-solvability of ill-posed problems is a worst-case phenomenon. It melts away in the average case for reasonable measures. Nothing has happened to make me change my mind that non-computability may

---

[25]See also J. F. Traub, A. G. Werschulz. 'Complexity and Information', Cambridge University Press, 1998, Chapter 9.

[26]R.L. Penrose. 'The Emperor's New Mind', Oxford University Press, 1989.

[27]A. G. Werschulz. 'What is the complexity of ill-posed problems?', *Numer. Funct. Anal. Opt.*, 9:945–967, 1987.

[28]J. F. Traub, A. G. Werschulz. 'Linear ill-posed problems are solvable on the average for all Gaussian measures', *Math. Intelligencer*, 16, No. 2: 42–48, 1994.

not be a cause for concern for physicists. As in the above example it may simply be a worst-case phenomenon.

CC: It seems to me your concern was that non-computability could be bad for physics. What about the possibility of being an asset?

JT: I agree that non-computability can cut in two ways. Its analogous to the situation in cryptography. We want secure encryption to protect out private information. On the other hand, we want to read encrypted messages between terrorists to foil the planning of attacks.

CC: Starting with Ralph Gomory's tripartite division of science into the known, the unknown which may someday became known, and the (most interesting) unknowable, the part which will never be known you've written "my goal is to move the distinction between the unknown and the unknowable from philosophy to science".[29] Did you make further steps towards achieving this goal, and if yes, can you summarise them?

JT: I'd like to begin with some background regarding my interest in this issue. The first time I wrote about this issue was in 1991.[30] I gave a talk on "What is Scientifically Knowable" at a symposium celebrating the 25th anniversary of the Computer Science Department at CMU and this reference is in the anniversary commemorative. Gödel's work has had a profound impact on mathematics. It established fundamental limits on mathematical proofs. It was an enrichment of mathematics. I hoped that establishing limits to science by proving that the answers to certain scientific questions were unknowable would be an enrichment of science. How might one prove that the answer to a question is unknowable? I've proposed several possible attacks. The first attack is the following. A scientific question does not come equipped with a mathematical model. Researchers develop models for scientific questions. Consider then all formal models that capture the essence of a scientific question. Prove that every formal

---

[29]That quote comes from J. F. Traub. "The unknown and the unknowable", *The Sciences*, 39, No.1: 39–44, 1999.

[30]J. F. Traub, "What is scientifically knowable?" in CMU Computer Science: A 25th Anniversary Commemorative", Addison-Wesley: 489–503, 1991.

model is undecidable or computationally intractable. It seems to me that would be one way of proving the answer is unknowable. However, although this might be a possible attack in principle it is far from evident that it could actually be carried out for any non-trivial question. Rather than a direct attack, which considers all mathematical models, perhaps an indirect attack would have more chance of success. Computational complexity might serve as a guidepost. The intractability theorems of IBC are not proven by varying algorithms. Instead, general theorems are proven from which we can infer intractability of specific mathematical problems. Can this procedure be adapted to derive negative properties (undecidability, intractability) which any mathematical model, for a certain scientific question, must possess? I still think the question of how to distinguish the unknown from the unknowable is an interesting question. However, since the papers I wrote in the 1990s I've moved into other research areas.

Chapter 9

Ian H. Witten: A Stroll Through the Gardens of Computer Science

Ian Witten, $http://www.cs.waikato.ac.nz/\sim ihw/$, is a Professor in the Department of Computer Science at the University of Waikato in New Zealand. His many research interests include information retrieval, machine learning, text compression and programming by demonstration. As head of the New Zealand Digital Library Research Group $http://www.nzdl.org/cgi-bin/library.cgi$, Professor Witten oversaw the development of Greenstone Digital Library software, used by the BBC, New York Botanical Gardens and UNESCO. He has written several books, the latest being Data Mining *(2000),* How to Build a Digital Library *(2002) and* Web Dragons: Inside the Myths of Search Engine Technology *(2007). His Birthday Book, 2007 ($http://www.nzdl.org/Books/Birthday/index.html$) includes contributions from collaborators, friends and students, from all around the world. Professor Witten is a Fellow of the ACM and the Royal Society of New Zealand. He was awarded*

*the IFIP Namur Prize (2004) for "contributions to the awareness
of social implications of information technology... and the need for
a holistic approach in the use of information technology that takes
account of social implications", and won the 2010 World Class New
Zealand Award. In 2012 he was appointed Chief Scientific Advisor at
Pingar* http://www.pingar.com *to provide advice on developing
technologies and solutions to augment enterprise ability to manage
unstructured data.*

CC: How was computer science during your studies at Cambridge
University (MA in Mathematics), the University of Calgary (MSc in
Computer Science) and Essex University (PhD in Electrical Engi-
neering)?

Very different from today! At Cambridge in 1968 I took a course
on numerical analysis from the famous computer science pioneer
Maurice Wilkes, but I'm sorry to say I found it very boring. I wrote
a couple of programs in a language called Focal, a precursor to
Basic I think. At Calgary in 1969–1970 I met both Fortran (punched
cards) and a PDP-12 (teletype and paper tape), which I used inter-
actively — very cool, because I could actually see the computer! At
Essex in the early 1970s I was bequeathed an ancient PDP-1, and
had a lab of several PDP-8s, each with 4 KB RAM — one even had a
massive 10 KB disk. Around 1976 I installed the second UNIX installation in the UK. I loved UNIX because of its openness (still do). All
of these computers had less power than a digital watch does today.

CC: Did the education in three subjects — mathematics, computer
science and electrical engineering — help you well in your career?

IHW: It's a great selling point to have degrees that cover these
three fields; everyone's terrifically impressed. But in actuality my
Computer Science MSc and Electrical Engineering PhD were in very
similar fields, which would be more accurately called applied statistics. I do think that mathematics is a great foundation for thinking in
general, though I have no regrets about abandoning my early aspira-
tions to become an actuary in favour of moving to computer science.

CC: You have lived in three corners of the world and eventually
settled in New Zealand in 1992. What was the motivation?

IHW: When others ask me that I tell them that if they had ever been to New Zealand the answer would be obvious, but you know that already, Cris. It's like asking someone in heaven why they chose that over the alternative. I wanted a more relaxed lifestyle with a greater emphasis on a balanced life and more outdoor recreational opportunities, but also with a good hi-tech environment. New Zealanders are very quick to pick up on new technologies, particularly networking, which is obviously very important over here.

CC: As you said, I know and I fully agree. Tell us about Greenstone, the suite of software for building and distributing digital library collections.

IHW: Greenstone emerged from a desire to apply the *Managing Gigabytes* indexing and searching techniques on a grander scale. A key event was our involvement with UNESCO beginning around 1999/2000, which happened completely by accident. It made me aware of the enormous potential of end-user-built collections for disseminating information in developing countries. Of course, Greenstone is not just for developing countries — it's widely used almost everywhere, including the US — but I became passionate about its use in the developing world. We take libraries, and the Internet, and the ready availability of information, for granted; but life is very different in other places — and the degree of Western cultural hegemony is awful. Greenstone enables people to build and disseminate collections of their own information, in their own language — the interface has been translated, by volunteers, into over 50 languages, some of which you've probably never heard of. And it's been a tremendous personal opportunity for me as well: Greenstone has taken me to meet new friends in places like Cuba, Fiji, Micronesia, Nepal, Trinidad, as well as several African countries and all over India.

CC: Fascinating, I think you have a myriad of stories from these trips.

IHW: Stories and stories. I'll never forget a week-long workshop in a packed computer lab in Havana with ancient Windows computers and no air conditioning. It was glorious bedlam! — My first real encounter with the Hispanic temperament, I guess. People chatting and singing and flirting on the side, and me fighting to retain control. And then the computers started acting up. "Over here, Ian, Greenstone's stopped working on *this* one." "And here too!" I'd take a look: garish windows popping up autonomously all over the screen. Viruses. One by one the lab computers succumbed, until at the end only a couple were still usable. I have since learned that viruses, essentially invisible in my own, obviously well-protected, computer environment, are the curse of the developing world, a productivity sapping "white man's disease" created by affluent westerners which cripples poor countries that lack the technical support needed to fight them. Once (and only once) I passed my memory stick around a class in Africa to distribute sample files: it took just minutes to pick up hundreds of viruses! Spam email is a similar issue: virtually non-existent for me at home, but a plague in these people's lives. Imagine deleting hundreds of spam messages on a painfully slow Internet connection, every day. I have learned to respect other things that we take for granted, like electricity. Just minutes before starting a hands-on workshop in a computer lab in Kathmandu I was told of the scheduled rotating 8-hour electricity cuts ("didn't you know?"), and today's began... ("let me check the schedule")... now! And different cultural mores: after a conspiratorially whispered question "do you like alcohol?" (the answer is obvious to those who know me) I was hijacked from a lively and eagerly anticipated student party in India by smart-suited top officials who insisted I join them in a clandestine, prolonged and rather dismal drinking session.

CC: Please explain the importance of "keyphrase indexing" and your work in this subject.

IHW: Here's an area where computers outperform people at a task that is obviously human! When you choose keyphrases, or index terms or whatever you want to call them, for a document, the aim is to be consistent with what other people are likely to choose, because ultimately the terms are going to be used for searching and browsing by others in order to find the information they seek. The aim is consistency with others, doing what others would do — to be boring, if you like. And success can be measured in terms of the degree of agreement with other people who independently index the same documents. In terms of this measure — agreement with humans — our experiments have shown that computer indexing technology can outperform "ordinary" people and even rival specialists, including professional indexers. That sounded outrageous when my student speculated that it was possible, but she turned out to be right and I was wrong. This seems to happen a lot with me and my students.

CC: Your book *Managing Gigabytes* (co-authored with Alistair Moffat and Timothy C. Bell) published by Morgan Kaufmann Publishing, San Francisco in two editions, is about compressing and indexing documents and images. "This book is the Bible for anyone who needs to manage large data collections", wrote Steve Kirsch, co-founder of Infoseek. How do you see this subject after 18 years since the first edition and 13 years since the second one?

IHW: The Bible? — I know I live in heaven, but did Steve really say that?

CC: Yes, he did.

IHW: I also heard that the book was required reading for early employees at Google. We made a big mistake by saying in the first edition's Preface that maybe the second edition would be called *Managing Terabytes*, and we had to eat our words when we came to the second edition. I'd love to write Managing Terabytes, but in truth the problems are completely different when you move upscale. What amazes me about today's search engines is not so much that they can answer queries so quickly but that they can keep going in the face of continuous failure. With a hundred thousand disks, a dozen must fail every day; with a million, one must fail every ten minute. And it's not just disks...

CC: Data deluge is not a danger? Sciences are shifting to engineering by using statistical techniques to sniff through huge databases to find patterns, and, amazingly, with good and very good predictive results. This is fine unless this paradigm "kills" one of the important scientific quests, the effort to *understand*. This issue was discussed in a very interesting conversation between Noam Chomsky and Yarden Katz titled *On Where Artificial Intelligence Went Wrong*, recently published in *The Atlantic*.

IHW: Yep, understanding is indeed degenerating in favour of publishable "results", and I regret to say that I have personally contributed to the problem. I cringe when I read papers that compare this machine-learning technique to that one on half a dozen standard datasets and present nothing but a nicely formatted table of statistical results (to 5 significant digits), with no insights at all. This is pointless research, Weka-enabled. The pressure to publish has become all-consuming. (The only upside, and it's not a very big one, is that such "research" does contribute to my citation count. (That was a joke, by the way.)).

As the years pass I've become less interested in philosophical issues surrounding artificial intelligence, brain theory, the mind/body problem, consciousness, and so on. However, one strand of my current work is stimulated by the need for computers to apply knowledge rather than, or as well as, statistics. I think that Wikipedia, although embarrassingly primitive and limited at present, signals a sea change in how our society deals with knowledge. A few hundred years ago, control of society's knowledge was wrested from the Church and relocated in academic institutions. Now, to the great chagrin of us university professors, our monopoly is under threat: society can collaboratively create, edit and refine knowledge artefacts without even asking us! (And we are threatened on the teaching side too by the rise of instant Internet universities and Massive Open Online Courses (MOOCs), but that's another story.) An important side effect is that computers can now peruse these knowledge artefacts and benefit from them too. So I'm interested in knowledge mining from Wikipedia and other public information sources. Also — remember Cyc, Doug Lenat's common-sense knowledge project from the 1980s? The project's still going, and although it may seem as though time (and crowdsourcing) has passed it by, Cyc does contain a wealth of core knowledge (about disjunctive concepts, for example, and argument restrictions) carefully hand-coded by professionals. Some of our current work is aimed at reaping that and using it for ontological quality control of information garnered from the Linked Data movement and inferred from less reliable sources such as Wikipedia.

CC: Your book *Web Dragons* was described as "not a resource on how search engines work, but rather what ideas and ideals have been realised in the development of search engines, the political and human challenges they face, and problems and opportunities they present to humans and to the nature of knowledge and information." How do you see the future of search engines? What about their social role?

IHW: Boy, if only I could answer questions like that! *Web Dragons* was written in 2006, before the astounding rise of Facebook and Twitter, and predicted a social dimension to information retrieval that has now become commonplace. But the future? I think people are less interested in information than I realised, and more interested in phatic communication. Obviously I think social interaction is important, but so is real information — and perhaps it's getting lost in our obsession with trivia. Personally I prefer my social interactions to be face-to-face. Several followers of my Twitter account are still eagerly awaiting my first post!

CC: Machine learning is another area in which your group has excelled over the years. You have written state-of-the-art software for developing machine-learning techniques and then applied it to real-world data-mining problems. Please describe the software Weka and Massive On-line Analysis (MOA).

IHW: When I came to New Zealand in 1992 I wanted to initiate a project that enabled people in the rather obscure little computer science department I had joined to work together and develop new lines of research. We hit upon machine learning as a technology that was interesting, futuristic sounding, and had potential relevance to agriculture, the staple regional and national industry. We began work on a C++ machine-learning workbench, which at the time was in stiff competition with Stanford's MLC++, and moved to Java early on, which was risky because of performance issues at the time but proved to be an excellent decision. Weka has really taken off — which is astonishing considering that it denotes a small flightless bird. But meanwhile I have moved on to other projects, and have not been involved with MOA, a stream-oriented ML project that stands for

Massive On-line Analysis and denotes a huge extinct New Zealand bird twice the size of an ostrich.

CC: What industrial applications have you developed?

IHW: I'm not very good at working directly with industry. Everything my students and I do is issued as open-source software, which is picked up by academics and industry alike. As well as the better-known Weka, Greenstone and Wikipedia Miner, we have Kea (keyphrase assignment), MAUI (multi-purpose automatic topic indexing), Realistic Books, Katoa (knowledge assisted text organisation algorithm), FLAX (flexible language acquisition), and, very recently, FFTS (the fastest FFT in the south, and considerably faster than FFTW, the fastest in the west). All done by my students, I should emphasise; not by me.

CC: Programming and proving are very similar mental activities. It took me a long time to understand that programming is more demanding than proving: the difference comes from the agent validating the product — code or proof, a computer or a human expert. What is programming by demonstration?

IHW: Programming by demonstration involves showing a computer what to do rather than instructing it in some programming language. People often have to do boring, repetitive tasks on computers — reformatting references or addresses, processing lists and drawing sequences of boxes. Given such a chore, perhaps you should write a program — or perhaps it's quicker to just go ahead and do the job manually. Some of my early research was on calculators that inferred iterative computations from the beginning of a sequence of keypresses, and a predictive typing interface that set the scene for predictive text entry on today's cellphones. My students and I created a "smart mouse" that automated repetitive graphical editing tasks, an instructable interface that acquired data descriptions and procedures by being taught rather than programmed, and a programming-by-demonstration agent that worked with a set of common, unmodified applications on a popular computer platform. This was amongst my best and most creative research: highly interactive interfaces that incorporate a learning component, with enormous potential to expedite many human-computer dialogues. But I became discouraged. Reviewers rejected our papers, demanding more tightly controlled human evaluation, which we could not deliver because interactions between a user and a "learning agent" evolve over time.

CC: Even top researchers can get discouraged...

IHW: I don't know about top researchers, but I certainly can. Discouraged and rejected. My dean once said "it's all right for you, Ian; no one ever rejects *your* papers". But nothing could be further from the truth! I'm sure there can't be many people who've had more rejections than me. Our book *Computer Science Unplugged* (with Tim Bell, principal author, and Mike Fellows) was rejected by 27 publishers before we gave up. Sixteen years later it has spawned a major movement in the teaching of computer science to schoolchildren all over the world, including the US and UK, and has been translated (with our permission) into Arabic, Chinese, French, German, Hebrew, Italian, Japanese, Korean, Polish, Portuguese, Russian, Spanish and Swedish. This has been possible because, since it's unpublished, we still own the copyright. The silver lining.

CC: If your dean thinks that *you* (read: as a top researcher) are spared the misery of rejection (sometimes without real base, using unnecessary, harsh arguments like "my weakest student would have done it better", "there is no subject for the paper"), imagine how the younger colleagues imagine the "status" of the academic establishment...

IHW: Well, this was just one offhand remark of one dean: other deans I have worked with are far better informed about the realities of academic publishing. However, I agree with you entirely: the academic establishment is often really tough on younger colleagues. And I have learned that university administrators tend to present different *persona* to senior professors than to junior staff (which I think is reprehensible), so that in many cases I experience entirely different, and more humane, personalities than my colleagues do. But neither do I think university academics should complain too much: life is far tougher, I believe, on most other working people, whether they are digging ditches, teaching school kids or staring into people's mouths all day. And when I look at referee reports, many of the really harsh ones come from younger colleagues. We all need to do better and be more understanding when evaluating each others' work.

CC: The story of your unpublished book is fascinating: please tell us more.

IHW: Unplugged and unpublished. The book, as the title implies, is about the teaching of computer *science* without using computers, in contrast with IT skills such as the use of Microsoft products, which is what many schoolchildren have experienced up until recently (and they think university computer science will be about advanced word processing). So it's intentionally revolutionary, or at least runs counter to the established culture in the teaching world. The publishers' responses were hilarious: hilarious, that is, if you hadn't invested a large chunk of your life in what they were rejecting. One wrote that they "will not pursue the idea of publishing the book", yet described it as "your wonderful volume..." and said it "would be a real pity not to have this book released". A children's publisher said it "may be too academic for children", while an academic publisher referred us to a children's publisher. One publishers' educational arm referred it to their computing department, who responded that they couldn't publish a book if it wasn't about how to do things on a computer. Yet now, if you Google "unplugged", we come in above Eric Clapton!

CC: What does it mean "unplugged"?

IHW: You know, stop fooling around, unplug your computer and start to learn some real computer *science*. As you know, probably better than anyone else, there are fundamental ideas about computation that do not depend on computers at all. *Computer Science Unplugged* has games and activities that teach kids about computation but do not involve computers. My favourite is a kind of formation dance that expresses a parallel sorting algorithm. Kids follow lines chalked on the playground that represent a sorting network and end up sorting N numbers in $O(N)$ time. The `http://csunplugged.org/` website has a video of 21 kids sorting 21 numbers in ...

um... about 7 seconds (admittedly the video is played in fast-forward mode).

CC: I have rushed to `http://csunplugged.org/` to download it as I will soon become a grandfather...

IHW: Congratulations! The activities are suitable for kids of all ages, 8–80. You'll have to wait a while to try them on your grandchildren, but you might be able to start with your parents!

CC: Recently you have been appointed Chief Scientific Advisor at Pingar.

IHW: Yes. Pingar is a small NZ company that is developing really interesting technology for document analysis and organisation. My ex-student Alyona Medelyan is their Chief Research Officer and it's great to keep in touch and involved with what they're doing.

CC: You play jazz...

IHW: Now you're talking. Yes. Live music is the really big thing in life, far more important than computers and technology. A couple of weeks ago at the SPIRE conference in Cartagena, Colombia, I had the great pleasure of jamming with a duo from Spain in their open-air concert and in the bar afterwards into the wee small hours of the morning. But I play classical music as well as jazz. I play second clarinet in the Trust Waikato Symphony Orchestra — this weekend we have a concert called the Waikato Proms, modelled after the famous BBC promenade concerts in London. And a clarinet group meets at my house every week. Often it's quartets or quintets, but last night it was trios — an excellent evening sight-reading 19th and 20th century music; a real challenge. I'm lucky enough to play with musicians who are better than me, so it's a constant learning experience. We play everything: classical, modern, light, jazz, and they say I have the most comprehensive library of clarinet ensemble music in the country. Currently, having spent two months in Buenos Aires last year, I'm obsessed with Piazzolla tangos.

CC: Your yacht Beulah is a 28-foot Nova, New Zealand designed, launched in the early 1980s, built of double diagonal kauri wood, fibreglassed over...

IHW: Ah yes. Sailing is my other passion, and part of the reason for moving to New Zealand from Calgary where the sea is a couple of day's drive away. I began sailing as a kid. Indeed I once raced internationally, picked to represent Northern Ireland against the South in a youth championships. We lost. And I was never chosen again. Moving quickly on, NZ's Hauraki Gulf is the best water in the world for the kind of weekend cruising that I enjoy now; hundreds of beautiful islands with lovely anchorages. Beulah, my pride and joy, is where I get away from it all: no computer, no Internet, no phone even — and we rarely use the engine. There's hardly any electricity, but of course there's live music wherever you go in Beulah. The simple life. We sail and swim and play with dolphins; watch the sun set, drink wine, eat well and sleep. And we have adventures. You can read about them in our annual family Christmas letters, which Google will find for you if you ask it nicely.

PART 2

Computing in Biology, Mathematics and Physics

Chapter 10

Jon Borwein: Experimental Mathematics

Professor Jon Borwein, http://www.carma.newcastle.edu. au/jon, is Laureate Professor of Mathematics at the University of Newcastle, Australia.

His interests span pure mathematics (analysis), applied mathematics (optimisation), computational mathematics (numerical and computational analysis), and high-performance computing. He has authored many books (several on experimental mathematics, the latest with the late Alf van der Poorten, Jeff Shallit and Wadim Zudilin, Neverending Fractions, to be published by Cambridge University Press in 2014) and over 400 refereed articles. He is a well-read blogger: http://www.carma.newcastle.edu.au/jon/blogs.html.

Professor Borwein has received many awards including the Chauvenet Prize (1993), Fellowship in the Royal Society of Canada (1994), the American Association for the Advancement of Science (2002) and the Australian Academy of Science (2010), an honorary degree from Limoges (1999), and foreign membership in the Bulgarian Academy of Sciences (2003). He is an ISI highly cited mathematician for the period 1981–1999.

CC: Born in St Andrews, Scotland, you received the DPhil from Oxford University as a Rhodes Scholar at Jesus College. Where is the mathematical gene coming from?

JB: I suppose it comes from a mix of inheritance and environment. My father David is an ex-President of the Canadian Mathematical Society and my younger brother Peter is a distinguished analyst and number theorist. David and my mother Bessie were the first in their families to go to University but their fathers were both remarkable men. They both got their families from Lithuania to South Africa before 1930. My maternal grandfather had studied to become a *Hasidic* rabbi in Lvov before losing his faith. He is still remembered in *Hasidic Yeshivas* as an example of the danger of free thinking. My paternal grandfather was an engineering student in Glasgow in 1914. He dropped out to join the Royal Flying Corp and the armistice found him in a German POW camp. It was a better war for a Jew to be in a German camp than the next one. My sister is a medical doctor with an undergraduate mathematics degree and her son has just finished a Caltech mathematics degree and has embarked on a mathematics PhD. One of my sons-in-law is a research mathematician. David did not hothouse any of us but he did offer a wonderful role model for an academic but engaged life.

Here and below I take the liberty of quoting from my own writings when I feel that I have already produced a good answer to part of the question.

> Both my brother and I ultimately became academic mathematicians and not surprisingly have from time-to-time mulled over what factors led us to take up the same vocation. I started University determined to be a historian. Neither of us was in any sense "hothoused". In my undergraduate career I had precisely one lecture from my father, otherwise he assiduously scheduled classes so as to avoid our meeting. The only exception being a five pound bet with his colleagues

in St Andrews — also for a large quantity of cheese — that he could teach his six-year-old son to solve two-by-two simultaneous linear equations by making it into a game. In recently post-war Britain I was so taught and, while conning neither reason nor rationale, I loved playing this mysterious game and taught my best friend also to play.

From then until I was a third-year undergraduate David's (Dad's) role in my education was restrained. I was offered very little overt enrichment. Nor in the politically heated and drug laden late 1960s would I have brooked much intrusion. But what I did infuse in confrontational discussions at the dinner table over Johnson and later Nixon, and more quietly, as we began to jointly solve problems posed in the *MAA Monthly* was the timbre of a to-the-manor-born academic, a man who nonetheless cared deeply about the external world; a man with a subtle and inexhaustible sense of humour; a man who would happily stay up all night polishing a proof or hunting for the resolution to an obdurately untameable mistake. Above all a man who demonstrated with every fibre that he was doing just what he wanted to be doing, that fads were fads but that scientific knowledge would not ever be entirely deconstructed. And so by 1971 when I graduated from UWO, and went somewhat uncertainly as a Rhodes Scholar to Oxford, he had helped me become inescapably a mathematician despite James Sinclair's (Pierre Trudeau's father-in-law) offer that if I studied PPE (Politics, Philosophy and Economics) in Oxford he would give me a cement factory to manage on my return[1]!

CC: You have worked in various universities around the world: Dalhousie, Carnegie Mellon, Waterloo, Simon Fraser and recently, Newcastle, Australia. Please describe the motivation in following this path.

---

[1]Excerpted from J. M. Borwein, "The best teacher I ever had: Personal reports from highly productive scholars", *Royal Society of Canada Volume*, A. Michalos, editor, Althouse Press, 2003. See also `http:///www.carma.newcastle.edu.au/jon/CMS/programme.htm`.

JB: My partner of 43 years, and wife of 40, and I met as undergraduate students at Western in London, Ontario. We promised each other we would never turn down interesting opportunities. This has left us experience-rich — if somewhat cash-poor as compared to a stay-in-one place strategy. My trajectory was Dalhousie Maths (1974), CMU in OR and in part GSIA (1980), Dalhousie Maths and CS (1982), Waterloo C&O (1991), SFU Shrum Chair of Science and then Canada Research Chair in Collaborative Technology (1993), Dalhousie Faculty of CS and CRC in Distributed Environments, then "finally", Newcastle as a Laureate Professor in Pure and Applied Mathematics.

The first job was the only one I applied for in a standard way. The others followed from either unsolicited or solicited invitations. So I can, with a straight face, claim to have been employed as most kinds of mathematical scientist other than as a statistician and have made only voluntary moves.

CC: You are a mathematician with expertise, interest and many achievements in computer science, especially in high-performance computing. Is computation relevant for mathematics?

JB: I think it is crucial to the future of mathematics. Much of what can be discovered without *digital assistance*[2] has been. This is why I have invested so much time in advancing technology-mediated experimental mathematics. I have recently written "The Future of Mathematics: 1965 to 2065" for the *MAA Centenary Volume*, 2015.[3] This was a daunting project as one wishes to be stimulating without seeming foolish in 10 years time. I concluded that article as follows:

> After 60 years with really only two input modalities: first *via* keyboard and command line computing; and then 30 years later with Apple's adoption of Douglas Engelbart's mouse[4]

---

[2]See my article on exploratory experimentation http://www.ams.org/notices/201110/rtx111001410p.pdf.

[3]See http://carma.newcastle.edu.au/jon/future.pdf.

[4]See http://sloan.stanford.edu/mousesite/1968Demo.html. Note that William Gibson was right — the future was already there for Steve Jobs to distribute.

along with iconic graphical user interfaces (GUI), we are now in a period of rapid change. Speech, touch, gesture, and direct mental control are all either realised or in prospect. As noted, the neurology of the brain has developed in 25 years from ignorance to a substantial corpus.

It is barely 20 years since the emergence of the World Wide Web[5] and it would be futile to imagine what interfaces will look like in another 20.[6] We are still exploring the possibilities suggested by Vannevar Bush in his seminal 1945 essay "As We May Think"[7] and some parts of Leibniz's dreams still seem very distant.

In any event, in most of the futures, mathematics will remain important and useful, but those of us who love the subject for its own sake will have to be nimble. We cannot risk leaving the task of looking after the health of our beautiful discipline to others.

CC: What is experimental mathematics, its objectives, tools and uses?

JB: Let me quote from my 2008 book with Keith Devlin (also the 'maths guy' on National Public Radio), *The Computer as Crucible: an Introduction to Experimental Mathematics*, AK Peters, 2008. ISBN-13: 978-1568813431. Japanese edition: (O'Reilly) 2009. This was our best shot at explaining modern experimental mathematics non-technically.

> **What is experimental mathematics?** United States Supreme Court justice Potter Stewart (1915–1985) famously observed in 1964 that, although he was unable to provide a

---

[5]On a slow news day in 2013, the Washington Post reposted a 1995 CNN report http://www.washingtonpost.com/ blogs/wonkblog/wp/2013/03/29/what-the-internet-looked-like-in-1995/?tid=pm_business_pop.

[6]A 2013 summary of applets useful in taming scientific literature can be read at http:// blogs.scientificamerican.com/ information-culture/ 2013/ 03/ 26/ mobile-apps-for-searching-the-scientific-literature/? WT_mc_id=SA_DD_20130326.

[7]See http://en.wikipedia.org/wiki/As_We_May_Think.

precise definition of pornography, "I know it when I see it." We would say the same is true for experimental mathematics. Nevertheless, we realise that we owe our readers at least an approximate initial definition (of experimental mathematics, that is; you are on your own for pornography) to get started with, and here it is.

Experimental mathematics is the use of a computer to run computations sometimes no more than trial-and-error tests to look for patterns, to identify particular numbers and sequences, to gather evidence in support of specific mathematical assertions, assertions that may themselves arise by computational means, including searches. Like contemporary chemists and before them the alchemists of old who mix various substances together in a crucible and heat them to a high temperature to see what would happen, today the experimental mathematician puts a hopefully potent mix of numbers, formulas and algorithms into a computer in the hope that something of interest emerges.

Had the ancient Greeks (and the other early civilisations who started the mathematics bandwagon) had access to computers, it is likely that the word *experimental* in the phrase "experimental mathematics" would be superfluous; the kinds of activities or processes that make a particular mathematical activity experimental would be viewed simply as mathematics. We say this with some confidence because, if you remove from our initial definition the requirement that a computer be used, what would be left accurately describes what most if not all professional mathematicians spend much of their time doing and always have done!

Many readers, who studied mathematics at high school or university but did not go on to be professional mathematicians, will find that last remark surprising. For that is not the (carefully crafted) image of mathematics they were presented with. But take a look at the private notebooks of practically any of the mathematical greats and you will find page after page of trial-and-error experimentation (symbolic or numeric), exploratory calculations, guesses formulated, hypotheses examined (in mathematics, a hypothesis is a guess that doesn't immediately fall flat on its face), etc.

The reason this view of mathematics is not common is that you have to look at the private, unpublished (during their career) work of the greats in order to find this stuff (by the bucketful). What you will discover in their published work are precise statements of true facts, established by logical proofs, based upon axioms (which may be, but more often are not, stated in the work).

CC: Please tell us about the software company *MathResources* you co-founded (1994) and the role of interactive software in school and university mathematics.

JB: In the mid-1980s I co-authored a Dictionary of Mathematics. The publisher, Collins, out of ignorance left us "the musical and electronic rights." As my co-author was in Glasgow and I was in Halifax we worked largely by sending floppy discs across the Atlantic and became the first book set from disk in Europe. This was an ugly experience but left us with a 7000 word database being used only as a recipe to print. I have written about this at some length in my review of The Oxford Users' Guide to Mathematics as a featured *SIAM Review* 48(3): 585–594, 2006.

When hypertext arrived in the late 1980s my friend and computer science/library science colleague Carolyn Waters (now Vice President academic at Dalhousie) started exploring its use. This lead to a prototype of my dictionary with maple and mathematica embedded inside it. It was very satisfactory but by 1994 we had given up on persuading mathematics publishers to go down the same road for calculus texts and were incorporated into a company run by the third partner Ron Fitzgerald who had worked for 15 years in publishing. The company, *MathResources*, is about to turn 20. We struggled to find investors before two wonderful angel capitalists took us on.

At that point we wrote a letter to HarperCollins (which had bought Collins) on the instruction of our lawyers. It ran "It is our understanding that we own the electronic rights to the HarperCollins Dictionary of Mathematics and we intend to exercise those rights." A month later a letter came back from Harper's head office "Dear Sirs, much as we hate to agree with you, you do indeed own the rights..."

MathResources has paid many salaries and has built many good products and taught me a lot about the issues in building an educational software company, the differences between commercial and research software, large regional development grants, IP issues, taking contract work to stay alive and much else. While I made no money out of this, and since a falling out with Ron Fitzgerald in 2009 have not had any connection with the company, it was a great experience. I still believe profoundly that good technology and computing need to be an integral part of mathematics education. I find it frustrating that there have been few real successes in integrating the process.

CC: You have been dubbed "Dr Pi" after developing, together with your brother Peter, extremely fast algorithms that enabled extremely large calculations of π. Why is π so interesting?

JB: For three reasons. (i) It is arguably the only object from the first stratum of mathematical research still being seriously studied today and the underlying mathematics is deep and beautiful, (ii) fast computation of elementary functions relies on being able to quickly compute π and this has become a benchmark for various types of computation and (iii) π has some resonance with the general public and so makes for great outreach. I keep an up to date "beamer talk" on these matters at `http://carma.newcastle.edu.au/jon/piday.pdf` and Dave Bailey and I write about these matters for the March 2014 (3.14) edition of the *MAA Monthly* with the title "Pi Day is upon us again and we still do not know if Pi is normal".[8] I find the concrete complexity reduction required for Pi computation—reducing the time to multiply trillion digits numbers from eons to hours is key—still really exhilarating.

CC: Quite unusual for a prolific mathematician, you have a vast scientific administration experience: Governor at large of the Mathematical Association of America (2004–2007), past president of the Canadian Mathematical Society (2000–2002), chair of (the Canadian National Science Library) NRC-CISTI Advisory Board (2000–2003), chair of various of NATO's scientific programs, chair of

---

[8]See `http://carma.newcastle.edu.au/jon/pi-monthly.pdf`.

the International Mathematical Union's Committee on Electronic Information and Communications (2002–2008), currently Chair of the Scientific Advisory Committee of the Australian Mathematical Sciences Institute (AMSI). What is the motivation and the reward?

JB: Since high school I have always been politically engaged (25 years ago I was briefly treasurer of the Nova Scotia New Democratic Party, which now governs the province) and find such activities both stimulating and a good antidote from the somewhat autistic life-of-the-mind that many good research mathematicians lead. I think I am a pretty good administrator in part because I actually want the meetings to end so I can go back to my real profession reasonably quickly. Quite often I agree to take on jobs after I ask "who precisely will do this if I do not" and the answer is unpalatable. The consequence of these experiences is that I have an unusually varied and, I think, nuanced world view. For example, I was at NATO headquarters the night before Kosovo was bombed.

I have been fortunate to occupy research chairs for more than 20 years and view scientific administration and expository writing as part of my obligation that comes with the job. I am now actively often blogging with Dave Bailey for the Conversation and the Huffington Post.[9] I see that as a small attempt to be a public intellectual.

CC: Can you explain one of your favourite mathematical results?

JB: Since I work in several fields I cannot pick one. In applied functional analysis my favourite is Ekeland's variational principle (1972) which says that a lower semi-continuous function on a complete metric space can be slightly perturbed to attain its infimum at a point near to any approximate minimum. I was able to produce a smooth version in 1987 which has proven almost as useful as the original and view this as one of my best contributions to non-linear analysis.[10] In number theory my favourite results are those in Jacobi's amazing *Fundamenta Nova* in which, like Athena from the head of Zeus, the

---

[9]See http://www.carma.newcastle.edu.au/jon/blogs.html.

[10]J. M. Borwein, D. Preiss. 'A smooth variational principle with applications to subdifferentiability and to differentiability of convex functions,' *Transactions of the American Mathematical Society* 303: 517–527, 1987.

subject of elliptic and *theta* functions emerges almost fully complete. In 1991 my brother Peter and I were able to find "A cubic counterpart of Jacobi's identity and the AGM,"[11] and it was wonderful to be treading so closely in the footsteps of Jacobi and Gauss.

CC: Please tell us about your long collaboration with David Bailey.

JB: David contacted us early in 1986 after reading an article Peter and I wrote on fast computation[12] in *SIAM Review*. He wanted to implement our algorithms for π and those for elementary functions as part of commissioning the first CRAY 2 at NASA's Ames Lab. This led to a record computation of π, a lot of press and a 1993 shared Chauvenet prize.[13] It also uncovered subtle hardware and software errors on the CRAY that led to the algorithms being run as part of CRAY's in-house test suite for many years.[14]

We have now written more than 30 joint papers, and several books on experimental mathematics, and since 2009 have blogged together. This is really an exemplary story — when we wrote our SIAM article we were new to the fields involved and did so with some trepidation. It was the first of many times that I have been rewarded for taking some risks. In July 2013 I attended an after-dinner talk by Australia's Chief Defence Scientist. He listed the mathematical science areas that his portfolio needed people working in. He started with statistics and ended with experimental mathematics. When David and I started working together "experimental mathematics" was viewed as an oxymoron. I am pleased to think we have help change its status.

CC: Can you comment on today's fraud in science from the historical perspective, for example, given by the book *Free Radicals* http:// www.freeradicalsbook.com by Michael Brooks?

---

[11] J. M. Borwein, A. Lewis, "On the convergence of moment problems", *Transactions of the American Mathematical Society* 323: 691–701, 1991.

[12] J. M. Borwein and P. B. Borwein, "The arithmetic-geometric mean and fast computation of elementary functions," *SIAM Review* 26(3): 351–366, 1984.

[13] For J. M. Borwein, P. B. Borwein, D. H. Bailey/ 'Ramanujan, modular equations and pi or how to compute a billion digits of π,' *MAA Monthly* 96, 201–219, 1989.

[14] This is one of many cases where "extreme mathematical computation" has laid bare problems with chips, storage or other computer issues that intensive but more routine tests did not.

JB: I was not aware of the book but from the preface I largely agree. My *experimental methodology* is also a call for honesty in how we describe what we do — to our colleagues, our students and the public. We are humans with all the foibles, vices and impulses which that implies. Science is one of the most successful human ventures. But as Richard Feynman neatly put it, somewhat less sensationally, in his Nobel acceptance lecture:

> We have a habit in writing articles published in scientific journals to make the work as finished as possible, to cover up all the tracks, to not worry about the blind alleys or describe how you had the wrong idea first, and so on. So there isn't any place to publish, in a dignified manner, what you actually did in order to get to do the work.

Having subsequently read Brooks' book, I think he exaggerates for effect. And — as some reviewers have noted — he indulges in (really engaging) anecdotal cherry-picking to knock down a straw man that no scientist truly believes exists. There may be more malarkey among "paradigm" shifter's, in Kuhn's sense. But, for every free radical like Einstein, Maxwell or Kary Mullis, there is a Darwin spending eight years on barnacles or worms ("its dogged that does it") or an Andrew Wiles refusing relentlessly to give up on "normal science" in his pursuit of Fermat's last theorem. Let me add that I think Frans de Waal's fine 2013 book *The Bonobo and the Atheist: In Search of Humanism among the Primates*[15] offers *inter alia* a better account of scientific misbehaviour though it is far from his central theme.

I am engaged in current related attempts for greater openness and reproducibility in computational science. This is quite urgent as is described in two recent articles.[16]

---

[15]See `http://www.scientificamerican.com/article.cfm?id=mind-reviews-bonobo-and-atheist`.

[16] "'Setting the Default to Reproducible' in Computational Science Research," *SIAM News*, 46(5): 4–6, 2013. Also D. H. Bailey, J. M. Borwein, V. Stodden, 'Set the default to open,' *Notices of the AMS*, 60(6): 679–680, 2013.

CC: Brooks' list may look cherry-picked, but it contains cold details about fraud committed by a long list of iconic scientists, a list which starts with Galileo, Newton, Maxwell, Einstein and ends with more Nobel laureates. Mathematicians don't get into this list as fraud comes mostly in experimental science...

JB: Well those folks are described as "frauds" but that is not entirely fair. They are, by Brooks' own description, largely guilty of selectively interpreting their data, bashing their critics or sweeping away unpleasant artefacts. Were they not ultimately proven right the story would look different. Barry Marshall (the Australian MD and 2010 Nobelist who discovered the bacterial basis of most stomach ulcers) is beautifully described. He ended up experimenting on himself (which is actually not taboo) and has now cured millions of diseases. Here is a committed free radical but no fraud.

On the 50th Anniversary of Keynes' death. Sir Alec Cairncross (in *The Economist*, 20 April, 1996) wrote "Keynes distrusted intellectual rigour of the Ricardian type as likely to get in the way of original thinking and saw that it was not uncommon to hit on a valid conclusion before finding a logical path to it". Many of Brooks' best descriptions discuss the consequence (from electromagnetism to prions) of such conviction. There are very few frauds described in his book. In our recent article, "Scientific fraud, sloppy science — yes, they happen",[17] Bailey and I wrote:

> Fraud. It's an ugly word, an arresting word. As with "cheating" it comes loaded with negative connotations, but can potentially lead to far greater penalties and consequences. And yet fraud in science is not unheard of. The world of economics was shaken two weeks ago[18] by the revelation that a hugely influential paper (by Reinhart and Rogoff) and accompanying book in the field of macroeconomics is in

---

[17]see https://theconversation.com/scientific-fraud-sloppy-science-yes-they-happen-13948.

[18]See https://theconversation.com/the-reinhart-rogoff-error-or-how-not-to-excel-at-economics-13646.

error, the result of a faulty Excel spreadsheet and other mistakes — all of which could have been found had the authors simply been more open with their data.

Yet experimental error and lack of reproducibility have dogged scientific research for decades. Recall the case of N-rays (supposedly a new form of radiation) in 1903; clever Hans, the horse who seemingly could perform arithmetic until exposed in 1907; and the claims of cold fusion in 1989.[19]

Medicine and the social sciences are particularly prone to bias, because the observer (presumably a white-coated scientist) cannot so easily be completely removed from his or her subject.

We went on to mention two other famous examples ignored by Brooks:

Of even greater concern are proliferating cases of outright fraud. The "discovery" of the Piltdown Man in 1912, celebrated as the most important early human remain ever found in England, was only exposed as a deliberate fraud in 1953. An equally famous though more ambiguous case is that of psychologist and statistician Sir Cyril Burt (1883–1971). Burt's highly influential early work on the heritability of IQ was called into question after his death.

After it was discovered that all his records had been burnt, inspection of his later papers left little doubt that much of his data was fraudulent — even though the results may well not have been.

Perhaps the most egregious case in the past few years is the fraud perpetrated by Diederik Stapel.

Stapel is/was a prominent social psychologist in the Netherlands who, as a November 2012 report has confirmed,

---

[19]None of these were mentioned by Brooks.

committed fraud in at least 55 of his papers, as well as in 10 PhD dissertations written primarily by his students.

(Those students have largely been exonerated; though it is odd they did not find it curious that they were not allowed to handle their own data, as was apparently the case.)

A 2012 analysis by a committee at Tilburg University found the problems illustrated by the Stapel case go far beyond a single "bad apple" in the field.

Instead, the committee found a "a general culture of careless, selective and uncritical handling of research and data" in the field of social psychology:

> [F]rom the bottom to the top there was a general neglect of fundamental scientific standards and methodological requirements.

The Tilburg committee faulted not only Stapel's peers, but also "editors and reviewers of international journals".

In a private letter now making the rounds, which we have seen, the 2002 Nobel-winning behavioural economist Daniel Kahneman has implored social psychologists to clean up their act to avoid a potential "train wreck".

We need mechanisms to catch folks like Stapel and behaviour like that of Reinhard and Rogoff, not to excoriate Maxwell's and Einstein's.

CC: Increasingly many offenders — from politicians and top-ranking military to businessmen — not only show no remorse, but try to keep former positions and even to capitalise on their experiences in the wrong. High-ranked politicians in the EU — including a head of state, a prime minister and a few ministers — have been recently exposed to have plagiarised their PhD theses. Some resigned, but not all (e.g., a prime minister). It seems that "dying of shame" is morphing into "the death of shame". Do we see this trend also in research and academia? If, yes, to what extent?

JB: My impression is that in academia one can survive almost anything except unambiguously forging academic credentials or research — if one has a thick enough skin. Amusingly, a mathematician acquaintance of mine is married to the new (and presumably scandal-free) German Education Minister. In Germany, almost uniquely, there is great prestige in public life to being called "*Doktor*". This explains some of the recent European scandals. By contrast, at a leadership competition 25 years ago for leadership of the Canadian NDP (currently the official Federal opposition) six of the seven or eight candidates had doctorates and they all actively avoided mentioning the fact. I have written recently that plagiarism is a symptom not a disease:

> Plagiarism is a bit like the weather. Everybody talks about the topic but nobody does anything much about it. Sure students are admonished not to and punished when caught; but that is about it, other than outsourcing much of the issue to money-making outfits like turnitin.com. There are many reasons for this and I intend to discuss a few of them.[20]

CC: "If enough eminent people stand together to condemn a controversial practice, will that make it stop?" This is the first sentence of *Nature News Blog* `http://blogs.nature.com/news/2013/05/scientists-join-journal-editors-to-fight-impact-factor-abuse.html` from 13 May 2013 regarding the San Francisco Declaration on Research Assessment `http://am.ascb.org/dora`. What is your opinion?

JB: I am well aware of the background to this. It cannot hurt and the goal is admirable. That said, after 20 years editing a book series for Wiley and Springer, and a great deal of diverse journal editing experience (I am currently co-editor in chief of the *Journal of the Australian Mathematical Society*), I am convinced that most mathematicians are deeply uninterested in most matters to do with publishing. I spent 10 years on the International Mathematical Union's electronic communications committee. We talked to everyone we could about

---

[20]See `http://experimentalmath.info/blog/2013/05/plagiarism-is-a-symptom-not-a-disease/`.

copyright, open access, abuse of metrics and much else. But the truth is most authors have no idea who published their most recent article unless — like the American Mathematical Society — it is in the name of the journal. In the decade after the AMS changed its rules to allow authors to keep copyright and just give adequate permission to publish, only a handful exercised that right.

Likewise. Tim Gower's recent crusade against Elsevier struck me as somewhat ill-conceived. The "big E" is by no means the worst of the commercial publishers. Finally, it is my impression that the impact factor is not used as substantially in mathematics and computing as in the hard sciences. Mathematics is often forced into a model that works for neuroscience or astrophysics, where funding models, journal culture and much else are very different and poorly suited to our needs.

Chapter 11

Douglas Bridges: Constructive Mathematics

Professor Douglas Bridges has authored more than 190 research papers, and 8 books, on constructive mathematics and mathematical economics. The books include 'Constructive Analysis' (with Errett Bishop) and 'Varieties of Constructive Mathematics' (with Fred Richman), which together were the definitive reference works on (Bishop-style) constructive mathematics for over 20 years. In 2006, he and Luminiţă Vîţă published 'Techniques of Constructive Analysis', the only exposition of the major developments in constructive analysis in the preceding 25 years. In 2011, he and Vîţă published 'Apartness and Topology: A Constructive Development', which is a full exposition of their constructive approach to general topology.

Bridges has been chairman/head of department in three universities, including the University of Canterbury, where he has been Professor of Pure Mathematics since 1999. He is a former

President of the New Zealand Mathematical Society. Professor Bridges has been awarded many distinctions: DSc by Oxford University (2000), Fellow of the Royal Society of New Zealand (2000), and Corresponding Fellow of the Royal Society of Edinburgh (2004). He has been a visiting professor in several institutions, including New Mexico State University (1979 and 1988), Cornell University (1993) and Ludwig-Maximilians-University of Munich (2003, 2009 and 2010). He is the New Zealand member of a consortium of mathematicians from Europe and elsewhere that has been awarded two large grants, one for 2009–2010 and a new one for 2014–2017, under the EU IRSES Marie Curie banner.

CC: Tell us a short history of constructive mathematics.

DB: Although the origins of constructive mathematics can be traced to people like Kronecker in the late 19th century, the subject made its grand entry on the mathematical stage when L.E.J. Brouwer (also famed for his contributions to classical topology) published his doctoral thesis "*On the Foundations of Mathematics*" in Amsterdam in 1907. In the thesis, Brouwer expounded his mathematical philosophy of "Intuitionism", in which mathematical objects are creations of the human mind rather than objects in some extra-mental universe. A consequence of Brouwer's philosophy is that, in proving the existence of some mathematical object, the intuitionist has to show, at least in principle, how that object can be constructed/computed. This process contrasts sharply with the pervasive mathematical practice of proving that some object x exists by first assuming that it doesn't, then deriving (by correct logical deductions) a contradiction, and finally concluding that the object had to exist after all; that process does not enable you to construct the desired object. Brouwer's approach to mathematics was highly controversial, and eventually resulted in a major breach between the small group of intuitionistic mathematicians and the dominant group, led by the enormously talented and influential David Hilbert, of "classical" mathematicians, for whom Brouwer's constructive methods were too restrictive.

Since very few mathematicians took up Brouwer's ideas in their daily mathematical practice (though some — notably Hermann

Weyl — were sympathetic to his views), it appeared for some decades that, as Bourbaki[1] famously claimed, *the intuitionistic school would be a "memory ... no doubt destined to remain only as a histori-cal curiosity"*. In the late 1940s in the Soviet Union, A.A. Markov developed an alternative form of constructive mathematics in which, rather than using Brouwer's special intuitionistic principles (his con-tinuity principle and fan theorem), one worked with recursive func-tions and used intuitionistic logic (a logic that had been abstracted from intuitionistic mathematical practice). Markov's school of recur-sive constructive mathematics (RUSS) had some successes, but the restriction to recursive functions was also seen by many as a major hurdle to its acceptance in general.

Things changed considerably from 1967 onwards. In that year, Errett Bishop, a young American mathematician who had already established a formidable reputation for his research in functional analysis and several complex variables, published *Foundations of Constructive Analysis*, in which, single-handedly, he developed con-structive treatments of large parts of real, complex and functional analysis, including measure theory. Initially, only a few mathemati-cians took up Bishop's challenge to work in Bishop-style constructive mathematics (BISH, which in practice is mathematics carried out with intuitionistic logic and an appropriate set-theoretic foundation, but without any of Brouwer's principles or the Markovian restriction to a recursive-function-theoretical framework). However, the rise of computer science, with the resulting increase in awareness of issues of computability/constructibility, gradually created growing interest in BISH, and since 2000 there have been several conferences largely devoted to constructive mathematics and related issues.

CC: How relevant is philosophy in constructive mathematics?

DB: It is relevant to one rationale for working constructively: namely, that a subscriber to Brouwer's intuitionistic philosophy or something close to it would regard a constructive approach as the

---

[1]N. Bourbaki. *Elements of the History of Mathematics*, Springer-Verlag, Berlin, 1998.

only justifiable, meaningful one for mathematics. It is less relevant to most constructive mathematical practice, in the sense that even a Platonist might appreciate that the use of intuitionistic logic (and an appropriate set theory) is a good idea if one wants to distinguish between constructive and non-constructive aspects of mathematics. Such a distinction is a meaningful one. Moreover, Bishop-style constructive proofs come with a bonus: not only can implementable algorithms be extracted from them, but the proofs are themselves proofs that those algorithms are correct (meet their specifications). You don't need to be a committed philosophical constructivist to see the merit in such a proof; but you do need to be prepared to work with intuitionistic logic if you want to get your hands on one.

CC: Constructive mathematics is particularly relevant in computer science. Can you elaborate on this issue.

DB: I've really done this in my previous answer. Constructive proofs contain algorithms that can be (and in many cases have been) extracted and implemented, the proofs also showing the correctness of the extracted algorithms. This has considerable significance for theorem-proving systems and the like, several of which have been created over the past quarter of a century.

CC: Can you illustrate the role of constructive mathematics for theorem-proving systems?

DB: This is an area about which I am woefully ignorant. However, although I understand that one can use classical logic in proof assistants, it seems to me that using constructive logic is the right thing to do when one is interested in algorithmic proofs. For example, what would be the point of, say, using classical logic to prove the correctness of an implemented constructive proof, when that proof already embodies a constructive correctness proof? On the other hand, there is the work of Kohlenbach, who uses classical logic to extract computational content from classical proofs; but that work, though technically impressive, is heavily logic based and so, in my view, rather unlikely to attract the interest of non-logicians (and there is no evidence that it could handle highly abstract proofs of existence by contraction in functional analysis).

To tell the truth, these are matters that do not interest me that much. I'm definitely a mathematician (an analyst), not a logician or a computer scientist. However, in the last year I have returned to work on constructive Morse set theory, which first appeared in my Oxford DPhi. thesis. This set theory is developed in a kind of pseudocode that definitely looks promising as a basis for developing a theorem-proving expert system.

CC: Give us a simple example of a classical theorem which is not constructively valid? What is the main reason?

DB: A nice example is the intermediate value theorem, which says that if a continuous function f is negative at 0 and positive at 1, then it must take the value 0 somewhere strictly between 0 and 1. Our geometric intuition tells us that this is obvious, as first-time students of analysis are likely to point out. But the theorem does require proof, the usual proof being based on an interval-halving argument: if $f(1/2) = 0$, we are through; if $f(1/2) < 0$, repeat the whole process using the interval $[1/2, 1]$; and if $f(1/2) > 0$, repeat the process using the interval $[0, 1/2]$ and so on. This produces a nested sequence of closed intervals whose intersection is the desired point c with $f(c) = 0$. Unfortunately, this proof, and the theorem itself, is non-constructive: for at the very first step we may not be able to decide whether $f(1/2)$ equals, is less than, or is greater than 0. We could get away with a decision that $f(1/2) \geq 0$ or $f(1/2) \leq 0$, but even that is not possible constructively. In fact, the intermediate value theorem in its full classical form is constructively equivalent to the statement

$$\forall_{x \in \mathbf{R}}(x \geq 0 \vee x \leq 0),$$

where $\mathbf{R}$ denotes the set of real numbers. This statement is false in a recursive interpretation and is constructively equivalent to the "omniscience principle"

> **LLPO**: For each binary sequence $(a_n)_{n \geq 1}$ such that $a_m a_n = 0$ for all distinct m and n, either $a_{2n} = 0$ for all n or else $a_{2n+1} = 0$ for all n,

a weak form of the law of excluded middle.

Fortunately, there are versions of the intermediate value theorem that do go through constructively. One is a "same hypotheses, weaker conclusion" version: under the usual hypotheses of the intermediate value theorem, for each $\varepsilon > 0$ there exists (we can construct) c with $0 < c < 1$ and $|f(c)| < \varepsilon$. Another is a "stronger hypotheses, same conclusion" version: if our continuous function f is locally non-zero, in the sense that for each $x \in [0,1]$ and each $\varepsilon > 0$ there exists $y \in [0,1]$ such that $|x - y| < \varepsilon$ and $|f(y)| > 0$, then there exists c with $0 < c < 1$ and $f(c) = 0$. The latter version applies to virtually any situation in real analysis that one can think of.

CC: Can you reminisce about Bishop with whom you co-authored a very important book?

DB: I have to be cautious here, as I only met Bishop twice: once, over coffee, when my wife and I visited San Diego in 1979, and later, at the end of 1982, when I had the privilege of staying with Errett and Jane Bishop in their home in La Jolla while he and I were working on the book. My first actual contact with Bishop (other than reading his book and papers) was while I was a DPhil student at Oxford and we engaged in some correspondence over some small things of mine on function algebras. What I wrote must have seemed pretty obvious and trivial to Errett, but he was kind and encouraging in his replies. I believe that kindness and encouragement towards developing mathematicians were a feature of the man. When I stayed with the Bishops in 1982, I was treated as one of the family, which was very good of them: having an almost stranger as a house guest is seldom easy.

What impressed me most about Errett's mathematical abilities was the combination of speed and depth: I have never dealt with a mathematician whose deep thought processes were as fast. I mentioned this some years later to Paul Halmos, who had been Errett's PhD supervisor at Chicago. His response was that he had met one other mathematician who was as fast a thinker as Errett: von Neumann! (In his early career, Halmos had been von Neumann's research assistant).

Errett had wide-ranging interests. He was a keen, highly competitive tennis player (wiping me off the court on the one occasion we played). He collected geodes and other rocks. He was widely read in many subjects. Altogether, he was one of the most remarkable intellects and people that I have ever met. It was a great tragedy when he succumbed to cancer in the spring of 1983, a mere four months after I left his home.

CC: Bishop is also famous for the essay "Schizophrenia in Contemporary Mathematics" (1972). His analysis included the following "principles" (which are relevant for the foundations of constructivism, but seem to go beyond them):

- (A) Mathematics is common sense.
- (B) Do not ask whether a statement is true until you know what it means.
- (C) A proof is any completely convincing argument.
- (D) Meaningful distinctions deserve to be preserved.

How relevant are his ideas today?'s Is today's mathematics less or more 'schizophrenic' than in 1972?

DB: I always thought that "schizophrenia" was an odd word to use, and was never quite sure what he meant by it. Perhaps he was referring to the mathematicians' desire to have their cake and eat it, by accepting non-constructive proofs as adequate for establishing the existence of objects that, at heart, one would really like to "grasp" in some way. I'm reminded of the days when I started a PhD on von Neumann algebras (a PhD I gave up in order to go teaching in high school for a few years). In that subject, a typical argument had the following form. You want to prove the existence of a projection with a certain special property in the von Neumann algebra, so you begin by assuming that no such projection exists; using Zorn's lemma, you then "construct" a maximal family of projections of some type or other, a type that exists because of your initial assumption; after some pages of careful and deep argument, you arrive at a contradiction, from which you conclude that the projection you originally sought was there after all. These proofs were very clever and beautiful, but left me with a vague sense of unease, which became less vague once I found Bishop's 1967 book. Proofs of that sort still abound in mathematics, and it is hard to see how at least some parts of our subject could be handled in any other way: think of the work on higher cardinals. But what we have seen is a substantial increase in awareness of, and interest in, constructive/computable mathematics in the past 20–30 years.

It is a lot easier these days than it was when I started giving seminars in the 1970s to persuade mathematicians that the distinction between "constructive existence" and "idealised existence" (i.e., existence proved by a contradiction argument) is meaningful. In the earlier days, many excellent mathematicians seemed incapable of appreciating this distinction, I suspect because they had been brought up in the dominant Bourbaki tradition. I imagine that the improvement in perception of constructive issues has originated, in part, from mathematicians having computers on their desks and quickly becoming aware that it is not as easy as they though to write programs that work.

Incidentally, Bishop told me that one of the things that made him enter the constructive domain was an unsuccessful attempt he made to picture certain hypersurfaces in complex n-space, as part of his famous work in several complex variables. My recollection is that he had tried to program a machine to draw those surfaces, and had convinced himself that this was an impossible task. In fact, he may have come up with a Brouwerian example showing this; if so, he never made it available to others. Whatever the case, constructive mathematics and its relatives are definitely held in higher, or at least less low, regard in this century than they were in 1972.

Anyway, to get back to Bishop's four principles. Of those, (B) and (D) seem reasonable and ever-applicable, especially (D). Principle (A) is a value judgement, and is perhaps a bit dubious: things may be "common sense" to the super-gifted like Errett, but totally mysterious to us lesser mortals. Principle (C) does not, I think, stand up to philosophical scrutiny. What does it take to be "convincing"? How do I know that I am convinced? And even if I am convinced, how do I know that my conviction coincides with reality? (There are, it is said, still some people who are convinced that the earth is flat).

CC: Martin-Löf's constructive type theory is very important in theoretical computer science. Is Martin-Löf's theory used in constructive mathematics?

DB: Martin-Löf's type theory is a very important part of constructive mathematics, so much so that (see my article *Constructive Mathematics* in the *Stanford Online Encyclopedia of Philosophy*) it can be regarded as a variety of constructive mathematics akin to, but not identical with, that of Bishop. Type theory plays a big part in foundational issues and in the formal (point-free) topology of Sambin and Martin-Löf.[2] One advantage of Martin-Löf's type theory over most other foundations for constructive mathematics is that it really is a kind of programming language. I recall years ago seeing a preprint by Jan Smith, which dealt with something like Quicksort in Martin-Löf's type theory.

Among the other foundations for constructive mathematics we have various set theories such as Myhill's CST,[3] Friedman's IZF,[4] and the Aczel-Rathjen CZF[5] that is currently the most favoured of the three.

As I mentioned above, I have recently revisited the constructive development of Morse's very formal set theory.[6] By the time this interview is published, this theory should be freely available online, as "Morse Set Theory as a Foundation for Constructive Mathematics".

CC: How much constructive mathematics should go into the curriculum of mathematics and computer science?

---

[2]G. Sambin. *The Basic Picture (Structures for Constructive Topology)*, Oxford Logic Guides, in preparation.

[3]Myhill. Constructive set theory, *J. Symbolic Logic* 40(3), 347–382, 1975.

[4]H. M. Friedman, Set theoretic foundations for constructive analysis, *Ann. Math.* 105(1), 1–28, 1977.

[5]P. Aczel, M. Rathjen, *Notes on Constructive Set Theory*, Report No. 40, Institut Mittag-Leffler, Royal Swedish Academy of Sciences, 2001.

[6]A. P. Morse. *A Theory of Sets* (2nd Edn.), Academic Press, New York, 1986.

DB: At the undergraduate level, little if any. What I think is important in mathematics at that level is (as I do) to point out the "meaningful distinction" wherever it arises, so that students are well aware that much of the mathematics they see has either little or very obscured computational content. At the honours level it is reasonable to present some constructive analysis in specialised courses — for example, ones on the foundations of mathematics.

As regards computer science courses, I'm not really qualified to comment on how much constructive mathematics would be appropriate, or which course it would go into. Certainly, in New Zealand it would be almost inconceivable to generate interest in constructive mathematics among computer science majors — except perhaps in your university, where you have managed to build up a strong group of researchers and teachers in theoretical computer science.

CC: Professor Giuseppe Longo has remarked that for physics, non-computability is more important than computability. Is there a similar phenomenon for constructive mathematics and physics?

DB: The relation between constructive mathematics and physics has been the subject of some controversy, with one philosopher arguing strongly and from several physical perspectives that constructive mathematics cannot be applied to physics. I believe, and have written papers to that effect, that this view is based on technical misunderstandings. But it remains to be seen how, if at all, work like we do in constructive analysis can be applied to theoretical physics. To date, the one major piece of work in that area is Richman's proof (with minor assistance from me) of Gleason's theorem[7]: but that theorem, though deep and interesting in its own right, does not seem to have much real influence on the foundations of quantum theory. In order to make major applications to modern physics, we would need, on the one hand, a constructive development of operator-algebra theory (of which we have very little at present) and, on the other, constructive development of the theory of differential manifolds (some of which

---

[7]F. Richman, D. S. Bridges, A constructive proof of Gleason's theorem, *Journal of Functional Analysis* 162, 287–312, 1999.

has been given by Diener.[8] One thing seems clear, though: since, in constructive mathematics, we do not distinguish between "computable" and "non-computable" objects — if an object is well defined constructively, it has to be computable — non-computability will not be a part of Bishop-style constructive physics. Of course, we may produce Brouwerian examples showing that certain classical theorems cannot be proved constructively, and we may even go so far as to work in the recursive model of Bishop's mathematics, in which explicit examples of non-computable things can appear; but as long as we work within Bishop's framework unadorned with such extras as the Church–Markov–Turing thesis, then we will be producing only positive results, such as (perhaps) a constructive proof of the existence of a black hole under certain hypotheses.

CC: Please comment on the relevance of constructive mathematics for economic theories.

DB: In view of the allegations made about the role of mathematical models in the recent global economic collapse, one might ask what is the relevance of *any* mathematics for economic theory. Now, as you are aware, I have indulged in some constructive aspects of economic theory, such as the existence of preference relations and demand functions. While these investigations were extremely interesting to me, and in some cases spawned non-constructive work by me and others, it would be ridiculous for me to claim that their outcome had any real relevance to economics. I suspect that this holds for much of the classical work going on in mathematical economics: it generates beautiful, hard mathematics based on, but very far removed from, real-world economic problems. That is not to say that one shouldn't continue looking constructively at problems that arise from an economic situation. We just need to be realistic about the non-mathematical merits of our solutions to them.

CC: Tell us about your extra-mathematical interests.

---

[8]H. Diener, *Compactness under Constructive Scrutiny*, PhD thesis, University of Canterbury, Christchurch, New Zealand, 2008.

DB: Until my knee succumbed to years of running, I was an active runner and cricketer, playing for the Staff XI at Waikato University during my tenure there. At that time I also coached junior football (not rugby, but the real game, with the round ball), starting with my elder son's team of 12-year-olds and going right through his high-school days. I have now more or less given up golf, and cycle a lot less than I used to or would like. When I retire, Vivien and I hope to do some cycling holidays in NZ and abroad.

These days my major interest is classical music, and in particular, listening to Bach, Beethoven and Schubert (especially piano music). Also, I sing as a first bass in the Christchurch City Choir, our city's symphonic choir. I read a great deal, with particular interest in biographies. And once a month I am Service Leader at St Christopher's Church.

Chapter 12

Gregory Chaitin: Mathematics, Physics, Biology and Philosophy

Professor Gregory Chaitin, $https://ufrj.academia.edu/$
$Gregory\ Chaitin$, *is at the Federal University of Rio de Janeiro in Brazil, where he is working on a mathematical theory of biological creativity. He is also a co-founder of the algorithmic information theory to which he made seminal contributions, including the Omega number. Chaitin's latest book,* Proving Darwin: Making Biology Mathematical, *has also been published in Spanish, Italian and Japanese.*

CC: I suggest we discuss the question, *is mathematics independent of physics?*

GC: Okay.

CC: Let's recall David Deutsch's 1982 statement:

> *The reason why we find it possible to construct, say, electronic calculators, and indeed why we can perform mental arithmetic, cannot be found in mathematics or logic.* **The reason is that the laws of physics "happen" to permit the existence of physical models for the operations of arithmetic** *such as addition, subtraction and multiplication.*

Does this apply to mathematics too?

GC: Yeah sure, and if there is real randomness in the world then Monte Carlo algorithms can work, otherwise we are fooling ourselves.

CC: So, if experimental mathematics is accepted as "mathematics," it seems that we have to agree that mathematics depends "to some extent" on the laws of physics.

GC: You mean maths conjectures based on extensive computations, which of course depend on the laws of physics since computers are physical devices?

CC: Indeed. The typical example is the four-colour theorem, but there are many other examples. The problem is more complicated when the verification is not done by a conventional computer, but, say, a quantum automaton. In the classical scenario the computation is huge, but in principle it can be verified by an army of mathematicians working for a long time. In principle, theoretically, it is feasible to check every small detail of the computation. In the quantum scenario this possibility is gone.

GC: Unless the human mind is itself a quantum computer with quantum parallelism. In that case an exponentially long quantum proof could not be written out, since that would require an exponential amount of "classical" paper, but a quantum mind could directly perceive the proof, as David Deutsch points out in one of his papers.

CC: Doesn't Roger Penrose claim that the mind is actually a quantum computer?

GC: Yes, he thinks quantum gravity is involved, but there are many other possible ways to get entanglement.

CC: How can such a parallel quantum proof be communicated and checked when it exists only in the mind of the mathematician who "saw" it?

GC: Well, I guess it's like the design of a quantum computer. You tell someone the parallel quantum computation to perform to check all the cases of something, and if they have a quantum mind maybe they can just do it. So you could publish the quantum algorithm as a proof, which the readers would do in their heads to verify your claim.

CC: On paper you have only the quantum algorithm; everything else is in the mind! What about disagreements, how can one settle them "keeping in mind" (no pun!) that quantum algorithms are probabilistic? Aren't we in danger of losing an essential feature of mathematics, the independent checkability of proofs in finite time?

GC: Well, even now you don't publish **all** the steps in a proof, you depend on people to do some of it in their heads. And if one of us has a quantum mind, then probably everyone does, or else that would become a prerequisite, like a high IQ, for doing mathematics!

CC: Theoretical physics suggests that in certain relativistic space-times, the so-called Malament–Hogarth space-times, it may be possible for a computer to receive the answer to a yes/no question from an *infinite computation* in a *finite time*. This may lead to a kind of "realistic scenario" for super-Turing computability.

GC: Well, to get a big speed-up you can just take advantage of relativistic time dilation due either to a very strong gravitational field near the event horizon of a black hole or due to very high-speed travel (near the speed of light). You assign a task to a normal computer, then you slow down your clock so that you can wait for the result of an extremely lengthy computation. To you, it seems like just a short wait, to the computer, aeons have passed...

CC: Physicist Seth Lloyd[1] has found that the "ultimate laptop," a computer with a mass of one kilogram confined to a volume of one litre, operating at the fundamental limits of speed and memory capacity determined by the physics of our universe, can perform 10^{51} operations per second on 10^{31} bits. This device sort of looks like a black hole.

GC: And he published a book called *Programming the Universe*. The basic idea is that the universe is a computation, it's constantly computing its own time evolution.

CC: What about the Platonic universe of mathematical ideas? Is that "muddied" by physics too? To exist mathematics has to be communicated, eventually in some written form. This depends upon the physical universe!

GC: Yes, proofs have to be written on paper, which is physical. Proofs that are too long to be written down may exist in principle, but they are impossible to read.

CC: Talking about writing things down, logicians have studied logics with infinitely long formulas, with infinite sets of axioms, and with infinitely long proofs.

GC: How infinite? $\aleph_0$, $\aleph_1$, $\aleph_2$?

CC: Could it be that such eccentric proofs correspond to something "real"?

GC: Well, if people had $\aleph_2$ minds, then formulas $\aleph_0$ characters long would be easy to deal with! There's even a set-theoretical science fiction novel by Rudy Rucker called *White Light* in which he tries to describe what this might feel like. I personally like a world which is discrete and $\aleph_0$ infinite, but why should Nature care what I think?

In one of his wilder papers, physicist Max Tegmark suggests that any conceptually possible world, in other words, one that isn't self-contradictory, actually exists. Instead of conventional Feynman path integrals summing over all histories, he suggests some kind of crazy

---

[1]S. Lloyd. 'Ultimate physical limits to computation,' *Nature*, 406, 1047–1054, 2000.

new integral over all possible universes! His reasoning is that the ensemble of all possible universes is **simpler** than having to pick out individual universes!

Leibniz had asked why is there something rather than nothing, because nothing is simpler than something, but as Tegmark points out, so is **everything**. In his approach you do not have to specify the individual laws for this particular universe, it is just one of many possibilities.

CC: What about constructive mathematics?

GC: Of course the mathematical notion of computability depends upon the physical universe you are in. We can imagine worlds in which oracles for the halting problem exist, or worlds in which Hermann Weyl's one second, half second, quarter second, approach actually enables you to calculate an infinite number of steps in exactly two seconds. But I guess computability can handle this, everything relativises, you just add an appropriate oracle. All the proofs go through as before.

CC: Are you talking about a physical Church–Turing thesis?

GC: Yes, I am. — But I think the notion of a universal Turing machine changes in a more fundamental way if Nature permits us to toss a coin, if there really are independent random events. (Quantum mechanics (QM) supplies such events, but you can postulate them separately, without having to buy the entire QM package). If Nature really lets us toss a coin, then, with extremely high probability, you can actually compute algorithmically irreducible strings of bits, but there's no way to do that in a deterministic world.

CC: Didn't you say that in your 1966 *Journal of the ACM* paper?

GC: Well yes, but the referee asked me to remove it, so I did. Anyway, that was a long time ago.

CC: A spin-off company from the University of Geneva, *id Quantique*, markets a quantum mechanical random number generator called *Quantis*. *Quantis* is available as an OEM component which can be mounted on a plastic circuit board or as a PCI card; it can supply a (theoretically, arbitrarily) long string of quantum random bits sufficiently fast for cryptographic applications. A universal Turing machine working with *Quantis* as an oracle seems different from a normal Turing machine. Are Monte Carlo simulations powered with quantum random bits more accurate than those using pseudo-randomness?

GC: Well yes, because you can be unlucky with a pseudo-random number generator, but never with real random numbers. People have gotten anomalous results from Monte Carlo simulations because the pseudo-random numbers they used were actually in sync with what they were simulating.

Also real randomness enables you, with probability one, to produce an algorithmically irreducible infinite stream of bits. But any infinite stream of pseudo-random bits is extremely redundant and highly compressible, since it's just the output of a finite algorithm.

CC: In a universe in which the halting problem is solvable many important current open problems will be instantly solved: the Riemann hypothesis or the Goldbach conjecture.

GC: Yes, and you could also look through the tree of all possible proofs in any formal axiomatic theory and see whether something is a theorem or not, which would be mighty handy.

CC: Talking about the Riemann hypothesis, which is about primes, there's the surprising connection with physics noticed by Freeman Dyson that the distribution of the zeros of the Riemann function looks a lot like the Wigner distribution for energy levels in a nucleus.[2]

And in an inspiring paper on "Missed opportunities" written by Dyson in 1972, he observes that relativity could have been discovered 40 years before Einstein if mathematicians and physicists in Göttingen had spoken to each other.

GC: Well in fact, relativity **was** discovered before Einstein by Poincaré — that's why the transformation group for Maxwell's

---

[2]Andrew Odlyzko and Michael Berry continued this work. And recently Jon Keating and Nina Snaith, two mathematical physicists, have been able to prove something new about the moments of the Riemann *zeta* function this way.

equations is called the Poincaré group — however Einstein's version was easier for most people to understand.

But mathematicians shouldn't think they can replace physicists: there's a beautiful little 1943 book on *Experiment and Theory in Physics* by Max Born where he decries the view that mathematics can enable us to discover how the world works by pure thought, without substantial input from experiment.

CC: What about set theory? Does this have anything to do with physics?

GC: I think so. I think it's reasonable to demand that set theory has to apply to **our** universe. In my opinion it's a fantasy to talk about infinities or Cantorian cardinals that are larger than what you have in your physical universe. And what's **our** universe actually like?

- A finite universe?
- Discrete but infinite universe ($\aleph_0$)?
- Universe with continuity and real numbers ($\aleph_1$)?
- Universe with higher-order cardinals ($\geq \aleph_2$)?

Does it really make sense to postulate higher-order infinities than you have in your physical universe? Does it make sense to believe in real numbers if our world is actually discrete? Does it make sense to believe in the set $\{0, 1, 2, \ldots\}$ of **all** natural numbers if our world is really finite?

CC: Of course, we may never know if our universe is finite or not. And we may never know if at the bottom level the physical universe is discrete or continuous...

GC: Amazingly enough, Cris, there is some evidence that the world may be discrete, and even, in a way, two-dimensional. There's something called the holographic principle, and something else called the Bekenstein bound. These ideas come from trying to understand black holes using thermodynamics. The tentative conclusion is that any physical system only contains a finite number of bits of information, which in fact grows at the surface area of the system and not as the volume of the system as you might expect, whence the term "holographic."

CC: That's in Lee Smolin's book *Three Roads to Quantum Gravity*, right?

GC: Yes. Then there are physical limitations on the human brain. Human beings and computers feel comfortable with different styles of proofs. The human push-down stack is short. Short-term memory is small. But a computer has a big push-down stack, and its short-term memory is large and extremely accurate. Computers don't mind lots of computation, but human beings prefer ideas or visual diagrams. Computer proofs have a very different style from human proofs. As Turing said, poetry written by computers would probably be of more interest to other computers than to humans!

CC: In a deterministic universe there is no such thing as real randomness. Will that make Monte Carlo simulations fail?

GC: Well, maybe. But one of the interesting ideas in Stephen Wolfram's *A New Kind of Science* is that all the randomness in the physical universe might actually just be pseudo-randomness, and we might not see much of a difference. I think he has deterministic versions of the Boltzmann gas theory and fluid turbulence that work even though the models in his book are all deterministic.

CC: What about the axioms of set theory, shouldn't we request arguments for their validity? An extreme, but not unrealistic view discussed by physicist Karl Svozil, is that the only "reasonable" mathematical universe is the physical universe we are living in (or where mathematics is done). Pythagoreans might have subscribed to this belief.

Should we still work with an axiom — say the axiom of choice — if there is evidence against it (or there is not enough evidence favouring it) in this specific universe? In a universe in which the axiom of choice is not true one cannot prove the existence of Lebesgue non-measurable sets of reals (Robert Solovay's theorem).

GC: Yes, I argued in favour of that a while back, but now let me play devil's advocate. After all, the real world is messy and hard to understand. Maths is a kind of fantasy, an ideal world, but maybe in order to be able to prove theorems you have to simplify things, you have to work with a toy model, not with something that's absolutely right. Remember you can only solve the Schrödinger equation exactly for the hydrogen atom! For bigger atoms you have to work with numerical approximations and do lots and lots of calculations...

CC: Maybe in the future mathematicians will work closely with computers. Maybe in the future there will be hybrid mathematicians, maybe we will have a man/machine symbiosis. This is already happening in chess, where grandmasters use chess programs as sparing partners and to do research on new openings.

GC: Yeah, I think you are right about the future. The machine's contribution will be speed, highly accurate memory and performing large routine computations without error. The human contribution will be new ideas, new points of view, intuition.

CC: But most mathematicians are not satisfied with the machine proof of the four-colour conjecture. Remember, for us humans, *Proof = Understanding*.

GC: Yes, but in order to be able to amplify human intelligence and prove more complicated theorems than we can now, we may be forced to accept incomprehensible or only partially comprehensible proofs. We may be forced to accept the help of machines for mental as well as physical tasks.

CC: We seem to have concluded that mathematics depends on physics, haven't we? But mathematics is the main tool to understand physics. Don't we have some kind of circularity?

GC: Yeah, that sounds very bad! But if maths is actually, as Imre Lakatos termed it, quasi-empirical, then that's exactly what you'd expect. And as you know Cris, for years I've been arguing that information-theoretic incompleteness results inevitably push us in the direction of a quasi-empirical view of maths, one in which maths and physics are different, but maybe not as different as most people think. As Vladimir Arnold provocatively puts it, maths and physics are the same, except that in maths the experiments are a lot cheaper!

CC: In a sense the relationship between mathematics and physics looks similar to the relationship between meta-mathematics and mathematics. The incompleteness theorem puts a limit on what we can do in axiomatic mathematics, but its proof is built using a substantial amount of mathematics!

GC: What do you mean, Cris?

CC: Because mathematics is incomplete, but incompleteness is proved within mathematics, meta-mathematics is itself incomplete, so we have a kind of unending uncertainty in mathematics. This seems to be replicated in physics as well: our understanding of physics comes through mathematics, but mathematics is as certain (or uncertain) as physics, because it depends on the physical laws of the universe where mathematics is done, so again we seem to have unending uncertainty. Furthermore, because physics is uncertain, you can derive a new form of uncertainty principle for mathematics itself...

GC: Well, I don't believe in absolute truth, in total certainty. Maybe it exists in the Platonic world of ideas, or in the mind of God — I guess that's why I became a mathematician — but I don't think it exists down here on earth where we are. Ultimately, I think that's what incompleteness forces us to do, to accept a spectrum, a continuum, of possible truth values, not just black and white absolute truth.

In other words, I think incompleteness means that we have to also accept heuristic proofs, the kinds of proofs that George Pólya liked, arguments that are rather convincing even if they are not totally rigorous, the kinds of proofs that physicists like. Jonathan Borwein and David Bailey talk a lot about the advantages of that kind of approach in their two-volume work on experimental mathematics. Sometimes the evidence is pretty convincing even if it's not a conventional proof.

For example, if two real numbers calculated for thousands of digits look exactly alike. . .

CC: It's true, Greg, that even now, more than a century after Gödel's birth, incompleteness remains controversial. I just discovered two essays by important mathematicians, Paul Cohen and Jack Schwartz.[3] Have you seen these essays?

GC: No.

CC: Listen to what Cohen has to say:

> "I believe that the vast majority of statements about the integers are totally and permanently beyond proof in any reasonable system."

And according to Schwartz,

> "truly comprehensive search for an inconsistency in any set of axioms is impossible."

GC: Well, my current model of mathematics is that it's a living organism that develops and evolves, forever. That's a long way from the traditional Platonic view that mathematical truth is perfect, static and eternal.

CC: Tell us more about this model.

GC: Okay, as I'm sure you remember, John von Neumann observed in the late 1940s that the essential mathematical idea in biology is the same as the essential mathematical idea in computer technology: it's the idea of digital software. And according to von Neumann DNA is digital software, and that's what gives the plasticity of the biosphere. Nature discovered programming languages billions of years before we did.

CC: Really?

---

[3]P. J. Cohen. 'Skolem and pessimism about proof in mathematics,' *Philosophical Transaction of the Royal Society A*, 363: 2407–2418, 2005; J. T. Schwartz. 'Do the integers exist? The unknowability of arithmetic consistency,' *Communications on Pure and Applied Mathematics*, **LVIII**: 1280–1286, 2005.

GC: Yes there is digital software everywhere, in every cell, and it's ancient software. In fact, biology is just software archeology!

CC: Okay, that is basically in von Neumann's paper on *"The General and Logical Theory"* of what he called natural and artificial automata, namely biological organisms and computers. So what are you working on?

GC: Well, I am trying to find the simplest possible Pythagorean life form, the simplest possible system that provably evolves by Darwinian natural selection. And since real biology is a million-pound marshmallow, it is much too complicated, I am studying what I call meta-biology, which is the random evolution of mutating computer programs, instead of the random evolution of real DNA. That's a tractable mathematical problem, in fact, it's just a hill-climbing random walk in software space, and I am able to prove a few theorems, including the fact that Darwinian evolution works.

CC: Sounds like you are studying a highly simplified toy model of biology.

GC: Well, it is that, but it is also an attempt to extract the essential mathematical ideas from biology and develop them into an elegant mathematical theory. I have published a small book about this in an attempt to stimulate further work, but I'm afraid that it is a bit too theoretical, too philosophical and too interdisciplinary for most people's taste.

CC: It'll be interesting to see what happens with these new ideas. Talking about models, what about Einstein's famous statement that,

> "Insofar as mathematical theorems refer to reality, they are not sure, and insofar as they are sure, they do not refer to reality."

Still valid?

GC: Or, slightly misquoting Pablo Picasso, theories are lies that help us to see the truth!

CC: Perhaps we should adopt Svozil's attitude of "suspended attention" (a term borrowed from psychoanalysis) about the relationship between mathematics and physics...

GC: And about the relationship between mathematics and biology... Deep philosophical questions are never resolved, you just get tired of discussing them.

Chapter 13

Françoise Chatelin: Qualitative Computing

Françoise Chatelin http://www.cerfacs.fr/~chatelin *is the Emeritus Professor of Applied Mathematics at the University Toulouse 1 — Capitole and Head of the Qualitative Computing group at the Centre Européen de Recherche et de Formation Avancée en Calcul Scientifique (Cerfacs) in Toulouse, France. Her expertise includes many areas, from spectral theory for linear operators in Banach spaces to finite precision computation of very large matrix eigenproblems. Professor Chatelin has supervised 31 PhD theses and has authored five books; the first four are now classic references. A graduate from L'École Normale Supérieure Normale (Paris), Professor Chatelin taught at the Universities Grenoble 2 — Pierre Mendes-France and Paris 9 — Dauphine before moving to Toulouse. She was a visiting researcher at Berkeley and Stanford Universities, IBM San*

Jose (Ca) and Yorktown Heights (NY). For almost a decade (from 1984 to 1993) she was a scientific manager (in charge of intensive computing) at the Centre Scientifique IBM — France in Paris and the Laboratoire Central de Recherches Thales near Paris. Her book Valeurs Propres de Matrices *(Masson, Paris, 1988) has received the IBM — France prize for "Meilleure publication scientifique et technique 1988".*

CC: Your book *Qualitative Computing: A Computational Journey into Non-linearity* (World Scientific, 2012) develops a theory of computing — which you call qualitative — using certain multiplicative algebras. What is qualitative computing?

FC: Qualitative computing is a branch of mathematics which extends analysis and algebra over $\mathbb{R}$ and $\mathbb{C}$ by specifically looking at how the laws of *classical* computation (Euler–Cauchy–Riemann–Jordan–Puiseux) are modified when mathematical computation does not take place over a *commutative field*. This fills a gap since most college-level textbooks in mathematical analysis only consider numbers which are either real or complex. And modern abstract algebra is *not* driven by computation.

CC: So we are talking about numerical computation. Why are classical numbers not enough?

FC: Numerical in a broad sense, where "numbers" are defined as entities over which well-defined computation can be performed. There are important practical domains where classical numbers are too *limited*. Let me cite three different examples.

In physics, the quaternions which form a *non*-commutative field of numbers with four real dimensions are the language of Maxwell's electromagnetism and special relativity. In computer graphics, they are essential for 3D motion pictures. Another example is found in the booming field of numerical linear algebra: to speed-up computation, the basic "numbers" are often taken to be square matrices which form an associative *algebra* (over $\mathbb{R}$ or $\mathbb{C}$). This is essential for large computer simulations required by high-tech industries.

The third example is well known to computer scientists: it consists of vectors (or strings or sequences) defined over a finite ring of scalars. The scalars $\{0, 1, 2, 3\}$ in $\mathbb{Z}/4\mathbb{Z}$ have a *ring* structure with 2 as a zerodivisor ($2^2 = 0 \bmod 4$).

CC: In the first two examples multiplication seems to be associative too. What is the reason for dropping associativity altogether?

FC: To favour *recursiveness*, which enables complexification and creativity, two properties which are ubiquitous in life's phenomena.

CC: Why is non-associativity better suited for recursiveness and how does this feature "enable complexification and creativity"?

FC: I would rather say that the recursive definition of the 3 algebraic operations, addition, conjugation and multiplication, which complexifies real vectors in $\mathbb{R}^{2^k}$, $k > 0$, implies that multiplication becomes necessarily non-associative for $k \geq 3$. This does not happen when $\mathbb{R}$ is replaced by $\mathbb{Z}_2$, giving birth to binary sequences of length 2^k. Then conjugation reduces to the identity map, and multiplication remains commutative and associative. Complexification is defined below, and creativity is also related to paradoxes to be presented later.

CC: Is such a recursive definition for multiplicative algebra a new idea?

FC: Not at all: the idea — which goes back to the American mathematician Dickson — is about a century old! Originally, Dickson was looking for an algorithmic way to derive the multiplication table for the (non-associative) octonions $\mathbb{G}$ of Graves (December, 1843), from that for the (non-commutative) quaternions $\mathbb{H}$ of Hamilton (October, 1843). This led him to the discovery in 1912 of the recursive doubling process which defines an unbounded sequence of multiplicative real algebra A_k (over $\mathbb{R}$), $k \geq 0$ in $\mathbb{N}$. Let 1_k (respectively $\tilde{1}_k$) represent the real (respectively complex) unit in A_k, then

$$A_0 = \mathbb{R}, \quad A_k = A_{k-1} \times 1_k \oplus A_{k-1} \times \tilde{1}_k, \quad k \geq 1,$$

where $1_k = (1_{k-1}, 0)$ and $\tilde{1}_k = (0, 1_{k-1})$ satisfy respectively $1_k \times 1_k = 1$ and $\tilde{1}_k \times \tilde{1}_k = -1$. Starting from $A_0 = \mathbb{R}$, one successively gets

$A_1 = \mathbb{C} = \mathbb{R} \oplus i\mathbb{R}$, $\tilde{1}_1 = i = (0,1)$ for $k = 1$, and $A_2 = \mathbb{H} = \mathbb{C} \oplus \mathbb{C} \times j$, $\tilde{1}_2 = j = (0\ 0, 1\ 0)$ for $k = 2$.

In the complexification process where A_{k-1} yields A_k, the complex unit $\tilde{1}_k$ is constructed by assimilation of a vector foreign to A_{k-1}. Therefore each "complex" algebra A_k possesses features which are not present in its "real" part A_{k-1}. This is an aspect of creativity resulting from complexification, non-linearity and induction $(k - 1 \longmapsto k)$. This vastly differs from the much simpler creative process known as mathematical induction. In Dickson algebra multiplication displays new features for each $k \geq 0$. By way of contrast, let us consider associative Clifford algebra C_k (over $\mathbb{R}$) used in high-energy physics. Their structure obeys the evolution law with period 8 given by $C_{k+8} \cong C_k \otimes \mathbb{R}^{16 \times 16}$ (Cartan, 1908). The sequence C_k is completely determined by the 8 first algebra C_0 to C_7, where in particular $C_0 = A_0 = \mathbb{R}$, $C_1 = A_1 = \mathbb{C}$, $C_2 = A_2 = \mathbb{H}$ and $C_3 = \mathbb{H} \oplus \mathbb{H} \neq A_3 = \mathbb{G} = \mathbb{H} \oplus \mathbb{H} \times \tilde{1}_3$.

Vectors in general multiplicative algebra, have been called *hypercomplex numbers* (Frobenius, 1903). Accordingly, computation in A_k, $k \geq 2$, is an example of *hypercomputation*. The original idea of Dickson was later developed by considering scalars in algebraic structures other than $\mathbb{R}$. If one is interested in the various transformations of multiplication as the dimension 2^k of the numbers increases, then the case of scalars in a finite ring (leading to discrete mathematics) is no less important than that of real scalars (leading to continuous mathematics).

CC: Can you briefly describe the pros and cons of computing with elements in a real Dickson algebra A_k?

FC: Hard to be brief because each A_k, has specific properties which makes it unique in many respects. Any maths student knows that analysis over $\mathbb{C}$ differs greatly from analysis over $\mathbb{R}^2$, despite the isomorphism $\mathbb{C} \cong \mathbb{R} \times \mathbb{R}$. This is the simplest form of an underlying analytical engine in A_k, $k \geq 1$, which takes a specific form at each k. The first 4 algebras A_k, $k \leq 3$, are division algebras (without zerodivisors). They contain rings of integers of dimension 1 to 8 on which one can perform an euclidean division algorithm. Chapter 9 explains how classical arithmetic over $\mathbb{Z}$ is transformed over the integer rings of Gauss, Hurwitz and Dickson, leading to useful ways to process whole entities in dimensions 2, 4 and 8.

As long as multiplication remains associative ($k \leq 2$), non-linear computation in A_k remains classical and yields the absolute certainty that mathematicians are accustomed to, the very certainty that singles out mathematics from all experimental sciences. The situation changes drastically in the absence of associativity for $k \geq 3$.

In a nutshell, non-associativity induces measurement paradoxes which modify the local geometry and challenges classical logic. Paradoxes signal a clash between the global non-linear viewpoint and the local linear one. It turns out that paradoxes and freedom of choice between several computational routes can pop up anywhere. In non-associative algebra, only existing competing answers exist which are all tentative. Their validity becomes *relative* to a backward analysis test elaborated by the computing agent. Therefore the special status of classical mathematics does not hold without associativity. Maths becomes *experimental*: it tells us what "is possible" and no more what "is". The analysis based on paradoxical computation stops being deterministic *without* becoming random.

CC: Please describe a measurement paradox?

FC: A measurement paradox is related to the singular value decomposition (SVD) of the multiplication map. In dimension 16 and higher, a vector defining a multiplication may have up to 2^k, $k \geq 4$, distinct measures (which are the singular values of the corresponding multiplication map), with only one agreeing with Euclid's norm. Even more strikingly, the Euclidean norm of a non-zero vector may be computed as 0; hence Euclidean measurements may not be reliable. As I said earlier, there may be several different answers to the same question, depending on the chosen computational route. The two contradictory answers 0 and 1 may well be valid computational outputs, showing the limits of classical logic. Such a paradoxical phenomenon evokes the celebrated measurement problem in quantum mechanics. What looks like a logical nightmare can be interpreted as a blessing: the freedom to choose between several computational routes favours creativity. But extreme caution is necessary, since non-linear computation plays havoc in classical analysis when it becomes paradoxical.

CC: So, what do we compute?

FC: I assume that your question is about any sort of computation, in general as we can imagine it today. If we talk about conscious computing such as arithmetic and beyond, we should keep in mind that, if all human groups have developed language skills, not all count beyond "1, 2, many". So conscious counting is not necessary for survival... Computation which sustains life in organisms seems to take place mainly at an unconscious level, in which measurements play an important role because the flow of information has to be delicately balanced. Dreams often express a sort of symbolic computation within the human psyche.

But I guess that your question is more concerned with our technology-based society. For millennia, computing has been the driving force behind the development of mathematics. However in the 20th century, it has been used mostly to develop techno-science, science only driven by technology, for which classical mathematics is good enough. Moreover, the swift computerisation of our society is fuelled by the impressive feats of the computer science community, which receives invaluable help from numerical software developers. It may not be widely known that part of the worldwide success of Google should be credited to Gene Golub. This leading figure in numerical linear algebra was a very influential professor at Stanford for almost half a century. He was the scientific advisor for many numerical routines developed by his former students to create the first-rank search engine which led to the current supremacy of Google.

On the side of life sciences in the 21st century, Nature and lab experiments both indicate formidable difficulties: life defies classical logic. If we want to progress in our understanding of *life* beyond the simplistic picture that it emerges "in principle" from physics and chemistry, it may be wise to look seriously at the amazing properties of paradoxical computation.

CC: Which agents compute? Does Nature compute?

FC: Because mathematics is a creation of the human mind, it seems hard to maintain that other living beings are endowed with a man-created ability! However the celebrated "unreasonable effectiveness of mathematics in the natural sciences" (Wigner, 1960) indicates that scientists can safely reason *as if* they did, as if Nature had the ability to process information by mathematical computing. But they should never forget that any human explanation through a theory is anthropomorphic by necessity: it may be a far cry from a "natural reality" which lies possibly beyond man's intellectual grasp.

CC: What is the goal of computing for human beings?

FC: This is a vast question which is a matter of much debate between psychologists and neuroscientists. And today there is no consensus about what "computing for human beings" could mean "in reality." For the sake of this dialogue, let us assume that man-created computation in the broadest sense is a plausible model for some of the uncountably many ways by which the human mind can process information. I suggest that, deep down, we compute in an effort to understand life as we experience it, both in the world outside and in our own inner world. We try to order the world according to reason. The goal is to help build our *imago mundi*, that is an image of the world specific to each of us, and necessary to navigate in it.

In the book *Qualitative Computing* I postulate that hypercomputation in Dickson algebra is an important tool to explore the mind's processes which appear to us as non-linear computations. This shows in the subtitle of the book: "A computational journey into non-linearity." An essential epistemological tool for the construction in this specific context, is the notion of *algebraic irreducibility by linear derivation*, which characterises the limits of any explanation by *linear* causality within an inherently *non-linear* algebraic context when $k \geq 2$. The dimension of the irreducible nonlinear core of A_k is by definition the algebraic depth of A_k (over $\mathbb{R}$). It can be shown that the three division algebras $\mathbb{R}$, $\mathbb{H}$ and $\mathbb{G}$ have an algebraic depth equal to 1; all other A_k, $k \notin \{0, 2, 3\}$, have an algebraic depth ≥ 2.

The algebraic depth is a measure of *algebraic* complexity, not to be confused with the *descriptive* complexity (measured by the size of a computer program) in computer science.

CC: The computational world you describe, while fascinating, is about numerical computation, hardly suited to be the only model of *imago mundi*. Non-numerical computation is as important if not more important than numerical computation.

FC: I must confess that I do not find your distinction numerical/non-numerical as being helpful. The age-old mathematical tradition tends to accept as "numbers" all entities over which one can perform computations of some sort in a meaningful way. Nature has more imagination than mathematicians and computer scientists put together... And Nature's computation is a boundless domain, which extends far beyond what you call numerical computation (which, I suppose, refers to real scalars only). Since Viéte in the 16th century, mathematicians compute over *letters* rather than just over the "numbers" of school day arithmetic. In the book *Numbers in Mind. The Transformative Dynamics of Numerics* (World Scientific, in press), I explore the computational properties of general hypercomplex numbers as they were defined at the end of the 19th century and surveyed by Cartan (1908). This study recalls that besides complex numbers $x + iy$, $x, y \in \mathbb{R}$, $i^2 = -1$, two other types of 2D numbers of equal importance exist which are known as the bireal numbers in $^2\mathbb{R}$, of the form $x + uy$, $u^2 = 1$, $u \neq \pm 1$, and the dual numbers in $\mathbb{D}$, of the form $x + ny$, $n^2 = 0$, $n \neq 0$. Both sets have a *ring* structure with zerodivisors, which contrasts with the field structure of $\mathbb{C}$. The *complete* resolution of a quadratic equation with real coefficients yields 2, 4 or an uncountable infinity of solutions when the discriminant is negative, positive or zero. The bireals are used by physicists to explain special relativity in 1D time and space. The threefold algebraic nature of the numerical plane $\mathbb{R}^2$ underlies the flexibility of human thinking. And please observe that the above definition of 2D numbers uses exclusively letters, besides 0, $\pm 1 \ldots$

As open-ended as hypercomputation may be, it would be risky to claim that such a computational mode is the only model for the inner ways of the human mind. At best, such a model captures some important features which are not revealed by classical computation. It is clear to me that most features of the mind remain outside the reach of hypercomputation.

CC: Please explain the difference you make between 1D thinking vs 2D thinking. Is this related to the algebraic difference between the numerical line and plane?

FC: Yes, 1D thinking refers to $\mathbb{R}$ and to the extended line $\overline{\mathbb{R}} = \mathbb{R} \cup \{\pm\infty\}$ and 2D-thinking refers to the triple nature of the numerical plane. In the plane, $\mathbb{C}$ can be closed as the extended complex plane $\hat{\mathbb{C}} = \mathbb{C} \cup \{\infty\}$. Observe that $\overline{\mathbb{R}}$ (respectively $\hat{\mathbb{C}}$) is isomorphic to a circle (respectively Riemann sphere). Each set $\mathbb{R}$, $\overline{\mathbb{R}}$ and $\mathbb{C}$, $\hat{\mathbb{C}}$ is associated with a different causality which shapes the corresponding human thinking. For example, a realisation of the causality based on $\mathbb{R}$ is the scientific causality where cause always precedes effect. This is the causality that shapes the mind of an infant: the spoon invariably drops on the floor when not held in hand. And the completed numerical line $\overline{\mathbb{R}}$ can be associated with circular thinking, leading to the observation of many cyclic phenomena in Nature. Examples of causality based on the plane are not experimentally as obvious. We all know that Western science rules out any causality other than the one — originally suggested by empiricism — which is based on $\mathbb{R}$ (interpreted as the physical time line). However the Riemann sphere $\hat{\mathbb{C}}$ plays an essential role in general relativity which is the basis for our current understanding of cosmology.

The numbers 0 and 1, the elements of $\mathbb{Z}_2$, are the fixed points of real multiplication: they solve the equation (1) $x^2 = x$ over $\mathbb{R}$. Non-real vectors in two dimensions satisfying (1) are called *idempotent* in abstract algebra. Only hyperbolic numbers can be idempotent; two such 2D vectors $e_{\pm} = \frac{1 \pm u}{2}$ exist which are also zerodivisors: $e_+ \times e_- = 0$. They solve (1) together with the reals 0 and 1.

It follows that real Boolean logic based on 0 and 1 does not capture the inner creativity of hyperbolic numbers. This kind of creativity is exemplified by the explanatory role played by hyperbolic numbers for special relativity, a theory where the interpretation of light waves as electromagnetic waves appears as a fiat. This 2D hyperboliticity provides a mechanism by which *quantity* is turned into *quality*. The so-called light-cone in 3 space dimensions becomes two light-lines when space is the real line $\mathbb{R}$. And the light-lines are generated by the idempotent vectors of $^2\mathbb{R}$.

It seems plausible that 2D-thinking is at work in the creative act of mathematical understanding at once, in a flash of light, an act well documented in the writings of Poincaré (1908) and Hadamard (1945). In mathematics, understanding and discovery are global processes based on the plane of thought, whereas proofs and communication are sequential processes akin to language: they are based on $\mathbb{R}$ endowed with a natural order.

CC: Your views — from the perspective of continuous mathematics — on understanding, discovering, proving and communicating are very interesting. I would argue against the generalisation you made when you said "[i]n mathematics": in discrete mathematics, an increasing part of "mathematics", $\hat{\mathbb{C}}$ and $\overline{\mathbb{R}}$ play no role and understanding, discovering, proving and communicating appear in a different light.

FC: Of course there are discrete versions of $\mathbb{R}$- and $\mathbb{C}$-thinking adapted to hypercomputations realised on finite rings. Circles and spheres have to be replaced by regular polygons and polyhedra. The smaller the number of vertices, the greater the difference between certain aspects of discrete and continuous hypercomputation. Discrete thinking sheds a new light on the algorithmic role of old notions such as the Sierpinski's triangle (i.e., the arithmetic triangle mod 2). A good part of my 2012 book is devoted to the constructive interaction between the discrete and the continuous in computation (Chapters 6, 8, 10). A remarkable example of such a constructive interaction is provided by the Picard iteration for the fixed-point equation $x = rx(1 - x)$, with $-1/2 \leq x \leq 3/2$ and $-2 \leq r \leq 4$. The amazing properties of the logistic iteration: $0 < x_0 < 1, x_{n+1} = rx_n(1 - x_n), n \geq 0$ were first reported in the

West by the biologist R. May (1976). The descriptive complexity is low, but the global dynamics is complex (not real) in relation with the roots of $w^3 = -1$ and $z^6 = 1$ (Chapter 6). A complete analysis of these dynamics requires the cooperation of results by Fermat, Euler, Riemann, Cantor, Sierpinski, Sharkovski and Feigenbaum. These results run over a period of about three and half centuries. They deal with numbers in $\mathbb{N}, \mathbb{R}, \mathbb{C}$ and with actual infinity. The dynamical analysis blurs the three distinctions: discrete/continuous, real/complex, potential/actual infinity. These distinctions play an essential role in our current views about numerical computation. But they are intimately intermingled by the logistic iteration and defy separation. More is happening. At the three exceptional values $r = 1$ (respectively $-2, 4$), the iterate x_n can be expressed in closed form as a function of x_0, n and r by means of an exponential (respectively trigonometric) function. The algebraic and transcendental viewpoints coalesce at the three values $r \in \{-2, 2, 4\}$.

In the book in preparation, I elaborate on these results to construct a theory of information whose logic *evolves naturally* under the pressure of computation. This sheds more light on the irreducible difference between mathematical and mechanical computation, when the latter mode is operated under an *invariant* formal system of axioms. This radical difference was clearly understood by Gödel who wrote in 1972: "what Turing disregards completely is the fact that *mind, in its use, is not static, but constantly developing*, i.e., that we understand abstract terms more and more precisely as we go using them." (Italics in the original.) Despite the methodological warning of the great logician against naive extrapolation from machine to mind, the machine-program metaphor remains today the favourite concept of science to explain the life phenomena that we perceive.

CC: The discussion of the Borel–Newcomb paradox in your book is fascinating. Can you please summarise it?

FC: I am pleased that you ask this question because the Borel–Newcomb paradox, lies deep at the heart of non-linear computation, but has not yet received the serious attention it deserves.

In 1881, the American astronomer S. Newcomb noticed with amazement that the first decimal digit in numbers arbitrarily chosen among those produced by human computers or by Nature was about 6.5 times more likely to be 1 than 9. A paradox (Chatelin, 1996) emerges when one contrasts Newcomb's little known remark with the much better-known result by Borel (1909) from which follows that all (but the first being $\neq 0$) decimal digits of a real number x chosen at random are uniformly distributed with density $1/10$ (i.e., x is simply normal in base 10). The paradox can be easily resolved by the theory of P. Lévy (1939) about the addition of random variables mod 1. Borel and Newcomb do not look at the same numbers. The reals of Borel are abstract mathematical numbers free from any computational process. By contrast, Newcomb observes numbers which result from various *non-linear computations* performed by man or Nature alike. And Lévy proved that computation makes the first digit more likely to be 1. This is a fundamental, yet little known, consequence of the scientific notation for a positive real x in the base $b \geq 2$: $x = sb^{\nu}$, where $s \in [1/b, 1[$ is the significand and $\nu \in \mathbb{Z}$ is the exponent. Observe that $x = b^{\log_b x} = b^{[\log_b x] + \{\log_b x\}}$, so that $s = \frac{1}{b} b^{\{\log_b x\}}$, where $\{\log_b x\} \in [0, 1[$ is the mantissa of x. According to Borel (respectively Lévy) $\{x\}$ (respectively $\{\log_b x\}$) is uniformly distributed on $[0, 1]$.

Scientific computers use a version of the scientific notation adapted to the finite world (finite number of digits for the significand, finite range for the exponent): this is known as the floating-point representation of machine numbers. It is quite remarkable that floating-point computation transforms Borel-normality ($\{x\}$ uniform) into Lévy-normality ($\{\log_b x\}$ uniform). This indicates that the bad reputation of inexact computer arithmetic is largely undeserved. On the negative side, the arithmetic is *not* exact; but the inaccuracy can be kept under control by a careful use of reliable numerical software. On the positive side, this floating-point arithmetic endows a piece of hardware with an epistemological value. It is perplexing to realise that this amazing potential is either ignored or dismissed by most scientists. Finally, let me add that the complete theory of Lévy includes the case of scalars in any finite ring $\mathbb{Z}_n$, n composite ≥ 4 or field $\mathbb{Z}_p$, p prime ≥ 2.

CC: Do you subscribe to the view according to which "mathematicians think and reason, do not compute?"

FC: Literally speaking, such a view may describe some pure mathematicians of the 20th century only. From antiquity to the 19th century, all mathematicians did compute in the sense that their research as driven by the necessity to understand computation in order to solve equations. Fermat, Euler and Riemann are three famous examples of computing mathematicians in the 17th, 18th and 19th centuries. But this is looking at one side of the coin only. Since the 16th century and Viète's idea to use letters to denote arbitrary data or unknowns, algebra grew increasingly symbolic, showing that reason is partly an abstract computation. This complementary side of the nature of mathematics is illustrated by Bourbaki: maths is considered by bourbakists as an all-axiomatic, abstract, most general formal construction based on set theory. Both aspects are equally at work in mathematics, but they are unevenly distributed among mathematicians.

CC: The 20th century "paradigm shift" in computing appeared when, to cite from your book, the "notion of *mathematical computability*, crafted over millennia, was abandoned in favour of *mechanical* computability. . . " What is "millennia old" *mathematical computability*?

FC: The red thread which runs through the historical development of mathematics has been the crucial question of which entities could be accepted as *numbers*, so that one could confidently compute over them and get *meaningful* results. This epistemological question underlies "mathematical computability." Before they could be accepted as *bona fide* numbers, the status of the following entities has been passionately scrutinised: irrational numbers, zero and $\infty = \frac{1}{0}$, negative numbers, complex numbers, quaternions, to name a few familiar examples. The list of numbers is open-ended; it contains increasingly symbolic "numbers", most of which are yet to be thought of.

CC: We talk about numbers — old, new or yet to be discovered — but computing is not about numbers only. Computability theory, developed in the 20th century, is a mathematical theory of mechanical computing. It shows that one can compute not only with numbers (of any type), but also with strings over alphabets. The digital revolution has its main roots in the "computer on paper" imagined and studied in this field. The universal Turing machine is the theoretical model justifying the very existence of our current computers, from laptops to the super-computers. Gödel's incompleteness theorem (and many other results which followed) was proved in this framework. Still, you seem to hold strong negative feelings against this field...

FC: First, let me slightly disagree with you. Why should letters in an alphabet be considered of a different nature than numbers, if they enable well-defined computations? They are both symbols conceived by man and used on an equal footing by mathematicians since Viéte. In the past century, Poincaré and Hilbert pioneered the use of a (multiplicative) group to characterise all isometric transformations in geometry: multiplication is taken to be composition. Should we call these "numbers" or "letters"? Either way is fine of course. Under the influence of cybernetics and molecular biology, the more encompassing but vaguer term "information" seems to gain interdisciplinary acceptance.

The sweeping success of computers in our society owes something to the theory of computability. Arguably, it also owes a lot to the floating-point arithmetic of scientific computers. When talking about computers it seems fair to keep an equal balance between the two different species of computers to which the names of Turing and von Neumann (or scientific) have been attached by history. In addition to Turing's paper of 1936, the origin of the computer revolution could be assigned with equal rights to the year 1914 (a century ago) which saw the first known design of floating-point computer arithmetic, by L. Torres y Quevedo in Madrid. According to Knuth as well as to Assyriologists, the scientific notation was used implicitly in Sumer four millennia ago! Moreover, if scientific computers were to disappear tomorrow, this would deal a severe blow to the development of the scientific know-how at the two extreme scales, large and small, such as cosmology and highenergy physics.

Second, I want to protest. I certainly hold no negative feelings against the respectable field of computability theory. In our computerised society, it is very important to delineate the precise limits of mechanical computing, the limits of static formal axiomatic systems. And my new book will revisit that issue by means of a computational information theory. My reservations only concern the claims of some researchers which extend to mathematics, without further ado, results which have only been proved for Turing machines; they ignore the warning of Gödel himself against such a bold extrapolation which I recalled earlier.

CC: With your permission I wish to continue our disagreement. Floating-point computer arithmetic is part of numerical computing which has many applications in science and technology. However, we should not forget the equally (maybe more?) important area of non-numerical computation. The use of the Internet, social networking and many other non-numerical computations — the largest part of computer science daily used by laymen — are modelled by Turing computations, not by a computation in commutative or non-commutative algebra.

FC: What about Boolean algebras? And is not $\mathbb{Z}_2 = \{0, 1\}$ a commutative field? Your question is a good illustration of the current cultural divide between mathematics and computer science. A divide which expresses only a difference in perspective about computation. I have already explained why the dichotomy numerical/non-numerical that is put forth by computer scientists makes little sense for a mathematician. Turing's original diagonal argument (1936) tells us that the algebraic structure of $\mathbb{N} \times \mathbb{N}$ can be modified by computation: unbeknownst to the user, analysis creeps in...

Now, the opinion that computer science is more (or less) important than scientific computing is also a matter of perspective. Computers certainly have a visible impact on the organisation of everyone's life. The contribution of computer simulations in engineering is not obvious on a daily basis, but the results are highly visible in high-tech industries: from cellular phones to nanotechnologies they have changed ordinary life. Moreover, beyond academia, computers are not used as strict Turing machines. They harmoniously combine, whenever needed, the two aspects of computation which are logical and numerical. It is useful to contrast — but useless to oppose — these two kinds of computers.

CC: I certainly agree with your last point of view. But language itself can contribute to the mutual misunderstanding. For example, the name "scientific computing" seems unfortunate: it creates the (wrong) impression that any other type of computation is unscientific. Some terms like computability, complexity, hypercomputation, have different meanings in computability theory and in "classical mathematics". For example, the meaning of hypercomputation in the sense you cited is different from (and older than) the one practiced in computer science (which means "going beyond the computational capability of any Turing machine").

FC: This results from natural evolution: new fields of knowledge tend to drift away from their origin as they mature. This happened to computability theory which, in 80 years, evolved away from mathematics to become a vital part of theoretical computer science. Inevitably, this creates a semantic ambiguity which should be clarified when it arises. For example, what is mechanically computable differs greatly from what is mathematically computable.

CC: You write that "The *coup de force* was accomplished in the name of *rigour*, neglecting the fact that rich polysemic notions are necessarily ambiguous. Only trivialised notions can be crystal clear." Rigour doesn't oppose ambiguity (think about fuzzy sets theory or polyvalent logics).

FC: You are absolutely correct about the importance of alternative logics. The example of fuzzy logic is developed to some extent in my book (Chapter 10). My first comment is to recall that fuzzy logic (Zadeh, 1961) is extremely *controversial* in the West, despite its impressive successes for smart technology. This is not surprising since I show how it is related to $\mathbb{C}$-causality, a blind spot in current science. My second comment is that, when the *coup de force* took place in the 1930s, it was explicitly directed against geometry. It had been realised by then that geometric evidence was not fully rigorous nor always reliable. But mathematicians threw away the baby with the bathwater, and $\mathbb{C}$-causality was implicitly banned together with geometry. This explains the paramount importance given afterwards to axiomatisation and formal proofs in any mathematical work intended for publication (papers and textbooks). This formal approach — duly avoiding any reference to meaning and interpretation, not to mention significance for life — has deterred many a scientist and schoolchild from mathematics in the second half of the last century. But the modern structuralist emphasis seems to slowly go out of fashion nowadays, allowing the age-old computational perspective to re-emerge.

CC: Citing again from your book: "Turing's proof of the unsolvability of the halting problem is a mechanical version of Gödel's incompleteness result: because $\mathbb{Z}$ is algebraically too "poor", propositions written in a formal axiomatic system will always exist which happen to be true but are not formally provable within the system." Unsolvability and incomputability abounds in continuous mathematics as well. Just to quote a well-known example: Pour-El and Richards proved in 1979 that an innocent looking differential equation has uncountably many solutions, but does not have a computable solution.

FC: I stress in my book that the deep reason behind Gödel (1931) and Turing (1936) is the fact that the set of numbers that they consider has an algebraic depth equal to 1 rather than being ≥ 2. The algebraic depth is related to the purely algebraic notion of a derivation map. To recall, a derivation D over an arbitrary multiplicative algebra A is a linear map which satisfies, for any $x, y \in A$, the Leibniz formula: $D(x \times y) = (Dx) \times y + x \times (Dy)$. This extends the 17th century notion of a derivative for a function to a much broader context, which can be either discrete or continuous. Thus the question of discreteness ($\mathbb{N}$ or $\mathbb{Z}$) vs continuity ($\mathbb{R}$) is *not* essential. For example, Rumely (1986) showed that Hilbert's tenth problem is solvable over algebraic integers which have an algebraic depth equal to 2.

Therefore, the result of Pour-El and Richards is not surprising in the context of (mechanical) computability theory. However, in a continuous context, it is important to avoid the semantic ambiguity. A precaution not taken by these authors. Their equation is not difficult to solve on a scientific computer, which suffices for practical purposes.

CC: Maybe the result proved by Pour-El and Richards is not surprising today, but it belongs to a large list of undecidable problems in continuous mathematics, analysis, real or complex, topology, differential geometry, quantum physics, to name just a few. Apparently these results have nothing to do with algebraic depth.

FC: Pour-El and Richards illustrate vividly the difference between mathematical and mechanical computability, two theories based on *different* assumptions. Their result is a welcome reminder of computational *relativity*: natural phenomena (modelled by continuous mathematics) exist which are mathematically computable, but cannot be formally produced by mechanical computation. Unless one's mind is fully under the spell of finite algorithms, this should not come as a big surprise. Admittedly, the many Turing-like undecidability results in continuous mathematics have been proved without any explicit appeal to the notion of algebraic depth. However, this does not mean that the notion should play no explanatory role. Indeed, Rumely's result points in the other direction. But to perceive such an implicit role, it is useful to think outside the Turing box of mechanical computability, and apply the wisdom credited to Hadamard: to fathom the reals, go complex. One might benefit from expanding the framework of Turing computability to the broader one of hypercomputation, while staying within the scope of mathematical computability.

CC: Can you give your arguments refuting the Church–Turing thesis?

FC: This is certainly not an absolute refutation. Our dialogue has shown the importance of the algebraic *context* for any computability theory: binary vs real, rational vs irrational, algebraic vs transcendent, real vs complex and so on ... What I question is the claim to absolute universality of the Church–Turing thesis. If universality is meant *within today's machines* using classical technology, then I agree that the thesis is plausible. But if universality refers to mathematical computation, then the thesis is obviously too restrictive. It cannot account for the simple fact that $\sum_{k=0}^{\infty} 2^{-k} = 2$. The real number 1.1111... in base 2 is Turing-computable but cannot be identified with the integer 2 by any finite algorithm. This inability prevents the Turing machine achieving life's simplexity on its own. In addition, it is telling to contrast Turing machines and scientific computers. It is known that Borel-normal sequences appear random to any finite-state machine. Analogously, any Chaitin-normal sequence (i.e., algorithmically irreducible in computer science *parlance*) appears random to any Turing machine. From an epistemological point of view it does not pay to move from a finite-state to a Turing machine. You can only get an *aggravated* form of randomness (Chaitin, 1977). This makes a sharp contrast with scientific computers!

CC: A Tuatara machine (Calude, Stay, 2006) has the capability you seem to think a Turing machine may miss. Why do you think that, epistemologically, you don't need Turing machines, you can do everything with (the weaker) finite-state automata? Also, please explain "sharp contrast with scientific computers!"

FC: This is not at all what I think! Above, I only contrasted a finite-state automaton and a Turing machine from the point of view of the type of *randomness* they produce. I do not say that the epistemological alternative to a Turing machine is a finite-state automaton. I say that the alternative is a scientific computer. The contrast between the two computers appears in full light when one starts from a Borel-normal sequence which looks random to a finite-state automaton. By processing the sequence on a Turing machine, one is likely to get a Chaitin-normal sequence. Such an algorithmically irreducible sequence is tautologic: each of its bits has a value justified by no other formal reason than itself. In other words, the sequence is because it is; there is no deeper reason to be found. For x chosen at random in $[0, 1]$, the global identity $x \mapsto x$ becomes a string of tautologies at the bit-level inside x. Now, if we process a Borel-normal sequence on a computer endowed with scientific notation, one is likely to get a Lévy-normal sequence. The dynamics differ because the map $x \mapsto \{x\}$ is replaced by $x \mapsto \{\log_b x\}$. Instead of the *reinforcement of the identity* that is produced by a Turing machine, the scientific computer induces a *change of viewpoint*, from x to its *mantissa*. Interestingly, "*mantissa*" in Latin means "additional weight," whereas its Greek root "*manteia*" means "divination".

As I develop in my forthcoming book, a Turing machine is the tool of choice to analyse identity and invariance; it enforces the chosen law of logic. A scientific computer, on the other hand, is a tool best suited to model natural change and evolution, thanks to its floating-point arithmetic. The goal is no more to maintain the logical coherence, but rather to explore the evolutive diversity of Nature. In conclusion, neither of these two versions of computers can claim supremacy over the other. Both provide invaluable help in the scientific approach through computation of life's phenomena, which combines constructively invariance and change, conservation and evolution in amazingly inventive ways.

Chapter 14

Rod Downey: Computability, Complexity Theory, Reverse
Mathematics and Algorithmic Information Theory

Professor Rod Downey, http://www.mcs.vuw.ac.nz/~downey/,
*is a very well-known mathematician and theoretical computer scien-
tist. He works in classical and applied computability theory and in
complexity theory (mainly parameterised complexity), reverse mathematics and algorithmic information theory. Professor Downey is not
only "world famous in New Zealand" (as a local saying goes in this
country), but one of New Zealand's (NZs) best-known mathematicians. He has won numerous awards for his work on logic and his
work on theoretical computer science. These include the inaugural
MacLaurin Fellowship, a James Cook Fellowship, an Isaac Newton Fellowship, the Hamilton Prize of the RSNZ, New Zealand (NZ)
Association of Scientists Research Medal, the Hector Medal, ASL
Schoenfield Prize, EATCS Nerode prize, the NZMS Research Award*

and the Vice Chancellor's Award for Research. He was elected a Fellow of the ACM, AMS, Aust MS, RSNZ and the NZMS. He is an editor of numerous journals and chaired the prizes committee of the Association for Symbolic Logic. He gave an invited lecture at the International Congress of Mathematicians *(2006), and has given invited addresses at numerous conferences including the* International Congress of Logic Methodology and Philosophy of Science, *and the* IEEE Conference on Computational Complexity. *He is also an accomplished surfer and Scottish country dancer.*

CC: Were there any "mathematical genes" in your family before you?

RD: My family were really working class in Australia. I think I am the only person from either my mother's or father's side to ever go to university, and likely past 10th grade. My father, who left very early, was a lens grinder, and then a storeman and packer, but also a bookmaker (that is, the kind that takes bets for horse racing) on the side. I think that figuring out the odds so that you don't lose money needs at least a modicum of mathematical talent. But, of course, to realise such a talent you need the opportunities which my parents never had I guess. My mother also worked in the credit part of a large national company called Waltons, and she had to figure out repayments and the like. They did not really have very much respect for "university types" and really could not understand why I did it until I got paid for it!

CC: How did you first notice your mathematical talent?

RD: I guess I was always good at mathematics and my reports down through the years show this. Maybe I liked it as it needed less study than other subjects!

CC: Were you interested in Mathematical Olympiads?

RD: From the point of view of those doing it I think it's nice in that it encourages mathematics and more generally science. My eldest son was involved in the final few of the Chemistry Olympiad and had all that training. He did not make the team, but it was a great experience for him and encouraged him towards science. I believe that this is the really nice part of Maths Olympiad, programming contests etc. It is such a good benefit to those who participate, at all levels not just those who go away as finally selected. The only negative I have is that it encourages a certain view of mathematics as combinatorial exercises, which colours the views of young people about the nature of mathematics. Do successes from the Maths Olympiad go on to being good mathematicians? I don't know. But certainly one of my recent postdoctoral fellows, Antonio Montalbán, was very successful for Uruguay in the Maths Olympiad, and is regarded as one of the finest recent graduates in logic in the world. He is now a full professor at Berkeley and has won a Packard Fellowship and the AMS Centenary Fellowship amongst other accolades. Also the name Terry Tao springs to mind!

CC: Who were your first mathematical mentors?

RD: Hmm. What is a "mentor" varies with time. I have recollections about a number of these. The first person who I remember really exciting me was a headmaster, called Harry Seldon, in a little school I went to called Rainworth with only enough students to have one teacher and class for each year. This headmaster would take over from the other teachers at will, and try to inspire us with English poetry and mathematics. He was in his last years of teaching and had a very colourful past with many stories and "punishing" methods of class control, the cane being legal in those days. I still read and love poetry to this day, so maybe he had a big effect. I remember he challenged us by mocking "The Hollow Men" by T.S. Elliot, and later I went up to him and said that actually I liked it and thought it was a great poem. He berated me for not getting up in class and showing the courage of my convictions, a lesson which has stuck. He showed us the mysteries of Pascal's Triangle in Year 6, and I was captivated by the beauty. He encouraged me to study my sister's high school book on Euclidean geometry and again I was fascinated at those wonderful proofs about inscribed triangles and the like. At high school we had quality mathematics teachers, but at some stage I decided that I wanted to do logic and philosophy, a high school subject in Queensland, usually done as an easy option instead of mathematics. Clearly as a logician many years later, it was a good option. We had a great teacher there, Miss Jenela Miller, who had real insight into logic, and encouraged me by loaning me university texts.

Later, as an undergraduate at university, I was inspired by the teaching of the then youngish Phil Diamond, Barry Jones (a wonderfully disorganised but insightful algebraist who clearly loved mathematics) and a logician, Neil Williams, who challenged me with work by Tarski's student, Szmielew, on the decidability of the elementary theory of abelian groups. At Monash I was lucky to interact with the gifted Chris Ash, and a young student of Nerode called Rick Smith, who was very inspiring. But while he was kind of inspiring, one gift he made was asking me to prove a certain "theorem" which "ought to be routine". For a long time I thought I must be so stupid as I could not get the proof to work, until I realised that the reason was that the theorem was not true! This led to the discovery of a class of Turing degrees called the ANC degrees which I am still trying to understand to this day.

Finally, I think there is that time when you meet someone who really opens your eyes to the really right way to think about mathematics, and how things "really work". Often it is more than one person and to a lesser extent this has been true of my interactions with Richard Shore, Carl Jockusch and Mike Stob, but after talking with Ted Slaman I found my thinking had really changed and really opened up. The same was true later when I met Mike Fellows and his view of computer science.

Of course there are the other kind of mentors who you need I think. Those people who don't directly work with you but whose encouragement and sometimes influence help so much. For me I would especially single out Anil Nerode, who has been unwavering with his support and advice, though sometimes I ignored him (you must come to America to succeed, etc.). Here in NZ, Rob Goldblatt has been exceptionally supportive as has Vaughan Jones in other ways.

CC: Do you remember your first published paper?

RD: Yes. I had kind of two. The first was a research announcement, but the first real paper was published in the *Z. Math. Logik Grundlagen Math.* and I was so excited when the acceptance letter came on the recycled paper they used to use in East Germany. It wasn't much of a paper, but I was finally a published author!

CC: As I said in the introduction you are one of New Zealand's best-known mathematicians. But you don't work on "core mathematics", algebra, analysis, geometry. . .

RD: That's not completely true. It is just that when I do things like algebra, I do them from a logical point of view. I have always been fascinated by computation and complexity. For example, two of my recent papers appeared in the *Journal of Algebra* and are devoted to understanding computable aspects of ideals in computable rings, and a recent paper with Montalbán looks at the complexity of the isomorphism problem for torsion-free abelian groups. One consequence of the work with Montalbán is to show that the integral homology sequence is, for finitely presented groups, as bad an invariant as it can possibly be. Logicians have tools to attack questions like this: that is, when are no reasonable invariants possible for the classification of objects? As a computability theorist, showing that such a problem is Σ_1^1 complete means that any set of invariants must be as complex as the classification problem itself, and hence no reasonable invariants are possible. I have been interested in effective mathematics for a long time, but have always had the view from logic. I guess that it is just taste. In computer science, the problems are so easy to state and so hard; it is so fascinating.

I think it is also true that one's perception of "core" mathematics is kind of political. I think all mathematicians should know *epsilon delta* arguments, but by the same token, they should be forced to do logic.

CC: Very interesting. Do you present your papers in algebra to logic or algebra meetings?

RD: Almost always logic meetings, but I often use those papers based around algebra or combinatorics for colloquia in maths departments. I do *publish* is algebra journals such as the *Journal of Algebra*.

CC: Tell us about your work in reverse mathematics.

RD: Reverse mathematics in its modern form goes back to an ICM talk of Harvey Friedman and the efforts particularly of Harvey and Steve Simpson. The idea is that we try to understand the proof theoretical strength of various theorems of classical mathematics using calibrations in second-order arithmetic. This idea really has its roots in the Greeks: is the parallel axiom necessary? The outgrowth is not only a deeper understanding of these systems but also sometimes completely new proofs or, indeed, new mathematics. A great example of this is Montalbán's invention of totally new invariants (signed trees) to analyse the strength of various theorems concerning linear orderings. There are five basic systems coming from restricted comprehension axioms, saying that certain objects defined in a certain way can be "comprehended". The base system is called RCA_0 and is strong enough to prove basic facts, of, say, countable algebra including some strong results like "every field has an algebraic closure", whereas to prove *uniqueness* one requires what is called ACA_0, arithmetical comprehension. Roughly speaking this is like comprehending the Turing jump. There are other systems, WKL_0 saying that every infinite binary tree has a path, and higher systems ATR_0 and $\Pi_1^1\text{-CA}$. There are also a bunch of currently poorly understood systems at the bottom, such as those related to Ramsey's theorem for pairs. A nice example is the fact that the theorem that every countable commutative ring with identity has a prime ideal is equivalent to WKL_0 but if we replace "prime" by "maximal" then the result is equivalent to the *provably stronger* system ACA_0. The hidden fact is that there must be a different proof of the existence of a prime ideal to prove the prime ideal theorem. An excellent introduction is a classic paper of Friedman, Simpson and Smith in the *Annals of Applied and Pure Logic*: countable algebra and set existence axioms. One must be careful with the results as they tend to be representation dependent.

It is natural for someone working in computability theory to consider reverse mathematics, since often there is an alignment of the effective content of a computable version of a theorem with the proof theoretical content viewed *via* reverse mathematics. Many techniques are familiar to a computability theorist. But it is a mistake to think that they are the same but clothed differently. A good example is the Robertson–Seymour theorem that finite graphs are well quasi-ordered by the minor ordering. This theorem is true in computable mathematics, but, even the restricted form of the theorem where only graphs of bounded treewidth are considered, the Robertson–Seymour theorem is provably not provable in *any* of the systems above.

My own work has been mainly in algebra and combinatorics. With Stefan Lempp I investigated the well-know Dushnik–Miller result that every countable linear ordering has a non-trivial self-embedding using (for the first time) a priority argument to show that this is equivalent to ACA_0. I did some work on Hahn's theorem and on free groups with Reed Solomon, and also with Lempp and Hirschfeldt on questions about extensions of partial ordering to linear orderings. (For example, every well-partial ordering has a well-ordered extension; this is a very strong theorem as it turns out.) More recently, with Lempp and Joe Mileti we looked at the dumbest questions one might imagine. We showed that the "theorem" that every commutative ring with identity that is not a field has a non-trivial ideal is equivalent to WKL_0 but the "theorem" that it has a principal ideal is provable equivalent to ACA_0 and so provably harder! The same is true for vector spaces. Reverse mathematics is a really attractive subject, but I do think something could be refined here, such as the number of applications of the comprehension needed for the result. It is also related to proof mining I think, and I really like the work of Jeremy Avigad and his co-authors here.

CC: In your career what has given you the most satisfaction?

RD: Effecting change. I think I have really changed the thinking of a number of young people both in complexity theory and logic. It makes me really proud to see how many of them are succeeding all around the world. With the work of the NZIMA and the NZMRI I think we have been a truly positive force in New Zealand, with the brilliant Kaikoura, Nelson and New Plymouth conferences, as well as the Israel-NZMS and upcoming NZMS-AMS joint meetings. These were undreamed of when I came to New Zealand and I would like to think I was a positive force behind them. I also like to think I can ask good questions, and have effected change with parameterised complexity and with the current interest in the algorithmic information theory. I have plans for future directions such as trying to comprehend the great similarities between online and computable thinking, but who knows? Likely, most things will be done by the next crop of young people who seem to get smarter every year.

CC: What attraction can New Zealand offer to an Aussie mathematician?

RD: For me, New Zealand has been a great place to be a mathematician, and Victoria University has been exceptionally supportive. I came just before the WWW and the Internet. Early on, collaborative research was, send a letter, wait a month for the reply (probably solving the problem in the waiting time), occasionally visit a famous place. This has changed with email and web access. Also, there was almost no money for research for mathematics in the 1980s, but the Marsden fund has highlighted the world-class work that some mathematicians have done in New Zealand and we mathematicians are favourably viewed in New Zealand. Part of this is through the efforts of Vaughan Jones who, after winning the Fields Medal, worked on bringing world-class people to interact with New Zealanders and summer schools etc., especially through the NZMRI (directors Marston Conder, Downey, Vaughan Jones, David Gauld, Gaven Martin), and later the NZIMA. Up to the present year I believe that we have had a nicer place to do mathematics than, say, Australia. But recently the demise of the NZIMA because of changes to government policy perhaps spells problems ahead, though mathematics is still supported indirectly by computational biology which is big here in New Zealand with the work of Mike Steel, Charles Semple and others. The Marsden fund remains the main supporter and I have had a succession of very, very talented postdoctoral fellows to work (and compete!) with down through the years. Working with outstanding young people is so much fun.

Also New Zealand has good surf and is really a nice, albeit cool, place to live. And I get to work in 10 min. Whenever I go overseas (or to Auckland) I am reminded that life is too short to spend it in traffic.

CC: You are extremely prolific, publishing many multi-author papers. How do you organise this cooperation across continents?

RD: Part of the answer is above, *via* the Internet. There remain co-authors I have not met. I have found mathematics and CS as a social endeavour. It is so much fun to work with others. That is the only downside of New Zealand, you really do have to travel to see others and this is non-trivial. I remember in the early days when I had little money, I asked the travel agent to find me the *cheapest fare*. This turned out to be Wellington–Sydney–Tokyo–Amsterdam–Tel Aviv, (to go to Haifa) and there were bad connections. 54 hours! But mainly if I start working with someone then I will continue this for quite a while after they leave and expect them to do the same. I have also found that short sharp visits you work up to are very effective.

CC: Tell us about your "parameterised complexity theory".

RD: Mike Fellows and I met at a conference in Palmerston North over some fine New Zealand wine. He had come to New Zealand to surf, being inspired by the old movie *"Endless Summer"*. We discovered that we were both interested in complexity, something that I had been teaching myself at VUW. I had read his paper "Non-constructive Advances in Polynomial Time Complexity" and was telling him about this stuff, saying it resembled his talk, before he told me that he was the author. He gave me the (Abrahamson, Ellis, Fellows, Mata) PGT paper (*On the complexity of fixed-parameter problems*, FOCS, 1989) the first attempt to study n^c vs $n^{g(k)}$ asymptotic behaviour. The fact that there might be something interesting in this had been noted earlier in passing by Ken Regan, and also in 1982, Moshe Vardi had suggested that perhaps traditional complexity was wrong for databases, and a complexity based around the query size might be more appropriate. There was also some earlier work focusing on parametric issues without any completeness by Fellows and Langston in the mid-1980s. This Fellows–Langston work was an important conceptual precursor. Of course, as can be seen in, say, Garey and Johnson, it had long been realised that "some forms of intractability seem better than others" but there was no real formalisation I think, except for approximation.

The PGT paper was the first to setup a complexity theory to try to explain the behaviour. The setup was non-uniform, only really applied to parameterisations of NP complete problems and the notion of reduction was extremely clumsy. Additionally, the hardness results needed something like "P-space complete by the slice". It was not fine-grained enough also to address the final W-hierarchy. Still it is a seminal paper I think.

As Mike Fellows was well supported with loads of grant money, he asked me to visit him in Canada. We corresponded a lot, as this was the beginning of the Internet and email. Then at some stage, particularly on a surf trip around the North Island of New Zealand, we figured out the main definitions and proved some basic hardness results for the W-hierarchy, and some basic fixed parameter tractability (FPT) results. It was really exciting seeing it come out. Those first six papers we felt that we were really on to something. People like Anil Nerode were really supportive. I recently looked at one of the first announcements of the material at *Dagstuhl* in April 1992. I remember giving the talk as the first of the conference, and being totally jet-lagged arriving from New Zealand the day before, after maybe 40 hours travel. Someone at a recent *Dagstuhl* who was there said that at the time he thought that this was yet another uninteresting hierarchy in complexity theory, but he said to me how wrong he was. I found that comment very rewarding.

Practitioners of computer science will tell you that classical complexity often cannot be used to explain the computational behaviour of algorithms in real life. The idea is that we tried to design a complexity theory which perhaps better addresses this. The idea is to systematise the observation that sometimes when a parameter is fixed, perhaps a graph width metric in a hidden case, computational behaviour can be much better. The example always used is VERTEX COVER where for a fixed k, there are algorithms running in about $1.26^k k^2 + 2n$ for graphs of size n and these are implemented using simple reduction rules. They actually perform extremely well on, for instance, problems from computational biology, such as the work of

Mike Langston on genomic sequences on irradiated mice. On the other hand, there seem to be problems such as DOMINATING SET where the only algorithm essentially "tries all possibilities". Thus it runs in time n^{k+1} or worse. The point here is that k-VERTEX COVER is linear time for each k whereas k-DOMINATING SET has the exponent increasing with k. Of course being able to prove that this is really the case would show that $P \neq NP$. Thus we use a hardness theory to show that things like k-DOMINATING SET cannot be done in time $O(n^c)$ with c independent of k unless there is an algorithm running in time $O(n^{c'})$ for deciding if a Turing machine with arbitrary fanout has an accepting path of length k, c' independent of k.

There have been many surveys of this area (two in the *EATCS Bulletin*) and now there is a whole conference devoted to it, as well as three books (Downey–Fellows, Flum–Grohe, Niedermeier) with another on the way (Fernau), and several journal special issues (such as *The Computer Journal*), that I believe it has penetrated the consciousness to the extent that I won't develop this further here. (For details see my website.)

What is really nice is that it has been developed by lots of strong young people such as Martin Grohe, Rolf Niedermeier, Vantakesh Raman and their students, and the development is ever expanding. We know that you can use it to show no reasonable PTAS's and there are continuing interactions with things like ETH and non-approximations. We have even been successful in having real dialogue between people doing parameterised complexity and heuristics, such as the IWPEC and *Dagstuhl* series. It is really satisfying that our intuitions that this was something important turned out to be correct.

Actually, early on we had a lot of negative comments about the work, reports saying that there was too much work in this area, and one classic referee report saying "what this area really needs is for it to be developed by someone like (snip) (at a big name university like (snip))".

It is hard to get new ideas to penetrate I think. That first (Downey–Fellows) book was important as it allowed people to access the material, rather then relying on "big conferences". Whilst big conferences can have difficult deep work, I believe that the kinds of topics they publish tend to be quite conservative. That is, people will be a bit like reef fish, swimming around the current "hot" topic. (My current postdoc Barmpalias works on Schelling segregation; perhaps this explains the phenomenon.) Moreover, the obsession seems to be how hard the mathematics is rather than the actual computer science content.

Historically, I think, several conferences for particular areas have been spawned because those groups were unsatisfied with their treatment at the "big conferences" such as STOC/FOCS. I do think this comment is rather less true in Europe which seems to be a much more diverse place, not just socially, but in its scientific outlook in theoretical computer science at least. For example, ICALP strikes me as a much more diverse conference, than STOC/FOCS.

I remember saying to Mike, we should not worry: if our stuff is good and useful, people will take it up. We should write a book and make it easily accessible. As anyone who knows him will say, Mike always had absolute faith in the area.[1] Recently, Fellows and I have a new book, *Fundamentals of Parameterized Complexity*, along with those by Niedermeier, and by Flum and Grohe. Our new book clearly demonstrates how this subject has flowered in ways we certainly did not anticipate, particularly in the realms of systematic parameterised algorithm design. In some sense, we can now show that many algorithms are asymptotically optimal up to a big O term, assuming a reasonable complexity assumption.[2] So we have systematic ways of constructing algorithms and methods to show they are optimal. There has also been huge development in other methods of addressing the methodology, such as exploration of the limits of preprocessing. There are now a number of very gifted people working in the area

---

[1] For more on the history and development of parameterised complexity, one should have a wee look at the *Festschrift* volume for Mike Fellows LNCS 7370, particularly for the role of Mike Langston who was there from the start.

[2] Specifically, usually this assumption will be $M[1] \neq FPT$, which is equivalent to the ETH, n-variable 3SAT is not in DTIME($2^{o(n)}$).

extending the theoretical boundaries. There are also a number of people implementing the material. It will be interesting to see how this unfolds against the benchmark of ILP, and the effects of algorithm engineering.

This remains one of the nice things about Wellington, in that there is not much pressure on you to conform to the current fashions in research. I do not like the current CS culture of "what must I do to get into the next (STOC/FOCS/STACS/ICALP/CCC/etc.), the focus of research being the next deadline"; maybe this is a maths vs CS view. (But maybe it is because I have tenure!).

There is a huge amount to understand about practical computation. For example, we seem a long way from understanding why commercial SAT solvers are so effective when applied to practical problems, when SAT is such a generically hard problem. As Moshe Vardi once said in a talk when he was young, SAT was thought of as being akin to bubonic plague (my paraphrasing), and now it is routinely used. (That is, we want to solve a hard problem, then reduce it to SAT, and solve it! This works in practice). The same seems true for commercial uses of the automatic verification of properties. Perhaps there is some kind of parametric solution using the distributions. These seem such important problems to understand. Another example is the work of Abdulla and others using the well-quasi-ordering theory to verify infinite state systems, but then implementing something that should take the life of the universe to work, at least in theory, but then on real data it works very nicely thank you. There is no theoretical explanation for these phenomena. Surely if we understood why these things work in practice, then we would be better able to design and understand such tools.

For the present time, I am willing to accept that $P \neq NP$ as a working axiom. This axiom is far from describing all sorts of computational phenomena arising from practical computation. Much more fine-tuning is needed and specific tools designed.

Also, for instance, there have been astonishing results in complexity using pseudo-random generators and it would be nice to develop this theory in the parametric setting.

CC: Can you explain in plain English one of your favourite theorems, its meaning, significance, and, maybe, relevance outside mathematics?

RD: Do you mean favourite theorem of mine or of others?

CC: Yes, favourite and not necessarily yours.

RD: From others, my favourites include the calculation of the number of derangements (the beautiful fact that e comes in), the fundamental theorem of calculus (!), Kruskal's theorem that finite trees are well quasi-ordered by a minimal bad sequence argument, Cohen's invention of forcing to solve the Continuum hypothesis and Sacks' density theorem for the computably enumerable Turing degrees. I guess I am attracted to material by the depth of the ideas in the proofs. For my own, I would like to say one of the $W[1]$ hardness results, such as the early Downey–Fellows series, or the paper with Fellows, Geoff Whittle and Alexander Vardy on coding theory, which says a lot about practical coding questions for linear codes, or the requirement-free solution to Post's problem with Hirschfeldt, Nies and Stephan, but to be honest the paper which sticks in my mind as most beautiful is one about non-embeddings in initial segments of the computably enumerable Turing degrees. To me this is such an elegant non-uniform argument. Likely it has little meaning outside the area, but the ideas of the proof are so nice to me.

CC: You are regarded as one of the world's best in logic circles. Please share with us your vision about the future of this important discipline.

RD: Logic is a funny game. There is classical logic, being set theory, computability theory, proof theory and model theory which historically reflect classical mathematics. It is their classical forms, to me, that are important in that they give insights and alternative views of what mathematics is. For example, it is interesting that category theory gives one version of what a "natural" transformation is, yet in logic the idea of natural seems to go hand in hand with definable. Computability theory and complexity theory to me ask more deeply "what does it mean for there to be a solution". I was talking with one of Vaughan Jones' students who was studying "classical" mathematics, and found it hard to calculate various polynomials related to the Jones polynomial, and was totally unaware of what $\#P$ is. There seems now a trend that this classical form of logic is going back more to its roots and giving more insight back into classical mathematics. What is so sad to me is that because of hiring policies, there seems a loss of this expertise from many departments around the world. This is unfortunate as there seems no reason to limit your perspectives.

On the other hand, there has been a spectacular interaction between logic and computer science, with much of the world's best work in logic being in computer science. There are nice surveys in and around "On the Unusual Effectiveness of Logic in Computer Science" (Moshe Vardi). If you think about it this is really natural. For example, in parameterised complexity, and algorithmics more generally, there has been so much emphasis on logical structure and meta-theorems, rather than heroic case analysis. It is also a salutary lesson to us and maybe funding agencies. I remember when I was young a senior logician referred to fuzzy logic as "mathematical pornography", and now look how this has revolutionised the construction of, for example, washing machines. So much for intuition.

From my own point of view, there are some really brilliant young people in logic, both classical and applied, and in terms of results the future looks fine. Whether they will win things like Fields Medals or Turing Awards is not clear to me as awards are so political. The committees for such awards are full of people who think whatever *they* do is the hardest and deepest thing on earth. I found it a real tragedy that Shelah did not win the Fields Medal, in spite of the enormous depth and breadth of his work. But then again, neither did Lovasz nor Szemeredi.

CC: In the last years you have intensively and extensively worked in algorithmic information theory. Tell us about your long anticipated (and extensively cited before its publication in 2010) book *Algorithmic Randomness and Complexity* (with Denis Hirschfeldt).

RD: In many ways this book was your fault Cris. One of my post-docs, Richard Coles, was working with you in Auckland and had come down with a question you had asked. This was immediately after attending a series of talks by Lance Fortnow in our NZMRI conference in Kaikoura (which appears in a collection of talks on basic complexity in a volume *Aspects of Complexity*, (with D. Hirschfeldt, editors), de Gruyter Series in Logic and Its Applications, Volume 4, 2001, vi+172 pages). Denis and I worked on this problem for some time, and then discovered this huge and rather neglected area with exciting interactions between computability, complexity and randomness. We then made the possibly foolish decision to try to organise a mass of, difficult to obtain, material such as Solovay's wonderful notes, material from Russian literature and other unpublished material such as Stuart Kurtz's thesis. Much of this material was really hard to find, and in some cases even harder to understand. The main point of some of these papers seemed to be to claim the theorem rather than to make the reader understand. We felt that we should present this in an accessible form, plus a few results we had recently proven, little imagining what was about to happen. Having got Solovay's and Stuart Kurtz's permission, we began the project, as usual thinking this would take two years... Simultaneously there was an explosion of work with many new theorems and avenues for exploration found by lots of gifted people, such as André Nies, Wolfgang Merkle, Jan Reimann, Antonin Kučera, Jack Lutz, Ted Slaman, to name a few, and then the book kind of took on a life of its own. In particular, I had some really gifted postdocs and co-authors, Denis Hirschfeldt, Joe Miller and Yu Liang who really discovered a lot. Eventually it took 6 years and 855 plus pages.

The main theme is what do levels of randomness and levels of computational power have to do with one another. Li-Vitanyi is a good basic introduction to the whole area of algorithmic information theory, as are other books such as yours and Ko's, but our book is really an in-depth concentration on randomness for real numbers and the relationship of this fact with computational power. For example, it has been shown recently things like Chaitin's Ω, which are random but have high computational power, are quite exceptional amongst randoms, and almost all randoms have almost no computational power. This requires careful explanation, so *buy the book!*

The survey *"Calibrating Randomness"*[3] in the *Bulletin of Symbolic Logic* gives a reasonable idea, as well as a couple of relevant papers of mine *"Five Lectures on Algorithmic Randomness"* and *"The Sixth Lecture on Algorithmic Randomness."* It remains a source of amazement to me that the material on lowness has turned out to be so deep. This is also true of the connections between initial segment complexity and higher levels of randomness such as 2-randomness. The most obvious omission is resource-bounded material, but that must wait until later.

CC: Is mathematics relevant to computer science?

RD: Definitely and on many levels. There are the obvious algorithms behind many programmes, there is the obvious use of mathematics in design, the use in complexity theory, and many less obvious examples. Look at the work verifying safety and liveness properties using automata and WQO (well-quasi-ordering) theory look at Kleinberg's work with Google and small worlds. There are so many examples. On the other hand, practitioners doing something like software engineering maybe don't see the obvious mathematics in the same way the people running helical CT scans don't see the mathematics and CS behind these things. This is always the trouble trying to support mathematics and/or theoretical CS; that somehow we must constantly be expected to prove to everyone why we are important, and underlay many of the main advances.

Of course, prejudices go the other way. CS has so many problems that are gifts to mathematics, but many traditional mathematics programmes completely ignore these areas.

CC: We have a strong group in theory in Auckland and we work hard to integrate ourselves: we teach theory courses, but we also "infuse" small theory chapters in applied CS classes. I will quote you a comment posted on a stage one forum by a CS student: "Most

---

[3]The paper won the 2010 Shoenfield Prize for writing in logic.

of us are doing or have already finished maths 108/150, some are even doing level 2 maths subjects. I understand maths 108 is the minimum requirement for most computer science level 2 subjects. Just wondering what would be the best course of action for someone like us that hasn't taken a maths course yet. A lot of computer science students I know only care about the courses they're interested in and passionate about, and usually maths isn't their passion. It just seems a shame to have to take up maths when some of the best programmers I know get by fine without knowing it as extensively as 108/105. Please don't suggest a change of education provider. I am doing maths myself, just curious and asking for a friend". What would you respond?

RD: Difficult question. I am sure that there are a lot of students in first year who think that they could design all of their degrees etc. Young people have very strong opinions. All I can say to them is that we believe that mathematics will enrich their understanding of CS and their view of the world. Students also benefit I think from doing philosophy and English and the like. This student question comes mainly from areas such as CS where the university experience is seen more like an apprenticeship, rather than one which is a broadening experience. We also see the other side of the coin. We have students planning to be CS majors and discovering that university mathematics, especially the discrete, has little resemblance to high school maths, and is fascinating. These are often the very best students who finish up doing our LOCO (logic and computation, half mathematics and half CS) stream.

One of the other problems we have is that CS students often don't give mathematics their best shot as they are too busy writing code. When students come to me with complaints that their time is taken up with COMPXXX then I suggest to them that "so the reason you are not doing *my* course with a *reasonable* work load is that you are choosing to work on *another* with an *unreasonable* one, is that correct?" This usually has the desired effect.

My eldest son Carlton is doing a PhD at Carnegie Mellon on machine learning. He tells me that he had to do huge amounts of maths to be able to succeed in the programme. Especially linear algebra and calculus! In fact he asked me "why did I not teach him the "right" linear algebra!"

CC: You play tennis, badminton and table tennis. What else?

RD: So long as my knees hold up I will continue with them. I also swim, surf and teach Scottish country dancing and an learning ballroom dancing. None of this seems to completely halt the onset of the permafat of middle age. Of course, it is a bit harder after the surgery (I had a "resection" of half of the gastrocnemius for the treatment of soft tissue sarcoma in 2008), but you should always struggle on. Actually, I devise Scottish country dances and have three books with one more on the way. Devising dances is kind of like proving theorems, where you see flow through space.

CC: Are your children interested in mathematics or computer science?

RD: The oldest one came to university to be a chemist, but has been lured to the dark side of CS. He is very practically orientated and is horrified how little I know about (e.g.,) Java. Carlton has an MSc from VUW, and is doing a PhD in Machine Learning at Carnegie Mellon University. Doing machine learning at CMU means that he now has to do a lot of heavy-duty mathematics, particularly linear algebra, Bayesan statistics, and analysis. The younger boy is more attracted to design and art, and plans a career in design. He is definitely not attracted to mathematics. Alex has a degree in design and is now a professional designer, currently working for the Wellington City Council, and doing freelance work.

You don't really know CS until you come to university I think. In New Zealand there is no computer *science* taught at schools, only a little *computing*. Both are addicted to computer games of strategy.

CC: Data deluge is growing. The theory of big data — data science — is to have no theory at all. You just accumulate massive amounts of data, observe the patterns and estimate probabilities. Google's philosophy is to "observe" that a page is better than another one without knowing why. Google's translation works reasonably well by "observation", but not well enough to be used at the

UN — without knowing any grammar. No semantic or causal analysis is required to make those "observations" because with enough data, numbers seem to speak for themselves. Causation is replaced by correlation. Big data can help answer many questions, but knowing why is a missing realm. Is the (traditional) scientific method becoming obsolete?

RD: Maybe you should ask my son at CMU! This is exactly the kind of stuff they are grappling with there and the inherent mathematical challenges. In truth, my understanding of the scientific method is as follows: we observe. We hypothesise and test our theory. The theory is wrong if it does not align itself to reality. This has been the way of science forever. The difference is now the amount of data we observe is so large that we have immense trouble analysing it, and then trying to interpret it. But it is clear that progress is being made. The history of, for example, physics is littered with observations awaiting explanations. Think of Faraday and electric motors well before Maxwell told us why Faraday's field theory was correct. I just think we are at the stage with our understanding big data where the Greeks were explaining the earth's motion using a complex wrong model, and then someone like Galileo comes along and explains things. Unfortunately, lots of scientific research, particularly medical, seems based on statistical analysis of big data, and the core question is the validity of the analysis and the data. Anyway, this is speculation on my part. The challenges ahead in this area are really exciting and this is a wonderful area for young people to move into. The data will get ever bigger.

CC: Your work is very theoretical. Have you been tempted to look for "real world" (a horrible expression) applications of results in your areas of interest?

RD: I know my work has been applied in biomathematics and other applications such as social choice, databases, etc. The reason for the large funding going to parameterised complexity in Europe is that it can, and is, applied. Currently, I speculate on using some new randomness material in physics. I am currently looking at applicable material on incremental models of computation. The deal is that a big advance here could well have a significant impact on our understanding of large computation. To be honest, though, I am attracted to what my intuition tells me is interesting. This does not *exclude* applications, and I would argue that parameterised complexity is driven by an attempt to understand the complexity of real data, as is my recent work on generic computation. But the key here is that I want to *understand* rather more than to actually implement. I guess I really should be more like Mike Langston at Tennessee, for instance, who can do it all. If a nice applied project comes along, I will be keen. But also these things are very hard. In my experience, changing areas, getting real understanding of any new area of maths takes at least a couple of years to get up to speed. Getting a deep understanding of some area of *science* so that it becomes intuitive takes a huge investment of time and effort. I am not sure I have it in me, especially with all the great problems in my current areas I am still trying to solve.

Chapter 15

Jozef Gruska: Informatics, Physics and Mathematics

Professor Gruska, http://www.fi.muni.cz/usr/gruska, is well known not only for his results but also because he has been "everywhere" — he's had 33 long-term visiting positions in Europe, North America, Asia and Africa. He introduced the descriptional complexity (of grammar, automata and languages) and is one of the pioneers of parallel (systolic) automata. Professor Gruska is the co-founder of four, regular series of conferences on informatics and two in quantum information processing, and the founding chair (1989–1996) of the IFIP Specialist Group on Foundation of Computer Science.

He has been awarded my distinctions including Computer pioneer (IEEE, 1996), the Bolzano medal of the Czech Academy of Sciences (2003), elected member of the Academia Europaea (2006), Doctor

Honoris Causa, Latvian University (2013), IFIP Silver Core Award (1995) and Slovak Literally Fond Awards (1998, 2000).

His other research interests include parallel systems and automata, and quantum information processing, transmission and cryptography.

CC: A century ago hardly anyone would consider information an important concept for physics.

JG: Correct. One can even say that at that time one could hardly see information as a scientific concept at all. In spite of the fact that quantum entropy had been known since 1932, and actually before classical entropy, it was only due to the seminal work of Shannon, *A Mathematical Theory of Communication*, in 1948, that (hard) science started to see the concept of information as a scientific one.

CC: Shannon's concept is very important, but it does not fully capture the intuitive concept of information. There are many other models for information (a "Workshop on Information Theories" was held in *Münchenwiler*, Switzerland, in May 2006).

JG: I think philosophers still consider the concept of information as one we have no full understanding of yet. Historically, they see its origin from the Latin words *informatio* and *informare*. In scholastic terms one would see information as a *representation of matter through a form*. Information usually has three dimensions: syntactic, semantic and pragmatic. An important philosophical approach to this concept was developed by Carl Friedrich Weinzsäcker in *Information is das Maß eine Menge von Form* ...; it comes from his *Ur-theorie*.[1] There is lots of interesting material written about *information* from the point of view of philosophers, but hardly anything "really useful". Shannon's approach, motivated to a significant extent by war problems, considers "only" quantitative aspects of information, from the point of view of transmission, as a key ingredient of communication. This semantic-less concept has turned out to

---

[1]Sadly, Weinzsäcker died on 28 April 2007.

be extremely important and one of the success stories of modern (applied) mathematics.

CC: My colleague, Garry Tee, pointed out to me that Edmond Halley published his great geomagnetic map of the Atlantic Ocean in 1699, and for centuries thereafter immense efforts were devoted to measuring precise information about the earth's magnetic field. And from 1850 to 1890 Kelvin, Maxwell, Jenkin, Rayleigh and other British physicists devoted immense efforts to establishing accurate measurements of electricity. However, probably the first important use of information in a more abstract way in physics was related to an explanation of the Maxwell demon paradox.

JG: This is correct. In spite of the big role that Galileo's famous dictum played in science, *"measure what is measurable, and make measurable what is not."* However, a really significant breakthrough in the relation between physics and information came, I think, actually only after Landauer's observation that *information is physical* — that is to say that physical carriers are needed to store, transform and transmit information, and therefore the laws and limitations of physics also determine the laws and limitations of information processing. An additional breakthrough came later with the view usually attributed to John Wheeler: *physics is informational*. Information processing phenomena, as well as their laws and limitations, are of key importance for understanding the laws and limitations of physics. Another big issue was also the discovery of the information paradox of black holes — the term also attributed to Wheeler. It is known that black holes absorb information and do not let it out. However, quantum mechanics says that information cannot get lost!

CC: Wheeler summarised his position with the now famous "it from bit" (*Sakharov Memorial Lectures on Physics*, Vol. 2, Nova Science, 1992). This "thesis" is well discussed in many publications, for example, in Tom Siegfried's book *The Bit and the Pendulum* and in Seth Lloyd's book *Programming the Universe*.

JG: Wheeler explained in more detail his position as follows: *"It from bit* symbolises the idea that every item of the physical world has at the bottom — at the very bottom, in most instances — an immaterial source and explanation. Namely, that which we call *reality* arises from posing of yes-no questions, and registering of equipment-invoked responses. In short, that things physical are information theoretic in origin." Worth noting is David Deutsch's "updating" of Wheeler's "it from qubit" and Wheeler's confession: "I think of my lifetime in physics as divided into three periods: in the first period... I was convinced that everything is particles; I call my second period everything is fields; now I have a new vision, namely that everything is information."

CC: Wheeler's position is close to digital physics (a term coined by Fredkin), which proposes to ground much of physical theory in cellular automata by assuming that the universe is a gigantic universal cellular automaton. Gregory Chaitin, Edward Fredkin, Seth Lloyd, Tomasso Toffoli, Stephen Wolfram and Konrad Zuse are some of the main contributors to this new direction.

JG: A. Zeilinger has a similar position. In his article with Caslav Brückner they note that "quantum physics is an elementary theory of information". However, as one can expect, not all physicists share such a view of the physical world.

CC: The first workshop "Physics of Computation", organised at MIT in 1981, played a key role in understanding the role of information in physics and can be seen as inaugurating the field of quantum information processing, communication and cryptography.

JG: It was the workshop organised by Tomasso Toffoli and of the utmost importance was the keynote talk of Richard Feynman in which he argued that classical computers cannot efficiently simulate all quantum processes. This motivated David Deutsch to come in 1985 with a model of a quantum computer — the quantum Turing machine. In addition, Deutsch was able to show the existence of universal quantum Turing machines capable of simulating any other quantum Turing machine. Unfortunately, the simulations were not always polynomial — a big weak point that was overcame in 1993 with the result of Bernstein and Vazirani. However, I think, none of these pioneers could imagine how revolutionary their ideas would be even for quantum physics.

CC: At that time quantum physics was considered deeply mysterious ... even for its fathers.

JG: Indeed, Niels Bohr is often quoted to say that "everybody who is not shocked by quantum theory has not understood it." And even the same Feynman used to say, in 1965, in the introduction to his book *The Character of Physical Laws*: "I am going to tell you what Nature behaves like... However do not keep saying to yourself, if you can possibly avoid it, 'but how can it be like that?' because you will get 'down the drain' into a blind alley from which nobody has yet escaped." Interesting, beautifully said, however, no longer fully acceptable.

CC: The situation has changed nowadays, when a lot of hopes (and money) are put into quantum information processing.

JG: A new understanding of the quantum world had already started to appear by the late 1980s. This was nicely summarised in 1990 by T. James who said: "today we are beginning to realise how much of all physical science is really only *information, organised in a particular way*. But we are far from unravelling the knotty question: *to what extent does this information reside in us, and to what extent is it a property of Nature?* Our present quantum mechanics formalism is a peculiar mixture describing in part laws of Nature, in part incomplete human information about Nature — all scrambled up together by Bohr into an omelette that nobody has seen how to unscramble. Yet we think the unscrambling is a prerequisite for any further advances in basic physical theory." All this, of course, does not mean that Feynman was wrong. We may never fully understand how can Nature behave as it does.

CC: I think there is little doubt that we will never know the whole story. As Popper recognised a long time ago, scientific theories cannot be proved correct, they could only be disproved. But a better grasp of quantum information and information processing could have a deep impact for our understanding of the physical world and computer science, or, as you prefer, informatics.

JG: The impact on our understanding of the quantum world and physics is already really significant. To start with, let us observe that in parallel to the algorithmic Church–Turing thesis since 1985 we have the physical Turing principle, formulated by Deutsch: *every finitely realisable physical system can be perfectly simulated by a universal computing machine operating by finite means.* This principle can be seen as one of the guiding principles of physics. Today, we are witnessing an emergence of so many new views and approaches in quantum physics motivated mainly by paradigms, methods and results of quantum information processing. Some of them have strong informatics background as the emerging NP-*principle*: "NP-complete problems are intractable in the physical world."

CC: What actually are the main contributions of quantum information processing and communication (QIPC) to (quantum) physics?

JG: They are numerous. On a very general level, QIPC should be seen as both an attempt to develop a new, more powerful, information processing technology, and as a new way to get deeper insight into the physical world, into its laws, limitations, phenomena and processes. QIPC gave rise to quantum informatics as the area of science combining goals and tools of both physics and informatics. QIPC is an area that brings new paradigms, goals, value systems, concepts, methods and tools to explore the physical world, and its potential for information processing and communication is significant. On a more particular level, QIPC provides (quantum) physics with new concepts, models, tools, paradigms, images and analogies, and makes many old concepts quantitative and more precise. In some cases, this even allowed solving old problems. For example, an application of computability and complexity theories allowed the vision that some old ideas about the physical world are very likely wrong and that various proposals of the modification of quantum mechanics are unlikely to work because they would allow the physical world to "easily" compute what is very likely beyond the complexity classes BPP and BQP, currently regarded as not feasible. Moreover, QIPC helped not only to understand the various phenomena considered for years as strange, counter-intuitive and even mysterious, such as entanglement and non-locality, but to show that they are powerful resources for information processing which can provide better a quality of security.

CC: Could you explain, in simple terms, just one example?

JG: OK. Quantum entanglement, that is the existence of quantum states of composed quantum systems that cannot be decomposed into the states of subsystems, was, for a long time, considered a strange consequence of (an imperfect?) quantum theory. Nowadays, there are many books discussing this precious, though hard to create and preserve, information processing resource, its laws and limitations, and there are a huge variety of measures of entanglement with deep informatics and physics interpretations.

CC: Please explain the one-way computation.

JG: In the so-called one-way computation one starts with a special entangled state, the so-called cluster state, a source, and then one performs only one qubit measurement. The discovery that this is a universal way of doing quantum computation has been a big surprise.

CC: Which discoveries made QIPC one of the hottest topics of science and technology?

JG: It was the discovery of quantum teleportation by Bennett *et al.* (1993), Shor's polynomial integer factorisation algorithm (1994), Shor's proof of the existence of quantum error correcting codes (1995) and of quantum fault-tolerant computation (1996).

CC: Did QIPC contribute to foundational issues?

JG: One cannot say that the contributions of QIPC to foundational issues have been breathtaking. Perhaps the main effort of QIPC has concentrated so far on the question "why quantum mechanics?" with the goal of finding *natural*, information-theoretic, or even information-processing cast, axioms of quantum mechanics.

CC: Clifton, Bub and Halverson (2003) showed that one can derive quantum mechanics from the following three (negative) "axioms": no superluminal communication, no broadcasting and no unconditionally secure bit commitment. This suggests that quantum theory should be regarded as a theory of (quantum) information rather than a theory about the dynamics of quantum systems. Technically, it seems that the proof needs the assumption that quantum mechanics is formulated in C^*-algebra terms.

JG: Indeed, this has been demonstrated by an counterexample due to J. Smolin.

CC: What we have been discussing so far seems to indicate a certain similarity, or at least an interesting relation, between the scientific goals of physics and informatics.

JG: The main scientific goal of physics is to study concepts, phenomena, processes, laws and limitations of the physical world, and the main scientific goal of informatics is to study concepts, phenomena, processes, laws and limitations of the information world. In order to integrate these positions, I would like to see physics and informatics as two complementary windows to observe, explore and understand our world.

CC: What actually is the information processing world? How different is it from the physical world?

JG: Of course, no one seems to have clear ideas about that. However, physics also does not have an absolutely clear idea about the physical world and, in spite of that, it has been extremely successful in studying it and in producing beautiful, powerful and useful results. And so does informatics in spite of not having a clear understanding of what information processing worlds are about...

CC: Please give some examples.

JG: Even understanding time and space is still one of the grand challenges of current physics. Did time exist before the Big Bang? Is time an emerging concept? Are time and space illusions? Also, the nature of dark matter and dark energy is still a mystery.

CC: Contrary to the digital physics view, you seem to believe that these worlds are distinct. Then, which of these two worlds is the most basic one, if any?

JG: It is too early to answer this question. We need a lot of research to explore the relations between the basic concepts, principles and so on of these two worlds. However, it may be one of these eternal questions. Actually, this is the most likely development.

CC: An instance of the question regarding which of the two worlds — physical or informational — is more basic appears in the process of understanding the nature of quantum states: do they represent an objective physical reality, real physical objects or do they have a subjective information character as a compendium of probabilities for the outcomes of potential operations we can perform on them?

JG: The information view of quantum states — as a description and or compendium of our knowledge (or beliefs) concerning probabilities of the measurement outcomes — is on one side strange, all of us would like to have some physical reality behind it. But, on the other side, it allows us to see the collapse of quantum states upon measurement as something that does not contradict much of our common sense.

CC: On a more practical level, what can one say about the overall impact of physics and informatics on the rest of science, technology and society?

JG: Physics used to be seen as an area of science that has the largest impact on all natural sciences. This has been, in a condensed way, well captured by a famous remark of Ernest Rutherford (1912): *"in science there is only physics, the rest is stamp collecting."* However, I believe that this has changed a lot recently and one can nowadays say, without exaggeration, that informatics is currently the leading science and technology discipline with enormous impact on all other sciences, technologies, industry, economics, health and environment care, liberal art and so on — guiding them and serving them. I dare say that informatics can now be seen as a new, powerful, wise but nice, queen and, at the same time, as an incredibly useful, intelligent, powerful and diligent servant of all sciences and technologies (and most, if not all, other major areas of society). In particular, informatics can be seen as having a bigger potential to contribute to two current mega-challenges of science, technology, medicine and mankind in general: (a) to beat human intelligence and (b) to beat natural death. Both as much and as soon as possible.

CC: You have strong views concerning the relation between informatics and physics. How about the relation between informatics and mathematics?

JG: On the scientific level, I see mathematics as a part of informatics, as it used to be actually for centuries. In addition to being a science, I see mathematics as a basis of the so-called theoretical methodology that science has (as a sort of complement to the experimental methodology) and I see informatics as the basis of a new, third, informatics-driven methodology of science. I even envision that our — so-called Galilean science — where producing outcomes in a mathematical form was often seen as the main goal of research, is quite fast developing to a new era of science, where results of our research are going to be much, much more demonstrated by "informatics products" such as information models, simulation systems, visualisation systems, algorithms and their analysis, and so on. In other words, instead of trying to understand our world in mathematical terms, and in this way to make our findings available for future generations to utilise them, we will try, in future, to understand our world in informatics terms (that includes, of course, all mathematical terms).

CC: Well, informatics didn't exist for centuries like mathematics... One could argue, for example, that mathematics is not only about computation or information. Mathematicians have routinely studied non-computational mathematics, non-real, non-physical and many-dimensional spaces. In the last century we saw the transition from mathematics understood as calculation to mathematics considered as qualitative reasoning.

JG: Well, you have addressed several important issues and let me comment on them briefly. First of all, informatics has also existed for centuries and its origins are at least as old, if not much older, as those of mathematics. Modern computers have brought only a new dimension into many areas of the field — for example, an understanding of the deep impact of the study of various complexity problems and the study of specification, reasoning and verification systems. Informatics is not only about computation and information. Far from that — as I have already mentioned, one of its main goals is to study the laws, limitations, phenomena and processes of the information processing.

Concerning the transition mathematics went through, I would like to add that Halmos even said that applied mathematics is important, interesting, but bad mathematics. Until quite recently, mathematics saw computational and information processing of mathematical problems also as interesting and important, but far from being "The Mathematics". Look, the book *Mathematical Thoughts from Ancient to Modern Times* (1200 pages on the history of mathematics) published in 1972 by Maurice Kline, does not contain a single occurrence of the term *algorithm*.[2] It mentions al Khwarizmi, Turing, and even Babbage and many scientists behind informatics, but, clearly intentionally, avoids the term *algorithm*. This indicates to me how deformed the mathematical thinking was of that time (and, often, still is). I see nothing in the development of mathematics that would convince me that mathematics should not be seen and developed as a part of informatics, for the good of all.

CC: Mathematical generalisations and abstractions turned out to be very powerful.

JG: Correct, but both of them are used and even more needed in informatics. One of the reasons is that informatics also has to develop tools to specify, design and analyse some of the most complex systems mankind has created. To do that many levels of abstraction are needed. In addition, informatics needs to develop a large number of logics, calculi and other formal systems. Moreover, some of the very basic concepts used to study the potential of information processing are complexity classes and the feasibility concepts that are both

---

[2] Actually one, referring to the Euclid algorithm — that was likely very hard to omit or rename.

down to earth and highly abstract ones. Developments and the study of virtual worlds are new steps along these lines.

CC: It won't be easy to make such a view acceptable...

JG: Separations, unifications or even the death of some areas of science always take time. But in our case the process can be more straightforward and faster than one can think, and there are already many steps indicating that. In connection with that I would like to recount one story. At the reception of the World Computer Congress in 1989 in San Francisco I asked Donald Knuth, who was the main keynote speaker of the congress, whether we should not do more to promote computer science. His response was, freely cited, that there is no big need to do something because in 50 years half of the members of the academy will have a strong computer science background and support will come naturally. Now I believe, to make an analogy, that in 50 years half of mathematicians in the Academy will be actually computer scientists and the development will go along the lines I have indicated.

Here is an idea. It could be a great contribution to mathematics and informatics, and to science in general, to write a book about the history of mathematics with similar goals as the one of Kline, but demonstrating that the history of mathematics is a part of the history of informatics. And also to show that the main impact of mathematics thinking on the development of society came primarily through new computation (and information processing) methods and tools.

CC: How do you see the relation between informatics and mathematics in the future?

JG: I can imagine that in some places one will study mathematics as a special direction/subarea within informatics departments. Actually, that would be very beneficial for both. In some places, we will have departments of mathematics in parallel with departments of informatics.

Another option, of course, is to start to see mathematics as having as its problems and tools (almost) as informatics has. This is actually happening ... Here is an example: the monthly magazine ERCIM

News of the European Research Council for Informatics and Mathematics publishes more, actually far more, articles on informatics than in mathematics. From 94 issues, 88 are devoted to informatics and the rest to mathematics, but basically to computational ones.

CC: Are you not going too far?

JG: I do not think so and all that is not to underestimate the importance, contributions and beauty of mathematics — by the way I graduated from pure mathematics. Actually, I would like to go even further. Mathematics departments have usually three goals: service, research and coaching a new generation of mathematicians. I am more and more convinced that informaticians, those theoretically oriented, could do the service better than (most) mathematicians.

CC: When you talk about informatics, it seems that you (mainly) have in mind theoretical informatics.

JG: Not really, but I like to see theoretical (or perhaps better scientific) informatics as a much broader and deeper area of science than it is mostly assumed. Not only as the one where mathematical methods dominate, but as the one that has as one of its goals to also study the laws and limitations of (information processing of) the universe, evolution, life, intelligence and so on.

CC: Your picture of science and technology raises many questions. . .

JG: Processes of differentiation and integration in science go often beyond all expectations (physics actually grew from medicine). In addition, the absolute truth is not always important; it may even not exist. What counts is whether a point of view is useful and can significantly contribute to the development of science (involved sciences).

CC: Let us go back to our discussion of classical and quantum worlds. To explore the relations between the classical and quantum worlds is another challenge.

JG: Views on these two worlds can be very different. Here are three examples. N. Bohr: "there is no quantum world. There is only an abstract quantum physical description. It is wrong to think that the task of physics is to find out how Nature is. Physics concerns what we can say about Nature." A. Zeilinger: "the border between classical and quantum phenomena is just a question of money." D. Greenberger: "I believe there is no classical world. There is only the quantum world. Classical physics is a collection of unrelated insights: Newton's laws, Hamilton's principle, etc. Only quantum theory brings out their connection. An analogy is the Hawaiian Islands, which look like a bunch of islands in the ocean. But if you could lower the water, you would see, that they are the peaks of a chain of mountains. That is what quantum physics does to classical physics."

CC: This is interesting.

JG: The search for such borders between classical and quantum worlds has recently been brought to the experimental level. An important recent research agenda is to find out for what kind of macroscopic objects such phenomena as superposition or entanglement hold. For example, these phenomena have been demonstrated already on an ensemble of 10^{14} atoms and on large molecules.

CC: Certainly your car mechanic is a classical mechanic, not a quantum one. General relativity and quantum mechanics do not combine well...

JG: Quantum mechanics surely brought a revolution in our view of the physical world. I would like to join those expecting that this revolution is not finished. One reason is that all attempts to get, within this theory, a unified understanding of time and space, particles and forces, cosmology and gravitation have failed so far. This is one of the reasons why quantum mechanics is still not "the theory" of the physical world. Smolin (see *quant-ph/0609109*) has explored the hypothesis that quantum mechanics is an approximation of another, cosmological theory, that is accurate only for the description of sub-systems of the universe. He found conditions under which quantum mechanics could be derived from the cosmological theory by averaging over variables that are not internal to the subsystem (and can be seen as non-local hidden variables of a new type). Actually, one of the grand challenges of physics is to find out whether quantum theory (or theories) and general relativity are valid at all scales.

CC: Should informatics get involved in such mega-problems?

JG: I would even like to argue that this is one of the main challenges and tasks for theoretical informatics. These are really the *problems* theoretical informatics should try to deal with instead of being concerned so much with numerous attempts to close various $\log^* n$ and $\log \log n$ gaps, to say it metaphorically.

CC: This brings us to the question: what really are the main reasons to pursue QIPC?

JG: I see the following reasons:

- QIPC is believed to lead to a new quantum information processing technology that will have a deep and broad impact.
- Several sciences and technologies are approaching the point at which they badly need expertise with the isolation, manipulation and transmission of particles.
- It is increasingly believed that new, quantum information processing-based tools for understanding quantum phenomena can be developed.
- Quantum cryptography seems to offer higher levels of security and could soon be feasible.
- QIPC has been shown to be more efficient than its classical counter-part in interesting/important cases.

CC: May I observe that with the exception of the last "reason" everywhere else you have used terms like "it seems", "it is believed". Could you give us the simplest example of a *provable* QIPC solution which is more efficient than any classical solution (except Grover's algorithm)?

JG: Several quantum teleportation cannot be made classically; if communicating parties share entanglement this may increase the capacity of their classical channel; in the area of quantum communication complexity, exponential separation has been proven for some problems. Finally, let me mention Simon's problem: check whether a given finite function is one-to-one or two-to-one. In this case it has been proven, in a reasonable sense, that the quantum solution is exponentially faster than any probabilistic solution — the weak point of this result is, however, that it is a promise problem and we work with query complexity.

CC: Deutsch's problem — test whether a bit-function is constant or not — was considered for many years the simplest example of a problem in which the quantum solution is superior to any classical solution; apparently nobody really checked this claim. Some years ago I showed that classical solutions as efficient as the quantum one exist. Are any of the above listed examples in the same category?

JG: Your classical solution of the Deutsch problem has been a big surprise. People have realised that what has been claimed to be a more efficient quantum solution of the Deutsch problem is actually a solution of a different problem, with a different black box and inputs. It was only believed that this is not something essential, but you have shown that it is. I tend to believe that this will not be the situation in the cases mentioned above, but I have to admit that I am not fully sure. Another surprising recent result along these lines is the discovery (see *quant-ph/0611156*) that quantum fourier transform over $\mathbf{Z}_q$, which has been thought to be the key quantum ingredient of Shor's algorithm, can be simulated on classical computers in polynomial time. All that actually demonstrates how little we actually know about the computational power of quantum phenomena — entanglement, superposition and measurement.

CC: In connection with that, it is perhaps useful to mention that many solutions offered by quantum information processing make crucial use of several counter-intuitive phenomena such as randomness of quantum measurement, the existence of entangled states and quantum non-locality, and even the more weird quantum counterfactual phenomena. Could we now turn our attention to them and perhaps start with quantum measurement?

JG: Results, both classical and quantum, of the basic quantum projection measurement should be random and should result, in general, in a 'collapse' of the state being measured. Erwin Schrödinger had problems accepting it and his position is well known: "had I known that we are not going to get rid of this damned quantum jumping, I never would have involved myself in this business." Albert Einstein, famous claims "God does not play dice" got a superb response from Niels Bohr: "the true God does not allow anybody to prescribe what he has to do." However, experiments seem to confirm randomness — summarised by Nicolas Gissin in his "God tosses even non-local dice". Interestingly enough, physicists seem to have more problems accepting randomness than informaticians, because informatics has a lot of technical results showing the power of randomness for computation and communication. I would therefore like to say that *"God is not malicious and provides us with useful randomness."* One should notice there are still very prominent old physicists and some bright young physicists having problems accepting the randomness of quantum measurement. However, I have different problems concerning quantum measurement. A key step in some quantum algorithms is the measurement at which Nature finds, in a single step, for a given (actually any) integer function f, and randomly chosen y from the range of f, all x such that $f(x) = y$, and then incorporates all such x into a superposition of basic states. I really have problems believing it fully in spite of the fact that the mathematics behind it is perfect once we accept the principles of quantum projective measurement.

CC: Entanglement is an even more esoteric phenomenon.

JG: Again, mathematically the existence of entangled states is very easy to understand. However, when physical consequences are to be considered, the situation is different. Look, a very simple CNOT-gate should be able to process two independent particles in such a way that they get entangled and stay entangled no matter how far away they move. This is extremely hard to believe, though experiments (not really perfect) confirmed entanglement: for example, for photons and atoms at a distance of 144 km (as recently demonstrated, see `http://arxiv.org/pdf/1403.0009.pdf`) — a quite shocking recent experimental outcome. In addition, using the process called entanglement swapping, one can make entangled particles that have never interacted.

CC: In spite of that entanglement is an important information processing resource.

JG: Some even say that it is a new gold mine of the physical world because entanglement allows creating such events, impossible in the classical world, such as quantum teleportation, to create quantum algorithms that are faster than any known classical algorithm (for the same problem). Entanglement is a key tool to make some communications, even exponentially, more efficient than what one can classically achieve, to increase the capacity of communication channels, to act as a catalyst and so on. In addition, entanglement allows the creation of pseudo-telepathy. Asher Peres pointed out nicely that "entanglement allows quantum magicians to do things no classical magician can do".

CC: Possibly the most controversial issue concerning entanglement is the existence of non-local correlations created by a measurement of entangled states. Could we discuss this counter-intuitive phenomenon?

JG: Not many realise that "physics was non-local since Newton times with the exception of the period 1915–1925", as recently Nicolas Gissin pointed out. In 1915, Albert Einstein came up with the theory of relativity that denies the existence of immediate non-local effects, but quantum mechanics then brought certain non-local effects back into the mainstream physics.

CC: Newton himself noticed counter-intuitive consequences of his theory of gravity.

JG: Yes, for example, Newton realised that according to his theory if a stone is moved on the moon, then the weights of all of us, here on the earth, are immediately modified. However, he actually believed that the reason is an imperfection of his theory. His words on this subject are very interesting: "that gravity should be innate, inherent and essential to matter, so that one body may act upon another at a distance through a vacuum, without the mediation of any thing else, by and through which their action and force may be conveyed from one to another, is to me so great an absurdity, that I believe no man who has in philosophical matters a competent faculty of thinking, can ever fall unto it. Gravity must be caused by an agent acting constantly according to certain laws, but whether this agent be material or immaterial, I have left to the consideration of my readers."

CC: Newton's observation may further complicate attempts to lose weight... More seriously, Leibniz criticised Newton's theory of gravity as a revival of the "occult properties" of medieval philosophy. However, quantum non-locality is different. It does not allow superluminal communication and therefore it does not contradict relativity. Did Einstein realise that? Can we have stronger correlations than those induced by entanglement without contradicting the relativity theory?

JG: There have been many interesting recent developments in entanglement and non-locality. For example, Methot and Scarani in *quant-ph/0601210* pointed out that there are good reasons to consider quantum entanglement and quantum non-locality as two independent resources. Namely, they have shown that for the main known measures of non-locality, not maximally entangled states are maximally non-local. However, the main new impulse for the study of non-locality came from the introduction of so-called PR-boxes by Popescu and Rohrlich in a 1997 paper that started to attract attention only fairly recently.

CC: The introduction of PR-boxes was an unexpectedly stimulating idea.

JG: They were intended as a toy tool that demonstrates (in a reasonable sense) a non-locality stronger than quantum non-locality which does not contradict relativity. PR-boxes are easy to describe. Indeed, a PR-box can be seen as consisting of two black boxes operated by two (very) distant parties that cannot have any direct communication. If one party, say A, puts on the input of its subbox a (random) bit x_A, then it gets, immediately, as an output, a random bit y_A. The same for other party, B. However, in spite of the fact that each of the inputs and outputs are random, the outputs should always be correlated with inputs as follows: $x_A \cdot x_B = (y_A \oplus y_B)$.

PR-boxes could be very powerful. Indeed, having enough of them we could have unconditionally secure bit commitment and, moreover, each distributed computation of a Boolean function could be done using only one bit of communication, something no one could believe. This quantum communication complexity result implies that PR-boxes cannot exist physically. This result was again one of the impressive contributions of the complexity theory to quantum mechanics.

CC: Quite interesting! Counterfactual effects are other mysterious phenomena.

JG: I see them as another indication that something may not be OK in our understanding of the physical world. Counterfactual effects allow, for example, for the possibility to get the result of a quantum computation without actually performing the computation. O. Hosten, M.T. Rakher, J.T. Barreiro, N.A. Peters and P.G. Kwiat have presented the first demonstration of counterfactual computation using an optical-based quantum computer (see *Nature* 439, 2006).

CC: A deeper understanding of all these phenomena is a challenge for physics.

JG: And for informatics too. There are of course many other very big challenges. Let me mention some of them[3]: is our universe computable? Efficiently computable? Is our world a polynomial or an exponential place?

---

[3]As pointed out by Scott Aaronson.

CC: Could our world be exponential?

JG: Well, without believing in the exponentiality of our physical world we could have problems explaining some experiments already performed. We do not consider as feasible a computation requiring an exponentially growing number of steps, but no one actually seems to complain to have exponentially large probability distributions. The situation with exponentially is therefore far from obvious and far from simple. As pointed out by Goldreich, we may need more realistic complexity models of quantum computations and, I think, also of communication.

CC: Can we really build a powerful quantum computer?

JG: This challenge is an important current research agenda for physics and informatics. Could it happen that quantum mechanics "breaks down" before factoring large integers? Landauer was perhaps the first sceptic and his statement, "one will need more than rain to stop this parade" reflects the feelings of his time, but these feelings keep coming back again and again.

CC: Why "quantum mechanics could break down before factoring very large integers"?

JG: There are many arguments to think this way. From the history of physics one can extrapolate that each theory has its limits and therefore one could expect that current quantum mechanics does not hold for scales which are too small or too by. Some believe that the size of measuring devices will have to grow exponentially. In addition, there are people who believe that we cannot fight decoherence and theoretical results which claim that if the reliability of elementary gates and "wires" reaches a certain threshold, then quantum information processing can be done in any time and space distance; they are wrong or the results have been improperly interpreted.

CC: By the way, how did you get involved in quantum information processing and the idea to write the book *Quantum Computing*?

JG: In 1989, after being appointed as the chairman of the newly created IFIP Specialist Group on Foundations of Computing (SGFCS 14), I worked out a very ambitious and idealistic programme on how SGFCS 14 could support the development of TCS. One of my suggestions was to create a working group "Informatics and Physics". No one complained, but such an idea turned out to be too much ahead of its time. In 1992 and 1993, during my three-year visit to the University of Hamburg, I ran, together with Manfred Kudlek, a physicist by education, a seminar "Informatics and Physics". One of the papers we discussed was Deutsch's paper where the model of a quantum Turing machine was introduced... To make a long story short, in 1997–1999 I wrote, partly on the beach in Nice, my book *Quantum Computing* that appeared in 1999 as both the first monograph and textbook in the field.[4] Initially the book was intended to be just a web chapter of my 730 page-book *Foundations of Computing* which appeared in 1997. This was the beginning of a long and, for me successful, story.

CC: In 2001 you initiated and organised, in Tokyo, the Asia Quantum Information Science Conference (AQIS). Since then you have been in charge of this annual and very successful conference. You have spent a lot of time in Asia countries to promote AQIS. How did all that happen?

JG: After coming back from my two-year position at the University of Minnesota, in 1971 I initiated two large conferences in Czechoslovakia, SOFSEM and MFCS, that still occur annually. After my arrival to Brno I also initiated two smaller conferences and, as the chair of IFIP SGFCS, I initiated, in 1992, the Latin conference in South America.

AQIS originated in quantum research project Erato Quantum Information Processing. During these years I visited Asian countries more than 40 times, gave more than 90 talks, got to know new and very interesting cultures with beautiful art...

---

[4]It was translated into Japanese in 2003.

CC: Could we now discuss the relations between physics and informatics. My first question is what should informaticians learn from physicists?

JG: I see three main directions: (1) physics sells itself better and in a more mature way, (2) physics is better organised and (c) physics has a better and more mature publication policy.

CC: What can physics learn from informatics?

JG: On a very general level, one can say that informatics offers (quantum) physics paradigms, concepts and results that allows physicists to reshape their ideas of reality and to revise their concepts of position and speed, cause and effect...

CC: We started our discussion with an observation that the concept of information plays such an important role nowadays for physics and our understanding of the physical world. A similar situation may apply to security and related cryptographic concepts. Is there an emerging security science and technology?

JG: I would also like to foresee a science not only for security providing technologies, but as a really fundamental science. And not only that.

It is well known throughout the history of mankind and can be seen, in a very simplified form, that it consists of the following three eras. Observe that their descriptions differ basically only by one word. The three magic words are *food, energy* and *information.*

Neolithic era: man learned how to make use of the potential provided by the biological world to have *food* available in a sufficient amount and whenever needed.

Industrial era: man learned how to make use of the laws and limitations of the physical world to have *energy* available in a sufficient amount and whenever needed.

Information era: man is learning how to make use of the laws and limitations of the information world to have *information* available in a sufficient amount and whenever needed.

In this context the following question arises: what can we expect to have as "being" in the fourth era to come? Of course, this is hard to predict. *Artificial* (worlds, intelligence, life…)? That may be the case, but I would like to foresee the fourth coming era as one in which the key concepts are those of security, safety, privacy, anonymity and so on. Modern cryptography, broadly understood, is the key science behind it.

CC: Why is cryptography so difficult?

JG: The general goal of modern cryptography is the construction of schemes which are robust against malicious attempts to deviate from a prescribed functionality. The fact that *an adversary can devise its attacks after the scheme has been specified* makes the design of such schemes very difficult — schemes should be secure under all possible attacks. It is very difficult to specify a cryptographic scheme with sufficient precision to ensure it's perfectly secure.

CC: We have several concepts of security.

JG: Correct: informational security — an enemy does not have enough information to break the scheme; computational security — an enemy cannot have enough computational power to break the scheme and so-called unconditional security — an enemy cannot break the scheme, due to physical laws, no matter how much computational power she/he has.

CC: How successful actually is our "fight" for security?

JG: In this area we have a constant fight between "good" and "bad". Both sides are trying to (maximally) use whatever science and technology bring us. Adi Shamir said that in security *"we are winning battles, but losing wars"*. One of the key issues is that society still has problems to realise and must accept that security is very costly, requires sophisticated tools, and we have to pay for it with time and freedom.

CC: Please highlight a simple result in quantum cryptography.

JG: Unconditionally secure generation of classical keys and the impossibility of having unconditional secure bit commitment are theoretical highlights. However, even more surprising, at least for me, is that using a simple quantum version of a one-time pad cryptosystem one needs only two bits to perfectly hide any qubit, even if its specification requires an infinite amount of classical bits.

CC: How about relations between cryptographic concepts and foundational issues of quantum mechanics?

JG: One of the big things of interest to foundational people is whether we can derive quantum mechanics from some simple axioms that have a natural physical, or information processing-based, interpretation. Fuchs and Brassard suggested considering as axioms (a) the existence of unconditionally secure cryptographic key generation and (b) the impossibility of secure bit commitment.

CC: At first glance, it seems odd that quantum mechanics could be derived from the axioms (a) and (b).

JG: Actually, it is not. Look, unconditionally secure key generation is possible only if the no-cloning theorem holds and quantum measurement causes a disturbance of quantum states. Unconditionally secure bit commitment is impossible only in the case where we have correlations similar to those quantum entanglement provides. And here we are.

CC: You have used several times the term "unconditionally secure". What does it mean? Is the goal to get *perfect* or *unconditional* security (anonymity, privacy, authentication) unachievable as perfect/unconditional security cannot exist in the same way as pure/perfect/true randomness was proved to be vacuous?

JG: The often used term "unconditional security" in connection with quantum generation of classical random keys is actually misleading. It sells very well, but its real meaning has actually very little to do with perfection. A more correct statement is that *undetectable eavesdropping is not possible (unless you break some law of current physics) when quantum means are used to generate a classical*

*binary key that would be perfectly random and an eavesdropper would
have received zero information about the generated key.* The terms
"detectability", "possibility" and "amount of the received information" are actually meant only in an asymptotic way, that is, they go
exponentially to zero with respect to the size of the generated key.
In short, the usual formulation is actually false but let laymen get
the truth "almost" correctly.

CC: In a presentation titled "Crypto Won't Save You" at the
AusCERT Conference (May 2014) my colleague Dr P. Gutmann
demonstrated — with a variety of examples, from Amazon Kindle to
the Sony Playstation and Microsoft Xbox consoles — that the weakest point of cryptography is typically in its implementation rather
than in the maths itself. Hackers have been successful not because
of weak cryptography, but due to poor deployment of security mechanisms, which were bypassed by attackers. His message was: "no
matter how strong the crypto was, the attackers walked around it."

JG: Correct, and the situation is getting worse fast. R. Rivest, a
security guru and the Turing Prize recipient, said in 2004: "in security
we won some battles, but we are losing the war". The fact that it is
harder and harder to make important information processing systems
secure creates enormous danger for society. Security can be broken
on many levels and surprisingly also on the physical level. This starts
to be fully realised...

CC: We can therefore expect interesting developments at the intersection between informatics and physics.

JG: Of course, and at the end of our discussion I would only like to
mention several citations to illustrate how the views of physics and
the physical world keep changing. For Democritus (400 BC) *"nothing exists except atoms and empty space; everything else is opinion"*
while for Rutherford (1912) *"all science is either physics or stamp
collecting."* My position is that *"physics is not the only science capable of producing a deep understanding of physical world. Informatics
can and should help. Or, even, it should take the initiative."*

CC: Are you saying that informatics should work on almost all key problems of science? Is this not too ambitious?

JG: Yes and no or no and yes, both to some extent. However, this is not a lack of modesty. And also nothing is very new in science. Here is an example. Physics keeps being seen by many as the science with an impact on almost everything of importance and some prominent physics institutes take such a view of physics. Once we accept that informatics is of equal if not more importance, the "no borders" view of the field not only has sense but it is the one that could and should be taken, for the benefit of society.

Chapter 16

Giuseppe Longo: Computations and Natural Sciences

Giuseppe Longo, a well-known mathematician and computer scientist, is a former Professor of Mathematical Logic and Theory of Computing, at the University of Pisa (Italy) and, since 1990, Directeur de Recherches at (CNRS) and at the École Normale Supérieure in Paris. Professor Longo has extensively published in many areas including logic and computability, type theory, category theory and their applications to computer science, and interfaces between mathematics, physics, biology, and the philosophy of mathematics. His current work focuses on theories of organisms, in conjunction with evolutionary theories. Since 2013, he is also Adjunct Professor at the Department of Integrative Physiology and Pathobiology, Tufts University School of Medicine, Boston.

Giuseppe Longo is the editor of the book series "Visions des sciences", *Hermann, Paris, and is serving as an editor to the following academic journals:* "Mathematical Structures in Computer Science" *(editor-in-chief),* "Information and Computation", "Theoretical Informatics and Applications", "JUCS", "La Nuova Critica", "The European Review", "Journal of Mind Theory" *and* "Biology Forum". *Professor Longo has supervised 33 (research-oriented) master's theses and 19 PhD theses. He has been an invited lecturer at 40 international conferences and has given more than 160 seminar talks at universities or research institutions in Europe, US and Asia. Professor Longo has been a member of Academia Europaea since 1992.*

CC: Your academic career has taken you from Pisa (where you graduated *"Laurea"* (*cum laude*) in mathematics and then spent 15 years as an academic) to the US (UC Berkeley, MIT and Carnegie Mellon for three years) and then to the École Normale Supérieure (ENS) in Paris (since 1989, as an invited professor). How enriching have these moves been?

GL: Learning from others, the exchange with others is crucial, in scientific work. Very few researchers can do relevant work without interaction. I learned a lot from these very enriching contexts, beginning with the extraordinary *milieu* of mathematics and informatics in Pisa, in the 1970s and 1980s, and the subsequent American experience. Some collaborations, in particular at MIT and Carnegie Mellon, but also in Britain (R. Hindley) and Holland (H. Barendregt) were fundamental for me. And then there is the complex network of interactions with colleagues of three disciplines I am enjoying in Paris, in particular, with the physicists F. Bailly and T. Paul. The main lesson I try to give to my students is that "two interacting brains think and produce much more than the double". But collaborating is very hard: good researchers are very careful in choosing collaborators and the exchange itself is difficult, in particular the interdisciplinary exchange.

There is a growing fashion instead in the use of words referring to "competition" in research. But this is not how science goes: the difficult and productive side is collaborating, exchanging, learning from others and...to go further on, together. If, time to time, one has to compete for finite resources or for a position, this is part of the game, not the purpose nor the joy of science.

Stressing competition of teams and individuals is a real disaster for scientific research. And it is largely borrowed from the current cultural hegemony of the financial markets, where traders are in continual competition and they compete on a mostly empty economic/productive content. As a further imitation, many institutions entrust "independent evaluation agencies" (like those that evaluated Enron in 2001 with the highest score and Lehman Brothers in 2008, until the "week before" their default...) for judging scientific work. And self-appointed, "science independent" agents provide automatic indexes for classifying researchers. I proposed an "Editor's Note: Bibliometrics and the Curators of Orthodoxy" (downloadable from my web page) for Mathematical Structures in Computer Science, the CUP journal I direct, on this theme. It was approved by all 34 members of the board, from 11 different countries. A more recent invited lecture on these issues (and bibliometrics), at an Academia Europaea meeting, is downloadable from my web page. Yes, in contrast to competition, collaboration and exchange are fundamental and moving enhances them greatly.

CC: Moving is a joy and a pain. How hard was it for your family, especially, your daughter?

GL: Hard, but stimulating. My wife started a new career, first by a master's degree in Pittsburgh, when I was teaching at CMU, then a PhD in Paris, finally a university position in France, but this was tough on her. My daughter moved between the age of 5 and 8 between three very different school systems (US, Italy, France), not easy for a child. Now she is trilingual, though, and she can... "adjust" to almost any life context. And she is completing a beautiful thesis on Italian *Quattrocento* paintings, in Paris, with very frequent trips to Italy.

CC: We share two main interests: incompleteness and randomness. Let's talk about incompleteness first.

GL: OK, but I prefer to tackle the issue by relating it to some mathematics of physics, in a preliminary way. In a short note in 2001, I suggested that Poincaré's three-body theorem is an epistemological predecessor of Gödel's undecidability result, in particular because Hilbert's completeness conjecture is a meta-mathematical revival of Laplace's idea of the predictability of formally (equationally) determined systems. For Laplace, once the equations are given, you can completely derive the future states of affairs (with some, preserved, approximation). Or, more precisely, in *"Le système du monde"*, he claims that the mathematical mechanics of moving particles, one by one, two by two, three by three... compositionally and *completely* "covers" or makes the entire universe understandable. And, as for celestial bodies, by this progressive mathematical integration, "we should be able to deduce all facts of astronomy", he says.

The challenge, for a closer comparison, is that Hilbert was speaking about *purely mathematical "yes or no"* questions, while unpredictability shows up in the relation between a physical system and a mathematical set of equations (or evolution function). That is, in order to give unpredictability, Poincaré's negative result, as he called his proof of the non-analyticity of the equations for a three-body system, needs a reference to physical measure. Measure is always, in classical (and relativistic) physics, an interval, that is an approximation. And non-observable initial fluctuations may give *observable*, thus deterministic, but unpredictable, evolutions, in the presence, typically, of the non-linearity of mathematical modelling (main reasons: the initial interval expands exponentially — this is measured by Lyapunov exponents — and it is "mixed" — its order is not preserved; the choice of a path, in the presence of a bifurcation, depends on minor fluctuations).

In order to relate consistently unpredictability to undecidability, one needs to effectivise the dynamical spaces and measure theory (along the lines of Lebesgues's measure), the loci for dynamic randomness. This allows having a sound and purely mathematical treatment of the epistemological issue (and obtaining a convincing correspondence between unpredictability and undecidability). I will go back to the work on this while answering your next question, on randomness.

As for Gödel's incompleteness, when studying Poincaré's theorem, I understood that the two results also share a methodological point: they both destroy the conjecture of predictability/completeness from inside. Poincaré does not need to refer concretely to a physical process that would not be predictable, by measuring it "before and after". He shows, from the pure analysis of the equations, that the resulting bifurcations and homoclinic intersections (between stable and unstable manifolds) lead to deterministic unpredictability (of course, the equations are derived in reference to three bodies in their gravitational fields, similarly as Peano axioms are invented in reference to the ordered structure of numbers). Gödel as well, by playing a purely formal game, formally constructs an undecidable sentence, with no reference whatsoever, in the *statements* and *proofs* in his 1931 paper, to "semantics", "truth" or alike, that is to the underlying mathematical structure.

Modern "concrete incompleteness" theorems (that is, Gödel–Girard's normalisation, Paris–Harrington or Friedman–Kruskal theorems) resemble instead Laskar's results of the 1990s, where "concrete unpredictability" is shown for the solar system. In reference to the *best possible astronomical measures*, Laskar shows that the evolution of our beloved system is provably unpredictable, globally, beyond one million years (100 years, when only considering earth). Similarly, concrete incompleteness for arithmetic was given by proving (unprovability and) truth over the (standard) model. More generally, I view the incompleteness of our formal (and equational) approaches to knowledge a fundamental epistemological issue. And this is why we permanently need new science: by inventing new principles of conceptual constructions we change directions, propose new intelligibilities, grasp or organise new fragments of the world. There is no such a thing as "the final solution to the foundational problem" in mathematics (as Hilbert dreamed — a true nightmare), nor in other sciences.

And finally, then, my other current interest, biology. The "incompleteness" of the molecular theories for understanding life phenomena is a similar issue. There is no way to completely understand/derive embryogenesis nor phylogenesis (evolution) by only looking at the four letters of the bases of DNA (the formal language of molecular biology). More precisely, in this very different context, "completeness" philosophically corresponds to the largely financed myth that the *stability* and the *organisation* of DNA, and the subsequent molecular cascades, completely determine the *stability* and the *organisation* of the cell and the organism. This is false, since the *stability* and the *organisation* of the cell and the organism causally contribute to the *stability* and the *organisation* of the DNA and the subsequent molecular cascades. Thus the analysis of the global structure of the cell (and the organism) must parallel the absolutely crucial molecular analyses. The hard philosophical point to explain now, to my friends in molecular biology, is that "incomplete" does not mean useless: formal systems are incomplete but . . . very useful, of course (well, I worked most of my life on type theory, *lambda*-calculus and related formal systems. . .). The point is that we badly also need an autonomous theory of organisms and further develop the (fantastic) Darwinian theory of evolution.

By the way, randomness plays a crucial role in evolution, but also, and it is increasingly believed so, in embryogenesis. But. . . what kind of randomness? Physics, classical/quantum, proposes two distinct notions of randomness. . . .

CC: What aspects of randomness interest you?

GL: Classical (physical) randomness is the unpredictability of deterministic systems in finite time (dice trajectories are perfectly determined: they follow the Hamiltonian, a unique geodetics; yet, they are very sensitive to initial and contour conditions. . . : it is, in general, not worth writing the equations). Now, Martin-Löf's (and Chaitin's) number-theoretic randomness is for infinite sequences. How would this yield a connection between Poincaré's unpredictability and Gödel's undecidability?

As I said, physical randomness, as deterministic unpredictability, is a matter at the "equations/process" interface by measurement and shows up at finite time. Yet, physical randomness may also be expressed as a limit or asymptotic notion and, by this, it may be soundly turned into a purely mathematical issue: this is Birkhoff's ergodicity (for any observable, limit time averages coincide with space averages). That is, physical randomness, as a mathematical limit property, lives in formal systems of equations or evolution functions: in their measurable spaces, they may engender infinite random trajectories or generic points, in the ergodic sense. And this sense applies in (weakly chaotic) dynamical systems, within the frame of Poincaré's geometry of dynamical systems.

As for algorithmic randomness, Martin-Löf randomness is a "Gödelian" notion of randomness, as it is based on the recursion theory and yields a strong form of undecidability for infinite 0–1 sequences (in short, a sequence is random if it passes all *effective statistical tests*). Recently, M. Hoyrup and C. Rojas, under Galatolo's and my supervision, proved that dynamic randomness (*a la* Poincaré, thus, but at the purely mathematical limit, in the ergodic sense), in suitable *effectively given* measurable dynamical systems, is equivalent to (a generalisation of) Martin-Löf randomness (Schnorr's randomness). This is a non-obvious result, also based on a collaboration with P. Gacs, spreading along two "entangled" doctoral dissertations (defended in June 2008, a nice example of how two collaborating individuals may produce more than the "double").

In the last few years, I have been teaching a course at ENS, in Paris (and once in Rome III), along these parallel lines, from Poincaré and Gödel to algorithmic randomness. The course (the program and one video-recording is on my web page) was first organised with a colleague in quantum mechanics at ENS, Thierry Paul: we alternated one two-hour lecture each and he introduced the Einstein–Podolsky–Rosen (EPR) paradox (Einstein's and others' paper on entanglement) and its modern consequences, quantum computing. As Thierry moved to *Polytéchnique*, I took up part of his lectures since we had been doing some joint work on a logical and (modern) physical understanding of EPR. By the way, EPR is dedicated to prove the incompleteness (!) of QM. Their argument is (beautiful, but) wrong as it is based on the impossibility of entanglement.

As for quantum randomness, note that now, because of entanglement, it differs from classical: if two classical dice interact and then separate, the probabilistic analysis of their values are independent. When two quanta interact and form a "system", they can no longer be separated: measures on them give correlated probabilities of the results (mathematically, they violate Bell's inequalities).

CC: What is the link between computability, continuity and the Church–Turing thesis?

GL: The idea hinted at in the book and in several papers with Bailly and Paul, two physicists, is that the mathematical structures, constructed for the intelligibility of physical phenomena, according to their continuous (mostly in physics) or discrete nature (generally in computing), may propose different understandings of Nature. In particular, the "causal relations", as structures of intelligibility (we "understand Nature" by them), are mathematically related to the use of the continuum or the discrete and may deeply differ (in modern terms: they induce different symmetries and symmetry-breakings, see a 2014 paper with Montévil).

But what discrete (mathematical) structures are we talking about? I believe that there is one clear mathematical definition of "discrete": a structure is *discrete* when the discrete topology of it is "natural". Of course, this is not a formal definition, but in mathematics we all know what "natural" means. For example, one can endow Cantor's real line with discrete topology, but this is not "natural" (you do not do much with it); on the other hand, the integer numbers or a digital database are naturally endowed with discrete topology (even though one may have good reasons to work with them also under a different structuring).

Church's thesis, introduced in the 1930s after the functional equivalence proofs of various formal systems for computability, only concerns computability over integers or discrete data types. As such, it is an extremely robust thesis: it ensures that any sufficiently expressive *finitistic formal system* over integers (a Hilbertian-type logic-formal system) computes exactly the recursive functions, as defined by Gödel, Kleene, Church, Turing... This thesis therefore emerged within the context of mathematical logic, as grounded on formal systems for arithmetic computations, on discrete data types.

The very first question to ask is the following: If we broaden the formal framework, what happens? If we want to refer to continuous (differentiable) mathematical structures, the extension to consider is to computable real numbers. Are, then, the various formalisms for computability over real numbers equivalent, when they are maximal? An affirmative response could suggest an extension of Church's thesis to computability on "continua". Of course, the computable reals are countably many, but they are dense in the "natural" topology over Cantor's reals, a crucial difference, as we shall see. With this question, we begin to get near to physics, since it is within spatial and often also temporal continuity that we represent dynamical systems, that is, most mathematical models for classical physics. This does not imply that the world is continuous, but only that we have said many things thanks to continuous tools which were very well specified by Cantor (but his continuum is not the only possible one: Lawvere and Bell, say, proposed another without points).

Now, from this equivalence of formalisms, at the heart of Church's thesis, there remains very little when passing to computability over real numbers: the theories proposed are demonstrably different, in terms of computational expressiveness (the classes of defined functions). The various systems (recursive analysis, whose ideas were first developed by Lacombe and Grezgorczyk, in 1955–1957; the Blum, Shub and Smale (BSS), system; the Moore-type recursive real functions; different forms of "analogue" systems, among which threshold neurones, the GPAC...) yield different classes of "continuous" computable functions. Some recent work established links, reductions between the various systems (more precisely: pairwise relations between subsystems and/or extensions), yet, the full equivalence as in the discrete case is lost. Moreover, and this is crucial, these systems have no "universal function" in Turing's sense. And it this, for a fundamental reason, which has to be analysed closely.

If one endows non-trivial space continua with interval topology (the "real" topology), there is no way to have an isomorphism between spaces of different dimensions (see further). This isomorphism, instead, is needed for having the universal function (Turing's universal machine) and, in general, for computability of the discrete. Its work spaces may be of any finite dimension: they are all effectively isomorphic, "Cartesian dimension" does not matter!

This is highly unsuitable for physics. First, dimensional analysis is a fundamental tool (one cannot confuse energy with force, nor with the square of energy...). Second, dimension is a topological invariant, in all space manifolds for classical and relativistic physics. This is shown by the fact that if two such spaces have isomorphic open subsets, then they have the same dimension. This is one of the most beautiful correspondence between mathematics and physics. Take physical measure, which is always an interval (it is approximated, by principle, classically), as a "natural" starting point for the metric (thus, the interval topology), then you *prove* that this crucial notion for physics, dimension, is a topological invariant. Discrete computability destroys this: a cloud of isolated points has no dimension, *per se*, and you may, for all theoretical purposes, encode them on a line. When you have dimension back, in computability over continua, where the trace of the interval topology maintains good physical properties, you lose the universal function and the equivalence of systems. Between the theoretical world of discrete computability and physico-mathematical continua there is a huge gap. One cannot even extend to the second a sound form of Church's thesis. While I believe that one should do better than Cantor as for continua, I would not give a penny for a physical theory where dynamics takes place only on discrete spaces, departing from physical measure, dimensional analysis and the general relevance of dimensions in physics (again, from heat propagation to mean field theory, to relativity theory... space dimension is crucial).

As for the relevance discrete, quantum mechanics it started exactly by the discovery of a key (and unexpected) discretisation of light absorption or the emission spectra of atoms. Then, a few dared to propose a discrete lower bound to measure *action*, that is, of the product energy × time. It is this physical dimension that bares a discrete structure. Clearly, one can then compute, by assuming the relativistic maximum for the speed of light, a Planck's length and time. But in no way are space and time thus organised in small "quantum boxes". And this is the most striking and crucial feature of quantum mechanics: the "systemic" or entanglement effects, which yield an inseparability of observables. No discrete space topology is natural. That is, these quantum effects are the opposite of a discrete, separated organisation of space, while being at the core of its scientific originality. In particular, they motivate quantum computing (as well as our analysis of quantum randomness above). As a matter of fact, Thierry Paul and I claim that the belief in an absolutely separable topology of space continua is Einstein's mistake in EPR.

A final remark. In general, the discrete is not an approximation of classical continua. In even weakly chaotic systems, a difference by approximation (below measure, typically) quickly leads to major (observable) differences in evolution. And the approximation relation is at most reversed. In some, not all, dynamical systems, the "shadowing lemma" holds: for any discrete trajectory, there is a continuous one approximating it. The quantification is the other way a round. This is an important result in numerical analysis, as it guarantees that a discrete trajectory on the screen is not meaningless: one can find a continuous one approximating it. Of course, it does not start with the same initial point, in general.

In summary, continua, Cantorian or not, take care rather well (they are not an absolute) of the approximated nature of physical measure, which is represented as an interval: the unknowable fluctuation is within the interval. Classically, I insist, the relevance of measure is derived from Poincaré's results (changes below measure induce major differences over time). And physical measure is our only form to access "reality". The arithmetising foundation of mathematics went along another (and very fruitful) direction, based on perfectly accessible data types. Poincaré firmly opposed the underlying philosophy of knowledge, by deep, but informal, reflections on "action" in the physical world.

CC: We have entropy and negative entropy. You invented anti-entropy.

GL: Traditionally, information is considered as negentropy (Brillouin). Then, by definition:

(1) the sum of a quantity of information (negentropy) and an equal quantity of entropy gives 0;

(2) information (Shannon, but also Kolmogorov) is "insensitive to coding" (one can "encrypt" and "decrypt" as much as one wishes but the information content will not be lost/gained, in principle).

I believe however, that this notion, of which the applications are numerous, is not sufficient for an analysis of the living state of matter. DNA (usually considered as digital information) is the most important component of the cell, as I said, but it is necessary to analyse the *structure* of the organism, as an observable specific to biological theorisation.

Here, the collaboration with Francis Bailly, a physicist also interested in biology, has been very important. He was actually my teacher in many aspects of natural sciences (Francis recently passed away: a recorded conference in his memory may be accessed from my web page). Concerning biological (morphological) complexity, we have proposed the notion of anti-entropy to define it (or quantify it in terms of complexity of cellular, functional and phenotypical differentiation). In short, biological complexity may be understood as "information specific to the form", including the intertwining and enwrapping of levels of organisation. Its use in metabolic balance equations has produced a certain number of results mentioned in a recent long article (and summarised in the 2014 book with Montévil). We have, in particular, examined systems far from equilibrium and analysed diffusion equations of biomass over biological complexity as anti-entropy, following Schrödinger's "operational method" in quantum mechanics. This has enabled operating a mathematical reconstruction of this diffusion, which corresponds to the paleontological data presented by Gould for the evolution of species.

Anti-entropy is compatible with information as negentropy, but it must be considered as a *strict* extension, in a logical sense, of the thermodynamics of entropy. Typically, the production of entropy and that of anti-entropy are summed in an "extended critical singularity", an organism, never zero, in contrast to Brillouin's and others' negentropy. As it is linked to spatial forms, anti-entropy is *"sensitive to coding"*, contrarily to digital information (it depends on the dimensions of embedding manifolds, on folds, on singularities...).

In short, over the last six or more years, in several collaborations and by (co-)supervising several theses, we have compared physical (dynamic) randomness with algorithmic randomness (at the centre of *algorithmic theories of information*); we worked on a theory of "extended criticality" (living objects persist in an "extended critical state"); we have added anti-entropy (a *"geometrical* extension" of the notion of information) to thermodynamic (in)equalities and balance equations; we modelled biological rhythms and time in two-dimensional manifolds, a sort of non-trivial geometrisation of time (and, perhaps, a quite useful one, for the digital simulation of cardiac rhythms, developed by M. Montévil). The scientific finality of this work may also entail some epistemological consequences, I hope: it should participate in the epistemological debate regarding the notion of information, the updating of its theoretical principles, as part of the many existing interactions with physics and biology. A possible outcome of these interactions could be to start thinking about... the next machine. Aren't we a little tired of this, nice, but mathematically rather old "discrete data types machine"?

CC: Is it possible to summarise the ideas of your book *Mathématiques et Sciences de la Nature. La Singularité Physique du Vivant* (Hermann, Paris, 2006) with F. Bailly? Is there an English version?

GL: Yes, there is a translation in English (*Mathematics and the Natural Sciences: The Physical Singularity of Life*, published in 2011, by Imperial College Press, London). In the book, Francis and I attempt to identify the organising concepts of some physical and biological phenomena, by means of an analysis of the foundations of mathematics and physics, in the aim of unifying phenomena, of bringing different conceptual universes into dialogue. The analysis of the role of "order" and of symmetries in the foundations of mathematics is linked to the main invariants and principles, among which the geodesic principle (a consequence of symmetries), which govern and confer unity to various physical theories. Moreover, we attempt to understand causal structures, a central element of physical intelligibility, in terms of symmetries and their breakings. The importance of the mathematical tool is also highlighted, enabling us to grasp the differences in the models for physics and biology which are proposed by continuous and discrete mathematics, such as computational simulations.

As for biology, being particularly difficult and not as thoroughly examined at a theoretical level, we propose a "unification by concepts", an attempt which should always precede mathematisation, that we later tried in some papers. This constitutes an outline for unification also basing itself upon the highlighting of conceptual differences, of complex points of passage, of technical irreducibilities of one field to another. Indeed, a monist point of view such as ours should not make us blind: we, the living objects, are surely just big bags of molecules or, at least, this is our main metaphysical assumption. The point though is: which *theory* can help us to better understand these bags of molecules, as they are, indeed, rather funny (singular?), from the physical point of view. Technically, this singularity is expressed by the notion of "extended criticality", a notion that logically extends the pointwise critical transitions in physics. Further work is summarised in the book with M. Montévil (*Perspectives on Organisms: Biological Time, Symmetries and Singularities*, Springer, 2014).

CC: I like this statement: "Further work is summarised..." in a book.

GL: The idea is to work towards a theory of organisms analogue and along the theory of evolution, where ontogenesis could be considered as part of phylogenesis. As a matter of fact, the latter is made out of "segments" of the first: phylogenesis is the "sum" of ontogenetic paths and they should be made intelligible by similar principles. To this aim, we look at ontogenesis from different perspectives: the peculiar role and structure of time, the relevance of critical transitions, the increasing complexity of many phenotypes in evolution, the structure of causality in phylogenesis and ontogenesis. By this, we tried to shed some light on the unity of the organism from different points of view, yet constantly keeping that unity as a core invariant. As a matter of fact, the analysis of *invariance*, as the result of theoretical symmetries, and of *symmetry changes*, is a key theme of the approach in the book.

CC: In a recent paper you rightly say that:

> "... randomness ... is not in the world, it is in the interface between our theoretical descriptions and 'reality' as accessed by measurement. Randomness is unpredictability with respect to the intended theory and measurement."

Randomness like determinism, chance, number and speed are only theoretical concepts with no *direct* counterpart in Nature.

GL: These concepts remarkably organise Nature. And this is far from arbitrary: our knowledge construction is designed by us on a phenomenal veil, by a concrete friction on the world and "reality" canalises our "endeavour towards knowledge", to put it in Herman Weyl's words. So, our theoretical proposals may be incomplete for several and different reasons: unpredictability, whether deterministic, like in classical dynamics, or indeterministic (the determination of a law or amplitude of probability), is a form of "incompleteness", in a broad sense. It is so by principle, because the approximated nature of classical measurement and quantum indetermination are fundamental principles of the interface between us and the world. We have no other form of access to the world, but by measurement, and this is what it is: always approximated or indeterminate. Then the theory says what unpredictability or randomness is, exactly, in that intended frame: classical deterministic unpredictability, quantum indetermination... or the one that future theories may give us.

CC: How does randomness appear in biology?

GL: In some writings, in collaboration, I focused on the various possible notions and instances of this essential component of biological dynamics, contingency as randomness. Randomness in biology deserves a proper analysis, along the lines, but well beyond the many deep ones, carried out within the various theories of the inert. Classical and quantum physics each propose different forms of randomness, as we know. These, in our view, are both relevant for understanding biological randomness, as they are both present at the molecular level, at least.

In short, in the classical Darwinian perspective on selection, the unfit or the less adapted are eliminated. However, low or high adaptations are relative and may depend, of course, on the possible presence of other avatars of competitive species or variants within a population which, locally and on specific aspects, may perform better or worse in reproduction, possibly in correlation to access to limited resources. However, even minor changes in the environment, undetectable at any particular time, may subsequently show that different causes may render the organism or species more or less adapted, adaptation standing as the only general criteria for natural selection. And in no way, by looking at one specific evolutionary moment, may one predict which individuals or species will be less or more adapted in thousands or millions of years.

So, we compared the different notions of randomness in physics with those implicit in current biology, for the purposes of the study of contingency in the two main biological processes, development and evolution. Quantum and "quantum-like" effects may happen jointly to classical dynamics and their proper forms of randomness, i.e., they take place simultaneously and affect each other via intracellular processes, as shown by robust evidence today. Moreover, different levels of organisation, in a multicellular organism (as well as in "colonies" of unicellular ones), may interact and produce stabilising and destabilising effects. This form of integration and regulation also includes random phenomena or amplification of randomness, and we called it "bio-resonance", an analogy to the well-established notion of resonance in physical non-linear dynamics.

CC: What is the relation between randomness and diversity in biology?

GL: Small differences may also be present in the DNA, at each cell reproduction. The sensitivity to the context at transition may contribute to cell differentiation; it surely contributes to diversity (in unicellular, first, but also in multicellular organisms). Note that disorder may go from molecules (mutations, typically, but also proteome changes or irregular split) to the whole organism, the latter being the key component for the exploration of diversity, proper for instance of the Evo-Devo systems.

Moreover, the analysis of randomness, in biology, cannot be isolated from a context: it is always a more or less highly canalised phenomenon. Even the Brownian motion of molecules, in a cell, is highly canalised by membranes and compartmentalisation or even by the coherent structure of water. The role of randomness is a crucial and fully general point. In particular, the many-folded forms of randomness, which manifest themselves within integrating and regulating activity, are at the core of variability and diversity, thus of evolution and development. That is, they also contribute to the peculiar stability of phylogenesis and ontogenesis. As a matter of fact, these are possible since they are adaptive and constantly explore possibly diverging paths, under different and ever-changing constraints.

Our work opens the way to a new conceptual and mathematical challenge: describing biological randomness also as unpredictability of the very phase space, well beyond the existing analyses in physics, where randomness is given in a predefined space of possibilities (phase space). And this is so, in the presence of dynamics where variability, adaptability and diversity are among the main invariants and contribute to the structural stability of organisms and species. And variability is (largely? only?) a consequence of randomness.

CC: In what sense do you think physical or biological processes "compute"?

GL: The discrete state machines that compute are a remarkable invention, based on a long history. As I hint in the paper "Critique of Computational Reason in the Natural Sciences", this story begins with the invention of the alphabet, probably the oldest experience of discretisation. The continuous song of speech, instead of being captured by the design of concepts and ideas (by recalling "meaning", like in ideograms), is discretised by annotating phonetic pitches, an amazing idea (the people of Altham, in Mesopotamia, 3300 BC). Meaning is reconstructed by the sound, which acts as a compiler, either loud or in silence (but only after the IV century AD we learned to read "within the head", in silence !).

I insist that the crucial feature of alphanumeric discretisation is the invention of a discrete coding structure, which is far from obvious. Think also of the originality of Gödel-numbering, an obvious practice now, but another remarkable invention. Turing's work followed: the logical computing machine (LCM), as he first called it, at the core of our science (right/left, $0, 1 \ldots$). Of course, between the alphabet and Turing, you also have Descartes' "discretisation" of thought (stepwise reasoning, along a discrete chain of intuitive certitudes. . .) and much more.

When, after 1948 or so, Turing again gets interested in physics, he changed the name to his LCM: in the 1950 and 1952 papers, he calls it discrete state machine (this is what matters for its physical behaviour). And twice in his 1950 paper (the "imitation game"), he calls it "Laplacian". Its evolution is theoretically predictable, even if there may be practical unpredictability (too long programs to be grasped, he says).

So, we invented an incredibly stable processor, which, by working on discrete data types, does what it is expected to do. And it iterates, very faithfully. Primitive recursion and portability of software are forms of iterability: iteration and update of a register, do what you are supposed to do, respectively, even in slightly different contexts, over and over again. For example, program the evolution function of the most chaotic strange attractor you know. Push "restart": the digital evolution, by starting on the same initial digits, will follow exactly the same trajectory (on a paper on Turing's imitation game I discuss the simulation of the double pendulum, a chaotic device). This makes no physical sense, but it is very useful (also in meteorology: you may restart your turbulence, exactly, and try to better understand how it evolves. . .). Of course, you may imitate unpredictability by some pseudo-random generator or by. . . true physical randomness, added *ad hoc*. But this is cheating the observer, in the same way Turing's *imitation* of a woman's brain is meant to cheat the observer, not to "model" the brain. He says this explicitly, all the while working in his 1952 paper, at a *model* of morphogenesis, as (non-)linear dynamics. Observe, finally, that our colleagues in networks and concurrency are so good that programming a network is reliable: programs do what they are supposed to do, they iterate and... give you the web page you want, identically, one thousand times, one million times. And this is hard, as physical space-time, which we better understand by continua and continuous approximations, steps in, yet still on discrete data types, which allow perfect iteration.

Those who claim that the universe is a big digital computer, miss the originality of this machine of ours. It is like believing that, when we speak, we produce sequences of letters: this is a cartoon's vision of language and misses the originality of our invention, the alphabet, an early musical notation (Chinese children have a different view: their cartoon bubbles evoke concepts). When we construct computers, we make the far from obvious construction of a reliable, thus programmable, physical device, iterating as we wish and any time we wish, even in networks: this happens very rarely in physics. One should not miss the principles that guided this invention, as well as the principles by which we understand physical dynamics.

By the way, a question for those who claim that the universe is a big Turing machine: are the main physical constants, G, c, h, *computable* (real numbers)? They appear in all equations and all dynamics... Of course, it depends on the choice of the reference system and metrics. So, fix $h = 1$. Then, you have to renormalise all metrics and re-calculate, by equations, dimensional analyses *and* physical measurement, G and c. But physical measurement will always give an interval, as we said, or, in quantum frame, the probability of a value. If one interprets the classical measure interval as a Cantorian continuum, the best way, so far, to grasp fluctuations, then... where are G and c? "Non-computable reals, or even Martin-L" of random reals form a set of Lebesgues measure 1, so... there is a probability of 1 that the main physical constant (except one, the one you prefer) are random reals (an asymptotic game, the one preferred by God, for sure).

Yet, the most striking mistake of many "computationalists" is to say: but, then, some physical processes would super-compute (compute non-computable functions)! No, this is not the point. Most physical processes, simply do not *define* a mathematical function. In order to have a classical process to define a function, you have to fix a time for input, associate a (rational) number to the interval of measure and ... let the process go. Then you wait for the output time and measure again. In order, for the process to define $f(x) = y$, at a rational input x, it must always associate a rational output y. But if you restart, say, your physical double pendulum on x, that is within the interval of the measure which gave you x, a minor (thermal, say) fluctuation, *below that interval* x, will yield a different observable result y' after a very short time. So, a good question would be, instead: consider a physical process that *defines* a (non-trivial) function, is this function computable?

The idea then would be that the process is sufficiently insensitive to initial conditions (some say: robust) as to actually define a function. But, then one should be able to partition the world into little cubes of the smallest size, according to the best measure as for insensitivity (fluctuations below that measure do not affect the dynamics). If the accessible world is considered finite (but... is it?), then one can make a list out of the finite inputoutput relation established by the given process. This is a "program": is it compressible?

As for biology, what can I say? 40% of fecundations in mammals fail (they do not reach a birth): a very bad performance for DNA as a program. While iterability is at the core of software (and hardware) design, our fantastic invention, the key principle for understanding life, at the phenotypic level, is *variability*, a form of non-iterability. It is crucial for evolution, but also ontogenesis, that a cell is never identical to the mother cell. So, the principles of intelligibility are the exact opposite: the failure of lots of fecundations corresponds to the possibility that a mutant better fits a changing environment (affecting the mother's womb, say). Of course, some molecular processes iterate, but there is an increasing tendency to analyse molecular cascades in terms of statistical phenomena (and this is where good computational imitations may help to understand, by some use of pseudo-randomness or by network interactions). This opens the way to an increasing role of epigenetic and, thus, to the relevance of downwards regulating effects, from the cell and the organism to DNA expression.

CC: You argue that incomputability phenomena are more important to physics than computable ones? After all, the laws of physics seem more computable than incomputable?

GL: Your second question refers to the effectiveness of our *mathematical writing* of physical invariants: of course, equations, evolution functions... are given by sums, products, exponents, derivations, integrations... all effective operations. Moreover, no one is crazy enough to put an incomputable real as a coefficient or exponent in an equation (even if h could be so..., so we just take an approximation of it, don't we?). This gives us remarkable approximations and, most often, qualitative information: Poincaré's geometry of dynamical systems or Hadamard's analysis of the geodetic flow on hyperbolic surfaces, do not give predictions, but very relevant global information (by attractors, for example, or regularities in flows... that we beautifully see today, as never before, by fantastic approximations, "shadowed" on our computer screens).

By the way, to those who believe that "nature computes" like Turing in his child's notebook, I would like to ask whether Planck's h is a computable real number. Well, set $h = 1$, then renormalise c, G. As Martin-Löf UTF009A" of-Chaitin random numbers have measure 1 on the reals, I bet that these physical constants are random reals... an asymptotic notion of randomness, thus an infinitary game, the only one adequate to God.

I do not know the (absolute) laws of Nature, but our constructive theorising on the phenomenal veil, at the interface between us and the world. These active constructions are of course effective (we use the alphabet, effective operations and codings, I insist). While predictable processes are not many in Nature: you can predict a few forthcoming eclipses, on a human timescale, but the solar system is chaotic in astronomical terms, as Poincaré proved and Laskar quantified (and computed!). Unpredictable ones are the mathematical and computational challenges. And a computable physical process is, by definition, deterministic and predictable. In order to predict (*predicere*, "to say in advance" in Latin), just "say" or write the corresponding program and compute in advance; more precisely, the results discussed above, by showing the equivalence of unpredictability and (strong) undecidability, and ML-randomness, prove this fact, by logical duality. Unpredictability may pop out in networks and this is because of *physical* space-time (we then make them computable and predictable-reliable by forcing semaphores, handling interleaving. . .). In Nature, many (most, fortunately) processes escape predictions, thus our computations. Fortunately, otherwise there would be no change, nor life in particular: randomness is crucial. And when we compute unpredictable evolutions, we just approximate their initial part, as I said, or give qualitative information, both very relevant tasks. But engineers put more cement than computed, to take care of vibrations below measure. . .

Now, the only mathematical way I know to define randomness, in classical physics, is Birkhoff's ergodicity. But it is very specific (certain dynamics). Otherwise, randomness is given in terms of probability measure. But this is unsatisfactory, as probability gives a *measure* of randomness, not a definition. It is the theory of algorithms, thanks to Martin-Löf, Chaitin and you, that gave a fully general, mathematical, notion of randomness, as a strong form of incomputability, independently (or on top) of the probability theory. Again, physical (classical) randomness is deterministic unpredictability and, by the results above and more in the literature, the role of computational randomness further comes to the limelight. In particular, it provides a very flexible theory of randomness: you can adjust the class of effective randomness tests (Martin-Löf, Schnorr. . . and many more). Our joint hope is that this may help to better grasp, for example, the mathematical difference between classical and quantum randomness.

CC: If all papers and books would be destroyed by a disaster, but you could keep just one, which one would you choose? Why?

GL: I do not think I would survive with this, but, just to give a partly random answer: Weyl's "*Philosophy of Mathematics and of*

Natural Sciences". Along the lines of *"Das Kontinuum"*, it radically departs from the Hilbertian alphabetic myths. Mathematics, actually human thought, for formalists and computationalists, is reducible to the matching and replacement of sequences of letters: no geometric judgements, no association of *gestalts...*, this is why Laplacian mechanics of thought is incomplete. The proof also has a "geometric structure", a remark by Poincaré, and, by this, it is "sensitive to codings". This is also why its formal coding is incomplete. Reasoning is not a chain whose strength is that of the weakest ring, as Descartes claimed, but a network, a rope made of many interlaced wires, as suggested by Peirce, reinforcing each other and coupling to meaning and to forms of life. And Weyl globally develops a deep and broad philosophy of knowledge, well beyond the parody of his views in predicativist or intuitionistic terms.

CC: If all your papers and books were destroyed by a disaster, but you could keep just one, which one would you choose? Why?

GL: The paper on "anti-entropy", where some (minor) aspects of evolution are mathematically described, because... it is the less quoted one (too "strange" a paper) and because, while working at it, I increasingly learned to love Darwin.

Chapter 17

Yuri Manin: My Life Is Not a Conveyor Belt

Professor Yuri Manin,[1] *http://www.mpim-bonn.mpg.de/ node/99, is a member of three institutions based in three different countries: the Max Planck Institut für Mathematik, Bonn, Germany, Steklov Mathematical Institute, Academy of Sciences, Moscow, Russia and Northwestern University, Evanston, USA.*

Professor Manin was educated at Moscow University; his graduate studies were supervised by I.R. Shafarevich. He has obtained famous and important results in extremely diverse mathematical areas — algebraic geometry, number theory, mathematical logic, mathematical physics, and informatics. "The field of quantum computing was first

---

[1]Picture courtesy of Tatiana Plotnikova.

introduced by Yuri Manin in 1980 [2] and Richard Feynman in 1981 [3], [4]".[2]

Professor Manin is not "a monomaniac mathematician, but... a deep scholar with wide interest, for whom penetration into the mystery of knowledge is much more important than professional success".[3] *He has also published extensively in literature, linguistics, mythology, semiotics, physics, computer science, the philosophy of science and the history of culture. His very long list of honours and awards includes invited lectures at universities and congresses,*[4] *prizes, membership in learned academies, honorary degrees and visiting appointments from prestigious organisations around the world. The books* Mathematics and Physics *and* Mathematics as Metaphor *provide a deep insight in his philosophy of science. He has supervised 49 PhD students, some outstanding mathematicians themselves.*

CC: What was your motivation to move from one area to a completely different one, not once, but several times? Did these transitions affect your "productivity" in the short term?

YM: I love mathematics, this great vast realm of human spirit, I am interested in its various aspects, I would like to understand as much of it as I can, and there is no other way than studying and working in various areas in turn. Productivity?? My life is not a conveyor belt, this word is not in my vocabulary.

CC: The inscription (promoted by academic bureaucrats) "publish or perish" is on all graduate schools walls. There is no better rebuttal than your statement: "Productivity? This word is not in my vocabulary".

YM: "Publish or perish" is a joke, of course... And a mild joke with a grain of sadness is the best way to cope with existential anxiety.

---

[2]Wikipedia, "Quantum Computer" https://en.wikipedia.org/wiki/Quantum_ computer.

[3]http://www-history.mcs.st-and.ac.uk/Biographies/Manin.html.

[4]Among them, a plenary and five invited lectures at International Congresses of Mathematics, 1966–2006.

CC: Mathematical logic is not a core subject for the working mathematician. It is not even taught in many mathematics departments: its home nowadays is in philosophy departments and mainly in computer science departments. How did you get interested in mathematical logic?

YM: I started thinking about mathematical logic when I had already published several dozens of research papers in the domains I was trained in (algebraic geometry, number theory) and felt the need to expand my overall view of mathematics. Moreover, it was the time when Matiyasevich made the last decisive step in the proof of the theorem that all enumerable sets are Diophantine. I could easily understand what Diophantine sets were, but enumerable ones required some study. Turning to books and articles on logic, I met again what was already a familiar problem: I could not achieve understanding by just reading, other people's texts did not tell me what I felt I needed to know.

The remedy was also, by this time, well-rehearsed by me: I taught a course on mathematical logic, this time not even in Moscow University where I served as professor (although my principal job was research at the Steklov Institute for Mathematics), but at the Moscow Institute of Electronic Engineering. My notes of the course were published in 1974, and they became the first draft of my book on mathematical logic published by Springer in 1977.

CC: You have developed your own formulation of Kolmogorov complexity in the idiosyncratic book on mathematical logic. In spite of being incomputable, you have successfully applied Kolmogorov complexity to mathematics, physics and linguistics. Your ideas, presented a few years ago at the CiE conference, the largest and arguably most important meeting dedicated to computability theory, have attracted a lot of interest.

YM: But the mathematical theory of computations is interesting *exactly* because it delineates precise boundaries of the computable realm, and most interesting things happen when we cross these boundaries! Kolmogorov complexity turned out to be the great bridge from the land of computable to the vaster realm of mathematics, unconstrained by computability, and, I hope, to physics as well.

I am very happy that during the last several years this vague feeling found justification in three papers of mine, where Kolmogorov complexity plays the role of "energy" in three very different contexts: renormalisation in computation, asymptotic boundaries for error-correcting codes as phase transition curves (joint work with Matilde Marcolli), and quite recently, a mathematical explanation of Zipf's law.[5]

CC: Please explain one result in which Kolmogorov complexity works as "energy".

YM: Consider a finite alphabet A consisting of q letters. An error-correcting block code is a subset $C \subset A^n$, $n \geq 1$ (I am speaking about unstructured codes, but the results I will explain hold, with appropriate modifications, also for linear codes etc.). Each such code C defines a point in the unit square of the plane ($R:=$ *transmission rate*, $\delta:=$ *relative minimal distance*). Now, what will you see if you look at the cloud of *all* code points (in a fixed alphabet)?

In 1981, I proved that this cloud is dense everywhere below the graph of a certain continuous function, $R \leq \alpha_q(\delta)$, whereas above it each graph point is isolated. This curve $R = \alpha_q(\delta)$ ("silver lining" of the cloud) is called *the asymptotic bound*. In dozens of papers various upper/lower estimates of this function were obtained, but up to now, its exact values are unknown (outside the trivial range), and even whether this function is theoretically computable is open.

In our paper, with Matilde, we constructed a partition function on the set of all codes, in the sense of statistical physics, in which the energy of the code is exactly its (logarithmic) Kolmogorov complexity. It turned out that after a simple renaming of coordinates, the asymptotic bound becomes the phase transition curve in the (*temperature, density*) plane.

---

[5]Zipf's law states that in a natural language corpus, the frequency of a word is inversely proportional to its rank in the frequency table.

CC: What led you to think about quantum computing?

YM: First, contemporary computers were electronic devices. They were supposed to produce *exact* results at the level of single bits, hence they had to be designed to suppress quantum effects inherent to any electronic device. Ongoing micro-minituarisation was making this task more and more difficult, so it was natural to think about *using* quantum effects rather than suppressing them.

Second, as I wrote then, *"the quantum configuration space is much more spacious that the relevant classical one: where in classical physics we have N discrete states, in the quantum theory, allowing their superposition, there are about c^N states. The union of two classical systems produces $N_1 N_2$ states, whereas the quantum version has $c^{N_1 N_2}$ ones."*

CC: The ancient Greek poet Archilocus observed that "the fox knows many things, but the hedgehog knows one big thing". For Freeman Dyson, foxes are mathematical birds (who "fly high in the air and survey broad vistas of mathematics out to the far horizon") and hedgehogs are mathematical frogs (who "live in the mud below and... solve problems one at a time"). Mathematics needs both birds and frogs.

Dyson called you a bird. While "globally" this seems to be true, I think that "locally" you have alternated between a bird and a frog. Are you a Francis Bacon's mathematical bee (who "extracts material from the flowers of the gardens and meadows, and digests and transforms it by its own powers")?

YM: The Swiss writer Max Frisch published in 1953 the ironic comedy *"Don Juan oder die Liebe zur Geometrie "*.[6] I find its title a wonderfully concise description of my mathematical personality.

Yes, I am a mathematical Don Juan. I still love all my loves, and when I meet an old flame, she can seduce me once again.

Yes, perhaps, all these loves are just incarnations of my deep love for "geometry" (the latter including algebraic geometry, homotopy topology, quantum field theory... and what not).

---

[6]Don Juan, or the Love of Geometry.

CC: In a memorable interview published in 1998, you said that "the mathematics of the 20th century is best presented around programs". Is this trend visible in the 21st century? Is the same true for computer science?

YM: Probably, it is too early to speak about the trends of the 21st century: imagine an interview on the trends of the 20th century in 1913 ...

But anyway, I see the full of energy development of programmes I most cherished in 20th century mathematics: Grothendieck's vast enterprise expanding in many directions thanks to the efforts of many strong minds; Langlands' program; Turing and von Neumann's programs (each new computer virus is a poisonous descendant of von Neumann's imagination).

CC: The "computer-assisted proofs, as well as computer-unassisted ones, can be good or bad. A good proof is a proof that makes you wiser" is nowadays less controversial than 15 years ago when you made it. How can a computer-assisted proof make you wiser? What about a quantum computer proof?

YM: A good proof starts with a project connecting your expected theorem with other results, opening vistas to interesting variations and generalisations. When you develop a detailed plan of it, it might happen that on the road you will have to make a complete list of some exceptional cases, or marginal situations, in which something is not quite as it is "generally", and that making such a list requires a search in a finite but vast set of *a priori* possibilities.

Then a good computer program that makes this work for you will not spoil the quality of your proof. If the computer is a quantum one, then of course you must additionally convince yourself, and others, that the answer given with a "probability close to one" is in fact a correct one.

CC: A paraphrase by Chris Anderson (in Wired Magazine) falsely attributed to Google's research director Peter Norvig, claims that "all models are wrong, and increasingly you can succeed without them". An example is Google's capability to match ads to content without any knowledge or assumptions about the ads or the content, and to translate languages without actually "knowing" them. Why? Google doesn't know why web page A is better than web page B. However, "if the statistics of incoming links say it is, that's good enough. No semantic or causal analysis is required". From here to the aggressive proclamation of the death of science was just one step: data deluge makes the scientific method obsolete.

YM: I'll start with stressing that we are speaking about the science rather than market managing.

Now, what Chris Anderson calls "the new availability of huge amounts of data" by itself is not very new: after the spreading of printing, astronomic observatories, scientific laboratories and statistical studies, the amount of data available to any visitor of a big public library was always huge, and studies of correlations proliferated for at least the last two centuries.

Charles Darwin himself collected the database of his observations and the result of his pondering over it was the theory of evolution.

Even if the sheer volume of data has by now grown by several orders of magnitude, this is not the gist of Anderson's rhetoric.

What Anderson actually wants to say is that human beings are now — happily! — free from thinking over these data. Allegedly, computers will take this burden upon themselves, and will provide us with correlations — replacing the old-fashioned "causations" (that I prefer to call scientific laws) — and expert guidance.

Leaving aside such questions as how "correlations" might possibly help us understand the structure of universe or predict the Higgs boson, I would like to quote the precautionary tale from J. Groopman, *The Body and the Human Progress, New York Review of Books*, Oct. 27, 2011:

"[...] *in 2000 Peter C. Austin, a medical statistician at the University of Toronto, and his colleagues conducted a study of all 10,674,945 residents of Ontario aged between 18 and 100. Residents were randomly assigned to different groups, in which they were classified according to their astrological signs. The research team then searched through more than 200 of the most common diagnoses of hospitalisation until they identified two where patients under one*

astrological sign had a significantly higher probability of hospitaliza-
tion compared to those born under the remaining signs combined:
Leos had a higher probability of gastrointestinal haemorrhage while
Sagittarians had a higher probability of fracture of the upper arm
compared to all other signs combined.

It is thus relatively easy to generate statistically significant but
spurious correlations when examining a very large data set and a
similarly large number of potential variables. Of course, there is no
biological mechanism whereby Leos might be predisposed to intesti-
nal bleeding or Sagittarians to bone fracture, but Austin notes, 'It is
tempting to construct biologically plausible reasons for observed sub-
group effects after having observed them.' Such an exercise is termed
'data mining', and Austin warns, 'our study therefore serves as a
cautionary note regarding the interpretation of findings generated by
data mining' [...]".

Hence my answer to Anderson's question: "what can science learn
from Google" is very straightforward: "think! Otherwise no Google
will help you."

CC: Ramsey's theory has shown that complete disorder (true randomness) is an impossibility. Every large database (of numbers,
points or objects) necessarily contains a highly regular pattern. Most
patterns are not computable. Can content-based correlations be distinguished from Ramsey-type correlations?

YM: I am not an expert. I did not wander far away from the noto-
rious motto[7] about "lies, damned lies and statistics".

CC: How do people make decisions?

YM: I know only how they *do not* make them: they certainly do not
"maximise their self-interest". Kahneman and Tversky demonstrated
this in their experiments in 1979, although I always thought that this
was so banally obvious that any clear-minded person knew it.

A little personal anecdote. When I turned 50, one of my former
students, I'll call him Z, visited me and, after a cup of tea, told me

---

[7]Benjamin Disraeli.

a story, about how he had chosen me as his advisor many years ago, when he was an undergraduate student.

"I consulted several people, and everybody advised me against asking you. They told me, I would never be able to continue graduate studies, get a decent job etc., if Manin becomes my advisor" (this was the time of certain "political" troubles).

Amazed, I asked: "but then, why did you ask me?"

For about a minute, Z looked at the ceiling, and then said: "I do not know".

CC: Richard Hamming famously said that "the purpose of computing is insight, not numbers". Do you agree? Do you think that mathematics will continue to be relevant to computer science?

YM: Yes, and yes.

CC: Will mathematics die? But linguistics?

YM: Archilocus' fable involving the fox and hedgehog was reintroduced in our contemporary cultural household by Isaiah Berlin. Berlin had a keen ear for compressed wisdom, and called another of his book of essays after Immanuel Kant: "*The Crooked Timber of Humanity*". Berlin's message was that all global social projects were doomed: one cannot build a house from crooked timber.

However, we want to be optimists and to believe that human civilisation, as we have known it for the last 2000 years, survives. Then mathematics will survive as well. It is incredibly resilient! My favourite example recently was Pappus' hexagon theorem (Alexandria, about 330 AD), a jump through millennia from Euclid to modernity.

CC: How interesting. Can you explain some details?

YM: Trying to explain its statement without a picture, I would first suggest imagining six points in a plane, numbered cyclically ("vertices of a hexagon"). Two consecutive points define a line, passing through them, "one side" of this hexagon, there are all-in-all six sides. Two opposite points define another line, "a diagonal" of this hexagon, there are all-in-all three diagonals. For each diagonal, there are exactly two sides intersecting this diagonal *not* at the vertices. I will say that this diagonal has *Pappus property* if this diagonal and the respective two sides have just one common point. *The Pappus theorem* now says that if two of the three diagonals have Pappus property, than the third one has it as well.

What immediately strikes anyone looking at the Pappus theorem, is its totally "non-Euclidean" character: neither its statement, nor its proof depends on angles and distances. In fact, it took more than a millennium to understand that Pappus' theorem refers to the (real) projective plane, uses only the relation of incidence between lines and points, and, in a hidden form, basic properties of the addition and multiplication of real numbers.

A couple of centuries later, it became clear that Pappus' plane's combinatorics is *completely equivalent* to the axiomatics of abstract fields and abstract projective geometry over them: essentially, his statement taken as an *axiom* is equivalent to the fact that the combinatorics of the incidence relation is an instance of (linear) projective geometry.

Then the whole nonlinear algebraic geometry over algebraically closed commutative fields was rewritten in the incidence terms, vastly generalising Pappus, using the theory of models, a chapter in mathematical logic.

And during the last 20 years, the abstract Pappus theorem/axiom was used in order to achieve an essential progress in Alexander Grothendieck's *anabelian program*.

Chapter 18

Solomon Marcus: Mathematical Analysis, Languages and Fractals

Solomon Marcus is a member of the Romanian Academy and Emeritus Professor of the University of Bucharest. He has published about 50 books in Romanian, English, French, German, Italian, Spanish, Russian, Greek, Hungarian, Czech, and Serbo-Croatian, 400 research articles on mathematical analysis, mathematical and computational linguistics, computer science, poetics, linguistics, semiotics, philosophy and history of science, education, relations between science, humanities, philosophy and religion and several hundreds of papers on various cultural topics of general interest. Professor Marcus wrote a paper together with Paul Erdös in 1957 which gives him an Erdös number of 1. He is recognised as one of the initiators of mathematical linguistics and mathematical poetics.

CC: Professor Marcus, congratulations on your 89th anniversary. This is a wonderful opportunity to talk about your activity. How did you start your career as a mathematician?

SM: You said "mathematician". I am very cautious to use this word as far as I am concerned. Norbert Wiener wrote "I am a mathematician", but Paul Halmos, an excellent scholar, who, however, cannot compete with Wiener, used a different title: "I want to be a mathematician".

CC: Then, let us refer to your relation with mathematics.

SM: My first attraction to mathematics appeared during the summer of 1944, when I was 19. I read something about non-Euclidean geometry. Its coexistence with the Euclidean one, each of them perfectly consistent, but contradicting the other, impressed me first of all from a logical viewpoint. Then, in October 1944, when I had to make a choice, my option for the study of mathematics was mainly of a negative nature. I did not like subjects like natural sciences or history, requiring a huge memory effort (at least this was their image in the high school textbooks of the time); mathematics seemed to me less demanding in this respect. Visiting the Faculty of Science (Maths section), of the University of Bucharest, I got new arguments for the same choice: titles of courses such as 'Infinitesimal Analysis', 'Transfinite Cardinals and Ordinals' and 'Probability Theory', although not very clear to me at that time, it made me very curious; I had a vague feeling that I would like them.

CC: If these are the only motivations which brought you to mathematics, they don't seem to be very serious.

SM: You are right. In November 1944 my strategy was to check for one year my interest and capacity to assimilate mathematics, and then had to decide later whether I continued this adventure or I moved to a different place. It happened that the first alternative proved to be valid. Moreover, the experience of the first year gave me more substantial reasons to continue my mathematical activity.

As a matter of fact, before paying attention to mathematics, I was attracted, as a teenager, by poetry. I read poetry much beyond what was required in school. I used to transcribe in special notebooks pieces of poetry I liked the most, from Poe and Baudelaire to Rilke and Esenin, but giving priority to Romanian poets such as Eminescu, Arghezi, Blaga and Barbu. I was also attracted by theatre: I was fascinated by Ibsen, Wilde, Shaw and Caragiale. So, you may wonder why I did not choose the Faculty of Letters (Arts). There are two reasons. First of all, as a survivor of the Second World War, I got a sense of the gravity of life and of the need to have a sure profession; mathematics, as a basic support for engineering, gave me a feeling of stability, I was convinced that, in the unforeseeable world opened by the Second World War, any further evolution would need teachers of mathematics. Second argument: literature seemed to me a topic I could know without university studies, while a similar possibility for mathematics appeared less plausible. So, I chose mathematics.

CC: Wouldn't it have been better to choose engineering, which is more practical and includes mathematics too?

SM: I have never liked technical activities, although later I discovered that the distinction between science/engineering is not as sharp as I had supposed. It seemed to me to be very risky to choose a profession for which you don't have a strong attraction.

Many of those who made the same choice left mathematics after the first year of studies, either because they moved to engineering or because they were not able to face the rigour of examinations. As I said, it was not my case.

CC: As a student in mathematics, what new arguments did you get for your option?

SM: I enjoyed university mathematics, but my way to approach it was strongly influenced by my (existing) passion for poetry and theatre. Against common opinion, according to which poetry and mathematics are rather opposite than similar, for me university mathematics had from the very beginning, something of a natural, synergetic relation with poetry. With poetry I experienced for the first time the feeling of infinity, of paradox, of frustrated expectation, while the *epsilon-delta* approach to calculus led me to similar situations, revealing to me the world of processes with infinitely many steps and, as a consequence of this infinity, the results conflicted with our intuitive expectations. When you learn that the square has the same number of points as the cube and that the Riemann alternate series $1 - (1/2) + (1/3) - (1/4) + \cdots$ may have the sum equal to any arbitrarily given real number, as soon as you modify conveniently the order of the terms, then you decide that mathematics is both amazing and funny.

CC: Sometimes you wrote about the role of analogy in mathematics; is it also a common pattern with poetry?

SM: Obviously. The power of analogy in both poetry and mathematics is explained by the crucial role metaphors have in both subjects. All generalisation processes, so important in mathematics, are based on cognitive and creative metaphors. It is not by chance that the International Congress of Mathematicians in 1990 selected "The Mathematical Metaphor" as a topic of an invited address. I also enjoyed projective geometry, with its duality theorems, but I learned only some years later that this chapter of geometry was the mathematical product of some great artists of the Renaissance, from Leonardo to Dürer, in connection with the phenomenon called "perspective".

CC: Did you intend from the beginning to become a researcher in mathematics?

SM: School mathematics did not give me the impression that something was left to be discovered in this field. On the other hand, I was ignorant about the existence of a profession called "mathematics researcher", with the same status as engineering, medical doctor, teacher, accountant, etc. In the horizon of the late 1940s, my only aim was to become a school teacher and I was happy that I found a possible profession giving me an intellectual satisfaction.

CC: Your Erdös number is 1, with a paper dating from 1957. Please tell us about it. Where did you meet Erdös?

SM: I met him for the first time at the Fourth Congress of Romanian Mathematicians, in Bucharest (1956).

CC: Were you already familiar with his mathematical work?

SM: I knew some of his papers were very near to my interests at that time, specifically combinatorial set theory, the Borelian hierarchy and measure theory. At that moment I was involved in a problem proposed by Émile Borel in 1946: "is there a decomposition of the real line in a finite number > 1 or in a countable infinity of homogeneous sets?"

CC: What does "homogeneous set" mean?

SM: According to Borel, a set E in the n-dimensional Euclidean space is said to be homogeneous if, for two arbitrary points X and Y in E, the translation XY transforms E into itself. It was introduced in his paper "Les ensembles homogènes" (*C.R. Acad. Sci. Paris*, 222, (1946), 617–618).

CC: I guess you mentioned this problem to Erdös...

SM: One day of the congress was dedicated to a trip to the Carpathian Romanian mountains. I observed that Erdös did not pay much attention to the beauty of nature. I approached him, being curious to experience a dialogue with this mathematician already known for his eccentricities. I introduced myself and his reaction was: "do you have an interesting problem?" I told him about my approach to Borel's problem. He showed much interest, we continued to dialogue about it during the respective trip and then by mail. The result was a joint paper "Sur la decomposition de l'espace enclidien en ensembles homogènes" (*Acta Math. Acad. Sci. Hungaricae* 8, (1957), 3/4, 443–452).

CC: So, what is the answer to Borel's problem?

SM: In our paper, we solved Borel's problem completely, but we also solved the corresponding problem in any poly-dimensional Euclidean space. The answer we got was negative in the case of a finite >1 decomposition and positive in the case of a decomposition in m

homogeneous sets, where m is a transfinite cardinal smaller than the continuum.

CC: Why did you publish it in French? Did Erdös understand French?

SM: I am afraid that Erdös did not speak French and perhaps he did not understand it. At that time, my English was more broken than it is now, so I wrote it in French. As far as I know, Erdös always left his partners to write the final variant, valid for publication, of his joint papers.

CC: Did you continue to work on similar problems?

SM: In 1960, in a joint paper with another Hungarian mathematician, A. Csaszar (*Colloq. Math.* 7, (1960), 2) we proved, in connection with a result by J. Mycielski, that no decomposition of the interval $(0, 1)$ in $n > 1$ disjoint sets, pairwise superposable by translation exists; the same holds true for the interval $[0, 1]$.

CC: Do you know how many researchers have got the Erdös number 2 as a result of having a joint paper with you?

SM: I have joint papers or books with mathematicians, computer scientists, linguists, literary researchers, semioticians, political scientists, chemists and a medical doctor. At first glance, the only one of them having an Erdös number equal to 2, not only due to his collaboration with me, but also his collaboration with another author, seems to be the chemist A. T. Balaban, who, besides his four joint papers with me, is also author of some joint papers with Frank Harary, whose Erdös number is surely 1. But who knows? There are 9267 authors[1] who have an Erdós number equal to 1, this makes the number of authors having Erdös number equal to 2 (among them is Einstein too!) extremely large and we are still ignorant whether Gauss has or not a finite Erdös number!

---

[1] See `http://www.oakland.edu/enp/thedata` visited on 13 May 2014.

CC: Trying to connect your work in mathematical analysis, set theory and topology, on the one hand, and your work in formal language theory, on the other, I observe a key word belonging to their common denominator: *symmetry*. This word appears in the title of many papers you have published from the 1950s to the 1990s and they culminate with a paper published in 2000, on "Real Analysis Exchange", whose title refers to a synthesis of your whole work referring to symmetry. Please give us some details.

SM: After working in excellent fields of continuous mathematics (mathematical analysis and general topology), I moved to fields predominantly of a discrete nature. The continuous-discrete distinction is not so old in mathematics, it became important only in the second half of the last century, under the stimulus of the emergence of the information paradigm. Working in discrete fields, I tried to take advantage of my experience in continuous fields. I was also curious to find out to what extent notions and results from the latter have their correspondent in the former ones. Discreteness and continuity are different faces of the same coin, so there are aesthetic reasons (symmetry reasons too) to expect a strong analogy between these two branches of science that need each other.

CC: One of your first works concerning symmetry refers to a problem of Hausdorff. What was it?

SM: Hausdorff's problem (*Fundamenta Math.* 25, (1935), 578) is the following: let f be a real function of a real variable, symmetrically continuous for any real x (i.e., the difference $f(x + h) - f(x - h)$ tends to zero when h is approaching zero): (a) is it possible for f to have an uncountable set of points of discontinuity? (b) given the real set D of Borelian type F_σ (i.e., a countable union of closed sets), does symmetrically continuous function having D as its set of points of discontinuity always exist? We will leave aside here question (a). H. Fried proved in 1937 that for D of the second Baire category the answer to (b) is negative, so (b) was replaced by (b'), obtained from (b) by replacing "F_σ" with "F_σ and of the first Baire category".

CC: This is perhaps the moment when you entered the scene?

SM: Right. It is to (b') that we gave a negative answer by proving that the Cantor ternary set cannot play the role of D (*Bull. Polish Acad.* 4, (1956), 4, 201–205). Further improvements were obtained by other authors, but a characterisation of the set D is not yet available.

CC: But there is an earlier paper you published on symmetry.

SM: It happened in 1955 when I proved that any F_σ real set is the set of points where a convenient real function of a real variable is not symmetrically continuous; but the problem characterising the set of points where an arbitrary real function of a real variable is not symmetrically continuous is still open. (It is known that the condition to be of F_σ type is both necessary and sufficient for a real set to be the set of points of discontinuity of a real function of a real variable.)

CC: Did you find a correspondent of these results in discrete mathematics, more specifically, in the formal language theory?

SM: I did not try it, but notions of continuity of a function don't seem to be compatible with discreteness. The situation changes, however, when we are dealing with symmetry of sets. In this respect, I will refer to another problem, raised by H. Steinhaus (Fund. Math. 1, (1920), 93): what can be said of a real set A such that, if x and y are in A, then $(x + y)/2 \notin A$? In this way, we are led to the notion of anti-symmetry of a real set A in a point a: if $x \in A$, then $2a - x \notin A$. This notion can be localised, by requiring the respective condition only for a suitable interval with its centre in a. S. Ruziewicz (*Fund. Math.* 7, (1925), 141) proved that if A is locally anti-symmetric in each point of A, then its interior Lebesgue measure is equal to zero. In this respect, we have shown that, generally speaking, local symmetry and local anti-symmetry of a real set impose the same measure-theoretic and the same topological (the Baire category) restrictions: any locally symmetric real set with void interior is of measure zero as soon as it is Lebesgue measurable; the same is true for any locally anti-symmetric real set (its interior is obligatory empty). Any locally symmetric real set with and empty interior having the Baire property is of the first Baire category; the same is true for any locally anti-symmetric real set (its interior is obligatory empty).

CC: Constructive analogues of the Lebesgue measure and the Baire category have been intensively studied in computability and complexity theory. What about formal language theory, did you find analogies?

SM: There are, but the analogy with real sets is more subtle, I would say, it is surprising or at least unexpected. The discrete analogue of "measure zero" and of the "first Baire category" is the property of a language to be regular, while the discrete analogue of measurability and of Baire property is the property to be in Chomsky's hierarchy (or, at least, to be context sensitive).

CC: Please give us some references for your results.

SM: A general account on symmetry of sets and functions was given in my 'Symmetry in the Simplest Case: the Real Line' (*Computers and Math. Applications* 17, (1989), 1/3, 103–115), while the discrete analogue was considered in "Symmetry in Languages" (joint work with Gh. Păun, *International Journal of Computer Mathematics* 52(1/2): 1–15, 1994); 'Symmetry in Strings, Sequences and Languages' (joint work with A. Mateescu, Gh. Păun and A. Salomaa, *International Journal of Computer Mathematics* 54(1/2): 1–13, 1994).

CC: Should we go back briefly to Erdös. After your joint paper, did you have any contact?

SM: In one of my papers, there is a reference to a letter I received from Erdös, including an idea helping me to find an example of a real set which is both of Lebesgue measure zero and of the first Baire category, but which is not a countable union of sets of Jordan measure zero (S. M., *Bulletin Mathematique de la Societe des Sciences Mathematiques de Roumanie* 2(50): 433–439, 1958; *Communi carile Academiei R.P.R.*, 12(3): 281–286, 1962).

CC: What is the significance of such an example?

SM: The negligible sets in the theory of the Riemann integral are just the sets which are countable unions of sets of Jordan measure zero. Such sets are, obviously, of Lebesgue measure zero and of the first Baire category, but the converse is not true, as the example we are talking about shows.

CC: Taking into account the long history of the Riemann integral, it seems strange that such an example came so late.

SM: O. Frink Jr. gave such an example in the 1930s, but it was in the plane and he concluded his work with the opinion that a similar example on the real line seems to be more difficult to be obtained. I was struck by this statement, I had never met a problem which was less difficult in two dimensions than in one dimension. However, he was right.

CC: Did you have any other interactions with Erdös?

SM: He published a paper giving the answer to a problem I had posed.

CC: There is one more word appearing in titles of your works in real analysis and in one of your papers on formal languages: 'convexity'. Is there a link between them?

SM: The link is similar to that related to "symmetry". Like the latter, the former is a universal pattern in mathematics and it is legitimate to look for the common denominator of convexity in continuous structures and in discrete structures. The discreteness-continuity interaction has been for me a permanent object of interest, not only within the framework of mathematics, but also as a general problem in science and philosophy, as I tried to explain elsewhere (S. Marcus, Discreteness vs Continuity: Competition or Co-Operation, *Essays in Poetics, Literary History and Linguistics*, OGI, Moscow,(1999), 659–665.) In real analysis, I was struck by the fact that Jensen convexity has the same measure-theoretic and the same Baire-category structure as its polar opposite, called "anti-Jensen convexity". I recall that a real set A is J-convex if for $x, y \in A, (x + y)/2 \in A$; it is anti J-convex if for $x, y \in A, (x + y)/2 \notin A$. In a joint paper with J. Dassow and G. Păun (Convex and Anticonvex Languages, *Int. J. of Computer Math.* 69, 1/2, (1998), 1–16) similar notions are defined for

. formal languages and similar results are proved, with the modification that the discrete analogue of measure and the Baire category is Chomsky hierarchy (as with symmetry).

CC: It seems that the story of symmetry and convexity you described is part of a more general strategy you have adopted: the transfer of some notions or/and results from one field into another.

SM: Yes, I realised that a lot of opportunities in science are missed because we don't look enough around us, in neighbouring fields, but also in fields having apparently no relation with our field of research. As an instructor of mathematical analysis, for instance, I observed that we don't pay enough attention to the analogy between, the link between sequences and series, on the one hand, and derivative and integral, on the other (again the discrete-continuous interaction); so, we fail to notice that what is called "hospital theorem" in differentiation theory is equivalent to "Stoltz–Cesaro theorem" about sequences. So, I asked a student to pursue this research and a paper was published on this topic, about 10 years ago.

CC: Can you give similar examples from your own research?

SM: There are a lot of such situations. "Analogy" was for me a permanent guide. My first papers were concerned with the transfer of "Denjoy approximate continuity and derivative" from their measure-theoretic context into the context of the Baire category. I introduced in this way the new notions of "qualitative continuity" and "qualitative derivative", which became such familiar tools in real analysis that it is no longer necesary to indicate their author. On the same line of thinking, I studied the category analogue of Lusin's property N (see my paper in *Colloq. Math.* 7, 2 (1960), 213–220) and the bi-dimensional analogue of Banach's properties T1 and T2.

CC: Did you apply a similar strategy in the measure theory?

SM: Yes, I observed the existence of a strong link between atomic measures and series with positive terms (see my papers in *Revue Roumaine de Math. Pures et Appl.* 7, 2 (1962), 327–332 and 11, 6 (1966), 641–646).

CC: Can you give now a similar example related to your research on formal languages?

SM: I will refer to the strong analogy between formal languages and infinite words. The latter field is older than the former, but they almost ignored each other. For instance, slender languages, introduced by G. Păun and A. Salomaa in the 1990s, are defined by the same property that Morse and Hedlund used in the 1930s, in order to characterise periodic infinite words. This fact suggests looking for the kind of periodicity slender languages could have. As soon as bridges are built between infinite words and formal languages, transfers from the former into the latter become possible and we can define meaningful notions such as "Sturmian language".

CC: I know you liked to find uniform treatments for apparently different problems. Can you illustrate this by an example?

SM: I will choose an example equally relevant for both mathematical analysis and formal language theory. In the 1950s and 1960s, I was involved in the study of various classes of functions defined by inequalities: Jensen convex functions, subadditive functions, internal and internal in the generalised sense functions. For each of these classes, it was important to determine conditions assuring their continuity. Particularly, some classes of functions, defined by certain functional equations, were also concerned. Each of these classes had its own literature and its specific approach. It happened that at that time I read the books (in French) by Sophie Piccard concerning, one of them, the sets of distances and, the other, the perfect sets. To each set A in a metric space we can associate the set $D(A)$ of distances between points of A. When A is a real set, we can also associate to it the set $S(A)$ of sums between elements of A. It was also a theorem by Steinhaus saying that if A is a real set of positive Lebesgue measure, then $D(A)$ contains an interval of the form $[0, a]$, where $a > 0$. There are several sets defined in the same way, for instance, we can define the sets $A + B$ of numbers $x + y$ where x is in A and y is in B and so on. Using tools of this type, I obtained a uniform treatment of all classes of functions mentioned above.

CC: And what is the counterpart of this situation in formal language theory?

SM: In many problems concerning formal languages it is relevant to consider the gaps between the lengths of the words in a given language, for instance, when you are interested in the asymptotic behaviour of an infinite language. I tried to introduce adequate notions in this respect in my paper "On the Length of Words" published in the *Festschrift* devoted to Professor Arto Salomaa on his 65th anniversary (Springer). Arranging the lengths of the words in the language L in increasing order, you are immediately led to consider the sequence of the differences between the consecutive terms; the sequence $g(L)$ of the gaps so obtained contains important information about the asymptotic behaviour of L.

CC: Should we stress the importance of having a good knowledge of the mathematical literature?

SM: There is a considerable waste of time and energy resulting from the ignorance of what was already done. Old fields of research such as mathematical analysis are especially concerned with this danger. Some of my papers in the 1950s and 1960s had their purpose to call attention to such situations. For instance, in 1939, A. S. Kronrod gave a four-page proof for the necessary condition required to a real set A for the existence of a function discontinuous at each point in A and differentiable at each point outside A. However, the respective result was an immediate corollary of a theorem obtained by W. H. Young in 1903 (S. M., *Comunicarile Acad. Rom.* 12 (1962), 3). M. K. Fort, Jr. proved in 1951 that the set of points of differentiability of a real function having an everywhere dense set of points of discontinuity on the real line is always of the first Baire category; but he ignored that his theorem was a direct consequence of Brudno's 1939 result. Karl Bogel developed in the 1930s a whole bi-dimensional analysis based on the expression $f(x + h, y + k) - f(x + h, y) - f(x, y + k) - f(x, y)$ replacing the classical difference $f(x + h, y + k) - f(x, y)$ and only recently it was pointed out that the same idea had already been developed, 50 years before Bogel, by the Italian Betazzi. F.B. Jones proved, in 1942, the existence of a Hamel basis including a non-empty perfect set, but this result is an immediate consequence of a theorem obtained in 1928 by John von Neumann (S.M., *Bull. Math. Soc. Roum. Math. Phys.* 1, 49: 4, 1957).

CC: I am afraid that such phenomena are unavoidable, even in fields younger than mathematical analysis.

SM: Yes, but we should try to reduce them, by promoting review articles stimulating researchers to look around their field too, not only in its interior. For instance, I realised how useful it is to look carefully in the review journals, not only in the sections directly concerned with your own field.

CC: I guess that some of your papers have their starting point just in bridging facts/phenomena in different sections of such review journals.

SM: Right. For instance, my results concerning the commutativity of the second-order cross partial derivatives were motivated by the idea of using, in their study, a notion apparently having nothing to do with partial derivatives: the notion of quasi-continuity introduced by S. Kempisty in 1932. One of the consequences was the fact that if $f(x,y)$ has partial derivatives of any order and of any type in the unit square, then all mixed partial derivatives are commutative (S.M., *C.R. Acad. Sci. Paris* 246 (1958), 4).

CC: One of your papers has the name of Kempisty in its title. Do you remember it?

SM: I published it in *Colloq. Math.* 8 (1961), and it is one of my most cited articles. A mapping f defined on a topological space, with values in a topological space, is quasi-continuous at x if for any neighbourhood U of x, and for any neighbourhood V of $f(x)$ there exists an open set G included in U such that $f(G)$ is included in V. Looking around, I realised that "quasi-continuous" was equivalent to what W. Bledsoe called in 1952 "neighbourly", while H.P. Thielman's "cliquish functions" (1952) were an extension of quasi-continuous functions. So, my advice is: look around!

CC: In younger fields, such as theoretical computer science, we may hope that a new generation of authors does not have difficulties in being aware of the contributions of previous generations. . .

SM: Unfortunately, the collective memory of science here too faces some difficulties. It is true that the history of theoretical computer science is much shorter than that of mathematical analysis, but most methods and tools used in theoretical computer science are inspired from classical fields, such as algebra, combinatorics, logic, set theory, etc. Only a few researchers have a good knowledge of all of them. So, many things are repeated in a different jargon and in a different order of ideas, in most cases with no reference to the previous research done in this respect.

CC: Any concrete cases?

SM: A very clear example is the theory of semi-groups, which was already a well established chapter of algebra when mathematical linguistics and formal language theory emerged, in the late 1950s and early 1960s. When I began to be involved in the study of mathematical modelling of natural languages, their framework was given by some free monoids, a well-known type of algebraic structure. The problems raised and the notions introduced in this respect in the study of languages were, to a large extent, different from those considered in pure algebra. If you compare books by Preston and Hammer or Ljapin, on the one hand, and the book on semi-groups by Michael Arbib, on the other, you will find that they are very different, despite the fact that they are concerned with the same basic structure. This happens just because their motivations and their problems are different. I remember Arbib's polemical reaction to the publication of S. Eilenberg's treatise on automata. However, this does not mean that purely algebraic works are useless for computer scientists; they deserve attention, because, ultimately, science is only one, as Rudolf Carnap stressed.

CC: Eilenberg's treatise was cited by many authors in automata and languages. . .

SM: Working on some mathematical models of grammatical categories, I observed that some notions of contextual domination, contextual equivalence, and distributional classes appear in some papers of algebra by B.M. Shein, in a different terminology; some theorems were also there. A very interesting situation was revealed by comparing two papers coming from completely different directions. One of them belonged to Antoine Sestier (late 1950s), who was interested in the Galois connection between sets of strings and sets of contexts with respect to a language L over a given alphabet A. He defines the contextual closure of a set E of strings over A, with respect to L, by first taking the set $C(E)$ of all contexts over A accepting in L all strings in E, then by taking the set $S(C(E))$ of all strings over A accepted in L by all contexts in $C(E)$. Ten years later, starting from problems related to the German language and with motivation related to computational linguistics, Jürgen Kunze introduces a contextual operator to model the notion of a grammatical category in German; a previous model of a grammatical category, introduced with motivation coming from Slavic languages, valid also for Romance languages, proved to be inadequate for German (in view of the specific behaviour of personal pronouns in German). Kunze ignored the work of Sestier, but I had the satisfaction of realising that, despite their completely different cloths, Kunze's contextual operator and Sestier's closure were the same mathematical object; I took advantage of all consequences of this equivalence.

CC: Sestier's paper was in French, while Kunze's paper was in German. Probably, they did not know the language of the other.

SM: This may be an explanation, but there are review journals helping in just such cases. Unfortunately, many researchers don't read them. But it happens that some authors no longer remember their own ideas. I will refer, as an example, to a famous theorem: any real function of a real variable is the sum of two Darboux functions (defined by the property to map any interval onto an interval). This theorem was published by W. Sierpinski in 1953. However, in 1927 this theorem was anticipated (without proof) by A. Lindenbaum.

I had under my eyes a paper by C. Kuratowski and W. Sierpinski, published in *Fundamenta Mathematicae* in 1926, dealing with an apparently different problem; however, deeply hidden in one of the proofs there, I found the fact that any real function of a real variable is the sum of two Darboux functions. Did Lindenbaum take profit of Kuratowski–Sierpinski paper? Was Sierpinski aware of what was hidden in his joint paper with Kuratowski? I told this nice adventure in *Com. Acad. RPR* 10, 7 (1960), 551–554.

CC: A similar situation occurred with Sudan's recursive function which is not primitive recursive.

SM: This is just what I had in my mind. Let us recall the facts. A short time before his death, Gr. C. Moisil told me that Gabriel Sudan, former student of Hilbert, was the author of the first example of a function which is recursive but not primitive recursive. Such an example is usually attributed to Ackermann. Moisil died before giving me any details. I told you this in 1973, when you were still a student, proposing you to investigate this matter. Ionel Ţevy was also invited to join in this research. It happened that no paper published by Sudan, had in its explicit purpose, the presentation of a function with the properties mentioned by Moisil. At that moment, we were faced with a real detective problem. You became passionately involved in this research and you told me later that this adventure decided your option for the direction of research you have choosen. I realised your satisfaction when you succeeded in putting your finger on Sudan's paper, locating the desired example. But obviously Sudan was not aware of the fact that the respective example was just what made the name of Ackermann famous in the same way in which Sierpinski was not aware of the potential presence, in his 1926 joint paper with Kuratowski, of the theorem he stated and proved in 1953, after it was conjectured by Lindenbaum in 1927. Science requires explicitness and clarity, in contrast with art, dominated by implicitness and vagueness.

CC: Many of your results in real analysis, a field in which you have published about hundred papers (some of them presented for publication by A.N. Kolmogorov, W. Sierpinski, P. Montel and M. Picone) point to counter-intuitive, pathological phenomena. Why were you interested in them?

SM: Science shows its power by making intelligible a lot of things that are beyond what is visible, or, more generally, beyond what can be perceived by our senses. This discrepancy between intelligible and sensible increased tremendously in the last century. Mathematics is full of results illustrating this assertion: most continuous functions are nowhere differentiable, so they are monotonous in no interval; any real function defined in the real interval I has a continuous restriction on a suitable dense subset of I; for any positive integer n, there exists in the plane n domains, having the same frontier; most recursive functions are not primitive recursive; algebraic numbers form a negligible set, because it is countable, in contrast with transcendental numbers, forming an uncountable set. All these results are surprising in respect with our intuitive expectations. We could state a general principle: *common situations, we meet in our everyday practice, become exceptional, as soon as we consider them from a theoretical standpoint.* So, there is a genuine conflict between individual instantiations of a concept and its general, theoretical status. This happens because most mathematical concepts and properties have a meaning which go beyond their intuitive representation. For instance, intuitively the property of continuity is confused with the Darboux property; however, the latter is much more general than the former. Let us observe that the world of convex bodies is full of situations of this type, as the papers by Tudor Zamfirescu point out.

CC: Are these things connected to Mandelbrot's fractals?

SM: Mandelbrot's fractal geometry of Nature has its origin just in the anti-intuitive objects rejected by Ch. Hermite and H. Poincaré as creations of the devil. They were considered as having nothing to do with the real universe. But even Poincaré may sometimes be wrong. In this respect, we should appreciate the premonitory vision of Arnaud Denjoy, who, in the 1920s, expressed the feeling that the classical properties of continuity and differentiability no longer fitted with the discontinuous structure of physical space, as it was revealed at that time. As a matter of fact, history was ironic in this respect, because Poincaré pioneered the field of deterministic chaos, where dynamical systems having fractals as they are now a normal pattern. Peano's curve, Koch's curve and many other similar objects are not less connected to reality than the circle and the square, but the latter correspond to the requirements of simplicity and symmetry of antiquity and the Renaissance, while the former are related to another prototype of beauty, expressed by high complexity.

CC: So, are you considering yourself as a "fractalist"?

SM: I could say, I was a "fractalist" *"avant la lettre"*, because many of my papers are concerned with objects which later became bricks, pieces of those structures receiving the status of fractals, and modelling real objects and processes such as snowflakes, ocean coasts and Brownian motion.

CC: From the several examples you have given, one can understand your interest in bridging works belonging to different authors who ignored each other.

SM: Unfortunately, authors ignoring each other, despite the fact that they work in similar or neighbouring fields, is a very frequent phenomenon. If we don't try to bridge such gaps, the progress would be very slow.

CC: Can you trace the roots of this phenomenon?

SM: The quantity of papers published in scientific journals is beyond the possibilities of researchers to capture, process and assimilate. To this objective reason we should add the insufficient care of some authors to pay attention to what was done by other authors. I have many colleagues who don't look systematically in the review journals, at least in the sections directly related to their interests. As a consequence, a large part of the scientific heritage remains underused. This is the paradox of scientific information: *it is both less than we need and more than we can use.*

CC: Please give us more examples.

SM: I have already given some examples: slender languages in the 1990s is a new variant of Morse and Hedlund condition of periodicity for infinite words in the 1930s. Karl Bogel rediscovers in the 1930s the Bettazzi derivative introduced in the 1880s. To them I would like to add that the finite-increment theorem, as it is stated in N. Bourbaki (*Elements de mathématiques*, livre IV, Hermann, Paris, (1949), p. 19) was stated and proved in 1884, by Ludwig Scheffer, as it was recently pointed out.

CC: It seems that the examples you provide show not only the presence of the same notion or the same result in a different "jargons", but also the connection between different fields, for instance, between formal languages and infinite words.

SM: Right. To give another example, this is what happened to me when I realised that the differential structure of functions having a dense set of points of discontinuity has a direct impact on the theory of Diophantine approximations. Usually, the negligible sets in this domain are of measure zero. The theorem I have proposed (*Math. Zeitschrift* 76, 1 (1961), 42–45) displays a negligible set of the first Baire category.

CC: What could be done, with respect to the global organisation of research, to increase the interaction between researchers?

SM: It is necessary to stimulate more and more authors to devote part of their effort to the elaboration of papers devoted to directions of research, by inspecting the quasi-totality of the bibliography of the respective subject. The profit is tremendous. I wrote such a paper for the topic of Pompeiu's derivatives (*Rend. Circolo Math. Palermo* II, 12, (1963), 1–36; they are non-negative derivatives, having a dense set of zeros, but being identically zero in no interval. I was able in this way to bring in a common framework things belonging to analysis, set theory, topology and differential equations. The simple comparison of various results and concepts led to many unifications and simplifications.

CC: Your "meeting" with Simion Stoilow's work in real analysis was a similarly interesting adventure...

SM: Stoilow attracted me by his interest for the differential structure of continuous functions. It is well known that before Weierstrass, the general belief was that differentiability follows from continuity. Weierstrass pointed out that the latter may exist in the absence of the former, in a whole interval. Denjoy, Young and Saks showed that a kind of regularity "almost everywhere", with respect to the disposal of derivate numbers, exists for any real function of a real variable. In 1924, Stoilow changed the perspective, by looking for negligible sets not in the domain of the definition, but in the range of the function. After reading his theorem, I immediately made a connection with some recent results. I realised that a whole chapter in S. Saks's book *Theory of Integration* (1937) follows elegantly from some parts of Stoilow's theorem. Similarly, some theorems of Banach (1926) and Minakshisundaram (1940) are consequences of Stoilow's result (S. Marcus, *Revue Roumaine Math. Pures et Appl.* 2 (1957), 409–412). The main point here is not Stoilow's chronological priority, but the capacity of his theorem to bring into a common framework things apparently coming from different directions. During 33 years, this beautiful theorem remained completely forgotten. No author working in the field had the curiosity to look back, in the history of the subject, in order to exploit what was already accumulated.

Today we observe how yesterday's researchers are victims of contemporary ones, tomorrow we could be similar victims of our successors.

CC: You have guided, advised and supervised many young researchers. Tell me about some of them.

SM: I could write a book with stories on the surprising experiences I accumulated in this respect. As a matter of fact, such a book was already written, it was published in 2010 under the title *Meetings with Solomon Marcus* (Bucharest, Spandugino, 1200 pages), but not by me. A large part of the book includes stories by my former students or other people, about their experiences with me and my work. In most cases challenging young people does not give you an immediate satisfaction — many of them don't react, some of them react with lack of passion — but if you persist in your attempts you may find, from time to time, the right people to whom you gave the right message at the right moment. You are in this respect, such a case. Proposing to you the investigation of Gabriel Sudan's paternity of the first example of a recursive function which is not primitive recursive, shaped your research direction for a long period. Gheorghe Păun, one of the top researchers in Formal Language Theory, explained in his autobiography my basic role in his research career and his consideration of me as his mentor. Andrew Bruckner, one of the leaders in the field of Real Analysis in the second half of the past century, explained in his contribution to the book cited above, how "much of the early part of my career was influenced by S.M." and concluded: "I learned a great deal from S.M.'s work and correspondences and I am grateful for that". I am one of the protagonists in W. Andries van Helden's two-volume book *Case ad Gender. Concept Formation between Morphology and Syntax* (Amsterdam and Atlanta, GA: Rodopi, 1993) for pioneering work in the field of algebraic analytical models. Mihai Dinu, a Romanian scholar at the intersection of Humanities and Mathematics, well known for his research in the mathematical approach to theater, was introduced to this subject by my course *Mathematics of the Drama* taught at the Faculty of Letters of the University of Bucharest.

In 1980 I put in the hands of my former student, the mathematician Dan Tudor Vuza, *The Book of Modes* (Editura Muzicala, Bucharest, English translation, 1993) by the composer Anatol Vieru. This book changed his life: the result was a series of articles in the American journal *Perspectives of New Music* in which he proposed a new theory of rhythm. Today Vuza is a leader in musical theory and composition, recognised as a continuator of Olivier Messiaen.

Important in all these examples is the *circularity* phenomenon. If initially I was for these people a reference, a guide, a mentor, in later stages they became for me a source of learning and discovery. My former disciples became my today teachers.

CC: What gave you most satisfaction in life?

SM: I learned to find a sense of life and a full satisfaction in the fact that I can move, I can look at the sky and the people around me,

I can trade a smile with a child, I can contemplate the spectacle of life, I can talk and, now, I can interact with people like you. I am in a permanent state of wonder. I wake up every morning ready to throw a fresh look on the world, I am happy to read and write. It is fantastic.

Chapter 19

Mioara Mugur-Schachter: Information,
Quantum Mechanics and Probabilities

Professor   Mioara   Mugur-Schachter, http://www.mugur-schachter.net *is a physicist, mathematician and philosopher specialising in quantum mechanics, probability theory, information theory and epistemology. Her PhD thesis (supervised by Nobel laureate Louis de Broglie) contains the first invalidation of von Neumann's famous proof stating the impossibility of hidden parameters compatible with the quantum mechanical formalism. This result was included in the volume* "Etude du caractère complet de la mécanique quantique", *(with a preface by L. de Broglie) published in the collection* "Les grands problèmes des sciences", *Gauthiers Villars, Paris, 1964, two years before Bell's invalidation.*

Professor Mugur-Schachter founded the Laboratoire de Mécanique Quantique & Structures de l'Information at the University of Reims, the Centre pour la Synthèse d'une Épistéémologie Formalisée and the L'Association pour le Développement de la Méthode de Conceptualisation Relativisée.

CC: You were born and educated in Romania. Tell us about your time at the University of Bucharest: subjects you studied, professors, general atmosphere.

MM-S: I began by studying mathematics and philosophy (especially logic and psychology). Then I chose to specialise in theoretical physics. For political reasons my studies suffered an interruption that seemed to be fated to be irreversible. But later events evolved and I was finally allowed to resume my studies. So I graduated with a Masters in Theoretical Physics. My professors, as I remember them, were very remarkable indeed. Profoundly educated persons and many among them endowed with genuine originality. The teaching was very thorough. For me however — from a subjective point of view — my student years were a deeply troubled time which I prefer not to focus my attention onto again. The general atmosphere after 1948, as I perceived it, was constantly growing more and more oppressive from a moral point of view.

CC: Your PhD thesis was elaborated in Bucharest and sent to Louis de Broglie before you came to Paris. How did you choose your subject? Did you have any supervision in Bucharest for this work?

MM-S: During a recent public visit to a town in the South of France, a young man asked how Louis de Broglie had recruited me? I answered that in fact it was me who tried — very hard indeed — to recruit Louis de Broglie.

When I graduated, my former Professor of Atomic Physics, Horia Hulubei (who was a pupil of Jean Perrin, in Paris, and after the war was called back to Romania to create an Institute of Atomic Physics) obtained a position for me in the team of theoretical physics at the new institute.

The subject of research assigned to me was to calculate, using the method established by van Vleck the interaction between three spins using the framework of quantum mechanics. While covering the matrix elements with metre-long sheets of paper intended for architectural projects, I constantly suffered from a very disagreeable feeling of not 'understanding' at all what I was calculating in the prescribed way. This was a new feeling. Newtonian mechanics seemed to me fully intelligible, and also thermodynamics, atomic physics, statistical physics and even Maxwell's electromagnetism. But in the case of quantum mechanics I simply did not grasp *how the mathematical formalism manage to carry definite meanings.*

In that state of mind, reading a textbook of quantum mechanics translated from Russian I found the assertion that a certain von Neumann had proved a famous theorem stating that "hidden parameters" that would "complete" the quantum mechanical formalism, making it intelligible, are impossible. The proof was not given. Immediately I reacted with a mixture of satisfaction and astonishment. I felt happy to learn that other people also perceived the unintelligibility and they were investigating it. But I was unable to imagine how it could be possible to prove a definitive impossibility. Inside what conceptual-formal environment could such a proof be achieved? Founded upon what assumptions? So I became very eager to examine the proof. I had a friend who worked at the library of the academy and I convinced him to order an English translation of the German book by von Neumann where the proof was first presented. The book eventually arrived, but its access was restricted to the library basement. Using a trick, I found von Neumann's book and took it home.

During the next months I became an expert in von Neumann's book. Meanwhile the calculus of matrix elements suffered a near total stagnation. At the end of the year I was downgraded for not having finished my assignment. On the other hand, I had written in English the first draft of what I thought to be an invalidation of von Neumann's proof.

I then began asking teachers and colleagues to read my work. But it appeared that nobody around was interested in von Neumann's proof. At the same time everybody was *a priori* convinced that it was a "definitive" result. This was my first collision with the social environment of scientific thought.

Meanwhile I kept improving the text. And when I finally thought it to be achieved I asked Professor Hulubei to do me the enormous favour of sending the manuscript by diplomatic courier (correspondence with the West was restricted at that time in Romania) to Louis de Broglie as I learned indirectly that he believed the theorem to be false. Professor Hulubei accepted, though assuring me that I would never receive an answer.

During the period that followed my husband (who was a Professor of Resistance of Materials at the Polytechnic Institute of Bucharest) decided that both of us should give up our professional positions in order to apply for a passport to leave the country without creating a dangerous and useless small scandal. We knew quite well how illusory such an action was, but we felt that we just had to try. So we coldly put an end to our Romanian "careers" and left Bucharest to start a long period of uncertainty (it lasted three full years) during which, *quasi incognito*, we wandered through the country with temporary jobs here and there. Which, unexpectedly, we enjoyed profoundly.

One morning, while we were living on a boat anchored on a void island in the delta of the Danube, where my husband was in charge of the construction of an irrigation system for a rice field, I rather miraculously got a telegram from my parents informing that Professor Hulubei wanted to see me as soon as possible. I left a small note on the boat, traversed swamps in a tractor, caught a train to Bucharest, and at the end of that very day I stood before Professor Hulubei. He said: "do you know what? Louis de Broglie answered you! And he agrees that you have invalidated von Neumann's proof!" He handed me a very brief letter addressed to "Mister Misare Mugur-Schächter" (I abandoned that precious letter in Romania, like any other handwritten document). In essence, Louis de Broglie's letter said that it was curious to see that two minds so different as his and mine, reached the same conclusion about von Neumann's proof. But since I had taken a logical approach and had genuinely demonstrated the circularity character of the proof, he would be happy if my work could one day become a PhD under his supervision.

From that moment on I nourished only one dream: to arrive in France. In 1962 this dream became true following an unrealistically adventurous detective path to obtain a passport. And in 1964 my PhD thesis, titled *Étude du caractère complet de la mécanique quantique*[1] was defended at the University of Paris and published by Gauthier Villars in the collection "*Les grands problèmes des sciences*", in a volume prefaced by Louis de Broglie (http://www.mugur-schachter.net). The first part of the volume contains a French version of my initial invalidation (practically unchanged); the second part contains the proposal of an experiment derived from considerations on the quantum theory of measurement and from de Broglie's reinterpretation of quantum mechanics (the experiment has not been realised, but it might be some day).

CC: You arrived in Paris in 1962. Can you reminisce about your first encounters with Louis de Broglie, the 7th Duke de Broglie?

MM-S: As if it were yesterday. It was towards the end of April. I immediately announced my arrival and obtained a "*rendezvous*". I was now waiting seated in the hall of the Academy of Science. An usher came and presented a silver tray asking me to put my visit card. I had no card, so I wrote my name on a piece of paper. And a little later Louis de Broglie himself arrived. He greeted me and invited me to follow him.

I shall never forget the instantaneous transition from the ocean of vague and moving inner images that had so long subsisted in my mind regarding the possible scene of my first meeting with Louis de Broglie, to that unique real scene, so radically definite in every detail, that was uncoiling with apodictic evidence. An upright, infinitely distinguished man, in a dark costume and a shirt with a broken collar, was there, in front of me, confirming that he would accept me to become his "last student". He was Louis de Broglie, and I was in Paris, France, seated in an office at the Academy of Science.

During the two subsequent years we met practically every Wednesday to discuss a fragment of my work that I had left in his letterbox from *Neuilly-sur-Seine*, at least two days in advance. He never forgot and never postponed something that he had announced

---

[1] *Study of the Completness of Quantum Mechanics.*

he would do. He never argued with an idea or a way of expressing something. He just stated his opinion. He also meticulously corrected my French. And very discreetly, he constantly helped me in essential ways to settle myself in France. His attitude influenced me profoundly.

CC: What was wrong with von Neumann's proof?

MM-S: It was simply circular. The hypothesis contained the conclusion. The conclusion of "definitive" (absolute) impossibility of hidden parameters was in fact derived inside the mathematical formulation of quantum mechanics, namely using the particular way of representing probabilities which is specific to Hilbert spaces, not of micro-states. (If micro-states are represented by another mathematical syntax, different from that of Hilbert spaces — as is indeed the case for the de Broglie–Bohm representation — then the proof ceases to hold).

But this is not the unique insufficiency of von Neumann's argument. In my thesis I brought forth the unacceptable global structure of von Neumann's argument. The inadequacies of this argument overflow abundantly due to the strictly logical-formal aspects. They leak out into epistemology, method and usual language. This "proof" can be regarded as a striking illustration of the extreme difficulty achieving a wholly and explicitly dominated mathematical representation of a domain of "physical facts". Such a representation involves quite essentially operations of various sorts, physical as well as abstract ones; it involves assumptions of a various nature, in particular, methodological choices and conventions; it involves *aims* of different natures, the aim to know in a precise way, of course, but also other aims that should all be composed under the constraint of a sort of global coherence. What thus comes out is a need of a sort of coherence that cannot be separated from a feeling of beauty, or on the contrary, of ugliness when certain slopes of it are violated in some unspeakable way. I had tried as much as I was able to bring all these aspects together into one representation and to extract the essence of the whole. But I was very young and this was my first research.

CC: You have also challenged Wigner's proof on the impossibility of a joint probability of position and momentum compatible with the formalism of quantum mechanics. Is this theorem false as well?

MM-S: I would not say that it is "false". I only showed that the asserted conclusion does not follow. I even identified a trivial counterexample and I showed how this counterexample is allowed to arise inside Wigner's construction. As in my experience with von Neumann's proof, as soon as I succeeded in achieving a sufficiently compact variant of this second critical work (which took more than two years and a long preliminary publication) I sent it to Wigner himself. Wigner invited me to visit him in his wooden house in Vermont, for a direct discussion. So I went there. He recommended the work for publication in the *Foundations of Physics*.

CC: What is the "opacity functional of a statistic" and how did you use it for a mathematical unification between the theory of probabilities and Shannon's theory of communication of information?

MM-S: This was my first constructive work. It is the result of an attempt at explaining why Boltzmann's statistical distribution tied with the Carnot–Clausius definition of physical "entropy", possesses a mathematical form that is identical with that of Shannon's purely mathematical concept of "informational entropy". My motivation came from the seemingly unconceivable fact that this formal identity between two concepts, that are so radically different in their semantic content, is just a coincidence.

The central idea of the approach was to construct — inside a Kolmogorov probability space — a purely mathematical definition of the probability of realisation of a given statistical distribution of elementary events of the space.

Consider a Kolmogorov space that contains a universe of elementary events and a probability law governing it. Consider a very long but finite random sequence of elementary events from this universe. The elementary events emerge inside this sequence in a certain order, and each elementary event possesses a certain relative frequency inside the sequence, which defines a certain "statistical structure" of the sequence. It is obvious that: a) a given statistical structure can arise for various lengths of the sequence, and b) for a fixed length, no statistical structure is possible.

Two questions can be examined. The first one is: what is the expression of the probability for the realisation of a sequence with a given statistical structure and abstraction being made of the order and length? We have proved that the Kolmogorov expression of the limit of the ratio between the probability of the sequence considered and the length of the sequence, is equal to the difference between two terms, the Shannon entropy of the probability law from the considered Kolmogorov probability space, and "the modulation of the probability law by the fixed statistical structure". I called this difference the *opacity* of the (fixed) statistical structure of the sequence of elementary events with respect to the probability law of the Kolmogorov probability space.

The second question is: how does this probability evolve when the length of the considered sequence tends to inifity? The answer is: if the length of the sequence of elementary events tends to infinity, then the opacity functional satisfies the weak law of large numbers.

The opacity functional realises an abstract unification between the probabilistic and informational approaches. This unification permits to construct deductively inside the theory of probability, the identity of form between, on the one hand, the concept of physical statistical entropy introduced by Carnot, Clausius and Boltzmann, and on the other, Shannon's concept of informational entropy of the probability law assigned to the signs from an alphabet of an information source regarded as elementary events. The formal identity can now be clearly distinguished from the semantic specificities (physical, informational), while the relations between formalism and semantics are clearly defined in each case.

CC: Your work on "formalised epistemology" was characterised by Jean-Paul Baquiast, editor of "Automates Intelligents", as *a revolution in the way of representing the processes by which we acquire knowledge...* Can you describe your method of "relativised conceptualisation"?

MM-S: The method of relativised conceptualisation (MRC) is similar to a grammar or "a formal logic", that give syntactic rules for making use of a set of signs. But instead of dealing with this or that "language" or symbolic way of constructing "rational truths" (conclusions established deductively), MRC concerns all of the human processes of conceptualisation: it is a general syntax for normalised creation of consensual knowledge. I say "normalised" in the sense of "methodologies": indeed, like any method, MRC is organically tied with aims, and the major aim of MRC is expressed in the following: the system of norms organised by MRC assures the realisation of "safe scientific knowledge", that is, of communicable and consensual knowledge where any possibility of emergence of false problems or of paradoxes is excluded by construction.

MRC establishes a bridge from my initial investigations — exclusively critical and achieved with reference to norms that worked only implicitly and were devoid of generality — to a quite general and explicitly organised methodological framework.

Let me detail a little more. Any piece of knowledge that can be communicated without resource restrictions (space or/and time) is a "description" (pointing toward something restricts the co-presence on a same place at the same time, so it does not give a "description"). What is not "described" cannot be communicated in unrestricted ways, even if it is known by someone. So, MRC is a method of scientific and safe description.

MRC is constructed in a deductive way and uses current natural logic. It involves 1 postulate, 3 principles, 1 convention, 22 main definitions and 6 proved "propositions". That is all.

A "description" consists of some 'qualification' — in a certain generalised adjectival sense — of some "entity-to-be-qualified". According to MRC-norms, any description has to be realised within a previously defined "epistemic referential" (G, V) which consists of an explicitly defined operation of generation G of the object-entity oe_G to be "qualified" ("described"), and a concept denoted V that is called a view which consists of a structure that precisely realises the desired sort of qualification.

The operation of generation G can consist of just selecting a pre-existing entity and assigning it the role of object oe_G for future qualifications; but G can also be a radically creative operation (as it happens indeed for a free micro-state to be studied according to quantum mechanics).

On the basis of very careful analyses, it appears that in order to avoid any arbitrary *a priori* restriction it is unavoidable to posit — even if *a posteriori* this posit is modified — that the object-entity oe_G stays in a one-to-one relation with its operation of generation G (this is expressed by the index G from the denotation oe_G). This *a priori* posit constitutes, inside MRC, an essential methodological decision.

The basic nature of V is analogous to that of a grammatical predicate. But its structure is far more complex, precise and general. A view V consists of a finite union $V = \bigcup_g V_g$ of aspect-view V_g. Each aspect-view V_g introduces a freely chosen "semantic dimension g" (for instance, the trivial one indicated by the word "colour", but also any other more unusual or sophisticated one) endowed with a finite set of "values" denoted g_k, where g is fixed and k varies in a finite set (for instance, for the semantic dimension of "colour", one could place just green, red and yellow, or these and also 15 other colours, etc.). An aspect-view V_g is "blind" with respect to the semantic dimensions different from its own, as well as with respect to any value g_k with which it has not been endowed by its definition: it is a filter. Moreover, each aspect-view V_g states explicitly (a) what conceptual-physical operations constitute an act of "examination by V_g", (b) what is the observable result of a given act of examination and (c) how this result is translated into a value g_k of V_g (when oe_G is not directly perceivable, this requirement is highly non-trivial).

For the sake of effectiveness in the sense of computability, MRC operates with operationally specified entities using finite constructions.

The relativised genesis of any MRC description induces a definite global structure for the whole evolving volume. This structure possesses the character of a network of chains of increasing complexity, subject to the explicit rules of mutual connection. Each relative description from this network reproduces the same basic epistemological structure $D = \{(g_k)\}$.

In the framework of MRC classical concepts and theories get a new form.

- The classical logic corresponds to a "genetic relativised logic" that entails calculus with relative descriptions.
- Classical probabilities correspond to relativised genetic probabilities.
- Genetic logic and genetic probabilities become essentially unified.
- Shannon's theory of communication of information, which by construction does not talk about the meaning of information, becomes relativised when it is embedded into the relativised theory of probabilities; some meaning can emerge.
- The MRC "complexity" can be expressed by a set of relativised numerical "measures" established by measurements.
- The concept of time acquires an explicit bi-dimensional representation.

New applications of MRC are developed. For example, a relativised concept of "system" was constructed in H. Boulouet's PhD thesis *Relativised Systems Theory* to be submitted to the University of Valencienne (2014).

Furthermore, all classical disciplines are constructed and presented as if the descriptions "mirror" things and facts that pre-exist quite independently of the model (even Wittgenstein's extraordinary analyses do not clearly challenge this conception). In contrast, MRC is explicitly founded on transferred descriptions. I dare assert that MRC is the first scientific general method of deliberate human conceptualisation.

CC: In what way did you recently collaborate with Giuseppe Longo, an expert in computability theory and discrete mathematics, areas seemingly far away from your main interests? Is this an indication that quantum physics might benefit from an interaction between these areas?

MM-S: I think so. For historical reasons, the beginnings of quantum mechanics have been marked by contributions expressed in terms of continuous mathematics; but also by contributions expressed in algebraic terms. I believe that in the future a discrete and finite, algebraic approach will predominate.

And I think the same is true for probabilities. (The functional opacity can be relativised and discretised).

Anyhow, MRC is quite essentially finite, hence discrete, by construction. With MRC I solved, I think, a major (though rarely discussed) difficulty of the classical probabilistic conceptualisation (see my paper "On the concept of probability", *Mathematical Structures in Computer Science*, special issue on "Randomness, Statistics and Probability", 2014 (24:3, e240309)). Namely, the lack of a general procedure for constructing the numerical distribution of probability to be used in a factual situation that is generally considered to be probabilistic. I called this difficulty "Kolmogorov's *aporia*" because starting from 1983 Kolmogorov himself denounced this startling and scandalous situation. For example, in the paper "Combinatorial Foundations of Information Theory and the Calculus of Probabilities", *Russia Mathematical Surveys*, 38, (1983), 29–40, Kolmogorov says:

> "The applications of probability theory can be put on a uniform basis. It is always a matter of consequences of hypotheses about the impossibility of reducing in a way or another the complexity of the descriptions of the objects in question. Naturally this approach to the matter does not prevent the development of probability theory as a branch of mathematics being a special case of general measure theory".

The MRC solution to Kolmogorov's *aporia* consists of an explicitly finite procedure for constructing, in a given factual probabilistic situation, the corresponding finite distribution of a numerically defined law of probability. Furthermore, an equation has been worked out, which expresses the formal consistency between the finite data, that characterise the above-mentioned procedure, and the mathematical theorem of large numbers.

Professor Longo was aware of this work and I think that he has understood its social difficulties. I must mention that the same special issue contains a very interesting discussion of probability from a

historical perspective, C. Porter, "Kolmogorov on the role of randomness in probability theory", of which I was unaware while developing
my work. In this way I learned that quite a number of mathematicians are well aware of what I have called Kolmogorov's *aporia*, but
they called it long before "the applicability problem", clearly a better
name.

Mathematicians seem to believe that the applicability problem
can be solved by purely mathematical means, while I believe that
this is fundamentally impossible. I believe that the semantic content
cannot be reduced to pure syntax, nor entirely "mimed" by it (in the
sense in which a mould can "mime" a face).

The special issue referred to above also contains a brief debate
between several outstanding contributors about the ways of connecting factual data with mathematical syntax. This debate brings into
evidence that the applicability problem — even though Kolmogorov
himself considered it so essential — not only is surprisingly little
known, but, even when it is raised in quite explicit and insistent
terms, it captures very little attention.

I believe that this state of facts deserves closer examination.
Human intuition is magic. Nevertheless, the introduction of explicit
principles and rules for matching a given semantic content and an
assigned syntactic expression, could be very fertile, acting like a
vehicle for rapid and precise understanding and consensus. People
lived before Aristotle's syllogistic, but its creation avoided heaps of
sophisms in heaps of lost time and effort. MRC offers a framework
for safely matching semantic contents and syntactic structures.

CC: Your last book *Principles of a 2nd Quantum Mechanics*
(arXiv:1310.1728, in French) presents yet another quantum mechanical formalism. What is wrong with the "1st quantum mechanics"?

MM-S: It is simply devoid of a theory of measurement acceptable
from a formal as well as from a conceptual point of view, with general
factual validity.

The von Neumann–Hilbert theory of measurement is, both, falla-
cious and devoid of general validity. As long as one is confined inside

the formalism itself it is very difficult to fully perceive this. (Personally, I am startled to discover what an incredibly long time I needed in order to acquire what I now believe to be a clear and coherent view on the global structure of the quantum mechanical formalism.)

The problem of "interiority", i.e., of ways of transgressing the limitations inside which one is imprisoned, is a very difficult problem indeed. If the imprisonment is absolute, this problem is radically devoid of a solution. This may seem trivial, but many fine authors act as if they were unaware of it, in particular, all those who make assertions concerning the entire universe. Wittgenstein stressed this epistemological fact in various contexts. He repeated that in order to be able to think of a "whole" one has to be able to be inside as well as outside of that "whole". To which he added his well-known injunction: *"whereof one cannot speak, thereof one must be silent"*.

Now, what happens when one wants to size up globally, as well as in its details, the structure of the quantum mechanical representation of micro-states? The imprisonment inside this representation, of course, is not absolute. One can place oneself outside it. But what is available outside, on which one can create a reference point for one's mind? There is classical physics and the whole classical thinking, with its "objects", its space-time and causal structures. But everybody says that quantum mechanics violates all this and nevertheless — marvellously — "is working". An organised formalism (outside of the quantum mechanical one) permitting to perceive consensually expressible specificities, or necessities, or impossibilities, does not exist.

And this is quite understandable. Indeed, quantum mechanics is the very first physical theory that introduces — implicitly — what I have called "transferred descriptions" of the physical entities. And, as I have already stressed, the whole organised thinking, which is exterior to quantum mechanics ignores, the concept of primordial transferred descriptions. So with respect to this concept an organised outside cannot exist.

As long as these conditions persist nothing can be asserted on the formalism of quantum mechanics in terms endowed with a precise meaning and with a character of objectivity. This, as a fact, is manifest for ten of years. What is cruelly lacking is an organised structure of reference, different from quantum mechanics itself, but constructed in a way that permits it to be clearly related with quantum mechanics, that admits a controlled comparison with quantum mechanics, in the details as well as globally.

So I constructed such an organised structure of reference. I maintained invariant that what is represented inside quantum mechanics, namely states of micro-systems, "micro-states", but I constructed another representation involving them. Quite independently of quantum mechanics, I brought into evidence just the necessary and sufficient conditions for constructing a communicable and consensual representation of micro-states, but nothing more. In this way an epistemological-operational-methodological representation of the genesis of very first pieces of the human knowledge on micro-states is obtained. I called this infra-(quantum mechanics) to be understood as "beneath the formalism of quantum mechanics".

By systematic reference to infra-(quantum mechanics), the formalism of quantum mechanics reveals unexpected deficiencies. Here are three of them:

- It does not distinguish clearly between the individual level of conceptualisation, and the statistical one. In fact it almost entirely occults the individual level.
- It does not represent at all, neither mathematically nor informally, the way in which a describable micro-state is generated. The process of generating a physical and individual micro-state is confused with something radically different, namely the process of "preparation for measurement of the mathematical state vector" that represents the statistics of results of measurement obtained with numerous replicas of the physical micro-state that is involved.
- Quantum mechanics lacks a generally valid theory of measurement.

I have sketched a 2nd quantum mechanics where the deficiencies enumerated above (and some others) have disappeared. This new representation — not a re-interpretation — introduces measurement operations based on the de Broglie–Bohm guidance relation, but assumed to be an observable process, not only a conceived process. And whether the process is indeed observable, or not... can be observed.

CC: Are you preparing an English version?

MM-S: I have already notably improved the French version and I shall soon update it on arXiv of quantum physics. As for the English version, it will be available before the end of July, I hope. Meanwhile I shall try to publish somewhere an extended abstract in English.

CC: Do you believe in the possibility of a grand unification between quantum mechanics and relativity?

MM-S: One can postulate that *if* one could directly observe microsystems *via* signals travelling with a universally invariant velocity, then we would construct descriptions of them that would obey Einstein's theories. There is a very strong tendency to extrapolate into absolute generality an approach that has produced remarkable successes in some given domain.

But — personally — I do not see any reason why that postulate should be particularly fertile. I do not believe that what is called a "grand unification" is the best choice of an aim for today's physics. I believe that the unique sort of a genuinely fertile unification of scientific rationality — in its entirety — can only be of a purely methodological nature. The contents should be left free of *a priori* constraints. They should emerge explicitly from all the specific conditions that are brought into play, so marked by unlimited diversity.

CC: As a researcher you have had good moments and bad moments. Can you recall one of them?

MM-S: By far the best moments that I have had as a researcher — and not very seldom — have been those that have emerged unexpectedly, when without any expressible specific cause I have suddenly felt a sort of inner certitude to have finally "understood" something that before, and for a long time, had stubbornly resisted my understanding.

Chapter 20

Grzegorz Rozenberg: Natural Computing

Professor G. Rozenberg is a Professor at the Leiden Institute of Advanced Computer Science of Leiden University, The Netherlands, and Adjoint Professor at the Department of Computer Science, University of Colorado in Boulder, USA. He has published over 500 papers, 6 books, and is a (co-)editor of more than 100 books on natural computing, formal language and automata theory, graph transformations and concurrent systems. He has founded a number of journals and book series in theoretical computer science and natural computing. He is often referred to as the guru of natural computing.

Professor Rozenberg is a Foreign Member of the Finnish Academy of Sciences and Letters, a Member of the Academia Europaea, and he is the holder of Honorary Doctorates from the University of Turku, Finland, the Technical University of Berlin, Germany, the University of Bologna, Italy and Åbo Akademi, the Swedish University in Turku, Finland. He has received the Distinguished Achievements Award of the European Association for Theoretical Computer Science.

With the artist name Bolgani, he is a performing magician specialising in close-up illusions.

CC: You commute between Boulder and Leiden. Untill very recently, you served, in various capacities, on 20 editorial boards, and used to chair quite a number of steering committees. How did you survive?

GR: The only recipe for survival is motivation and a *devotion rule* which says that one should not take any serious commitment unless one is sure that it can be fulfilled 150%. This gives you a safety margin: in unusually hectic times you can still fulfil your obligations in a satisfactory manner. My motivation also comes from a deep conviction that serving the scientific community is a very noble and satisfying activity.

CC: I did a Google search for "natural computing" and got 233,000 hits with Springer *Natural Computing: An International Journal* and the Leiden Center for Natural Computing on the first three. What is natural computing? You should know, since you coined this name and defined the scope of this area. Who were the precursors?

GR: Natural computing is the field of research that investigates both human-designed computing inspired by Nature as well as computing taking place in Nature. In other words it investigates models and computational techniques inspired by Nature, and it also investigates, in terms of information processing, phenomena taking place in Nature.

Representative examples of the first strand of research are: neural computation, evolutionary computation, quantum computing, molecular computing, cellular automata, swarm intelligence, artificial immune systems, and membrane computing. Examples of the second strand of research, computation taking place in Nature, are investigations into the computational nature of self-assembly, the computational nature of developmental processes, the computational nature of biochemical reactions, the computational nature of brain processes, and the system biology approach to bio-networks, where cellular processes are treated in terms of communication and inter-action, and hence, in terms of computation.

Research in natural computing is genuinely interdisciplinary, and it is concerned with theoretical, experimental and applied issues. As a matter of fact, natural computing forms a "natural" bridge between informatics and the natural sciences, both at the level of informa-tion technology and fundamental research. The interactions across this bridge are very fruitful: while the natural sciences are rapidly absorbing notions, techniques and methodologies intrinsic to infor-mation processing, computer science is adapting and extending its traditional understanding of the notion of computation, and compu-tational techniques, to account for computation taking place around us in Nature.

When I introduced this name in the 1980s it was considered to be a sort of science fiction, but today it has become very popular, and the science of natural computing is really flourishing: there are institutes, journals, book series, conferences, professorships... of/on natural computing.

It is difficult to pinpoint the real precursors of research in natural computing and it is always very difficult to give the just credit (to all involved) in such matters. Here are some names that come to my mind now: A. Turing (his work on morphogenesis and on connec-tionist models), J. von Neumann (biologically inspired computing), W.S. McCulloch and W. Pits (they viewed neurons as computational devices), R.P. Feynman (quantum computing), A. Lindenmayer (he considered the development of organisms as computational pro-cesses), J. Holland (who noticed that basic features of evolution can be utilised to design algorithms)... — once again, this is an *ad hoc* list. Perhaps one could also add Leonardo da Vinci to this list — he wrote in 1500 (*"Trattato della pittura"*): "those who took other inspi-ration than from Nature, master of masters, were labouring in vain."

CC: What is more important for research in natural computing: potential applications or understanding how "Nature" computes? Does "Nature" really compute?

GR: Advancing our understanding of the computation taking place in Nature will often lead to (potential) advances in human-designed computing, simply because usually the way Nature computes is superior to the way humans compute. In this sense, understanding how nature computes is "primary". But there is a catch here. Our classical notion of computation is rooted in the quest for formalising the way humans compute/calculate — it dates back (at least) to the work of Leibniz and it culminated in the first half of the 20th century with the research/results by Post, Church and Turing. Quite often, this (beautiful) notion/idea of computation does not really apply to the computation going on all around us in Nature because it violates various "underlying axioms" of the way that Nature works. I strongly believe that research into natural computing will eventually lead to a novel notion of computation, as a matter of fact to a new "science of computation" which will be developed by the interaction/co-operation of computer scientists, biologists, chemists, mathematicians, physicists... Indeed, the research into natural computing has already changed our understanding of what computing is about.

CC: Can you give examples of such differences in underlying axioms?

GR: An answer to such a question should be given by writing a series of papers but let me just mention one such difference, *persistence*.

In models of computation in computer science one assumes that if in a global state a local part of it is not "touched", then this local part will be preserved, i.e., it will be a local component of the successor global state. This does not hold in biology, e.g., when you model the living cell. An entity from a current state will be present in the successor state only if it is produced, hence sustained, by a reaction (or "thrown in" by the environment). This reflects a basic principle of bio-energetics: life must be sustained. Standard computer science models of computation would imply immortality!

CC: You have founded two journals and a book series dedicated to natural computing. Tell us more about them.

GR: The journals are: *"Natural Computing"*, originally published by Kluwer and then taken over by Springer, and the "Theoretical Computer Science, Series C: Theory of Natural Computing" (TCSC) by Elsevier and the book series is *"Natural Computing"* by Springer. *"Natural Computing"* is a journal of very broad scope: it covers experimental, applied and theoretical aspects of natural computing. There you will find publications by biologists, chemists, nanoscientists, physicists, mathematicians, computer scientists... — it really reflects the genuinely interdisciplinary nature of natural computing. It is an ideal journal for publishing special issues of interdisciplinary conferences such as, e.g., "DNA Computing". The TCSC journal, on the other hand, aims to publish theoretical papers that are in the style of the well established Theoretical Computer Science journal. The book series *"Natural Computing"* by Springer publishes both texts and monographs covering the whole spectrum of "natural computing" (theory, experiments and applications). All three publications were very well received by the scientific community. They are doing very well and will certainly grow and flourish in the years to come.

CC: You have edited four influential handbooks. The last one is the *"Handbook of Natural Computing"* which is really huge; tell us more about it.

GR: It is indeed huge: 4 volumes, around 2100 pages, over 100 contributing authors... This was the editing project which, by far, took most of my time and energy. But I am happy with the result.

The goal of the handbook was two-fold: (1) to provide an authoritative reference for a significant and representative part of the research into natural computing, and (2) to provide a convenient gateway to natural computing for motivated newcomers to this field.

Apparently, we have succeeded, as the handbook seems to be popular among both groups of readers; also, it has received very good reviews.

Sometimes one compares writing a book to writing a symphony and editing a book to directing an orchestra. I think that this is a nice and fitting comparison, except that there are two important differences between editing a book and directing an orchestra. Usually there is a rehearsal period (often intense) before an actual performance by an orchestra and mostly the individual players follow very closely (to the best of their abilities) the instructions of the conductor. Unfortunately in book editing (especially with a large number of authors, like, e.g., in a handbook) there is essentially no rehearsal and close following of the instructions by the editor is very difficult to enforce.

CC: You are also a magician...

GR: I am a performing magician, but I earn my living as a scientist. Both science and magic are beautiful and provide an exciting way of living. I feel very privileged that an interweaving of these two strands of creativity forms the double helix which determines my creative life.

Although science is very rational and magic is emotional, there are many similarities between them. Here are some similarities:

(1) First of all, both are based on creativity — the main source of success in both disciplines.

(2) An important lesson you learn from magic (either as a performer or as a spectator) is NOT to accept things on their face value (you just saw the King of Hearts in a deck of cards, but when you inspect the deck this card is not there!). Thus you need to question everything, which in fact is one of the key principles of an original research in science.

(3) Trying to achieve something astonishing/impossible is one of the key motives/incentives in both science and magic. In mathematics (theoretical computer science) we get great satisfaction if we settle a conjecture (preferably an "old" conjecture), because in this way we achieve something that was difficult/impossible for other scientists. Perhaps, the satisfaction is even greater when we disprove a conjecture, as then we are even closer to something impossible (something believed to be not true). Similarly, an important goal/essence of outstanding magic is to get as close as possible (close by *epsilon*) to something totally impossible, something that contradicts the reality (as we know it). My (magician's) business card says "Be Astonished by The Impossible."

However, there is also a cultural difference between scientists and magicians concerning achieving something "impossible". In my long scientific career I have witnessed, too often, situations where scientists (too quickly) have declared: "this looks impossible, let's do something else." On the other hand, in my long life in magic I have quite often heard a statement of this sort: "this looks impossible, let's work on it".

There are also other important differences — here is one of them. Magic is a performing art and the performance is the essence of magic. In science the standing/quality of a scientist is determined by her/his peers (e.g., the quality/acceptance of your publications is determined by reviews carried out by your peers). In magic there are essentially two ways in which your quality is determined/judged.

(1) The first one, the primary one, is the judgement by spectators — you are a good/great magician if this is the judgement by your audience (of laymen).

(2) Then there is a judgement by your peers, e.g., when you demonstrate/discuss magic in a magic club. The judgement of your peers may be very different, e.g., they may be fascinated by your mastery of a specific sleight of hand, while you may be a lousy performer. But... it is a performance that determines the emotional reaction of spectators — without it a lot of magic would be reduced to various kinds of puzzles!!!

As a matter of fact, the attitude of spectators is one of the problems facing magicians. Quite often, spectators (especially scientists or those who see a real magic performance for the first time) come to a show with the "puzzle attitude" — they sit there totally stressed, watching your every move, ready to catch you, to solve the puzzle. I always explain at the beginning of a show that this is the wrong attitude because illusions have no explanation and so there is nothing there to discover (to catch onto). In fact, if they ever got a glimpse of "something", then this particular effect was not an illusion. When I explained this to Mike Rabin (after performing for him and his wife) he called this "The Rozenberg Principle": an event observed disappears! Thus, there is a direct link between magic and quantum mechanics! Apropos, I have a magic show focused on explaining some of the principles behind various areas of natural computing — one of the card effects demonstrates some principles of quantum computing.

For several years now, many news items in a variety of media (newspapers, scientific journals, social media) have suggested that magic is just misdirection. I often get links to such news items from my friend Moshe Vardi (and he expects my comments). For example, some prestigious neuroscience journals publish studies which demonstrate how misdirection by a good magician (and some very good magicians are involved in these studies) can fool our brains and what it implies for the understanding of the functioning of the brain. Although some of these studies are interesting, a big flaw (in my opinion) is that the involved neuroscientists become convinced that they have become magicians (through conducting these experiments), and hence express opinions as if they were magicians, while the involved magicians become convinced that they have become neuroscientists (through their participation in these experiments) and hence express opinions as if they were neuroscientists. As a result, the studies/conclusions presented are often superficial. I wrote several times to Moshe that some beautiful magic effects indeed rely on misdirection, but on the other hand some beautiful magic effects have nothing to do with misdirection. You may be a top magician without ever employing misdirection — "magic by misdirection" is just a part of magic, in the same way as the graph theory or calculus are parts of mathematics.

Living in two worlds, science and magic, is also enriching from a social point of view. Through my life in magic I became embedded in a wonderful community of people (which is very different from the academic community). The notion of quality (of the magic performance) is central here and it is also easy to interact with other magicians. Once you have something interesting/amazing to show, a whole stream of interactions follows: you get comments, your spectators (magicians) show you their creations... naturally, very close contacts are established and they often lead to collaborations and friendships.

CC: How did your family react to your "magic"?

GR: When my son Daniel was a teenager, he was not really impressed by the fact that I was a university professor. But the fact that I was a magician was a different story. Once, when I got back home from my office and entered our house I found Daniel and his friend Ferdie in the hall. After Daniel introduced me to Ferdie I proceeded to the kitchen to have a glass of water. While drinking water I heard Ferdie asking Daniel "what is your father's profession?" to which Daniel replied "he is a university professor" and then a few seconds later Daniel added "but he is not stupid, he is a very good magician"! Also, my grandson Mundo is now very proud that his grandpa is a wizard.

Coincidence, predestination... are important concepts in magic. Thus, I wonder (magic, unlike mathematics, does not have to be rational) whether being a magician was my predestination. First of all, the maiden name of my mother was Zauberman (which translates into "magician") — I did not notice this connection until I was in my thirties. Then, my wife's name is Maja and during a trip to India we were told that in Hindu, Maja means "illusion". It is certainly great for a magician to be married to an illusion — this makes my magician friends pretty jealous!!!

CC: How do you see computer science after working in the field for about 50 years?

GR: The visibility and importance of computer science has grown very impressively during this period. The main reason is the spectacular progress in information and communication technology (ICT) which is very much driven by progress in computer science. This is a blessing but also a curse for computer science, because computer science is often perceived, by the public as well as by scientists from other areas of science, as a technological discipline, a collection of practical skills. Perhaps the most frequent perception of a computer scientist is that of a skilful programmer, an educated hacker. I remember that a long time ago at my university in Leiden, some physicists were not supporting the formation of the computer science department because "our people are also good programmers".

However, there is so much more to computer science than ICT. The only reasonable definition of computer science is that this is The science of information processing. If you consider a typical computer science department and observe the specialities of its faculty members, you will get a list of this sort: computer graphics, databases, human–computer interactions, natural language processing, computer architecture, programming languages, theory of computation, compiler construction, bio-informatics, concurrent systems... The only common denominator for all these research areas is that they are concerned with various aspects of information processing. As a matter of fact the term "informatics" used in Europe is much better than "computer science" which suggests that computer science is just focused on one specific device/instrument, *viz.*, computer.

Thus, informatics is the science of information processing and it is concerned with information processing in computers and elsewhere, e.g., in Nature. Therefore, informatics is a fundamental science for other scientific disciplines. This historical evolution of computer science into also becoming a fundamental science of information processing was strengthened by developments of some other scientific disciplines, especially in the second half of the 20th century, which adopted "information" and "information processing" as their central notions and thinking habits. Biology and physics are prime examples of such development — in both areas informatics provides not only instruments but also a way of thinking.

This is not just the opinion of a computer scientist, but also the conviction of top biologists and physicists. For example:

- Richard Dawkins, a famous evolutionary biologist, says "if you want to understand life, don't think about vibrant throbbing gels and oozes, think about information technology".
- Sydney Brenner, one of the best known living biologists, Nobel Prize winner, says "biology is essentially (very low-energy) physics with computation".
- John Wheeler, an eminent physicist, stated that while some time ago he thought that everything was particles, now he thinks that everything is information.

Since informatics is THE science of information processing it has a strong interdisciplinary character. As a matter of fact, I remember that in 1971 or 1972 when I was in the Department of Computer Science at the State University of New York, in Buffalo, a delegation from the national science foundation (NSF) was visiting there. Tony Ralston, our department chair, asked me (probably as a representative of the "European school") to present my vision of computer science to this delegation. I said then that I envisioned computer science departments of the future to be divided into groups dealing with the "core computer science", language processing (linguistics), artificial intelligence, biology, physics... In particular, I was arguing for biology where information processing is so apparent and so challenging to understand. Tony told me later that he heard from the delegation that they did not share my vision and, in particular, they thought that the relationship between biology and computer science was not as strong/intrinsic as I had suggested (in their opinion it was rather superficial). I am glad to realise that now, over 40 years later, everyone involved must realise that they were awfully wrong. As a matter of fact it is apparent today that the interdisciplinarity of informatics is one of the main forces driving the tremendous progress of our disciplines.

It is fashionable nowadays to discuss the grand challenges of informatics. I am myself convinced that one of the grandest grand challenges of informatics is to understand the world around us in terms of information processing. Each time progress is made in achieving this goal, both the world around us and informatics benefits. Natural computing is a natural avenue of research for achieving such progress!

CC: Please reminisce about your youth in Poland.

GR: I grew up in communist Poland, so my youth was dramatically different from the youth of my son in The Netherlands. It was not the best place to grow up, but on the other hand (seen from the perspective of time) in this way I got a deeper understanding of some important issues in life, deeper than that of my friends in my "new world". I strongly believe that deep matters in life can be understood only by experiencing them. As a matter of fact, I am often irritated by the attitude of many intellectuals who make statements of the sort "I understand what it means to live through a terrible war (or to live in a totalitarian system), because I have read many books about it".

I received my education in Warsaw, Poland. As everywhere else in the world, the quality of teachers in my schools determined my "initial" taste/liking for many subjects. Thus, I had an awful teacher of chemistry and so I did not like chemistry at all, while today I think that chemistry is relevant, fascinating and simply beautiful. On the other hand, I had a brilliant teacher of mathematics, his name was Taytelbaum. He became my idol and so I had already fallen in love with mathematics at school. Coming back to the issue of coincidences in magic, Eddy Taytelbaum, one of the nestors of magic in The Netherlands, became my idol and friend quite soon after I got embedded into Dutch magic (to understand this coincidence one has to realise that Taytelbaum is a very uncommon name in Poland and it is a very uncommon name in The Netherlands).

I chose to study electronics at Warsaw University of Technology, as then electronics was then a very modern direction of study, known for its high level of quality (entry exams were very competitive), and, most importantly, in this way I could combine my love for mathematics and physics with my curiosity about technology. It turned out to be a very good choice for me — I found many classes interesting and challenging, and, very importantly for my later life as a researcher (I am theoretician), I got an understanding/feeling, and a respect for, engineering.

For my master's thesis (for the master's degree in Computer Science) I chose "Theory of Algorithms". At that time in Poland this was a combination of Markov algorithms and Turing machines. My interest in the theory of algorithms was instigated through my study of the design of logic circuits, where a transitive closure of references led me to basic papers on automata theory.

As a matter of fact I got so fascinated by automata theory that, while I was still a student, I approached one of the assistant professors, Pawel Kerntopf (who became a very good friend of mine), and with his help organised a seminar on automata theory. This seminar involved both graduate students and faculty. It turned out to be very successful in many respects. When I recently gave a series of lectures in Warsaw, I was told by colleagues from my *Alma Mater* that at least 15 participants of my seminar later became professors in Poland and abroad!

While working on my master's thesis I met Andrzej Ehrenfeucht from the Mathematical Institute of the Polish Academy of Sciences. Meeting Andrzej changed my life in many ways. He became my source of wisdom on the theory of algorithms (my formal advisor from the department of electronics knew very little about this area). Moreover, it "clicked" between us and very quickly we became friends and later brothers by choice (we consider ourselves brothers). It is because of Andrzej that my love for the technology of information processing changed into love for the theory of information processing. We have just celebrated 50 years of scientific cooperation — during this period we have written hundreds of joint papers and spent thousands of hours talking to each other about scientific and many other matters.

Andrzej is a true Renaissance man, deeply knowledgeable about so many areas: mathematics, linguistics, geology, physics, biology, spiders, dinosaurs, fossils, history and the teaching of mathematics... Often, when I ask Andrzej a question I not only get an answer, I get a whole tutorial. Since 1971, I travel (on average twice a year) to Boulder, Colorado, where I am an Adjoint Professor in the Department of Computer Science of the University of Colorado. The main reason for me to travel there is to be with Andrzej. One of the many nice things related to our friendship/brotherhood is that Andrzej loves my magic — nobody else has seen as many of my magic shows, moreover, he is the best spectator I have ever had.

Andrzej is very interested in the history of mathematics and in the didactics of mathematics. He collaborates in research in these areas with Pat Bagget, his life partner — she is a Professor of Mathematics at New Mexico State University in Las Cruces. They are a very nice couple and it is always a pleasure when we three get together.

Telling political jokes in Poland was important for intellectual survival. This was the only way that one could beat the system into pieces. I had created many political jokes, which was pretty dangerous. As a matter of fact when I would tell a friend (whom I could trust) that I had a new joke, then he/she would first ask me "how good is this new joke?" and my typical answer would be "about 5 years" (referring to a punishment, the number of years in prison, in case I was "caught" when telling this joke). On my recent lecturing trip to Warsaw, when I met with a group of my colleagues and friends from my years in Poland, I was reminded about my creativity in inventing new jokes, and also reminded how dangerous it was. It was quite interesting for me to learn that some of my jokes are still in circulation today!

CC: Please tell us an "about 5 years" joke.

GR: Here is one. A huge factory was built in the Communist country. It was going to serve as a symbol of the superiority of the communist system, thus many visitors came to see it. Important visitors were given a tour of the factory by the mayor of the city. On one such tour when the visitors arrived at the entrance gate, the mayor proudly announced: "this is the biggest factory in the world employing 50,000 workers. It could be built only in a communist country." However, because of the noise of a truck passing by, one visitor didn't hear the first part of the sentence, so he asked: "how many people work in this factory?" The mayor answers: "oh, you mean *working* here. Perhaps two or three."

This joke describes in a compact way one of the big disasters of the communist system: the destruction of work ethic. For many years after I left Poland I had planned to write a book "*The Essence of Communism*" which would consist of a set of jokes illuminating various features of the system. Unfortunately, because of a chronic shortage of time, this project never materialised.

CC: You started your academic career at the Institute of Mathematics of Polish Academy of Sciences which was one of the world-famous mathematical research institutes...

GR: Even before I completed my master's thesis, I was offered a position at the Institute of Mathematics of Polish Academy of Science (Polish acronym: IMPAN) in the group of mathematical logic headed by Andrzej Mostowski. I was also offered a position in the electronics department, but I chose IMPAN because I wanted to pursue research in theory — this was among the best choices I have ever made! The senior members of the mathematical logic group were Mostowski, Grzegorczyk, Pawlak and Ehrenfeucht. Mostowski was a very "special" man: very kind with very good manners (a real gentleman) and genuinely friendly. He was very positive during my interview for the position in his group. He had only one small "objection", *viz.*, that I was very young. I still remember when, looking through administrative documents, he said "I see that you will be the youngest member of our group" and then he added "but this problem will resolve itself with time". I recalled this statement many times later in my life as I saw myself to be first the youngest professor, then a well-established member of a department, then a senior professor and then Professor Emeritus! The kindness of Mostowski also manifested itself in the fact that he always had time when I asked for a consultation on matters of logic. I had less contact with Grzegorczyk, but I had numerous discussions with him concerning computability theory, especially about his hierarchy of recursive functions. Grzegorczyk wrote a very good book on mathematical logic (in Polish) and I benefited a lot from discussing with him in-depth various topics from this book.

I spent a lot of time with Zdzisław Pawlak — we also became very good family friends. He was a wonderful person and a great scientist. He had a very good understanding of the applied aspects of computer science and an extraordinary talent for forming elegant, simple models capturing the essence of applications.

For a man of unusual talents he was very modest. He had a great sense of humour and loved good jokes — his laugh was very contagious. He was one of the few people whom I trusted with my new political jokes. Kayaking and walking were his two favourite physical activities. He had a great talent for writing rhymes and in the later phase of his life he painted — he was a good painter. His scientific talents are best illustrated by the framework of rough sets which he invented in his sixties. It is an area of research which is very impressive both its theory and applications, and it is immensely popular all over the world.

He was a delightful friend and I remember that I got very emotional when he told me that I was his best friend.

IMPAN was an "exclusive" institute as so many famous mathematicians worked there. Kuratowski was the director when I worked there. Among other famous mathematicians were Sierpinski, Łoś and Sikorski. I had quite frequent contact with Łoś, but especially with Robert Bartoszynski who worked with Łoś. Robert was a real *virtuoso* of, and so my main consultant on, probability theory. Because of my interest in linguistics, I also talked a lot with Robert's wife who was a linguist. I remember following some seminars by Sierpinski — he was quite old then, always taken care of by the famous, then young, number theorist Andrzej Schintzel. Because IMPAN was so well-known worldwide, we had a lot of visitors and this gave me a chance to meet a lot of famous scientists. For example, I met Solomon Marcus when he was visiting Pawlak. I spent a lot of time with him talking about science and many other matters, he also met my parents and my wife. I must have been among the first researchers he introduced to contextual grammars, a topic which I picked up again much later when I worked with Gheorghe Păun (a student of Marcus) on it. Marcus invited me to Bucharest to work together and I still remember a very nice visit there. Anyhow, I became an admirer of Marcus and remain so today. We meet from time to time at various events, and I cherish these meetings.

My relationship to Marcus also continued in a different way when during my later years in science, I became a collaborator, mentor and friend of many Romanian scientists educated/influenced by him. This group includes Lila Kari, Gheorghe Păun, yourself and Elena, Alexandru Mateescu and Ion Petre. I was always impressed by the mathematical and human qualities of the disciples of Marcus.

My first big new research topic at IMPAN was category theory — I got interested in both pure category theory and its potential to express and investigate computations. Concerning the former, I worked on axioms for the category of relations and this work brought me in contact with Samuel Eilenberg. I was very flattered by his interest in my work. We also remained in contact after I left Poland. He visited me in Utrecht and stayed in our apartment. His main passion outside mathematics was collecting certain types of figurines from Indonesia. Because of the long history of Dutch-Indonesian relationship, The Netherlands was a real gold mine for these figurines. So I visited a lot of "strange places" with him in Utrecht and Amsterdam.

At the beginning of my commuting to Boulder I met Stan Ulam, another famous Polish mathematician. Also, together with Aristid Lindenmayer, we invited Ulam to attend a symposium we organised in The Netherlands (on information processing in biology). Thus I had many conversations with Ulam and was fascinated by him. Mostowski, Eilenberg and Ulam were typical representatives of the famous old school of Polish mathematics. There was something common (in my perception) to all three of them: they were brilliant, erudite, well-mannered and had a very good sense of humour (I was certainly telling jokes to all three of them).

I was very much influenced by the paper "Finite automata and their decision problems" by M. Rabin and D. Scott — it was certainly one of the most important papers I have ever read. I started right away working on various problems inspired by it. In particular, I started to develop a theory of multi-tape automata, this was going very well and I hoped it would become my PhD thesis. Then one day Mostowski brought a manuscript (I think that this was an official report from Harvard, perhaps a PhD thesis) by Arnold Rosenberg on multi-tape automata, and asked me to look it up in connection with my own research. I observed that more than half of my results (with many of them already presented at our internal seminar) were covered by Arnold. I even remember making a joke that if Arnold's surname was written with "z" (hence "Rozenberg") then ALL my results would be covered by him! Mostowski then explained to me (he was always very kind and supportive) that in mathematics if you get "good" results and discover later that these results were proved by good scientists, then in this way you get the best possible confirmation that your research is on a good path. I decided then to switch to research on certain types of regular languages and got my PhD for this work.

This and a number of other events made me realise how isolated we were in Poland (nobody really cared about "us"!), even though through personal connections of Mostowski and others we were in a privileged position. I remember making a resolution then that if I ever got out of Poland, I would "do a lot for the scientific community" as opposed to "doing a lot only for myself". This resolution got strongly implemented when I left Poland. I have devoted a huge amount of my professional time to service for the academic community — this includes my work for EATCS, my work for organising conferences, my work for founding new journals and book series... Clearly, my list of publications would be much longer if I had not spend so much time in the service of the scientific community. But, I always remembered my resolution from Poland and really get a lot of satisfaction from serving the community and seeing many positive effects of this service.

To summarise, I was really lucky and privileged to work at IMPAN. It was a real oasis of tranquility: while there, the surrounding reality of the totalitarian political system was non-existent. The only thing that counted was science, there were no political activities. Clearly, the situation must have been very different for people running the institute, as they had to deal with the outside world.

CC: Why do you like Hieronymus Bosch's paintings so much?

GR: I was always interested in paintings and during my youth in Poland I was "possessed" by impressionism. I read everything that was accessible to me there about impressionism, I looked up all possible albums with reproductions, I even had reproductions of van Gogh and Monet hanging on the walls in my room. When I settled in The Netherlands, it was a sheer delight to visit museums here and see real paintings by impressionists as well as to go to Paris to see even more.

However, one day, just by chance, I bought a book with many Bosch reproductions, and right away I fell in love with Bosch (and the impressionists were moved to the back burner). This love for Bosch only intensified with time.

He is an enigmatic painter in many ways and therefore a difficult painter for art historians to analyse. Hence, e.g., we know very little about his life, we don't even know when he was born except for some reasoning which leads to "around 1450" — his funeral took place on 9 August 1516. This on its own is quite an obstacle in analysing his art. Furthermore, no more than 25 of his paintings survived and we are not even sure whether all of them are authentic. He signed only a few of these paintings and none of them are dated.

But what we know for sure is that he was a genius, who went his own way, and was very much ahead of his time — much of his creation is of timeless beauty. For me he is the personification of vision and creativity. My admiration for him is very well expressed by Jose de Siguenza (1544–1606) who was a historian, monk and prior of the monastery of *El Escorial* (a Spanish royal site close to Madrid). *El Escorial* was home to many Bosch paintings collected by Phillip II of Spain. Jose de Siguenza wrote that he was amazed that "a single mind could imagine so many things".

The best known of Bosch's paintings is "*The Garden of Earthly Delights*" in *Museo del Prado* in Madrid. Many art historians list it as one of the most remarkable paintings ever. For me Prado is the best museum in the world, as they have (in one room!) 5–6 paintings of Bosch (recall that no more than 25 paintings of Bosch exist today). Madrid is my favourite art city as they also have Bosch paintings in *Palacio Real* and close by in *El Escorial*. Then on top of this Madrid is famous for its school of card magic!!!

Bosch's drawings are less known than his paintings, but his drawings are also extraordinary. Again, no more than 40 of his drawings survived. He almost exclusively used only pen in his drawings. My favourite drawing by Bosch is "*The Wood Has Ears, the Field Eyes*", which depicts a larger tree in front of a grove of smaller trees, all set up in a meadow. The drawing shows a number of open eyes embedded in a meadow and two large ears embedded between trees of the grove. There is a later Netherlandish woodcut from 1546 (30 years after Bosch's death), possibly based on Bosch's drawing, which illustrates the same theme, where the inscription says "The field has eyes, the wood has ears, I will see, be silent, and listen." This demonstrates the timeliness of Bosch's art — think about today's concerns about privacy in the time of electronic media, surveillance cameras, etc. Even more interestingly, at the top of this drawing there is an inscription in Latin which says "For poor is the mind that always uses the ideas of others and invents none of its own." Most probably it was the "official motto" of his workshop, but it surely should be the motto for very researcher!

The larger central tree in this drawing has an owl sitting in a natural hollow opening in it. During this time period in this geographic location (Brabant) owls were a symbol of wickedness and evil spirits. Thus, the owl in the centre of the drawing was contributing to the intended theme of the drawing.

As a matter of fact, owls appear a lot in paintings of Bosch and also in his drawings. For example, another drawing of Bosch which I like a lot is "*Owl's Nest on a Branch*". Also, owls are quite central in "*The Garden of Earthly Delights*". Bosch was certainly fascinated by owls!

Since I am also fascinated by owls, this makes Bosch art even more dear to me. My interest in owls originated in science, more precisely in my collaboration with Juhani Karhumäki. I was his mentor when we worked on his PhD thesis with Arto Salomaa (today Juhani is one of the world leaders on the combinatorics of words). On one of his working visits to my home in The Netherlands, he brought many pictures of young (baby) owls in their nests. Juhani is also an ornithologist and spends a lot of time during the summers (mostly in June) banding young birds high in their tree nests (sometimes 30–40 metres high!!!). He is also an excellent photographer, so his pictures of young owls were really beautiful.

I fell in love, first with the pictures of owls, and then with owls in general. I started to read a lot about real owls but also about the images and the symbolism of owls in various cultures all over the world. Today I have a collection of over 2000 owls of all sorts: real stuffed owls, ceramic owls, glass owls, metal owls, silver owls, incrustrated owls. . .

A painting by Bosch which is well known to many magicians is "*The Conjurer*". It is a beautiful painting depicting a magician performing (most probably at a market).

I need now to make a digression into the history of magic. Unfortunately the history of magic is not so glorious, as magic was often used as an instrument of control and as a skill for cleaning people out of their possessions/money. As examples of the former, one can point out that pharaohs in Egypt had magicians in their entourage who performed all kinds of tricks which would prove that pharaohs did possess inhuman powers given to them by gods. As examples of the latter, one can point out magicians robbing people of money at markets by playing "very fair" cups and balls or 3-card monte guessing games. Thus cheating became closely associated with magicians. Magic became a performing art only in the 19th century (with a lot of credit for this transformation given to the famous French magician Robert Houdin). Today, magic flourishes as a performing art and is often referred to as the queen of the performing arts.

Going back to *"The Conjurer"* painting, it depicts a magician at one side of a table, with cups there and a small ball kept "professionally" in his right hand, clearly performing the famous cheating game of "cups and balls". A small group of spectators stands at the other side of the table with one of them "central" in this composition. This central spectator bends over the table watching the magician and is totally flabbergasted by the performance, so much so that a green frog jumps out of his gaping mouth (there was a proverb in Brabant at this time saying that you may be so flabbergasted that a frog will jump out of your mouth). While this spectator is so lost in the performance, a thief (perhaps a confederate of the magician) is cleaning him out of money kept in a leather pouch.

This beautiful painting shows Bosch as a keen observer of everyday life, while it also reminds magicians about the not-so-glorious history of magic.

I would like to add a comment about my love of visual arts. It began in Poland when I was a teenager, and it was purely "theoretical" in the sense that nobody in my family had any talent for painting. This situation changed dramatically when my son Daniel was born — it was clear since he was about three years old that drawing and painting were his vocation. Indeed, he became a very well-known visual artist — creations of DADARA (his artist name) are amazing. Since neither me, nor my wife Maja, had any talent for drawing/painting, in my lectures on molecular biology I gave Daniel as an example of a "beautiful mutation" — his talent came from "nowhere". It turned out that I was wrong: just a few years ago we discovered that Maja has a real talent for painting. In fact Daniel now says that his artistic genes come from her. Thus, when my love for paintings began in Poland I had just (cheap) *reproductions* of van Gogh and Monet hanging on the walls of my room. Now our home is full of *original* beautiful paintings by DADARA and Maja!

CC: You really love books. Which of them have influenced most your professional life?

GR: I have loved books all my life. My wife said once that I spend my money on books and playing cards! However I remember that when I was a teenager in Poland, there were non-monetary ways to get access to good books. Many good books from before World War II were not available in bookstores because they were "ideologically wrong". The way to get access to these books was through... rewriting. One could borrow such an unavailable book (or a hand rewritten copy of it) for a certain period of time, and during this time one would rewrite (a part of) this book. The borrowed book had to be returned, but one would have a handwritten copy that could be read several times. Such a copy could be also exchanged for a handwritten copy of another book. Rewriting a book by hand was very time-consuming, so one had to be a real book lover to engage in this way of collecting books.

During my study years and also during my work at IMPAN I profited a lot from the lawless pirating behaviour of the Soviet Union. They were translating scientific books published in the West on a massive scale, without respect for copyrights. Moreover, all Russian books were very cheap in Poland. In this way I read many excellent science books published in the West — without the lawless behaviour of the Soviet Union I would not have had access to most of these books!

One of the blessings of working at IMPAN was their mathematics library — certainly the best source of mathematical books and journals in Poland.

Also, the library of the Institute of Foundations of Informatics of Polish Academy of Sciences (Polish acronym: IPIPAN) in Warsaw had a very good library, especially of computer science and electrical engineering books. This was my library when I was a student. I would sit there for whole days, as many of the books there (especially British and American books) could not be moved out of the library. I became a good friend with the young librarian (her name was Lidia Miernicka) and at some point we were doing something illegal (which could have had bad consequences for her): when she was closing the library in the evening I was allowed by her to take with me (secretly) a couple of books which had to be back on the shelves when she opened the library in the morning. This meant that I was studying the books all night and waiting for her to open the library to (secretly) return the books. I was extremely indebted to her. When many, many years later Poland became a non-communist country and I learned that she was the main librarian of IPIPAN I began to buy books for her library as a way of saying "thank you" for what she did for me when I was a student. When I was lecturing at IPIPAN some time ago, I was shown a wall of shelves filled with "Rozenberg books" — to see this was very satisfying and emotional for me.

I should also mention that I have a really impressive collection of books on Hieronymus Bosch, perhaps one of the best private collections in The Netherlands. Indeed a lot of money and collecting effort went into establishing this collection, but it is very useful for my studies of Bosch.

As for the books that influenced my professional life, this would be a long list which would require a long time to construct (also because of my bad memory). But on a short call, and somehow *ad hoc* I would list the following books: "*Network Analysis* " by Van Valkenburg, "*Set Theory*" by Kuratowski and Mostowski, "*Abelian Categories*" by Freyd, "*Elements of Mathematical Logic*" by Rosenbloom, "*Automata Studies*" edited by Shannon and McCarthy, "*Computability and Unsolvability*" by Davis, "*Algebraic Structure Theory of Sequential Machines*", by Hartmanis and Stearns, "*Mathematical Theory of Context-Free Languages*" by

Ginsburg, "*Formal Languages*" by Salomaa, "*The Language of Life*" by Beadle and Beadle, "*Dealing with Genes*" by Berg and Singer, "*Recombination DNA*" by Watson, Tooze and Kurtz, "*Bioenergetics*" by Lehninger, and several books by Peter Atkins on chemistry and thermodynamics.

PART 3

Social Aspects of Computing

Chapter 21

Brian E. Carpenter: The Internet

Dr. Brian E. Carpenter, http://www.cs.auckland.ac.nz/ *~brian, is a distinguished computer scientist and engineer working on Internet standards and technology. The University of Auckland was privileged to attract Brian in 2007 and he was appointed professor in 2009. Before coming to Auckland, he led the networking group at CERN, the European Laboratory for Particle Physics and worked for IBM as a Distinguished Engineer. During his career he has published in various areas: automatic speech recognition, control software, programming languages, networking and the history of computing. Brian has chaired the Internet Architecture Board, the Internet Engineering Task Force, and served as a trustee of the Internet Society. Brian was heavily involved in the design and deployment of IPv6. He is also interested in the quality of service, management and measurement issues of the Internet. Brian was a member of the IBM Academy of Technology (membership lapses when one leaves IBM).*

CC: Can you please succinctly describe the history of the Internet?

BC: That's a tall order, but here goes. Packet switching was invented in the 1960s, by Paul Baran in the US and independently by Donald Davies in the UK. Various packet-switching networks were prototyped, most famously the Advanced Research Projects Agency Network (ARPANET) starting in 1969. In the early 1970s, the idea of interconnecting networks (hence *inter-net*) using a single logical addressing scheme and a common packet format was raised by Louis Pouzin in France, and rapidly adopted by the ARPANET community. This led to the pioneering design of the Transmission Control Protocol/Internet Protocol (TCP/IP) by Vint Cerf and Bob Kahn, which was also the first clear example of a layered protocol stack. TCP/IP was deployed on the ARPANET on 1 January 1983 and one can say that the Internet has existed since that day.

A key event was the availability of free TCP/IP software in the Berkeley Unix distribution 4.2BSD, also in 1983, which led to its rapid spread throughout the academic community and the emerging personal workstation market. As the 1980s progressed, there was an era of protocol wars, in which TCP/IP fought against proprietary protocols and against the "official" standards emerging from the International Telegraph Union (ITU) and the International Organization for Standardization (ISO). TCP/IP won for a variety of pragmatic reasons. At the same time, international connectivity appeared, spurred on by the continued progress of Unix in the academic world, as did the appetite for collaboration. For example, the first "high-speed" transatlantic link, at 1.5 Mbit/s, was installed between Europe (my team at CERN) and the Cornell node of the National Science Foundation (NSF) network, in March 1990. Probably the two most significant events since 1990 were the release of the Mosaic web browser in 1993 and the privatisation of the NSFnet in 1995; these together enabled the public emergence of the Internet as the medium for business, entertainment and social interaction that it has become.

CC: The Internet is a "network of millions of networks". Who owns the backbone of the Internet?

BC: Although one often speaks of the "backbone" or the "core" of the Internet, there truly is no such thing. The network is structured as a mesh, with surprisingly little hierarchy. One can think of it as a very large experiment in graph theory, with the added twist that nodes of the graph have minds of their own and may misbehave in various ways.

In as far as there is a hierarchy, it consists of local Internet service providers (ISPs) offering packet-level connectivity to individual subscribers and to enterprises, and upper-layer ISPs offering national and international interconnections. Another component of the mesh consists of Internet exchange points (IXPs) which act as neutral packet exchanges. All of the players — local and upper-layer ISPs, IXPs and enterprise networks — design their own network to provide the degree of redundancy they are willing to pay for.

Thus, one can see that the "backbone" of the Internet, which is really a mesh of meshes, has no single ownership — it's a giant cooperative. This cooperative works because it is mediated technically by the routing protocol known as border gateway protocol 4 (BGP4) and economically by business agreements between the ISPs — some of which are financial arrangements in which one ISP pays another for service, and some of which are peer-to-peer agreements to exchange traffic with no financial consequence.

The essence of packet switching using a protocol such as BGP4 is that when there is a breakage in the network for any reason whatsoever (natural disaster, man-made disaster, technical error or even bankruptcy), the routing system will automatically reconfigure itself to avoid the damage. Thus there *appears* to be a stable core but the reality is otherwise.

CC: How many ISPs deal with international interconnections? Are they private or government sponsored?

BC: I can't really answer numerically, but the typical pattern in a country of any size is that there are some purely local ISPs who only handle local customers, and therefore buy their international transit service from a larger ISP with direct international connections. These larger ISPs will also have their own local customers. It's pretty rare today for international connections to be government sponsored — presumably that happens in a few countries, but private enterprise rules the roost. There are a handful of major international ISPs who operate more or less on a global basis. It's ironic that the Internet, widely used as a communications medium by anti-globalisation campaigners, is itself the epitome of globalised free enterprise.

CC: The construction in 1985 by NSF of a university 56 kilobit/s network backbone was followed by a higher speed 1.5 megabit/s backbone — the NSFNet. The transition from academia to more commercial interests began in 1988. In spite of the fact that nobody is in charge of the Internet, it seems that there is a strong link, from the very first days, between the USA Government and the Internet. Is it true, and if yes, in what form?

BC: Certainly at its origin, the Internet was mainly funded by the USA through the Department of Defence, but as a research project; it was never used operationally for military purposes. Even the early international extensions to Norway and the UK, which were funded under NATO auspices, were pure research exercises. The switch to NSF funding really marked the recognition in the USA that the Internet was of general utility to the scientific research community (i.e., networking *for* research instead of research *about* networking). A similar pattern applied as the Internet grew in other countries, although in many cases the motive for government funding was the support of research *and* education; hence the designation National Research and Education Network (NREN) that is often used. For example, the growth of government- or university-funded NRENs in Eastern Europe after the fall of communism was spectacular.

When the NSFnet was closed in favour of commercial ISPs in 1995, two things happened. One was that a group of US universities created the Internet2 project, effectively a high-speed NREN for the USA. The other thing was that key administrative functions of the Internet, previously funded under contract by the USA Government, had to be housed somewhere. There was much discussion of what to do, revolving around the late Jon Postel, who had been running those administrative functions for many years. (I was chairing the Internet Architecture Board at that time, and thus found myself in a meeting in the Old Executive Office Building in Washington D.C. with Ira Magaziner, who was working on this issue for the Clinton/Gore Administration.) The result, considerably simplified, was that an independent not-for-profit corporation (ICANN, the Internet Corporation for Assigned Names and Numbers, see `http://www.icann.org`) was created to take over this administrative work. In the creation of ICANN, there was a triangular tension between commercial interests (who wanted a free-for-all), governmental interests (who saw the network as an emerging national asset) and the general Internet community (who saw the network as a worldwide communal asset). At the end of the discussion, and under heavy pressure from the USA Government, ICANN was set up independently, but operating under USA laws and under an agreement signed with the USA Department of Commerce. This was a compromise and like any compromise is disliked by some. As we speak, discussions about termination of this agreement are proceeding, with the same triangle of interests still evident. However, the Internet's administrative functions have continued without a break, from the beginning of the ARPANET until the present day.

BC: (2014) In early 2014, the US Department of Commerce announced its intention to end its contract with ICANN, leading to vigorous discussion with in the Internet governance community. We can come back to that later, because it has interesting ramifications.

CC: I tried to read more about the Internet2 project and found quite a wealth of information at `http://www.uazone.org/znews/internet2/internet2.html#Internet2`. In particular, there seems to be a mixture of projects going under the Internet2 umbrella, some sponsored by NSF, some by a consortium of universities, while others are funded by the USA Government. The project also includes Canada and some European partners as well.

BC: Yes. It's an important project, even though its name is a little confusing — it is a major R&D project that also provides services to US academia, and as you say it collaborates widely with other regions. We could also mention the many projects in networking sponsored by the European Union's R&D Framework Programmes, and similar projects in the major Asian economies. Generally speaking there is strong synergy between the NRENs and national or international R&D activities, continuing the trend set by the ARPANET 40 years ago.

CC: Are there basic goals for the development of the Internet?

BC: There are so many special interests today that there must be a hundred answers to that question, depending on who you ask. My personal opinion is "the three S's": scaling, stability and security. We need the Internet to scale-up to support a human population of ten billion people. We need it to be stable and reliable. We need it to be secure, both to protect privacy and freedom of information, and to minimise abuse.

CC: Who pays for the Internet?

BC: You do, Cris! In general, the network is user-funded (whether the user in question is a private individual, a business, or a research or education institute). Obviously in some cases the funds come ultimately from taxpayers, but outright government subsidy is rare.

CC: Is anybody (organisation) theoretically capable of shutting down the Internet?

BC: I don't believe so, although the difference between theory and practice is hard to define in this case. In what one might call theoretical theory, ICANN could instruct the operators of the 13 "root servers" of the domain name system (DNS) to cease operations; if they obeyed, nobody would be able to convert names to addresses any more. But in any realistic theory, some of those root server operators would simply refuse to obey, and only 1 of the 13 is needed for the network to carry on.

There is always the risk of cyber-sabotage to the DNS or the basic world wide routing system (the afore mentioned BGP4). However, those systems were designed to be resilient against partial failures, which makes total failure under software attack most unlikely.

CC: I like the syntagm "theoretical theory": it reminds me of Jaffe and Quinn "theoretical mathematics" (used in their provocative paper published in *Bull. Amer. Math. Soc.* 29 (1993), 1–13).

BC: Well, Internet engineers have a saying: in theory, there's no difference between theory and practice, but in practice, there is!

CC: Interestingly, we have 13 "root servers" of the DNS. Am I really wrong if I "theoretically" call them the "Internet core" (not backbone)? It would be interesting to know more about them: where are they located? Who owns them? Do they communicate between themselves in a special way?

BC: They are certainly crucial. Without them, users would be reduced to typing in numerical addresses. They are located in very secure buildings scattered around the world, and they are owned and operated by a variety of organisations, including Internet registries, NRENs, universities and three USA agencies. And by the way, although there is a technical limitation to 13 root server addresses, there are actually many copies of some of the root servers, using an addressing trick called "anycast", whereby multiple computers are able to answer to the same numerical IP address. There is a nice map at `http://www.root-servers.org/`. Root servers all supply the same information, which is supplied at global level by ICANN, so no horizontal communication between them is required.

CC: The Internet changes "in flight", to use one of your expressions. Given its huge size, how is it possible to be so robust?

BC: Firstly, the basic principle of connectionless packet switching is that each packet travels independently of its colleagues, and includes its own source and destination address. This in itself turns out to be a strong point for robustness under change (whether the change is essential or accidental): we basically have only one atomic operation to perform — send the packet in the right direction.

Secondly, from the beginning it was accepted that packets may get lost or damaged. This led to the "end-to-end principle" of design (first documented by Jerry Saltzer and colleagues at MIT). This states that the end systems in a communication should not assume any function inside the network *except* a best effort to deliver packets. All functions such as error detection, error correction, retransmission and security should be provided solely by the end systems.

Again, this principle is a very strong point for robustness — even if the network discards a noticeable fraction of the packets, end systems can and must recover the situation.

This principle hasn't been applied perfectly (firewalls are a counter-example) and cannot work perfectly (as glitches in voice over IP calls show) but it has kept the Internet up and running since 1983.

CC: What is the Internet Engineering Task Force (IETF, see `http://www.ietf.org`)?

BC: It's the self-organised community that develops and maintains the basic standards for IPs — the IP itself, transport protocols (TCP and others), elementary application protocols, and associated routing, security and management protocols. Although the IETF grew out of the original ARPANET project, it is now completely autonomous, very international in nature, and largely populated by engineers from companies in the networking and IT industries. It's organised in about 120 separate working groups, and holds three week-long meetings per year. However, most of the detailed work is carried out by email, allowing effective remote participation. The IETF's distinguishing characteristic is that it has no formal membership and no voting — decisions are taken by arguing to the point of rough consensus.

CC: There are a myriad of committees and organisations related to Internet standards (your web page once listed more than 50 such organisations you were aware of). Do they have any impact?

BC: Sometimes yes, sometimes no. We see cases of small industrial groupings creating a self-appointed "standards consortium" with quite expensive membership fees to develop a standard for a very specific technology. If the technology succeeds commercially, this rather closed "standard" can be very helpful to the companies involved (especially if the technology is patented). We also see cases of *ad hoc* consortia developing standards for a new general-purpose technology. If the consortium acts in an open manner and its technology succeeds in the market, everybody benefits. The IETF (founded in 1986) is indeed an example of this. The World Wide Web Consortium (founded in 1994, see `http://www.w3.org`) is another. In general, it seems that a standards organisation that has open debates and modest fees, and embraces general-purpose technology, has more impact than one with closed meetings and high fees that deals with very specific technology.

CC: "Spam, fraud, and denial-of-service attacks have become significant social and economic problems" — you wrote in your paper "Better, Faster, more Secure" (*Computer Architecture* 4/10 January 2007). Can we briefly discuss these three problems? Let's start with spam. A paper "Most Spam Comes from just Six Botnets" by John Leyden (posted at `http://www.theregister.co.uk/2008/02/29/botnet_spam_deluge`) claims that "Six botnets are responsible for 85% of all spam, according to an analysis by net security firm Marshal". What's a botnet?

BC: It's a large set of infected computers carrying a specific item of malware (malicious software), which acts collectively as a robot under the control of a *botmaster* who is a malicious individual. The infection is of course distributed like any modern virus, by infected email or websites.

CC: How does the scheme work?

BC: Simple enough. The malware might be constructed to pull a number of email addresses at random from the infected host's email address book, and send a particular spam message to those addresses. The botmaster, who sells his services on a black market, will broadcast the spam to all his bots, using intermediate hops to obscure his true location. His bots will then send the spam onwards, from and to seemingly random addresses. (It isn't sexist to say "his"; these people always seem to be male).

CC: The six botnets refereed to by Leyden are wellknown. Why is it so difficult to fight them?

BC: Firstly, botnets send spam and their own malware can be transmitted *via* infected spam. So the population of infected machines is self-propagating almost at the speed of light. Secondly, botmasters are hard to find, since they use intermediate hops as proxies. They *can* sometimes be found, as the example of the botmaster "AKILL" convicted in New Zealand showed.

CC: Who benefits from the "genuine" garbage spam?

BC: I think you mean spam that appears to have no coherent content in any language. Well, it could be a vector for infection. It could be practice for a botmaster, or a rather silly form of denial-of-service attack. Or maybe it's the Martians?

CC: What about fraud? Is authentication an enemy of privacy?

BC: Remember that authentication goes both ways. If I, as a customer, am connected to the genuine website of my bank, I expect the bank to authenticate me, and then to keep my transaction private, just as I would if standing at the counter. The real problem is in the other direction. If I mistype one letter in my bank's URL, and a criminal has created a perfect clone of the bank's website, whose only purpose is to extract my password from me, how do I know that I have reached a fraudulent website? For that, I would need to use the bank's public key in some reverse authentication mode. Personally, I'd rather be sure of mutual authentication before I start worrying about privacy. Cloned websites used without mutual authentication are probably one of the biggest dangers today.

CC: How difficult is it to check if a website has clones?

BC: Quite hard. The creator of the clone will not advertise except in fraudulent emails. The clone's URL name will be chosen to look visually as much like the original as possible (perhaps substituting a "1" for an "i", for example), so that the victim is unlikely to notice. Another trick is to incorporate a common typing error in the fraudulent name, in the hope that a few people will visit the URL purely by accident. Ideally, of course, public key cryptography and trusted certification authorities suffice to verify that a "bank" is really a bank, but can we expect 100% of the general population to understand the subtleties of this?

CC: What about denial-of-service attacks?

BC: Unfortunately these are built into the packet-switching model. If somebody chooses to send me an overwhelming flood of packets, the network does its job by delivering them. When a site is subject to such an attack, there are defensive techniques that can be used, but they are all palliatives — the rogue packets will continue to arrive. If they come from a single source, defence is relatively easy, and the source can be traced and blocked, but if the attack is launched by a botnet, defence is pretty tricky.

CC: What is the Internet quality of service?

BC: Traditionally, it's "best effort", i.e., packets will be delivered with high probability but not guaranteed. Some years ago when bandwidth was scarce, we could sometimes see appalling loss rates (up to 20% of packets lost) on congested routes; fortunately this is rare today.

There have been several attempts to improve on this, although in practice most ISPs simply tune their networks to minimise packet loss. The simplest solution to deploy is known as "differentiated ser-vices", in which packets are classified into a few classes of traffic as they enter the network, and the routers run a different queuing algo-rithm for each class of packets. For example, a very simple approach would be to put voice over IP packets in a fast queue, and everything else in a best-effort queue. As long as bandwidth remains cheap, this is probably all that is needed.

CC: How can you measure it?

BC: Traditionally one measures achieved throughput, loss rate, transit delay and jitter. The first three will be means over a given period and the jitter will express the variability of the transit delay. Throughput and loss rate are quite easy to measure using logging software at both ends; transit delay and jitter need synchronised clocks and driver-level software.

CC: How safe is the Internet? Some problems are clearly not "technological": we cannot stop somebody voluntarily giving their credit card details to a phishing site, can we?

BC: Exactly. But neither can we blame someone with poor eyesight for not noticing a mistyped URL, nor an ordinary consumer for failing to have fully up-to-date virus protection. However, I think it's hard to argue that the Internet is really more dangerous than the rest of society; there have always been conmen, and there have always been victims.

CC: Is Web 2.0 a meaningful concept?

BC: It's certainly true that there seem to be a number of new, dynamic application layer technologies sitting on top of the old static web and the first generation of interactive mechanisms. I find it very hard to see a break point where we changed from Web to Web 2; perhaps I've been watching the standards and technology evolve for too long. I think the keyword is "evolve", because nobody can afford discontinuity if they're trying to run a business. The notion of a website being "closed for maintenance" is not even funny! So I think that Web 2.0 is a nice marketing name for routine progress.

BC: (2014) The buzzword has changed since 2008: now the next new thing is HTML5. Again, it's really not much more than routine progress. But the problem caused by relying on new features when many users still run old browsers will only get worse.

CC: What about a "parallel" Internet? Is it possible? Is it going to be safer? Is it feasible?

BC: It's a delusion. Again, the Internet is a business now. Discontinuity just isn't an option. Anything new that comes along simply must plug into what we have. Of course, this doesn't preclude testing out new ideas on isolated test networks, but to be of real value, it must be deployed on the main Internet.

BC: (2014) We'll talk about the Snowden revelations later. However, one political reaction it has produced is the notion of a European network so that traffic doesn't pass through America to be spied upon. Again, it's a delusion. The Internet only has value because it's worldwide; and traffic can be spyed upon just as easily in Europe as in America. Similarly, attempts to limit Internet access to approved content, as some countries have tried to do, will ultimately fail. Where there's a will, there's a way around the filters.

CC: Please tell us more about IPv6.

BC: This is a case in point. The 1970s design of IP only allowed in theory for four billion addresses, and in practice we can't use them all. So we need a new version of IP, which because of a few false starts is version 6, allowing for an almost unlimited number of addresses. It's well defined and is included in many products now, but there are quite some practical challenges to get it into general use without discontinuity. This must happen over the next few years, because otherwise the Internet's address registries are expected to run out of address space in about 2010. I think this is an area, like the early Internet, where universities should take the lead.

CC: This is interesting, how "unlimited" is the number of addresses allowed by IPv6 and what is the reason for this huge jump?

BC: The decision was taken to expand the address size of the old IPv4 protocol from 32 bits to 128 bits in IPv6, which raises the size of the address space to the fourth power, or increases it by 29 orders of magnitude, to about 3.4×10^{38} addresses. Obviously, nobody expects to address that many objects on the Internet. The reason for the large increase is to allow some structure within an address, for example, to allow separate parts of the address to represent a particular subnetwork and a particular computer interface on that subnetwork.

CC: You have been heavily involved in the design of IPv6 — your talk on this topic given at IBM in Auckland a couple of years ago steered my interest in data communications. Please tell us more about your own contributions to the IPv6 project.

BC: I was fortunate enough to become an active participant in the IETF just when its study of "IP — the Next Generation", or IPng, was starting, in 1993. We considered several alternative proposals and finally a rough consensus was formed for what became IPv6. I helped in the analysis and comparison of those proposals, and I've been contributing to the standards development process ever since. Actually the basic IPv6 standard has hardly changed since 1996, although there has been constant tuning and refinement. What has proved very hard is developing operational solutions for the coexistence of the old IPv4 and the new IPv6 during the transition process. It's been described as attempting to change the engines on an aircraft in flight. Among other things, Keith Moore (University of Tennessee) and I contributed one of the mechanisms for connecting IPv6 "islands" together across an IPv4 ocean. Altogether, I've contributed substantially to numerous IETF "Request For Comment" documents on IPv6 topics. Today, I'm most interested in practical deployment issues.

CC: I know that predictions are hard, but I cannot resist asking you the obvious question: "what's coming next?"

BC: I hoped you weren't going to ask that. I certainly hope to see IPv6 in general use by about 2015 (five years later than my original hope). There will need to be some changes in the wide-area routing system to cope with continued growth, and active research is going on in that area. I hope we see security functions moving to their proper place in the end systems, with the role of firewalls declining. I think we'll see voice and video services in widespread use, although I doubt we will see the end of broadcast radio and TV. I'm sure that business use of distributed computing services will continue to grow. I'm really unsure what to expect in mobile services. Personally, I find it hard to believe that the things I do on my PC or watch on my TV will ever translate to a hand-held device with a tiny keyboard. Two things that are pretty certain, however, are that everything interesting will run over IP, and that we will be surprised and delighted by new, creative uses of this wonderful infrastructure.

BC: (2014) We are seeing decent growth in IPv6 now. The central registry (IANA) did indeed run out of IPv4 addresses in 2011, and the regional registries are now approaching the same point. As a result, content providers such as Akamai, Facebook and Google are reporting rapid growth in IPv6 traffic. All the same, many content providers and Internet service providers still have work to do.

CC: (2014) We've been reading a lot recently about Internet governance. What does that mean exactly?

BC: If you ask that question to 10 people, you will probably get 10 different answers, so I can only give a personal opinion. There are many aspects of Internet technology that need to be specified, administered and operated in a way that is really just a technical matter which doesn't deserve the term "governance." Also, there are many societal impacts of modern telecommunications that do require some kind of governance but are not specific to the Internet — essentially these are the effects on society that Marshall McLuhan predicted as effects of electrical communication long before the Internet was invented. These issues aren't contingent on the Internet as such, and society needs to deal with them regardless of Internet technology. Examples are freedom of information, privacy of personal information, consumer protection, electronic fraud and so on. However, between these very broad issues and the purely technical aspects of the Internet lie a number of issues of societal importance that are directly linked to specific aspects of Internet technology. These, in my opinion, are the proper subject matter for the discussion of Internet governance.

The problem we have is that, too often, the very broad societal issues are lumped together with both Internet governance issues and even some technical issues. This leads to very confused discussions and to false conclusions. A good example is pervasive surveillance, which we should also discuss.

CC: (2014) Which topics, in your view, really fit into the Internet governance rubric? And where should the other topics be discussed?

BC: I have quite a short list of Internet governance topics:
- The creation of new top-level domains in the DNS.
- The resolution of disputes about names within top-level domains.

- Privacy of registration data.
- Interconnection arrangements between ISPs.
- Coordination of security incidents with law enforcement.
- Tracking and tracing domain names and IP addresses across national borders for law enforcement purposes.

There may be others, but I apply a tight criterion: the issue needs to have societal impact and it needs to be contingent on specific Internet technology. Thus, for example, I exclude spam, which can be delivered by multiple technologies, not just the Internet, so it should be covered by laws and treaties about fraud and consumer protection. Perhaps surprisingly, I also exclude network neutrality, because it is a competition and consumer protection issue. This exemplifies the answer for all the other topics. They are issues that society has to manage irrespective of the Internet, by social contract, law or treaty as the case may be.

CC: (2014) What risks are there if the governance arrangements fail in some way?

BC: Internet engineers have a saying: "the Internet routes around damage." Originally this referred to resilient routing algorithms, but it's turned out to be much more generally true. I suspect that if something went seriously wrong in the governance area, people in the technical community would rather quickly get together and cobble a new organisation into existence, on a volunteer basis, probably over the weekend. The people who end up in Internet operational jobs tend to be can-do people who react quickly under pressure.

CC: (2014) You seem to be saying that pervasive surveillance isn't an Internet governance issue as such. Then whose problem is it?

BC: It's fundamentally a political problem. For students of the history of signals intelligence, there is a very direct line between Room 40 at the Admiralty in London during World War I, Bletchley Park during World War II, the equivalent activities in the USA and the widespread surveillance revealed by Edward Snowden. Since we're having this conversation in New Zealand, it's worth recalling that today's signals intelligence operation here, the Government Communications Security Bureau (GCSB) is the direct descendant of New Zealand's cooperation with Australia, Canada, the USA and the UK during World War II. It's absolutely no surprise that these activities, which started as literal wire-tapping on telegraph cables, have been extended to cover mobile telephones and the Internet. Of course, the extent of the surveillance, and the way it can touch ordinary citizens, is new and has shocked many people. And the only safe assumption is that all major governments are doing this, not just the Americans and their English-speaking allies.

Technically, what's going to happen is that standards and software, to make end-to-end encryption easier to use, will appear over the next year or two. But secret key management is an enormous challenge, even for sophisticated organisations. How ordinary citizens can be expected to do this is beyond me. Citizens need to be able to trust their own government and, worse, other governments too. That's a challenge for the democratic process and the rule of law.

CC: (2014) What about ICANN today? The USA Government has announced its intention to terminate the contract between the USA Dept. of Commerce and ICANN in 2015. Does this matter for global surveillance?

BC: As mentioned earlier, ICANN is a not-for-profit corporation which basically has an administrative job — registering and publishing the parameters needed by IPs. But that has an aspect that borders on governance: what policies should apply for assigning valuable resources? Fortunately, most parameters aren't valuable, but some are: especially IPv4 addresses, which are scarce, and top-level domain names, such as *.com* and *.nz*, which have clear marketing or political value. It's mainly the policy aspects of the latter that have been contentious at ICANN, and it is the oversight of domain name policy that the USA Government proposes to relinquish. In my view, there are several reasons why this has become a contentious question. Firstly, there is a great deal of money to be made out of registering individual names in popular domains like *.com*, so the right to operate such a registry is very valuable. Secondly, national domains like *.nz* have a political dimension, especially in countries with unstable politics. Thirdly, and most recently, domain names written in non-Latin scripts have a cultural and emotional power of their own.

But to answer your question: despite the contention about oversight of ICANN, nothing that ICANN does — all of which is fundamentally administrative in nature — has any effect on the ability of any government agency to spy on Internet traffic. The American agencies accused of breaching the privacy of others in this way aren't connected to the Department of Commerce, and in any case would have nothing to gain by interfering in the administration of Internet names, addresses or protocol parameters. And of course there is every reason to believe that many other governments also conduct such surveillance, at home and abroad.

CC: (2014) The NSA "persuaded" web-encryption company RSA to develop a "more vulnerable" random number generator. RSA said it should "have been more sceptical of NSA's intentions". In fact, any pseudo-random number generator (PRNG) is provably weak, so why are these methods still in use?

BC: I'm not a cryptographer, but in any case I suspect that the answer lies in economics (an equally black art). Asymmetric cryptography is computationally expensive. Efficient encryption and decryption needs some kind of shared secret that a third party finds unreasonably expensive to guess, both now and reasonably far into the future. I suspect the answer to your question is that for most purposes, the cost of a successful guess, even with a weak PRNG, far exceeds its value. Of course, the NSA is one of the few organisations in the world that we can assume is prepared to pay a very high cost to make a successful guess once in a while.

Also, as our colleague Peter Gutmann has pointed out, the vast majority of known security breaches (including ones known to have been made by the NSA) worked *via* bypassing encryption. That turns out to be much, much easier than cryptanalysis.

CC: (2014) Sir Tim Berners-Lee has marked the 25th anniversary of WWW (12 March 2014) by calling for a *Magna Carta* bill of rights to protect its users. Would this help in freeing the Internet from meddling governments?

BC: Every little helps. For example, in April 2014 a conference called NETmundial (or more formally, Global Multistakeholder Meeting on the Future of Internet Governance) took place in São Paulo, Brazil. It produced a sort of manifesto that goes in the direction Tim was talking about. In particular, it de-emphasises government inputs. However, a fact of life is that governments control what happens in their own countries, and that includes the Internet. So all Internet freedoms simultaneously depend on and enhance democracy and the rule of law. There is a good reason why reactionary regimes tend to dislike the Internet; it is indeed their enemy.

CC: (2014) But the recent announcement regarding Brazilian plans to divorce itself from the USA centric Internet is utopia, isn't it?

BC: I would even suggest that it's dystopia too, because such a network would lack one of the main features of the Internet: access to worldwide information and to worldwide users. In fact, the recently passed legislation in Brazil, known as the *"Marco Civil"*, has dropped the completely impractical requirement that all data about Brazilians must be stored in Brazil. The fact is that the Internet inevitably permeates national frontiers. Actually the Gutenberg revolution did that too, but in a less spectacular way. Society took a very long time to fully adapt to the printing press, and there is still a long way to go in its adaptation to electronic information.

Chapter 22

Eric Goles: Systems, Art and CONICYT

Professor Goles (full name: Eric Antonio Goles Chacc) obtained a Degree in Engineering from the University of Chile, a PhD in Computer Science and the Docteur d'État (Mathematics) from the University of Grenoble; he also studied philosophy for two years at the Catholic University in Santiago. After being a CNRS researcher in France for six years, he returned to Chile as Professor and Director of the National Centre for Mathematical Modelling at the University of Chile. Since 2000, he is the President of the National Commission for Scientific and Technological Research (CONICYT), http://www.conicyt.cl.

Professor Goles has published more than 120 papers, two books (Neural and Automata Networks: Dynamical Behaviour and its Applications, *Kluwer, 1990 (first edition) 1991 (second edition) and*

the co-authored with S. Martínez, was awarded the Prize "M. Montt")
and has edited 10 books. He has been honoured with many prizes and
distinctions, national and international (for example, the "Ordem do
Rio Branco Grau de Comendador" of the Brazil Government, 2002,
and the "Légion D'Honneur", of the French President, 2005). For
more details one can see the "Foreword" to the special issue of Theoretical Computer Science *(2013) dedicated to his 50th Birthday.*

CC: Why mathematics? Please describe your first steps and interests.

EG: My understanding of mathematics came very early, when I was 12 or 13 years old, but in an indirect manner, namely through chess. Near my house in the city of Antofagasta, there was a chess club. . . so I became a good player and I played chess until the age of 15 or 16. At that stage I changed my passion from chess to mathematics. When I finished high school I went to the engineering school where I obtained the degree of "mathematical engineer". In 1977, I went to France and between 1977 and 1984 I got two PhDs, one in Computer Science and the other one in Mathematics (Docteur d'État). In 1982, I was hired by CNRS and at the beginning of 1985 I came back to Santiago where I remain today.

CC: What subjects did you like in the beginning?

EG: I discovered very early on (1978) discrete dynamical systems (in time and space), cellular automata and threshold networks (today it is called neural nets). One of my first results was a proof that symmetric neural nets have only fixed-points or two periodic attractors. Two or three years before J. Hopfield proved a similar result in a more "physical" context.

I published many results on the dynamics and complexity of neural nets and their generalisations until the early 1980s. Then I got involved in sand-pile automata, their mathematical structure and complexity related to NP-completeness and universality, as well as in problems on discrete mathematics and modelling.

CC: You have dedicated a lot of time to mathematical modelling. Please give us an example of a problem you studied, and, if possible, describe briefly its solution.

EG: In the late 1980s I worked on learning algorithms to control the size of stones to feed industrial mills in Chilean copper mining. I developed mathematical models (granular materials and sand-piles) for the underground extraction of copper (the block-carving procedure). I developed, with some colleagues, software (and hardware) based on neural nets; it's still in use today.

CC: What are automata networks? What kind of simulations can you do with them?

EG: It's a graph, finite or infinite but finitely connected, such that each node is a finite deterministic machine depending (for inputs) on its neighbours. The evolution can be synchronous or asynchronous. When the graph is regular and the finite machine is the same for every vertex we have a cellular automaton.

My interest was studying the dynamics, i.e., to get short-cut theorems: given the graph, the local functions and the initial condition, find the attractors, time convergence, etc.; when this is not possible, try to determine the structure of computing capabilities, i.e., universality, can it simulate a universal Turing machine?

CC: How did you become interested in plastic artists?

EG: Three years ago I taught a general mathematics course open to all students at the University of Chile. There were students of science, law, medical sciences, architecture, and, of course, arts. Clearly, I could not teach a pure mathematical course, so I prepared a set of lectures (one semester, three times a week) about the evolution of calculability, from Ramon Lull[1] and it's first "naive" logical machine, through Leibniz, Boole, Cantor, Hilbert, Gödel until Turing. I presented, in an informal way, universal Turing machines and the Halting problem. One day, I was approached by a very shy art student (of painting) who had a canvas — a small one — to show me. I said, OK, and he showed me a very realistic painting: "the digital clock".

---

[1]See http://www.maxmon.com/1274ad.htm.

He asked me: "so, you see?", and, I replied, honestly, "no, I don't see anything special. Only that the seconds and minutes are very fuzzy". "Yes!", he said, "because my speed is not enough to capture the speed of numbers, and, also, I'm a machine... a Turing machine which observes the object and tries to copy it exactly..."

This was the beginning of a very fruitful adventure: in a couple of months this young artist has presented his first exhibition of paintings "as a Turing machine would do". For instance, he has several self-portraits looking into a mirror, so you see the copies of copies, and the question, as with Turing machines, is the Halting problem: could he stop, could he say when the canvas was finished? Because, as in Gödel's Incompleteness theorem, he has to climb outside its rules... I like this game. He is a very skilful painter, a man who wants to be a machine... maybe, the converse of AI.

In fact, this artistic episode not only didn't distract me from my mathematical activity, but it allowed me to think of other questions related to mathematics and computing. For instance, the notion of time in a painting: how much time does the artist need to copy a TV scene assuming that he has no memory and he can only copy a scene in real time? This assumes a very abstract canvas... Also, what is the relation, for a Turing machine, between the continuous and discrete times, or if the artist can accelerate his work (hyper-computation)?

CC: From 1997 to 2000 you have been the Director of the "National Centre for Mathematical Modelling" (NCMM). You are still affiliated with the NCMM. Please describe its main objectives and results.

EG: Between the late 1960s until the 1990s the Engineering School of the University of Chile sent its best students in mathematical engineering to be further educated in applied mathematics (also computer science) in France, to Grenoble, Paris, Lyon. So, in the late 1980s the school had an extremely good group of applied mathematicians — clearly the best in the country. Myself and some other colleagues began to think creating a centre to develop applications for problems in industry as well as continuing to develop theoretical aspects of some branches of applied mathematics: continuous and discrete optimisation, combinatorial problems, discrete mathematics, theoretical computer science, partial differential equations, probability and ergodic theory, etc. It took several years to get the financial support and to build a very modern building for the NCMM (about 2000 sqm).

Today our centre is well known in Chile and abroad; it is the first foreign centre in mathematics which is also a French CNRS unit. The NCMM is home not only to PhD students and postdoc fellows, but also to about 40 researchers working in applied and fundamental mathematics.

CC: Since 1996 you have regularly produced TV science programmes. They are amazingly popular in Chile, you are a real star. How did you become a TV producer? Tell us about your subjects and guests.

EG: Actually I am not a TV producer, I'm the manager of the TV programme "ENLACES" (links) dedicated to science and technology. It's a one-hour programme broadcast at prime time! That's unusual not only in our country, but in the world, for an open TV channel: Television National is the most important one in Chile.

The programme is broadcast each year for 2–3 months, one time a week, and every time it is seen by about one million people. It is really very popular; it won a lot of prizes in Chile and abroad (Canada, US, France, etc.). Last September we won the prestigious "Jules Verne" prize awarded by UNESCO and the French CNRS in Paris at the Eiffel Tour (at the recommendation of a committee chaired by the Programme CEO of BBC).

We had programmes about astronomy, creativity, depression, inventors, genetics, robotics, computing, food, global change, volcanos, eclipses, etc. I like a lot of this activity, to contribute to the script, to interview people like Penrose, Hawkings, Gell-Mann or Chaitin, etc. I like to know that people in Chile believe me, they believe in science as a possibility. I believe that there are several young people who are studying science because they were motivated by our programme. Maybe one of the most important recognition situations for me was in my city, in Antofagasta, when an Indian lady selling veggies in an open market recognised me and, with a very shy smile gave me... not a "flower", but a lettuce. She said: "I watch your programme with my children."

Over the years my "intersection" with TV was only a random event, a coincidence, but a friend told me that I was damned to be an artist: for years I tried to avoid it, to ignore that my father was a well known and popular musician — as an engineer — as well as my mother is (even now) a well-known actress in the North of the country. Who knows? For me doing mathematics is also an artistic performance: I do mathematics not "to eat", or to "get a salary", I do it to live!

CC: In 2006 we celebrated Gödel's centenary. I am not going to ask you about your article regarding Gödel's Incompleteness theorem, but about Borges' article. Did you meet Borges? How did you find that article?

EG: Gödel. I remember when in Cambridge, Massachusetts I was invited for a couple of months to the AI Lab at MIT (Minsky's Lab). I found Nagel–Newman's book *Gödel's Proof* in a "Harvard bookstore". Several months later I was invited by Dr N. Atlan to Jerusalem; I took the book with me as well as the more "formal proof" in Arbib's book. I read them both during a couple of weeks and I was fascinated by the result as a mathematician, but also as a lover of Borges' literature. Remember Borges' fixation for paradoxes, Achille and the Tourtle, the infinity, and Cantor's results. So, in some way, I read Gödel's proof like another piece Borges' fiction. Recently, just a couple of weeks ago, I found that Borges wrote a note in the women's magazine "Hogar" (I believe in the 1950s) about Gödel's theorem. I was in Buenos Aires when I learned about this note published in such a strange place... Actually, I have met Borges in Chile in 1975 or 1976. He told us about his well-known piece "*El Sur*" (The South).

CC: You have been the President of the National Commission for Scientific and Technological Research (CONICYT) for more than four years. What are the main activities of CONICYT? What is the role of its president?

EG: In Chile, CONICYT is a government agency for science. My direct "boss" was President Lagos. As in some other situations in my life, the chain of events leading to this position was a bit "strange". Seven years ago I had a position in science administration when I met President Ricardo Lagos, then a minister. Two years after that meeting he asked me to work for him in the campaign for the presidential elections in 1999. I said "yes", hence for a year and a half I travelled with him by plane, car, ship, visiting several cities, towns, speaking in various meetings. When he was elected, he proposed me to be the president of CONICYT and, naturally, I accepted.

CONICYT gives financial support for PhD fellowships, for individual research programmes, and for national/regional programmes in science, technology and innovation as well as in education. Before President Lagos, the CONICYT budget was about 43 million USD; today the CONICYT Budget is about 500–600 million USD. In 1999, the number of PhD fellowships awarded was about 60 per year; now we have (only in CONICYT) more like 1,000 PhD fellowships per year (700 for domestic students and 300 for international ones). To develop the national capacity — in industry and academy — to employ these people is one of the more important tasks for the near future. We also need more post-doctoral positions as well.

I feel that we have done quite a good job (of course, we've made some mistakes as well). There are no miraculous solutions, only stability, transparency and time — a lot of time and patience.

CC: How many countries did you visit as CONICYT President? Please enumerate a few political personalities you met.

EG: President Lagos believes in science as a tool to develop the country. As a consequence he invited me on his official visits around the world. I have been in Denmark, Finland, Russia, USA, New Zealand — where I met you — Brazil, Argentina, Uruguay... I have met several prime ministers and presidents. For me the most impressive were the presidents of China and Russia. I remember a small dinner in the Kremlin and a lunch at *Elysée* with President

Chirac. I forget a lot: I spent lots of hours in the sky over different continents.

CC: What are you going to do at the end of your term at CONICYT?

EG: Go back to research, creativity and intellectual activities. Technically, I will go back to my professorship at the Engineering School at the University of Chile, but I would like to "make" things happen, to initiate new programmes.

CC: You have recently founded the "*Valparaíso* Institute of Complex Systems". What are its objectives?

EG: As you know, over the last two years I have worked hard to create the ISCV, the *Valparaíso* Institute for Complex Systems. We started the project in 2002; now ISCV exists and operates in a nice, centennial house of 500 sqm on a beautiful hill looking over *Valparaíso* port (with a typical elevator) given by the Navy and is ours for the next 30 years. The initial funding came from the private sector, mainly from the "*Eslondida*" Mining Foundation ASFAL–Chile. In the first three weeks of operation, the ISCV activity was organised within the framework (and financial support) of the European Network of Complex System Institutes EXYSTENCE. This allowed us to invite several researchers from around the world, as well as from Chile, and 40 PhD students to discuss complexity in computer science, the foundations of mathematics, and biology. As lecturers we had Dr Atlan (from Jerusalem), Dr Chaitin (from New York), a distinguished group of researchers from France and yourself.

I will be more and more involved in the running of the ISCV: from March on I will spend at least one third of my time in *Valparaíso*. You know, *Valparaíso* is one of the dreams of humanity, a city in the Pacific with a lot of personality; it's not only a port for ships, but also for science as well. In some way I will be like a sailor . . . in search for new paradigms.

CC: I know that you have written fiction. Could you give us some details?

EG: The art comes from my parents and from my studies in philosophy. I really began to write fiction five or six years ago. This was like an obsession with, for me, a very strange historic event: Lady Lovelace who collaborated with Babbage to design the "analytical engine" (in some sense the first computer designed in the Victorian epoch). The trouble was that Lady Lovelace was the daughter of Lord Byron, famous for fascinating poetry and delicious scandals. Byron's residence in 1816 was *Villa Diodati*; the story goes by saying that he motivated Mary Godwin, better known as "Mary Shelley", to write "Frankenstein"... This is enough material from dreams, obsession and finally, after two or three years of work, the first *"nouvelle"*, which I think is not so bad. Maybe I will publish it in the near future... Now I am writing a second piece, pure fiction, which is set in the city of my childhood in the 1950s. Who knows, maybe in the next few years I will become a novelist...

Chapter 23

Yuri Gurevich: Mathematics, Computer Science and Life

Yuri Gurevich is well known to the readers of the Bulletin. He is a Principal Researcher at Microsoft Research (MSR), where he founded a group on Foundations of Software Engineering, and a Professor Emeritus at the University of Michigan. His name is most closely associated with abstract state machines (ASM) but he is also known for his work on logic, complexity theory and software engineering. The Gurevich–Harrington Forgetful Determinacy theorem is a classical result in game theory. Yuri Gurevich is an ACM Fellow, a Guggenheim Fellow, an EATCS fellow and a foreign member of the Academia Europaea, he has obtained honorary doctorates from Hasselt University in Belgium and Ural State University in Russia.

CC: Your background is in mathematics: MSc (1962), PhD (under P.G. Kontorovich, 1964) and Doctor of Math (a post PhD degree in Russia), all at Ural State University. Please reminisce about those years.

YG: I grew up in Chelyabinsk, an industrial city in the Urals, Russia, and was in the first generation of my family to get a systematic education. In 1957, after 10 boring years in elementary + middle + high school, I enrolled in the local polytechnic. I enjoyed student life, but I couldn't draw well and I hated memorising things. In the middle of the second year, one maths prof. advised me to transfer — and wrote a recommendation letter — to the maths dept. of Ural State University in Ekaterinburg (called Sverdlovsk at the time), about 200 km to the north of Chelyabinsk. One of the maths dept. profs there examined me, and I joined the class of 1962, on the condition that I pass all the maths exams taken during the last 1.5 years by my new classmates.

The maths dept., formally the dept. of mathematics and mechanics, was demanding. Typically, only a quarter of a class graduated after five years of study. I did my first little research in classical analysis, with Prof. V.K. Ivanov, the best known Ekaterinburg mathematician. Ivanov was a good man but a busy one, the "prorector" of science. He advised me to go to computational maths, because of its potential, or to join an active seminar. "You need interaction," he told me. Computational math seemed pedestrian to me at the time, and I joined the group-theory seminar of Prof. P.G. Kontorovich, the most active and competitive seminar in the Dept, with many enthusiastic participants and a list of open problems prominently posted on the wall. In my 1962 diploma thesis (article #1 of my website[1]) I solved the second problem on the problem list.

CC: P.G. Kontorovich, did he win a Nobel Prize in Economics?

YG: No, the Nobel Prize winner was L.V. Kantorovich. But my Kontorovich was remarkable in his own way. He went from an orphanage to founding the Ekaterinburg algebra school that is active to this very day. His humour was legendary and he knew seemingly all the languages. Once I found him reading some text and complaining that

---

[1]Here and below, references #n are to the Annotated Articles list at http:// research.microsoft.com/~gurevich/annotated.htm.

he understood the text but did not recognise the language it is written in. It turned out that the language was Esperanto, forbidden as a "product of *bourgeois* internationalism and cosmopolitanism" in the USSR.

Maybe I can use this occasion to say a few words about Ural State University. Compared to other Soviet institutions, my *Alma Mater* (at least the hard sciences part of it) was a rare oasis of good will. Senior professors, like Ivanov and Kontorovich, created an atmosphere of decency. Even our philosophical seminars, a necessary fixture in Soviet universities, were different. Typically, a philosophical seminar would be devoted to the study of the latest documents of the Central Committee of the Communist Party. The philosophical seminar of our maths dept. was devoted — surprise! — to philosophy, more exactly to the philosophical aspects of mathematics and mechanics. Later in my career, I spoke about logic at the seminar.

But I am getting ahead of myself. Upon getting my university diploma, I wanted to do maths research at a university or the Academy of Sciences, which offered better conditions than any university. Conveniently, the famous Steklov Math Institute of the Academy of Sciences opened a branch in Ekaterinburg and was hiring, and I applied there. But my chances were slim to none.

CC: Why? You were probably one of the best students or even the best student of your class.

YG: I might have been but Steklov was *Judenfrei*. Even Ural State University had limitations. They accepted me only as a PhD student by correspondence, but they hired me also as a lecturer. It actually worked well for me. I taught about 20 hours a week and did my maths. Today it sounds exhausting to me, but at the time I enjoyed it all and had time left to hang out with my dissident friends. I even remember feeling somewhat guilty for being paid to have fun.

CC: What does "PhD student by correspondence" mean?

YG: This is for people who have regular jobs. They may correspond with the university by mail.

CC: How did you move to mathematical logic? Did you study it at Ural State University?

YG: No, mathematical logic wasn't taught there. In fact there were few maths logicians in the whole USSR. Formal (as opposite to dialectical) logic had hard time in the USSR. However, things improved during the 1960s. Kleene's *"Introduction to Meta-Mathematics"* was translated into Russian, and I got it as a birthday present in May 1962. I studied it and fell in love with logic. But what could an algebraist do in logic?

In the 1962–1963 winter, a guest lecturer from Novosibirsk told us that a Polish student of Alfred Tarski, called Wanda Szmielew, proved the decidability of the first-order theory of abelian groups. A natural problem arose whether the first-order theory of ordered abelian groups is decidable. Szmielew and Tarski announced the decidability of that theory but then withdrew their claim. I worked on the problem. A big part of it was to understand when two ordered abelian groups have the same first-order properties. After a long chain of incremental advances, I proved that the theory is indeed decidable (#3). That became my PhD thesis which I defended in the spring of 1964 in Novosibirsk.

CC: Why Novosibirsk? Ural State University is not in Novosibirsk.

YG: By Soviet rules, you could defend your thesis in a science area X only at an institution with sufficient expertise in X. My choice was restricted to Moscow, Leningrad and Novosibirsk. Because of Maltsev's "Algebra and Logic" seminar, Novosibirsk was the best fit for me.

The 1964–1965 academic year I was teaching at the new Krasnoyarsk State University in Siberia. By the way the word "State" in the names of Soviet universities meant simply "of the Soviet state". In the middle of that academic year I attended an algebraic winter school near Ekaterinburg. There I met a third-year Ural State University student, Zoe, and I returned to Krasnoyarsk with a wife. We sought to move back to Ekaterinburg, and Ural State University accommodated us; the 1965–1966 academic year I was already teaching there. My obsession with logic was contagious and the logic seminar attracted the brightest students. During the winter breaks, we would rent a little house in the country to study but also to ski, play charades, etc.

CC: It sounds like scientific life in the Soviet Union was similar to that in the West.

YG: It was similar, at least where hard sciences were concerned. But there were important differences. We were poorer. For example, Ural State University had no foreign currency, and Western books and journals were not available in the library. More importantly, the totalitarian state was never far away. Here is an incident from one of those winter schools. One morning I woke up to much noise in another room, with none of my room mates in my room. I went to investigate. Two boys, surrounded by all the other students, were arguing whether there was state anti-Semitism in the USSR. Now all eyes were upon me. What could I say? The safe lie of denial was out of the question, but publicly accusing the state of anti-Semitism was too dangerous, especially for a teacher. The chances were that there was an informant present. I spoke and spoke trying to humour my audience. I used whatever parables and jokes occurred to me leaving it up to the students to interpret things. Eventually passions subsided and the attention deviated to other topics. I remember wishing to be able speak my mind.

But science and life also interacted independently of politics. Upon our return to Ekaterinburg, I had a bad motorcycle accident. In the hospital, they sewed me up but inadvertently infected me with hepatitis. As a result, I was quarantined for a month. No visitors were allowed in and there were few books to read there. I used the time to think about the classical decision problem — classify infinite fragments of first-order predicate logic, given by restrictions on quantifier prefixes and the vocabulary, into decidable (for satisfiability) and undecidable. The problem attracted the attention of great logicians including Gödel and there had been much progress in the early 1960s. If only one could prove that the $\forall\exists\forall\exists^*$ fragment with one binary relation is undecidable, the classification would be complete.

The ∀∃∀∃* problem was uniquely appropriate to my confinement. While the decision problem for ordered abelian groups required a long sustained effort and a long sequence of lemmas, each building upon the previous ones, the ∀∃∀∃* problem seemed to require just a clever combinatorial trick. It was like jumping over a barrier. You give it a try and you fall, then another try and another fall, over and over again. Indeed, by the end of my quarantine, I got lucky and jumped over that barrier. The fame of the problem helped me to defend my Doctor of Maths thesis later, in 1968.

CC: What is the Doctor of Maths degree for? The Russian system of academic degrees seems different from that in English-speaking countries.

YG: It is different. The first Russian postgraduate academic degree, an equivalent of PhD, is Candidate of science, and the second is Doctor of Science. Here "Science" is a variable to be replaced with "mathematics", "physics", etc. The Doctor of Science degree was a big deal at the time. If you taught at a university, the degree was a necessary and, in practice, sufficient condition for getting a full professorship. All academic degrees in Russia were — and are — subject to approval by the Central Attestation Committee of Russia.

CC: This was and continues to be the system in Romania: nowadays, this committee also includes Romanians from the diaspora.

YG: The system is supposed to impose some standards but of course it can be abused.

CC: Did you go to Novosibirsk to defend your Doctor of Maths thesis.

YG: No, the atmosphere in Novosibirsk changed for the worse, and a "Jewish dissertation" had little chance there. My dissertation also had a large algebraic component and thus qualified as algebraic. I defended it in Ekaterinburg, and the degree was eventually approved by the Central Attestation Committee.

CC: Your scientific activity splits into three periods: Soviet (up to 1973), Israeli (1974–1981) and American (since 1982). Let's visit them in that order.

YG: During the Soviet period I worked primarily on two subjects. One was related to the classical decision problem. The complete classification mentioned above comprised nine minimal undecidable classes and three maximal decidable ones. I wanted to understand whether there was an *a priori* reason that the classification resulted in a finite table. It turned out that indeed there was a rather general reason. That encouraged me to work on the extensions of the classification to first-order logic with equality or function symbols or both. I made good progress, and the Institute of Philosophy of the Russian Academy of Sciences asked me to write a book on the subject. I write too slow to produce a book, but I wrote a survey. It was withdrawn from publication upon our emigration from the USSR. Later the survey became the core of the 1997 Springer book *"The Classical Decision Problem"* by Egon Börger, Erich Grädel and myself.

The other subject was the decidability of algebraic theories. In particular, I continued my work on ordered abelian groups. It bothered me that theorems in the literature on the subject were not first-order; they were mostly in terms of so-called convex subgroups. I extended my analysis to the variant of the monadic second-order theory of ordered abelian groups where the set variables ranged over convex subgroups. Somewhat miraculously, the decision procedure not only survived but was simplified. The extended theory (and its easy further extensions) accounted for virtually all theorems in the literature. My attempts to publish these results in the USSR were unsuccessful (which is a separate story) but I published them after my departure (#25).

I also did some applied work. In my later undergraduate years, I worked at the university computing centre. Later I worked with the transportation industry on linking railway transportation to trucks. All that work influenced me and changed my attitude on pure vs applied science. You may have heard about a mathematician working on a difficult four-legged table problem. He generalised the problem to n-legged tables and solved the cases $n \leq 2$, the case $n = \infty$ and the case of sufficiently large n. In the process he advanced his career but the original problem remained open. That's pure science.

CC: Now, tell me about the Israeli period.

YG: That period started with a touch of drama, or comedy. The first few months we lived in Jerusalem and studied Hebrew. During my first trip to the Hebrew University, I met a young logician, Saharon Shelah. "Do you have an open problem," he asked me. I told him my conjecture that the ∃*∀∃* fragment of first-order logic with equality, one unary function and infinitely many unary relations are decidable for satisfiability. When I saw him again, a week or two later, he told me that he confirmed my conjecture. I smiled: "tell me about it." He did. I could not follow his explanation, partially because my Hebrew was still insufficient and my English non-existent, but I realised that he had all the intuition that led me to the conjecture and more. I was stunned. The first Israeli mathematician that I had a serious discussion with confirmed my conjecture. Maybe I should seek a university position in Israel. I asked Shelah whether he had an open problem. He gave me his paper on the monadic second-order theory of the real line; it was submitted to Annals of Mathematics and had many open conjectures.

The paper was full of original ideas, but it was difficult to read. It took me months just to understand the paper. After a year or so of hard work, I confirmed or refuted most of Shelah's conjectures. He was most kind; as he proofread his paper, he added footnotes announcing my results. The incident resulted in a fruitful collaboration with Shelah on monadic (second-order) theories. Survey #64 reflects a large initial segment of the results of the monadic project.

CC: Give me a flavour of that work.

YG: Shelah conjectured that countability is not definable in the monadic second-order theory $MT(\mathcal{R})$ of the real line $\mathcal{R}$ with just the order relation (and no addition or multiplication). In this connection I thought of the known and unsuccessful attempts to define countability in measure-theoretic terms. Of course sets of Lebesgue measure zero can be uncountable but also sets of universal measure zero (defined by Hausdorff) can be uncountable, and sets of strong measure zero (defined by Borel) can be uncountable under the continuum hypothesis. I expected the conjecture to be true but it turned out, somewhat surprisingly, that countability was definable in MT($\mathcal{R}$) under the continuum hypothesis. The construction built heavily on the methods developed by Shelah in his original paper.

One of the main results in Shelah's original paper was the undecidability of MT($\mathcal{R}$). The proof was a clever interpretation of first-order arithmetic in MT($\mathcal{R}$). In #57, Shelah and I interpreted second-order arithmetic in MT($\mathcal{R}$). Later, in apparent contradiction with these results, we discovered that first-order arithmetic, let alone second-order arithmetic, cannot be interpreted in MT($\mathcal{R}$) (#79). A closer examination of Shelah's original reduction revealed that it (and our generalisation of it) went beyond the standard model-theoretic notion of interpretability. And there was an interesting connection to set theory. If W is a model of ZFC, let W' be the model of ZFC resulting from the extension of W with a Cohen real, a real number that does not exist in W. Paul Cohen discovered a technique, *forcing*, that allows one to do things like that. Think of W as the current set-theoretic world and of W' as the next world. Our reduction in #57 was a reduction of the next-world second-order arithmetic to the current-world MT($\mathcal{R}$).

CC: Not too many mathematicians or computer scientists have a theorem bearing their name. Tell me about the Gurevich–Harrington Forgetful Determinacy theorem and how did you arrive at it.

YG: The 1980–1981 academic year was a logic year at the Hebrew University. Both Leo Harrington and I were there and proved the theorem independently; we talked about that, and I volunteered to write the theorem up for publication. I do not know Leo's motivation. On my side, laziness played a role. In 1969, Michael Rabin used nondeterministic finite automata on infinite (coloured) trees to prove the decidability of S2S, the monadic second-order theory of two successor relations. I understood the proof except for the complementation lemma according to which, for every tree automaton A, there is a complementary tree automaton that accepts exactly the trees that A doesn't. I kept thinking about the lemma but was reluctant to go through the difficult proof. And one day it occurred to me that it all, not only the complementation lemma but the whole paper of Rabin, was really about games. Things simplify (and become amenable to new useful generalisations) if you see them that way. For the games in question, the players can restrict themselves to "forgetful" strategies so that, at every point, the players need only to remember boundly many bits about the history of the current play. Even finite automata are able to execute forgetful strategies; hence Rabin's result.

CC: Eventually you moved to the US and to computer science. How did that happen?

YG: I had already been contemplating more applied research at the end of my Russian period but the Jerusalem logic seminar enthralled me. In spite of solving some high-profile logic problems, I was really a logic ignoramus. The seminar allowed me to learn cutting-edge logic developments. It was so much more efficient and so much more fun to learn things from seminar presentations than by reading papers. It was in Israel that I really became a logician, thanks to the logic seminar and joint work with Shelah. When the monadic project with Shelah began to wind down, I applied to computer science departments at some Israeli and US universities. All offers came from the US. I accepted a good offer from the University of Michigan and in the summer of 1982 we moved to Ann Arbor, Michigan. There was another reason for choosing the University of Michigan. Andreas Blass, the logician, was there, albeit in the maths dept. Andreas and I have been actively collaborating ever since.

CC: Tell me about your work on the finite model theory.

YG: Let me restrict myself to just one little story. At my first computer science conference, I heard a presentation by Moshe Vardi. He applied the interpolation theorem of first-order logic to relational databases viewed as first-order structures. I asked him whether his databases could be infinite and he said yes. But naturally databases are finite of course. I looked into the issue. As I suspected, most classical theorems of first-order logic, including the interpolation theorem, fail in the finite case (#60). I had a sense of *déjà vu*. First-order logic wasn't right for ordered abelian group, and it wasn't right for finite structures in the computer science context (#74).

Later on, a realisation came that real databases are not necessarily finite after all. For a simple example, consider a salary database of some organisation. The organisation may use a popular database-query language SQL to query the salary database. In addition to relational-algebra operations, SQL has so-called grouping and aggregation operations. This allows the organisation to compute various statistics over the database, e.g., the average salary and the total salary expense of the organisation. Note that the average salary may not occur in the database and, ignoring degenerate cases, the total salary surely does not occur. Thus, the database gives us a function from the employees to numbers, say rational numbers, and has rational arithmetic in the background. In that sense, it is not truly finite. To formalise this phenomenon of finite foreground and infinite background, Erich Grädel and I introduced *meta-finite* structures (#109). The meta-finite phenomenon is not restricted to databases. The states of an algorithm are often meta-finite. Most classical theorems of first-order logic, including the interpolation theorem, fail in the meta-finite case.

CC: Finite model theory has intimate relations with computational complexity but your complexity work went beyond that.

YG: It did. In particular, I worked on the average-case reduction theory pioneered by Leonid Levin. Consider NP-complete problems equipped with probability distributions on the instances. Some such problems turn out to be easy on average, but others remain complete even for the average case. Proving such average-case completeness results is difficult and the reason is this. While the range of a worst-case reduction may consist of very esoteric and unrepresentative instances of the target problem, the range of an average-case reduction should be of non-negligible probability. A popular article #85 argues in favour of an alternative, based on the average-case complexity, to the P=NP question. Consider a game between Challenger and Solver where Challenger repeatedly picks instances of a given NP-problem (with a fixed probability distribution), and Solver solves them. The idea is to measure Solver's time in terms of Challenger's rather than in terms of the instance size. It may take a long time to produce hard instances.

CC: Tell me about your work on ASM. In particular what motivated it?

YG: Right upon starting at Michigan, I volunteered to teach "Introduction to Computer Science with Pascal" to computer science majors. The dept. chair did not like the idea ("we hired you to teach theory") but agreed that I teach the course once. Preparing that course was instructive. I had not realised how much I had fallen behind in programming technology. At Ural State University, I programmed on the naked machine (01 for addition, 02 for substraction, etc.), and Pascal seemed advanced. The troubling part was that Pascal wasn't sufficiently documented. The interpreter on my Macintosh and the compiler on the university mainframe often disagreed on whether a given program is legal. Which of them, if either, was right? What was I supposed to tell my 250 or so students? That was scary and brought home the problem of the semantics of programming languages.

In this connection, I studied denotational and algebraic semantics but found them wanting. It seemed unfeasible to use them to specify the "dirty parts" of software. The celebrated declarativeness of denotational and algebraic specifications did not impress me. The advancers of the computer revolution weren't shy to program, specify and reason imperatively. There is a persistent confusion between declarative and high level. Declarative specifications tend to be high level, and executable specifications tend to involve unnecessary details. However, I saw no reason why high-level specifications could not be imperative and executable, amenable to testing and experimentation.

By Turing's thesis, every algorithm can be simulated by an appropriate Turing machine. Are Turing machines executable? In principle, yes, but of course this may be impractical. A bigger problem is that Turing machines work on the level of single bits. Are there more general state machines that specify algorithms on their natural abstraction level? Maybe that was too much to ask. But if yes then the reward would be high, for theory and practice. It would open a road to formalising the notion of algorithms. On the practical level, it would enable us to specify software on whatever abstraction level is desired.

It was that line of thought that led me eventually to ASMs. By the ASM thesis, every algorithm can be faithfully simulated by an ASM. We attempted to verify the thesis, which led to practical applications. There were also theoretical advances. The notion of sequential algorithms was formalised in #141; this formalisation was used later by Nachum Dershowitz and myself to derive Turing's thesis from first principles (#188). Parallel and interactive algorithms were also formalised (#162).

CC: How did you get attracted to Microsoft?

YG: I was convinced that the ASM approach was more practical than other formal methods but all methods work on small examples, and my attempts to find an industrial partner were unsuccessful. In the summer of 1998, I visited MSR, in Redmond, WA, by invitation of their crypto group. On that occasion I volunteered an ASM lecture. The lecture went rather well. There were many good questions. One of the MSR directors, Jim Kajiya, asked particularly astute and pointed questions. He said that he was surprised to see a formal specification method that seemed scalable. He proposed for me to start a new MSR group on the foundations of software engineering, and I jumped at the opportunity. The atmosphere and conditions at MSR are great, and the geographical area is spectacular. But what attracted me most was, of course, the opportunity to apply ASMs.

CC: Did it work? Could you apply ASMs at Microsoft?

YG: It was tough. I was lucky to hire the right people, and we built a tool, Spec Explorer, that facilitated writing executable specifications and playing with them. In particular, one could test the conformance between a spec and implementation. Spec Explorer was kept compatible with the Microsoft technology stack which consumed a lot of time and effort. The tech transfer was the biggest challenge. It is relatively easy to "sell" an incremental improvement to product groups. But Spec Explorer required learning and training, and product groups are busy. For a while we only had a few courageous groups here and there using Spec Explorer with our help. At a certain point, the European Union required, from Microsoft, high-level executable specifications of numerous communication protocols. The Windows division took over Spec Explorer and used it extensively and successfully.

CC: How applied is your work at Microsoft now? Do you use some theoretical results you proved as a "blue-sky researcher"?

YG: When Spec Explorer left MSR, I spent a couple of years catching up with theoretical work but then I returned to applications. Microsoft is an engineering place, and you catch the bug and want to influence technology. From time to time, I do internal consulting, developing efficient algorithms for various purposes. But my main current occupation is with distributed knowledge authorization language (DKAL). With the advent of cloud computing, a policy-management problem arises. In a brick-and-mortar setting, many policies may be unwritten. Clerks learn them from their colleagues. If they don't know a policy, they know whom to ask. In the cloud, the clerks disappear. The policies have to be handled automatically. The most challenging aspect is how to handle the interaction of policies, especially in federated scenarios where there is no central authority. DKAL was created to deal with such problems. The DKAL project has a large logic component so my logic expertise is useful.

CC: If you could dream about the year 3014, which result or concept would you like to see still "alive"?

YG: Hmm. "It's tough to make predictions, especially about the future," said Yogi Berra, the famous American baseball player and a philosopher of a kind. We live in quickly changing times. In the computer industry, longterm refers to just a few years ahead. It is an interesting question to what extent the future is predictable, even probabilistically. Let me just express the hope that humanity will survive until 2114 and that the scientific method will survive as well. It may seem that the second is obvious given the first, but it is not necessarily so. Lucio Russo convincingly argues in *The Forgotten Revolution: How Science Was Born in 300 BC and Why it Had to*

Be Reborn (2004) that the scientific method was not invented but reinvented by Galileo, Newton and their contemporaries, that science was discovered in the Hellenistic period and was then forgotten.

CC: How do you see the relevance of theoretical computer science for computer technology?

YG: Theory made weighty contributions to computer technology. Think of Alan Turing, John von Neumann and modern cryptography. The search technology that made Google rich is based on clever algorithms. One important theoretical contribution is for some reason less known to theorists than it deserves; I searched for it in vain in computation theory books. It is the 1965 discovery of $LR(k)$ languages by Donald Knuth: "a language can be generated by an LR(k) grammar if, and only if, it is context-free and deterministic, if, and only if, it can be generated by an LR(1) grammar." $LR(k)$ grammars can be parsed in time essentially proportional to the length of string, and their discovery revolutionised compiler construction.

But it is hard to influence computer technology by advancing theory, especially if the result is a non-incremental change in technology. "Nothing is more difficult than to introduce a new order," wrote Niccolo Machiavelli in *The Prince*, "because the innovator has for enemies all those who have done well under the old conditions and lukewarm defenders in those who may do well under the new." I lifted this quotation from a 2006 book *The Change Function: Why Some Technologies Take Off and Others Crash and Burn*. The author, Pip Coburn, argues that the chances of adoption of a new disruptive technology is given by:

$$\frac{\text{Pain of the crises}}{\text{Pain of adoption}}$$

To achieve successful technology transfer starting from just a theoretical advance is harder yet (though one may get lucky).

Chapter 24

Hermann Maurer: Computing and Thinking about the Future

Hermann Maurer, www. iicm. edu/ maurer, is a Professor at the Institute for Information Systems and Computer Media (IICM), at the Graz University of Technology. He has a number of advisory roles, the most significant one being a Member of the Board of the Academia Europaea, www. ae-info. org .

Professor Maurer has written more than 20 books and over 750 scientific articles in both theoretical and applied computer science, started or was involved with a number of companies supervised over 40 dissertations. He is a member of the Academia Europaea and the Finnish Academy of Sciences, has honorary doctorates from the Universities of St. Petersburg, Calgary and Karlsruhe, and was awarded the Austrian Cross of Honour for Science and Art and the Great Gold Medal of Honour of Styria.

Professor Maurer has also written a number of science fiction (SF) books, a few of which are available in English, see, e.g., www.iicm. edu/Xperts[1] *in which he employs metaphors such as telepathy and teleportation.*

CC: Let us start this dialogue by asking you to reminisce about your time as *EATCS Bull.* editor.

HM: I took this over from Maurice Nivat with No. 3 of the *Bulletin*, so we had to create the EATCS logo that still appears (after some 35 years!) on the first page of the *Bulletin* and also the picture of the automaton which always appears with the council composition. When I was secretary, the work in EATCS intensified a lot, so the *Bulletin* grew from some 20 pages to its current volume. The fact that the volume increased rather than decreased is due to G. Rozenberg, who took over the editorship of the *Bulletin* after me. His imagination, the various columns and cartoons from *Dardara* have influenced the *Bulletin* up to today in a decisive manner. I am happy I was able to be an active member of the community for about 10 years — after which my interests slowly changed to more applied areas — yet my allegiance to EATCS has never changed.

CC: You started your career by obtaining a doctorate in mathematics in 1965 under Professor Edmund Hlawka, with a dissertation entitled *Rational Approximations of Irrational Numbers*. Please comment on two results from your thesis.

HM: In the thesis I basically disproved the claim that using hypergeometric series would give better approximations to irrational numbers than were obtainable by continued fractions or similar methods. Since it is a negative result, in the sense of lower bound, the proof was reasonably tedious.

CC: Then you worked for IBM in Vienna...

HM: Before I worked for IBM I was an assistant to Professor John Peck, then from the University of Calgary, Canada, one of the leading

---

[1]He recommends (for anybody interested) to start with the "Paranet".

experts in programming languages. He was one of the inner group developing Algol 68. I am indebted to him for showing me the beauty of exact (formal) definitions for programming languages. I then had, far almost a year, a job as systems analyst with the Government of Saskatchewan, the first time I had a chance to apply computer solutions to large practical programs. On my return to Vienna I joined the IBM Research Lab in Vienna, headed by the father of computer science in Austria, Professor Zemanek. I developed a first list processing compiler and then worked in the group that eventually developed VDL, the Vienna Definition Language. In this group I was apprentice to powerful brains like the one of Peter Lucas: under his guidance (and that of Hans Bekic and Kurt Walk) the technique developed into what is today called Formal Methods Europe; it has survived four decades, something unheard of in computer science. Lest I am misunderstood: I was a tiny and unimportant part of this development, but I learnt a lot about formal methods.

CC: You have been an active — better still, hyperactive — member of the theoretical computer science community. In which areas have you worked?

HM: I continued my work in theoretical computer science when I re-joined the University of Calgary as assistant, later associate professor, in 1966. During my first years there I completed what was to be the first German pocket book on the theory (formal description) of programming languages: it turned into a bestseller. Nobody can still understand why this book sold some 50000 copies at a time (1969) when there were certainly not yet 50000 German-speaking computer scientists. For a number of years I continued in formal languages and automata theory.

CC: How was theoretical computer science in the 1970s?

HM: In the early 1970s the Formal Languages and Automata theory and related areas (like undecidability results and such) where the central focus of theoretical research. Towards the middle of the 1970s the theory of data-structures and algorithms gained more and more importance, and I started to work on this with a number of PhD students and postgraduates.

Some members of my group, like Professor Ottmann (University of Freiburg), Professor Albert (University of *Würzburg*), Professor Edelsbrunner (now Institute for Science and Technology, Austria), Professor Welzl (now at the Swiss Federal Institute of Technology in Zurich) or Professor Fellner (now *Darmstadr* and head of IPSI-*Fraunhofer*) are just a few of my early students who eventually became more successful than me.

CC: Please tell us your story about the famous MSW team?

HM: MSW stood for Maurer–Salomaa–Wood, with the person in the centre, Salomaa, also being the central figure. However, we really were a great team: two of us would get together and try to find new proofs and results, the third one was the one who would do the proofreading, trying to find holes in the proofs, etc. We became particularly wellknown for investigating L-systems and L-Forms, combining and extending ideas of the late Professors Ginsburg and Lindenmayer. Altogether we published some 50 journal contributions together and there was never the smallest amount of friction between us. Clearly, we have remained lifelong friends.

CC: How easy/pleasant was it to work jointly with Karel Culik?

HM: Karel Culik II has a brilliant mind. Working with him was not easy, however, since he was always ahead, but always also very intuitive. So when I worked with him I was never sure: am I not clever enough to understand what he says, or is he just arm waving. And it was always both: he had this incredible talent of immediately seeing the rough solution of very complicated problems, but the first idea had to be refined often dramatically to finally give a watertight proof. The story of the DOS sequence equivalence problem, where he submitted n versions (n quite large), each not correct, is typical for him: he eventually, however, managed to overcome all gaps in the original proof idea and solved this difficult problem.

CC: When and why did you switch from theory to applied computer science?

HM: My switch was fairly gradual, and much dictated by circumstances: first, formal languages, then algorithms, a bit of cryptography, then due to demand, applying this more and more to real-life problems, eventually reducing theory to just one of the things to do. It was also a pragmatic switch: it was much easier to get funding for applied projects than for very theoretical ones.

CC: Are there different skills required in doing theory vs applied computer science?

HM: I think to do good work in applied areas one does need a solid grounding in theory. The connection is not always clear to see, but the correlation is. There is, however, one basic difference: to be successful in applied work you have to be able to lead substantial teams, something less important for theoretical work.

CC: Can you compare your most important results in theory and applied computer science? Which gave you more satisfaction? Why?

HM: This is a very hard question. A good result in theory gives you the satisfaction of having solved a difficult puzzle that nobody has solved before, the satisfaction that you see things that were overlooked before. Applied projects give you the satisfaction that what you have done may be used by a large number of people, may lead to the formation of companies, to new jobs, and also to some recognition as an entrepreneur.

CC: Recently you gave a very interesting and provocative lecture in Auckland titled *Theory is Important but Dangerous*. What was its main message?

HM: The answer is almost in the title. We need theory, both to train students and to solve the theoretical basis for important problems. Examples are numerous: from cryptography to picture compression, from the organisation of data to computer vision, etc. At the same time, theory can be dangerous, mainly because negative results tend to scare people away from trying to solve problems whose exact solution may be very hard, but where there are very good approximate solutions.

CC: As in mathematics, in theoretical computer science beauty is a guiding principle as well as an ultimate indicator of value. Does it make sense to ask "How useful really is theoretical computer science"?

HM: No, the question does not make sense. If we did not have, did not teach, did not research in theory, we would not get anywhere in applications.

CC: What would be your principles in designing a balanced curriculum in computer science?

HM: A balanced curriculum must include a solid basis in mathematics and theoretical computer science, but must also teach more applied areas in a generic way. The emphasis here is on "generic". One must not study or work with concrete systems (software-packages) but one must make clear the underlying principles. Only in this way is it possible to make sure that the acquired knowledge does not obsolete too fast.

CC: Why has computer science has lost its appeal to the young generation?

HM: I really don't think it has. That numbers have dropped in some places is due to the negative PR around the "bust of the internet bubble" that suddenly created the wrong impression that computer science would not be important any more. However, this is definitely not so. The world needs many more IT specialists than are currently produced.

CC: You wrote extensively on the future of technology using metaphors such as telepathy and teleportation. Tell us more about these unusual writings?

HM: Basically, any technology that is far beyond our current one looks like a miracle. This statement is often attributed to Arthur Clarke, the SF writer, but actually goes much further back to around 1850! Just consider: if you had used a digital camera a few hundred years ago you certainly would have been burnt at the stake. Things like telepathy or telekinesis that sound impossible or miracles today will be implemented with suitable technologies before too long. Telepathy is almost a reality due to new brain-computer interfaces, and things like telekinesis will be handled (I quote Kurzweil) by swarms of nanobots. So: it is fun to write things that sound like SF but might well turn into reality at some stage, see XPERTS in `www.booklocker.com` or my homepage `www.iicm.edu/maurer`.

CC: "A lonely writer develops an unlikely relationship with his newly purchased operating system that's designed to meet his every need." Yes, this is the theme of the movie "Her".[2] Is socialising, even getting emotionally involved, with gadgets possible? Desirable?

HM: It is certainly possible and has happened, not just in that movie, but also in reality, like with the Tamagotchi[3] craze years ago. But we even had a program earlier that would play chess, pretend to be a person (Dave for women and Helen for men), and conducted superficial conversations *a la* Weizenbaum's Eliza[4] with a opponent via the net. Some did not realise they were communicating with a computer and in a few cases discussions got embarrassingly personal. However, I really doubt that it is desirable that gadgets are substitutes for real human contact. I feel more ambivalent about the role of avatars in, e.g., some virtual worlds: they may well be partial substitutes.

CC: How dangerous is Google?

HM: Google is THE largest data-mining company we have in the world. It knows more about people and organisations than any intelligence agency, and there is no control *via* data protection laws at this point in time. This gives more power into the hand of one particular company than is good for all of us. Actions will have to be taken to curtail those powers, and I know that such actions are on the way, without ruining the great advantages Google has for all of us due to its marvellous services, nor without ruining the value of the company for Google shareholders.

CC: You have served two successful full terms as Chair of the Informatics Section of the Academia Europaea. Can you briefly comment

---

[2]http://www.imdb.com/title/tt1798709/.

[3]A handheld digital pet, created in Japan by Akihiro Yokoi and Aki Maita; tens of million Tamagotchis have been sold worldwide.

[4]Mid-1960s computer program ELIZA written at MIT by J. Weizenbaum. DOCTOR — ELIZA simulation of a person-centred psychotherapist — provided an astonishingly human-like interaction with almost no information about human thought or emotion.

on the work done and, more importantly, on the work to be done. What is your vision about the role of the Academia Europaea?

HM: It was a pleasure to help grow the section from 70 rather exclusively theoretically oriented computer scientists to about 200, a growth in theoretical areas but also branching out in some more applied subjects. I am particularly proud that for the first time in 2014 the ERASMUS prize was awarded to a member of the Informatics Section, Professor Kurt Mehlhorn from Saarbrücken. My other main achievement was to set up a server showing the strength of the AE under,[5] yet (see below) the work on that server is not finished. Turning to with future. The informatics section is still small compared with other sections. However, the main task of the new chair will be to make sure that many members of the section contribute to workshops, seminars and other events of AE including the main conference (in 2015 to be held in Darmstadt). One might ask, why are such events organised by AE so important? Is there not a flood of more than enough such events already? The point is: the events of AE are most of the time much more interdisciplinary. Since informatics reaches so deeply into most other disciplines such interdisciplinary meetings are particularly important. Let me put this very bluntly: if an event is organised together by Sections X and Y, members of X may not go to the talks in Section X (presumably, they know most of that stuff), but could attend the talks of Section Y. This is also why the annual general meeting is such an interesting event: you can hear new stuff from top researchers in areas different from your own at a level that is comprehensible... at least this is what AE aims for. It is clear that the new chair will have an important role to make sure that members understand and accept that point. Also, the site www.ae-info.org (or equivalently, www.acadeuro.org) is not complete: some members are not presented fully yet, some material is obsolete, the presentation of news and aims of sections can still be improved. Again, all section chairs have an important role to play. Also members should realise that they can and should update

---

[5]www.ae-info.org.

their own contributions easily and the team in Graz will continue to help.

CC: Are you concerned about the massive global surveillance?

HM: We all have to be worried, but it must be clear that the Internet plays only one role in the continuing loss of privacy. Credit and bonus cards, surveillance cameras, drones, etc., make the situation worse. I believe that someone very worried about the loss of privacy will find ways for some protection, but I cannot explain what I see as partial counter measures on the horizon in a few sentences. Yet overall, the effect of the Internet and new ICTs is much more threatening in other areas, like cyber-warfare (much underestimated) and particularly in the effect of new technologies on the cognitive facilities of humans. There is no doubt that ICTs have caused losses of cognitive facilities in calculating, orientation, reading, writing, spelling, independent thinking and more. A viewpoint is presented in the paper "Is the Internet Turning us into Dummies?" which appeared in the *CACM* in 2014. Other papers that I (co)-authored, like "How Dangerous is the Web for Creative Work?" or "*Ueberwacht, verroht, bedroht und verdummt uns das Internet?*",[6] are dealing with such critical issues, and so are more and more books by various authors like Brabazon, Bauerlein, Carr, Keen, Spitzer, Weber and others. To put my *credo* into one sentence: *the reduction of our cognitive facilities* IS *indeed happening, yet this is OK if the loss is overcompensated by new technology* AND *we can survive massive network breakdowns* AND *we retain our facility for creative thinking: links in the web cannot replace synapses in our brain.*

CC: Sixty years ago, digital computers made information readable. Twenty years ago, the Internet made it reachable. Ten years ago, the first search engine crawlers made it a single database. Kilobytes are stored on floppy disks, megabytes are stored on hard disks, terabytes are stored in disc arrays and petabytes are stored in the Cloud. We

---

[6]See `http://www.iicm.tugraz.at/hmaurer/publications/by_date/2013` for details.

live in the *Petabyte Age*. Is the dying old-fashioned "science" quickly being replaced by "data science"?

HM: I think we should not put "science" and "data" on the same level. I believe we are slowly making progress to develop tools for handling and analysing huge amounts of data, even if much effort in this direction is still necessary and crucial. But if such tools will become available, they will not threaten science or research, but help them tremendously.

CC: What are your next decade projects?

HM: Open access scientific journals, helping to develop quality improved community encyclopaedias akin Wikipedia, and assuring that when we look for something on the Internet we don't find millions of pieces of information, but the knowledge we have been looking for.

Chapter 25

Moshe Y. Vardi: From Theory and Practice in Computing
to Research Ethics and the Surveillance State

*Professor Moshe Y. Vardi, www.cs.rice.edu/~vardi/ is the
George Distinguished Service Professor in Computational Engineering and Director of the Ken Kennedy Institute for Information Technology at Rice University. He is the author and co-author of over
450 papers, as well as two books: Reasoning about Knowledge and
Finite Model Theory and Its Applications. He is the co-recipient of
three IBM Outstanding Innovation Awards, the ACM SIGACT Gödel
Prize, the ACM Kanellakis Award, the ACM SIGMOD Codd Award,
the Blaise Pascal Medal, the IEEE Computer Society Goode Award,
the EATCS Distinguished Achievements Award and the Southeastern
Universities Research Association's Distinguished Scientist Award.
He is a Fellow of the Association for Computing Machinery, the*

American Association for Artificial Intelligence, the American Association for the Advancement of Science and the Institute for Electrical and Electronic Engineers. He is a member of the US National Academy of Engineering, the American Academy of Arts and Science, the European Academy of Science and the Academia Europaea. He holds honorary doctorates from the Saarland University in Germany and Orleans University in France. He is currently the Editor-in-Chief of the Communications of the ACM.

CC: You have referred to logic as "the calculus of computer science". Are mathematical proofs relevant for computer science? Can you cite a practical application of your results which can be understood by a non-mathematician?

MV: I should point out first that the most fundamental ideas in computer science, such as computability, universal machines that can execute arbitrary programs, the distinction between hardware (machines) and software (programs), and programming languages (formalisms to describe computations), all came out from an investigation in the 1920s and 1930s into the nature of mathematical proofs. Once people started programming in the 1950s and 1960s, they realised that reasoning about correctness of computer programs highly resemble reasoning about the correctness of mathematical theorems. This led to intensive research in "program verification". This research borrowed heavily from various branches of mathematical logic, such as lattice theory, model theory and automata theory. My own contribution has been in developing the connection with automata theory. Today there are industrial verification tools that are used daily, which are based on an "esoteric" concept such as "automata on infinite words".

CC: You have worked in many different subjects, including database theory, finite-model theory, knowledge in multi-agent systems, computer-aided verification and reasoning. Which of your results do you like most?

MV: I happen to like the most results which have been the most influential. As a PhD student I discovered that when analysing the computational complexity of database query evaluation one has to distinguish between the contribution of the data to that complexity and the contribution of the query. These are known as "data complexity" and "query complexity", and have become the standard way of looking at the complexity of query evaluation. I also discovered that query complexity is usually exponentially higher than data complexity. Fortunately for us, queries are typically short while databases are large. As a postdoc I discovered the automata-theoretic perspective to program verification. At first this did not lead to new algorithms as much as offered a very simple way to understand existing algorithms. (In fact, it was so simple that the paper was at first rejected when we submitted it to a conference). Over time, the automata-theoretic perspective has been highly useful, leading to many developments in automata-theory-based algorithms. This is is still a very active research area.

CC: You are a co-winner of the 2000 Gödel Prize. Do you see any relevance of incompleteness for mathematics or computer science?

MV: Gödel's Incompleteness theorems established limits on the power of the mathematical approach. It showed that mathematics is a human activity (or, as sociologists would say "a social construct"), with all the limitations that are implied by that. In a similar way, Church–Turing's Undecidability theorem established the limits of the computational approach. It showed that computing, which we tend to think of as a mechanical activity, is at its heart a human activity, since computers and programs are designed by humans.

CC: Is computer-aided verification "practical"? What about automated proof-checking?

MV: For many years there was a fierce debate whether computer-aided verification could ever be made practical. See, for example, the article by DeMillo, Lipton and Perlis on "Social Processes and Proofs of Theorems and Programs", *Commun. ACM* 22(5): 271–280

(1979). Today, model checkers such as FormalCheck, Rulebase, SPIN, and others are in standard industrial usage, so the philosophical debate has become somewhat moot. Proof checking is by nature more labour-intensive than algorithmic methods such as model checking, so its industrial applicability is more limited. Nevertheless, it is used to verify certain critical pieces of hardware designs, such as floating-point arithmetics. The development of highly scalable decision procedures for fairly expressive logics further reduces the distinction between model checking and proof checking.

CC: Please tell us more about the Ken Kennedy Institute for Information Technology (K2I) at Rice.

MV: The basic observation is that the information revolution is transforming society-creating new careers, new industries, new academic disciplines, and the need for new educational and research programmes. We wish to see Rice as a leading institution in the information age. For Rice to be an academic leader in the information revolution, it is imperative to make information technology a *key institutional priority* and take bold, coordinated, pervasive steps to enhance Rice's position in this area. The information technology initiative at Rice needs to encompass information technology research, the digital library effort, information technology education and information technology *in* education.

The role of the Ken Kennedy Institute (K2I) (`www.k2i.rice.edu`) is to complement the traditional academic structures of the university in order to provide more flexibility to respond to new educational and research needs in the fast-paced information age. K2I counteracts the compartmentalisation of the university by becoming a focal point for academic activities in information technology. It focuses resources to seed and nurture the development of both existing areas and emerging activities. It serves the broad and strong student interest in information technology, and incubates new concentrations, programmes, majors and departments as needs emerge. K2I faculty members tie their home departments to K2I and to one another, providing new channels for cross-disciplinary activity related to information technology. K2I is a home that encourages and facilitates exchanges between information technology and the broadest possible range of disciplines at Rice University.

CC: It seems that hardware evolves faster than software. Do you see in this trend any chance for theoretical computer science?

MV: Theoretical research can play different roles in computer science. On the one hand, its role is to clarify the fundamental principles of our discipline. These principles are quite independent from technical development. Much of complexity theory, for example, falls in this category. On the other hand, theoretical research can follow technical developments, trying to explain experimental observations, as well as solving technical challenges that practitioners face. For example, much of the current research on computer-aided verification is driven by the growing complexity of hardware designs. Thus, Boolean decision diagrams (BDDs), which are used to represent Boolean functions compactly, came out of theoretical research on automata theory and branching programs, motivated by the need to effectively manipulate very large Boolean functions.

CC: Improper scientific conduct undermines public trust in the results and methods of science, and threatens public funding and support for scientific research. You have organised a "Research Ethics Seminar" at Rice. Please tell us more about it.

MV: Researchers face ethical issues on a daily basis, managing research funds obtained from public sources, supervising graduate students whose educational interests may diverge from those of their supervisors, dealing with intellectual property issues and more. Even a decision on who should be an author on a paper has ethical dimensions. At the same time, graduate students, who are essentially apprentice researchers, typically receive little training and education in thinking about ethical aspects of research. The Research Ethics Seminar was an attempt to address that. It was a success and a failure at the same time. On the one hand, the students loved it. On the other hand, we did not find enough faculty members with an interest in the topic to make this seminar a regular course offering.

CC: Some public opinion leaders think that theoretical computer science has little relevance for core informatics. Many talented young people don't regard this subject as exciting. Do you agree? Please tell us about the challenges of teaching theoretical computer science.

MV: Twenty and thirty years ago, most computer science students arrived from mathematics. These students enjoyed learning theoretical computer science as a mathematical theory, so we taught theoretical computer science as a mathematical theory. Today's computer science students are interested in computing, yet we still often teach theoretical computer science as a mathematical theory. The challenge is on us to make the theory relevant to the practice of computing. For example, I teach "Logic in Computer Science" at Rice. Part of the final project of this course is for the students to implement a Boolean satisfiability solver and use it to solve "Einstein's Puzzle". This demonstrates to the students that Boolean satisfiability is not some abstract mathematical concept, but rather a very powerful generic problem-solving framework.

CC: Non-funded research seems to be declining. Do you agree? Is this a good trend?

MV: I am not sure I agree with that. If you go back to pre-WWII time, you see that the research enterprise was rather small. It grew enormously after the war, supported by research funding, when it became clear that research can contribute to national security as well as to economic prosperity. There is no question that today's funded research dwarves non-funded research, but it is not clear to me that non-funded research has actually declined. What clearly has declined is scientifically driven, industrially funded research. No industrial lab today is anything like Bell Labs in its heyday. That is a clear loss to science. Microsoft Research today is the only industrial research lab that supports curiosity driven research on a large scale. It will be interesting to see how it evolves in the coming years, as Microsoft loses its dominant position in the IT industry.

CC: Which topics cultivated today in theoretical computer science will survive the end of the century?

MV: If we just knew, we'd all be working on these topics! The most fundamental work will clearly survive. It is hard to imagine that the basic concepts and results of the complexity theory will not be used in 100 years (though if it turns out that P=NP, then much of current complexity theory evaporates!), including such fundamental algorithmic techniques such as breadth-first search and depth-first search. Some current theoretical topics, such as quantum computation, will either be extremely fundamental or completely irrelevant, depending on whether quantum computing will turn out to be a reality.

CC: In a recent editorial in *CACM* you pointed out that one role of theoretical computer science is to provide guidance to engineering. Referring to the Boolean satisfiability problem you noted that the current theories of complexity seem to offer little guidance for problems that are theoretically — worst case or average case — difficult to solve but tractable in practice. Could you give a more detailed picture of this phenomenon? Where a solution may be sought?

MV: I believe that complexity theory is facing a major challenge. This theory is based typically on worst-case complexity analysis, which focuses on instances that are the most difficult to solve. Worst-case complexity analysis has proven to be quite tractable mathematically, much more, than say average-case complexity analysis. It also seems intuitive from a practical point of view; for example, a worst-case upper bound for an algorithm offers an absolute upper bound on its running time in practice. Thus, worst-case analysis is the standard approach in complexity theory. What has become clear, however, is that worst-case analysis actually sheds very little light on the behaviour of algorithms in real-life instances. For example, theorists have demonstrated that current SAT-solving algorithms must take exponential time to solve certain families of SAT instances. Practitioners simply shrug at such bounds, while they continue to apply their solvers to very large but practically solvable SAT instances. Indeed, one role of theory is to provide guidance to engineering, but worst-case (and average-case) complexity seems to offer little guidance for problems that are difficult in theory but feasible in practice. What is needed is a new computational complexity model, which will better capture the concept of "complexity in practice". We need a new kind of complexity theory!

CC: In March 2013 you tweeted: "The Internet is a surveillance state". This was followed by an editorial in November 2013 in *CACM* titled "The End of The American Network" which ends with the statement:

> The real question, I believe, is whether we can have an Internet that is free, or at least freer, from government meddling than today's Internet. In view of the Internet's centrality in our information-saturated lives, this is a question of the utmost importance.

Meantime the US Government has signalled its intention to end its historical agreement with the Internet Corporation for Assigned Names and Numbers in late 2015, and ICANN will develop a new global governance model.

Do you see any significant improvement?

MV: This may be a positive development, but the devil is in the detail. While we are justified in complaining about the Orwellian activities of the US Government, other governments may not only eavesdrop by also censor. As we have also learned, it is not clear that we can trust corporations with stewardship of the Internet. Developing a new Internet governance model that is transparent and free of meddling by governments and corporations is not an easy task.

CC: How do you manage to do so many different things well?

MV: I do not. I have a huge pile of unfinished projects.

Chapter 26

Reinhard Wilhelm: Compiler Construction and Dagstuhl

Reinhard Wilhelm is Professor and Leader of the Chair for Programming Languages and Compiler Construction at Saarland University. He has been the scientific director of the Leibniz Centre for Informatics at Schloss Dagstuhl from its inception in 1990 until 2014.

Professor Wilhelm has obtained numerous results on compiler construction, static program analysis, embedded real-time systems, animation and visualisation of algorithms and data structures. He is one of the co-developers of the MUG1, MUG2 and OPTRAN compiler generators, which are based on attribute grammars. He is a co-founder of the European Symposium on Programming, ESOP, and the European Joint Conferences on Theory and Practice of Software.

Professor Wilhelm is a fellow of the ACM (2000) and a member of the Academia Europaea (2008); he was awarded the Alwin–Walther medal (2006), the Prix Gay–Lussac–Humboldt (2007), the Konrad–Zuse medal (2009), the Cross of the Order of Merit of the Federal Republic of Germany and the ACM Distinguished Service Award (2010); he has honorary doctorates from RWTH Aachen and Tartu University (2008). He is a member of the European Academy of Sciences and the German national academy of sciences, Leopoldina.

CC: You studied mathematics, physics and mathematical logic at *Westfälische Wilhelms*-University in *Münster*, computer science at the Technical University Munich and Stanford University, and obtained your PhD at TU Munich, quite a broad background. Please reminisce about this period.

RW: I studied at a time when the first curricula in computer science were being established. As a native of Westphalia, *Westfälische Wilhelms*-Universität Münster with its strong tradition in mathematics and mathematical logic was a natural starting point. Josef Stör, a numerical analyst from my home town, then on the faculty of USC San Diego, recommended switching to computer science, advice I followed after passing the Vordiplom exam in Münster. At TH, later TU Munich, I was among the first students of the new curriculum in computer science. I finished this obtaining a diploma degree, already oriented towards compiler construction. The German Academic Exchange Service (DAAD) offered one-year fellowships to study computer science in the US as they felt that the CS curricula did not yet have the same quality as the American curricula. I obtained such a fellowship and studied at Stanford University for one year. It was an exciting year with courses taught by Robert Floyd, Donald Knuth, Zohar Manna, John McCarthy, Robin Milner and Niklaus Wirth. Looking back, the semantics people, Floyd, Manna and McCarthy, seemed to have had the strongest influence on me. I gathered practical experience in compiler construction with my MS project, part of the port of the Zurich Pascal compiler to the IBM 360 machine.

CC: You discovered connections between code selection and regular tree automata, which are relevant for code generation.

RW: My group at Saarland University developed a formally based approach to compiler optimisations expressed as transformations of attributed trees. The necessary tree pattern-matching algorithm — identifying places where transformations could be applied — used a subset construction on non-deterministic tree automata as I learned later from Helmut Seidl. I found some informal proposals in the literature proposing to express code selection by tree parsing. This led to a beautiful and efficient approach using deterministic bottom-up tree automata, which could be nicely combined with dynamic programming to identify least-cost code sequences. However, reality, i.e., processor-architecture design, made this beautiful approach obsolete as real processor architectures did not offer the required regularity.

CC: Although your research is quite practical, the theoretical component is strong. How do you manage this?

RW: Well, my colleagues in the CS department at Saarland University have a strong conviction, that nothing is as practical as a good theory. This conviction has been a recipe for success. Our curriculum has always had a strong theoretical foundation on which one could build solid practical work.

CC: Yours and Dieter Maurer's book *Compiler Design* — written in German and translated into English and French — is a good illustration of the interplay between theory and applications: it offers a solid theoretical foundation for compilers for imperative, object oriented, functional and logic-based languages.

RW: I was not content with the Dragon Book, the dominant compiler textbook, which was, and is, by and large void of the theoretical foundations for compiler design. The underlying theory, however, is quite beautiful. So, I decided to write a book that I would like to teach from. I was fortunate to have Dieter Maurer in my group, who co-authored the first two editions. I have cooperated with Helmut Seidl and Sebastian Hack on a rather complete rewrite for the third edition. The virtual machines in this third edition are made more uniform. The code-optimisation part introducing static program analysis and program transformations has been largely extended. The code-generation chapters will be completely restructured and rewritten due to new insights into the code-generation process obtained in Sebastian Hack's dissertation.

CC: Please explain the shape analysis based on three-valued logic you designed.

RW: Static program analysis, which received most of its theoretical foundations from Patrick and Radhia Cousot in the 1970s, computes invariant properties of all behaviours of a program. Abstract interpretation, as the Cousots formulated it, uses an abstraction of the semantics of the programming language to determine these invariants at all program points. Due to the impossibility to be sound and complete at the same time, sound static analysis approximate these properties; they give up completeness, but maintain soundness.

A largely unexplored area was the static analysis of heap-manipulating programs. These offer particular challenges, namely dynamically created anonymous objects and linked data structures of unbounded size. During a sabbatical I spent in Israel I was fortunate to meet Mooly Sagiv, then a student at the Technion. He asked me for a good thesis topic, and I proposed to develop a specification language for static program analyses. Mooly and I cooperated on this topic for something like 16 years, joined by Tom Reps, whom I knew from our attribute-grammar times.

The breakthrough in our research came with the discovery that predicate logic was a good basis to express program semantics, and that a reinterpretation of the same semantics over a three-valued logical domain — the third value expressing *don't know* — could be used as an abstract interpretation. Our approach was parametric in the abstraction properties, i.e., different sets of predicates could be used to obtain different abstractions.

The *shapes* occurring in the name *Shape Analysis* were something like generalised *types* of data structures in the heap. Example are *singly-linked lists without shared nodes, balanced binary tree* etc.

CC: Your ACM fellowship citation refers to your research on compiler construction and program analysis. Can you discuss one or two important results in this area?

RW: A result of my group that had quite some impact is the development of an approach to derive run-time guarantees for real-time embedded systems, that is, to show that such systems satisfy their timing constraints. These are often quite tight; in the automotive domain, they range down to microseconds. At the same time, the execution platforms used to realise these systems have a huge variability of execution times: the execution time of an instruction depends on the state of the platform and may vary by a factor of 100 or more.

The engineers at Airbus in Toulouse called us to help them because they knew that their traditional methods, based on measurement, were not sound for the new architectures they were deploying in their planes. We were able to solve this problem and provide tools through a spin-off company, AbsInt, that Airbus could use. Meanwhile the long cooperation between Airbus, AbsInt, and my group at the university was so successful that several time-critical subsystems of the Airbus A380, the *big Airbus*, were certified with the AbsInt tool, which thereby became the only tool worldwide to be *validated* for the certification of these avionics applications. This work is considered as one of the major success stories of formal methods.

CC: One of your areas of research is *Algorithm Explanation*. Please "explain" it.

RW: Well, as an instructor of a course on data structures and algorithms you need means to show what an algorithm does on a data structure. A whole community has evolved, which has developed sophisticated animations showing executions of algorithms, or more precisely, programs implementing the algorithms, on sample input data. The student can then observe how the state of the data structure changes when an operation is applied to the data structure. My idea was that it is more relevant to show which properties of the state are invariant under the execution of the operations. The data-structure invariants are very important when it comes to proving the properties of algorithms. We had developed our shape analysis, which was in fact determining such invariants about data structures. So, the idea was to run a shape analysis as a preprocess and then visualise *abstract* instead of *concrete executions*, as the rest of the community was doing it. There were a number of obstacles; the number of shape graphs, representing such an invariant, could be rather large. So, we had to identify subsets that were large enough to explain the essentials about the data-structure operations. Also, our approach was in principle generic, i.e., the shape analysis as well as the visualisation should be generated from adequate specifications. This was a central achievement of our parametric shape analysis. But it turned out to be difficult for the visualisation. At least we couldn't find a satisfactory solution. However, it could be an interesting research programme for some brilliant young researcher.

CC: How do you see your book *Informatics: 10 Years Back. 10 Years Ahead* (Springer 2001), 13 years after its publication?

RW: That is hard to answer! I would have to reread the prognoses contained in it. In the domain of verification, I have recently co-authored a manifesto, *Modeling, Analysis, and Verification — The Formal Methods Manifesto 2010* attempting to describe the state of the art. This could be compared with the articles in the monograph you refer to.

CC: Please summarise your manifesto.

RW: The manifesto gives an overview of how far different formal methods, in particular the verification methods, have been taken up by industry. There are notable differences between hardware and software industries and also some between Europe and America. The acceptance of verification methods is related to the costs of potential failures. Chip manufacturers broadly adopted verification methods after the Pentium bug cost Intel a lot of money. The Ariane 5 disaster, due to a software bug, was very helpful in raising problem awareness in some parts of the embedded-systems industry. There is a somewhat surprising distribution of strongholds for the different verification methods; model checking is stronger in the US, abstract interpretation stronger in Europe, deductive verification initially stronger in the US, but is now strong in Europe.

One particular insight I gained in my work with industry and which is described in the manifesto is that the different verification techniques have a different distribution of roles, researcher, tool developer, user. In academia, typically the researcher also develops the tools based on his findings, and, of course, he is an enthusiastic user of his own tools. Some of the biggest disappointments resulted from the expectations raised by enthusiastic researchers/tool developers when the tools were deployed in industry and engineers could not use them.

CC: Since 1990 you have been the Scientific Director of the Leibniz Center for Informatics at *Schloss Dagstuhl*. What was the initial motivation of starting this centre? How did it evolve in the last 20 years?

RW: The Leibniz Center for Informatics was formed after the famous Mathematics Research Institute in *Oberwolfach*, in the Black Forest. Theoretical computer scientists had been guests there for a number of years and felt the desire to have an *Oberwolfach* for informatics. The German Informatics (GI) Society setup a search committee to identify an appropriate place for it. Several offers were made by the states *Baden-Württemberg, Rheinland-Pfalz* and *Saarland*. The search committee selected *Schloss Dagstuhl*, a late-baroque mansion, at that time a retirement home run by a nuns order. The Saarland Government agreed to buy the ensemble for the centre and the German National Science Council supported the decision to set the centre up in *Dagstuhl*.

Apparently, the informatics community had waited for this centre. Against my expectations it filled up rather quickly. An extension building was opened in 1995 together with a new kitchen and a restaurant. The greater capacity also filled up quickly so that lead times of far more than a year became common. You must know that meetings in *Dagstuhl*, the so-called *Dagstuhl* seminars, result from successful applications to a Scientific Directorate, which meets twice a year to decide about the submitted proposals.

CC: Yes, I indeed know as I was privileged to be invited to a few seminars. As a participant to both *Oberwolfach* and *Dagstuhl*, I noted similarities but also differences...

RW: Definitely, *Oberwolfach* was our role model when we set up Dagstuhl. When I had been convinced to run *Dagstuhl*, I went to *Oberwolfach* together with my colleague on the administrative side, Wolfgang Lorenz, to get advice from Martin Barner, the long-time Director of the Mathematical Research Institute, on what to do and, even more importantly, what not to do. Among the latter was his recommendation not to establish entailed estates, that is, long-running series of meetings, which ran too long to ever be stopped. We, therefore, established an iron rule that the organising team of a series had to, at least incrementally, change from instance to instance. This was not always well received by organising teams, but proved fruitful in the long run.

Another notable difference to *Oberwolfach* was that we charged participation fees right from the beginning. Computer scientists are usually better funded than mathematicians, and our fees were more symbolic than covering real costs.

Let me report an anecdote about where *Dagstuhl* profited from *Oberwolfach*. I was amazed by the fantastic music room on *Oberwolfach*. Great instruments and an extensive musical library! Actually, I had met Don Knuth and told him about our plans for *Dagstuhl*, and he had sent me a letter saying that he had always enjoyed playing the grand piano in *Oberwolfach*. The White Hall in *Dagstuhl*, a beautiful baroque hall, offered itself for our music room. I set out to buy instruments, a grand piano — not as grand as the one in *Oberwolfach* — a decent violin, a cello. The executive in the ministry in charge of supervising our efforts complained about us acquiring a grand piano. I sent him a copy of Knuth's letter to prove that luminaries like him would find their way to *Dagstuhl* because of the grand piano. This stopped the complaints.

Another anecdote on setting up the music library in *Dagstuhl*. Musical scores are very expensive. So I thought about how to save on buying a basic library. I knew that the German publishers had licensed editions to the Eastern countries not meant to be reimported, at least not on a large scale. At that time I was playing with a Hungarian pianist. I told him my problem and asked him to see how he could import Eastern editions of scores to *Dagstuhl*. Next time, a friend of his came to visit him, he had the trunk of his car full of scores, somewhat biased towards Southeast Europe, all that for just 1000 DEM. I was nervous about what would happen to the fellow and the smuggled scores at the Austro-Hungarian border, and, in fact, Austrian customs asked the fellow to open the trunk of his car. On top of all the scores, there was a 12-pack of cigarettes. They made him pay a fine for smuggling cigarettes.

CC: In addition to the music, the dedication to the fine arts is visible in *Dagstuhl*. What is the origin of this?

RW: Although I have a sister who is an artist my connection to the fine arts was not very strong. That changed when the extension building in *Dagstuhl* was finished. It is, I think, beautiful modern architecture based on a traditional concept, a monasterial building. The architects saw *Dagstuhl* as a scientific monastery. Our monastery has a cloister, a very nice opportunity for arts exhibitions. But what got me really involved with fine art and not so fine artists was the procedure for equipping the new building with artistic objects. Germany has a law requiring that public buildings should be furnished with pieces of art. A certain percentage of the construction money should go to the arts. A jury was set up, some groups of artists were asked to submit proposals. The architect and I were made members of the jury. When the submissions were discussed, I felt that something fishy was going on. I didn't know what. The jury, against my vote, selected some proposal that would deal with computer science in a pubertal way. I was quite upset and told the jury that this work would never see the centre. I was declared a philistine, ignorant of modern trends in the fine arts. A four-month battle behind the scenes led to the rejection of the jury's proposal by the minister in charge. As revenge, the jury decided to let the money in the arts budget fall back to the construction budget. We were left with empty walls! I then invented an arts donation scheme, see `http://www.dagstuhl.de/en/about-dagstuhl/kunst/`, which, with a little help by our friends, has helped us to acquire quite a few nice pieces mostly from exhibitions we have had in the cloisters.

CC: What is the "job description" of the scientific director of the Leibniz Center for Informatics?

RW: The scientific director is responsible for the scientific program in *Schloss Dagstuhl*. That is the primary duty. Unlike a conference hotel, the scientific directorate, and the whole scientific staff at *schloss dagstuhl* feel responsible to guarantee high-quality meetings. The participants, who spend considerable effort to travel to this remote place, expect a high return for this travel investment. A disappointed participant will most likely not accept another invitation.

The scientific director chairs the scientific directorate at its meetings, moderates the discussion, and executes the decisions taken.

He also develops or takes up new directions and functions of the centre. The Leibniz Center has extended its activities beyond the original function in several directions. It has become an open access publisher. The high-quality conference series, LIPIcs, provides a low-cost, open-access alternative to established publishers, who, under financial pressure from their owners, were forced to change their publication policy to increase their revenue.

Another new direction is the cooperation with DBLP, the renowned bibliographic database established by Michael Ley at the University of Trier. The Leibniz Center has agreed to secure the long-term existence of this important source of information for computer science. With support from the Leibniz Association and the Klaus Tschira Foundation, DBLP has strongly increased the coverage of computer science publications.

CC: Over the years you have witnessed many interesting events in *Schloss Dagstuhl*. Are there any such memories which you would like to share with us?

RW: Let me report about two events, one rather sad, one positive. We scheduled a meeting on computer science and astronomy at the time of last total solar eclipse covering central Europe. This meeting included computer scientists, astronomers and historians. As it brought together different communities that would hardly meet anywhere else it was a quite typical event for *Dagstuhl*.

One particular talk attempted to refute the then popular claim of some pseudo-historians that the solar eclipses, around 700–1000 AD didn't happen and had been invented. A historian had collected recordings about solar and lunar eclipses from that time. These were checked against an exciting software reproducing the planetary constellations at any time and any location. And indeed, all recorded eclipses were properly reproduced by this software. Another exciting experience at this event was that we selected exactly the right place to watch the eclipse. More or less all others in Britain, France, and Germany did not see anything due to rain and clouds, while we had a 20-minute hole in the clouds through which we could perfectly watch the eclipse.

Now to the sad side. As we know from history, total solar eclipses were always seen as bringing with them mischief, catastrophes and plagues. To support this old superstition, one participant had an accident coming to the meeting one fell ill during the meeting, and one had to leave early because his father died.

As mentioned above, it is very common that *Dagstuhl* meetings bring together different communities that don't have any conferences where they would meet. *Dagstuhl* thus often establishes absolutely necessary communication. Let me report about a meeting about scheduling. Scheduling is an important topic, which occurs in manufacturing and in logistics — this is typically dealt with in the operations research community — but also in computer science, and in computer science again in different subdomains, e.g., real-time scheduling, compilation and algorithms. A meeting in 2010 brought together the algorithms community the real-time scheduling community, and the operations-research community. Some real-time scheduling participants were asked to list their most interesting open problems, which were unknown to the algorithms community. They wrote-up a report about their most urgent open problems, and in the proposal to the successor meeting the proposers proudly presented

10 publications that had resulted from this meeting solving at least 5 of the listed open problems of the real-time scheduling community.

CC: I understand that under the German law you will have to retire soon. What plans do you have?

RW: I have already retired from the position of Scientific Director of the Leibniz–Center in *Schloss Dagstuhl*, but will still work for the open-access publication activities of the centre. I will become professor emeritus at the end of September 2014. There are still some doctoral students who need to be supervised, and I might get involved more in the operations of our spin-off company. I also enjoy our first grandchild very much. Seeing him growing up in a more relaxed time, compared to the time when our children grew up, is a lot of fun!

Cristian S. Calude: Postface

Editor: How did the project start?

CC: I was always fascinated by what happens "behind the grand scene" of science: how scientists get their inspiration, how they choose their problems, how they cope with success, and, more importantly, with failure. I was fortunate to meet eminent scientists, so I took the opportunity to ask them questions. These conversations have appeared over the years in the *Bulletin of the European Association for Theoretical Computer Science* and a selection of them evolved into this book.

Editor: Why computing?

CC: Computing is ubiquitous: it is everywhere and anywhere. The world's computational power has increased by 10,000% over a decade. Life would be inconceivable without it and the future even more. The sky is the limit.

Editor: In the digital world innovation is more than essential, it is vital.

CC: That's the stark truth: companies that fail to innovate risk extinction. Innovation laggards like Alta Vista, Kodak, Blockbuster, Borders are well-known victims.

Editor: Undoubtedly, this big optimisation coming from the computing revolution increases productivity, efficiency, reduces costs and generally makes life better. Surely, there is a price. . .

CC: First and foremost, the tsunami of information at our fingertips does not automatically imply knowledge nor wisdom. Big data can mislead.

Second, there are collateral damages: Wikipedia killed the encyclopaedia, smart phones killed cameras, maps, calendars, address books, calculators, watches, photo albums, etc. Lots of jobs are created but many are lost or radically changed. Middlemen and gatekeepers — agents of different kinds, travel, real estate, stockbrokers — are the most vulnerable.

Third, in the digital world privacy seems to be gone. Everything we click, like, post, email can be potentially and unexpectedly retrieved and used against our will: this varies from benign attempts to sell things we don't need to mischievous ways to evaluate/rob/embarrass/blackmail. Digital footprints tend to be very resilient, even if Google removes them from its searches.

Some of these important aspects are discussed in various conversations, preponderantly in those grouped in the section on social aspects of computing.

Editor: How far can the computing revolution go?

CC: Here are two computing challenges which may read like utopia: to beat human intelligence and to challenge natural death. Note first that these problems are computing problems, and, second, that they are solvable.

Editor: The title is very nice. Did you coin it?

CC: No. I had thought about a title for a long time without getting anything acceptable. Eventually I asked Solomon Marcus — whose linguistics imagination is unbeatable — and his proposal was

The Human Face of Computation. Then, Joseph Sifakis argued that "computing" is a better term than "computation", a suggestion immediately embraced by Marcus who also noticed that: "computing has only three syllables while computation has four; musically, the former is better than the latter".

Editor: How did you group the interviews?

CC: The main theme is computing, but conversations have different topics and accents.

The first group is devoted to computing science. In the second one, the main interest is in computing "outside computing": computing in biology, mathematics, physics and computing by imitating Nature. In the third group the social aspects are prevalent.

Of course, the thematic division is subjective, and, more importantly, interviews are to a large extent independent and can be read in any order.

Editor: There is a well-known view according to which mathematicians prove and reason, but do not compute. For the Fields Medallist R. Thom the question is *to dream or not to dream*:

> A great part of my discoveries arise out of pure speculation; one could undoubtedly think of them as manifestations of my dreaming. I'm happy with that, for isn't the act of dreaming a virtual catastrophe that gives birth to knowledge? At a time when so many scientists are busy computing, isn't it desirable for some of them — if they can do it — to dream?

CC: Mathematics is a "superposition" of modelling, reasoning and computing. These components are distributed in various proportions depending on time, subject, school or personal preferences. In some sense developing a "calculus" in an area of mathematics is a sign of maturity of that subject, but the process is cyclic. The development of experimental mathematics and proof assistants dramatically increases the use and importance of computing in mathematics.

Editor: Surely there are limits to what computing can do for mathematics.

CC: The main limit comes from Gödel's Incompleteness theorem. Still, under the advent of technology (hardware and software), proof assistants are better and better, and in the not too distant future mathematicians will use them as they use today LATEX.

Editor: Computing is changing science and even mathematics. What about philosophy or theology?

CC: Shortly before his death, Gödel proved the existence of (a "theoretical") God from a set of five axioms. Gödel's axioms were inspired by the premises used by the theologian and philosopher Anselm of Canterbury in his famous ontological argument. The discussion about the "obviousness" and "adequacy" of Gödel's axioms may never end. However, the choice of the axiomatic approach raises a mathematical important issue, namely, the lack of hidden contradictions of the axioms — technically, their consistency. This problem was open for 40 years. A recent automated analysis of (D. Scott's version of) Gödel's proof showed, with an unprecedented degree of detail, the consistency of the axioms and the correctness of the proof.[1] Significantly, the authors conclude their paper with:

> In case of logico-philosophical disputes, the computer can check the disputing arguments and partially fulfil Leibniz's dictum: *Calculemus* — Let us calculate!

Editor: This book couldn't have appeared without the help of many.

CC: My warmest thanks go to the eminent participants of the conversations reported here, to Erol Gelenbe for suggesting the project and recommending it to Imperial College Press, to Anil Nerode for writing the Preface, to Martin Davis and Maurice Nivat for the cover blurbs, to Jane Sayers and Catharina Weijman for their interest and support for the process of editing, and, last but not least, to you, the reader of the book.

---

[1]C. Benzmüller and B. Woltzenlogel Paleo. Automating Gödel's ontological proof of God's existence with higher-order automated theorem prover, *21st European Conference of Artificial Intelligence*, August 2014, http://www.ecai2014.org.

Printed in the United States
By Bookmasters